T0397916

The Prophet Is the People

Supplements
to
Vetus Testamentum

VOLUME 199

The titles published in this series are listed at *brill.com/vts*

The Prophet Is the People

An Answer to "Why Elijah?" in Second Temple Jewish and Early Christian Literature

By

Alicia R. Hein

BRILL

LEIDEN | BOSTON

The Library of Congress Cataloging-in-Publication Data is available online at https://catalog.loc.gov
LC record available at https://lccn.loc.gov/

Typeface for the Latin, Greek, and Cyrillic scripts: "Brill". See and download: brill.com/brill-typeface.

ISSN 0083-5889
ISBN 978-90-04-72976-6 (hardback)
ISBN 978-90-04-73469-2 (e-book)
DOI 10.1163/9789004734692

*With deepest gratitude
to my longsuffering Doktorvater,
Michael A. Lyons,
without whom the question of "why Elijah"
would, for me, be no closer to an answer*

∴

Contents

Acknowledgements

Since beginning this project, I have found myself drawn to the acknowledgement pages in other works. They have become relatable, offering a glimpse into the story behind the work and paying tribute to its central characters. I now fully understand just how impossible it is for an author to produce anything of value alone, and owe a debt of thanks to the people in my story.

First and foremost, credit for the very existence of this work goes to my doctoral supervisor, Dr Michael A. Lyons. From our first email exchange I sensed that he believed in this project, but I had no idea at the time just how true that would be. Throughout my PhD he read far more chapter drafts than any supervisor should be asked to read, allowing himself to become almost as fully absorbed in the project as I was. His influence is indelibly impressed on every page of this book, but he consistently pushed me to be confident in claiming my ideas and finding my voice. This study would not exist without his unwavering support, help, and fatherly encouragement, for all of which I am eternally grateful.

Thanks to the wonderful team at Brill and the Supplements to Vetus Testamentum series for their support and help in the publishing process; to Prof Dr Lena-Sofia Tiemeyer, to Laura Morris, to Nitzan Shalev, to Dirk Bakker, and to the reviewers who so heartily endorsed this project. Thanks to the faculty, staff, and administration at St Mary's College, University of St Andrews, who facilitated its initial completion, provided research support, and offered travel funding for conference presentations. Further thanks are due to the Eberhard Karls Universität Tübingen, above all by means of a very deep and heartfelt recognition of Prof Dr Jakob Wöhrle, who passed away suddenly and far too soon just as this book was going to print. Professor Wöhrle took a chance on a half-German international PhD candidate and gave me an opportunity to be part of his team. He never doubted that I could handle the challenge of teaching and researching in German, and he opened a world of possibilities both in me and for me that I never could have imagined. The future now contains a massive hole which no one will be able to fill, but we'll try to keep making you proud. Für immer Teil Deines Teams.

I owe thanks to numerous teachers and professors from earlier stages of my journey, without whom I never would have embarked on it in the first place. Thanks to Dr Kevin Peacock, whose Hebrew reading module on Elijah planted an idea for a master's thesis, and whose supervision of that thesis tended the seed of fascination that would become a dissertation and, finally, a book. Thanks to Dr Peter Engle, whose encouragement began in my first semester of undergraduate studies and has only increased since then. Thanks to Keven Funk, who opened my eyes to the world of biblical interpretation and lit a spark in me that has not gone out.

Many thanks go to my cheerful editor, E.M. Phillips, whose experienced eye, attention to detail, and inextinguishable enthusiasm saved me from numerous unfortunate errors. Heartfelt thanks also to Dr Lotta Valve of the University of Eastern Finland, whose insights into Elijah and Second Temple texts inspired me throughout this project, and who also provided helpful feedback in its final stages. Thanks to my Roundel people, to Jonny Schneider-Woods, Julia Glanz, and Haley Kirkpatrick, who have been both dear friends and valuable sources of discussion and feedback. Thanks to Tamara Mitton for always sharing my academic excitement and joy, and for understanding me in a way that very few could.

Finally, I would like to thank my parents, Fred and Priscilla Hein, for their unwavering love and selfless support throughout my life, but especially in the last fifteen years. They watched their daughter move first across the country of Canada and then across the world in pursuit of a path that made little sense at times, but they saw how much joy it brought me and have stood steadily by my side. I am who I am because of them. Thanks, Mom and Dad. I love you.

Abbreviations

AB	Anchor Bible
AcT	*Acta Theologica*
ANEM	Ancient Near East Monographs
ANTJ	Arbeiten zum Neuen Testament und Judentum
ApOTC	Apollos Old Testament Commentary
ATANT	Abhandlungen zur Theologie des Alten und Neuen Testaments
ATD	Das Alte Testament Deutsch
ATSAT	Arbeiten zu Text und Sprache im Alten Testament
AUMSR	Andrews University Monographs: Studies in Religion
AYB	Anchor Yale Bible
BBR	*Bulletin of Biblical Research*
BETL	Bibliotheca Ephemeridum Theologicarum Lovaniensium
Bib	*Biblica*
BibInt	*Biblical Interpretation*
BiThSt	Biblisch-theologische Studien
BK	*Bibel und Kirche*
BK(C)AT	Biblischer K(C)ommentar, Altes Testament
BN	*Biblische Notizen*
BNTC	Black's New Testament Commentaries
BR	*Biblical Research*
BSac	*Bibliotheca Sacra*
BTC	Brazos Theological Commentary on the Bible
BWANT	Beiträge zur Wissenschaft vom Alten und Neuen Testament
BZAW	Beihefte zur Zeitschrift für die alttestamentliche Wissenschaft
BZNW	Beihefte zur Zeitschrift für die neutestamentliche Wissenschaft
CBC	Cambridge Bible Commentary
CBQ	*Catholic Biblical Quarterly*
CBR	*Currents in Biblical Research*
DBAT	*Dielheimer Blätter zum Alten Testament*
DSD	*Dead Sea Discoveries*
EC	*Early Christianity*
ETS	Erfurter theologische Studien
ExpTim	*The Expository Times*
FAT	Forschungen zum Alten Testament
FRLANT	Forschungen zur Religion und Literatur des Alten und Neuen Testaments
HAT	Handbuch zum Alten Testament
HBS	Herders biblische Studien

HBT	*Horizons in Biblical Theology*
HdO	Handbuch der Orientalistik
HeyJ	*Heythrop Journal*
HNT	Handbuch zum Neuen Testament
HThKAT	Herders Theologischer Kommentar zum Alten Testament
HTR	*Harvard Theological Review*
HUCA	*Hebrew Union College Annual*
IB	*Interpreter's Bible*
IBC	Interpretation: A Bible Commentary for Teaching and Preaching
ICC	International Critical Commentary
IDS	*In die Skriflig*
IECOT	International Exegetical Commentary on the Old Testament
Int	*Interpretation*
JBL	*Journal of Biblical Literature*
JBLMS	Journal of Biblical Literature Monograph Series
JBQ	*Jewish Bible Quarterly*
JETS	*Journal of the Evangelical Theological Society*
JH	*Jewish History*
JHebS	*Journal of Hebrew Scriptures*
JJS	*Journal of Jewish Studies*
JNES	*Journal of Near Eastern Studies*
JR	*Journal of Religion*
JRT	*Journal of Religious Thought*
JSJ	*Journal for the Study of Judaism in the Persian, Hellenistic, and Roman Periods*
JSJSup	Supplements to the Journal for the Study of Judaism
JSNTSup	Journal for the Study of the New Testament Supplement Series
JSOT	*Journal for the Study of the Old Testament*
JSOTSup	Journal for the Study of the Old Testament Supplement Series
JTI	*Journal of Theological Interpretation*
JTS	*Journal of Theological Studies*
KAT	Kommentar zum Alten Testament
KKAT	Kurzgefaßter Kommentar: Altes Testament
LAB	*Liber Antiquitatum Biblicarum*
LNTS	The Library of New Testament Studies
LHBOTS	The Library of Hebrew Bible/Old Testament Studies
MNTC	Moffatt New Testament Commentary
NCB	New Century Bible
NIBC	New International Biblical Commentary
NICNT	New International Commentary on the New Testament

NICOT	New International Commentary on the Old Testament
NIDOTTE	*New International Dictionary of Old Testament Theology and Exegesis*
NIGTC	New International Greek Testament Commentary
NovTSup	Supplements to Novum Testamentum
NTD	Das Neue Testament Deutsch
NTL	New Testament Library
NTS	*New Testament Studies*
OTL	Old Testament Library
PHSC	Perspectives on Hebrew Scriptures and Its Contexts
PNTC	Pillar New Testament Commentaries
RB	*Revue biblique*
RevistB	*Revista bíblica*
RevQ	*Revue de Qumran*
RTR	*Reformed Theological Review*
SBibSt	Sources for Biblical Study
SBJT	*Southern Baptist Journal of Theology*
SBL	Society of Biblical Literature
SBLDS	Society of Biblical Literature Dissertation Series
SBLSCS	Society of Biblical Literature Septuagint and Cognate Studies
Scr	*Scripture*
SCS	Septuagint and Cognate Studies
SEÅ	*Svensk exegetisk årsbok*
SHBC	Smyth & Helwys Bible Commentary
SiChrSt	*Sino-Christian Studies*
SJLA	Studies in Judaism in Late Antiquity
SJT	*Scottish Journal of Theology*
SNT	Studien zum Neuen Testament
SNTSMS	Society for New Testament Studies Monograph Series
SOTSMS	Society for Old Testament Studies Monograph Series
StBiSl	*Studia Biblica Slovaca*
Tg Ps-J	Targum Pseudo-Jonathan
THKNT	Theologischer Handkommentar zum Neuen Testament
TKNT	Theologischer Kommentar zum Neuen Testament
TNTC	Tyndale New Testament Commentaries
TOTC	Tyndale Old Testament Commentaries
TWNT	*Theologisches Wörterbuch zum Neuen Testament*
TynBul	*Tyndale Bulletin*
TZ	*Theologische Zeitschrift*
VEccl	*Verbum et Ecclesia*
VT	*Vetus Testamentum*

VTSup	Supplements to Vetus Testamentum
WBC	Word Biblical Commentary
WMANT	Wissenschaftliche Monographien zum Alten und Neuen Testament
WUNT	Wissenschaftliche Untersuchungen zum Neuen Testament
ZAW	*Zeitschrift für die alttestamentliche Wissenschaft*
ZECNT	Zondervan Exegetical Commentary on the New Testament
ZNW	*Zeitschrift für die neutestamentliche Wissenschaft und die Kunde der älteren Kirche*

CHAPTER 1

Introduction and Approach to the Texts

1   Introduction

> A positive feedback loop developed: the more central a figure was, the more it became a 'magnet' for issues and images that stood at the community's core (including and involving matters of self-characterization, identity, and ideology). Conversely, the more such matters and images were associated with [this figure], the more central he became.[1]

Though Ehud Ben Zvi writes the description above of Moses and Abraham, it seems to me to address exactly the question that lies at the heart of this study in reference to Elijah. In all of the diverse studies that have emerged on Elijah within the last century, there has been no encompassing answer to the question of why he, in particular, takes on an apparently timeless relevance in an incredibly broad range of texts. His narrative cycle in Kings is linked closely to that of Elisha, yet Elisha receives no further mention in the Hebrew Bible.[2] Elijah's importance in later texts is most closely comparable to that of Moses, but while Moses is a primary character in four Hebrew Bible books, the Elijah narrative proper spans only six chapters.[3] No convincing answer has been offered as to why the Elijah of Kings comes to embody the hope of future restoration described in Malachi and expanded in other Second Temple texts.

---

1   Ehud Ben Zvi, "Exploring the Memory of Moses 'The Prophet' in Late Persian/Early Hellenistic Yehud/Judah," in *Remembering Biblical Figures in the Late Persian and Early Hellenistic Periods: Social Memory and Imagination*, ed. Diana V. Edelman and Ehud Ben Zvi (Oxford: Oxford University Press, 2013), 335; cf. idem, "The Memory of Abraham in Late Persian/Early Hellenistic Yehud/Judah," in *Remembering Biblical Figures in the Late Persian and Early Hellenistic Periods: Social Memory and Imagination*, ed. Diana V. Edelman and Ehud Ben Zvi (Oxford: Oxford University Press, 2013), 6.

2   He is mentioned by name once in the New Testament (Luke 4:27), as well as in Sir 48:12–14 and several fragmentary texts (CD-A viii20–21; 4Q382 frags. 9; 11; 4Q481ᵃ).

3   By "Elijah narrative," "Elijah cycle," or "Kings cycle," I refer to the chapters in 1–2 Kings in which Elijah is explicitly mentioned during the period of his narrative life: namely, 1 Kgs 17–19 and 21, and 2 Kgs 1–2. While the intervening chapters of 1 Kgs 20 and 22 are literarily linked to the Elijah cycle, Elijah himself does not figure in these chapters. In the current arrangement of Kings, the Elisha cycle acts as a continuation of Elijah's power and prophetic work, while likely also representing the literary source behind some of the Elijah material. An examination of the Elisha cycle beyond a few select mentions is beyond the scope of this book.

This study aims to answer, from the perspective of the texts at hand, the question of "why Elijah?" While this question has been raised by a few scholars previously, it has always appeared as a secondary concern, or in studies too small to address it in its broader textual context.[4] In this book I will therefore offer a literary analysis of the texts referencing Elijah throughout the Hebrew Bible, Second Temple Jewish literature, and the New Testament, attempting to examine them together through the lens of this question to an extent that has not been undertaken before.

Two shortcomings in past studies reveal the need for such a broad-spectrum approach. First, those studies that have analysed the Second Temple expectation of Elijah's return have done so often with only cursory reflections on its connection to the Kings narrative. This rather one-sided perspective is typified in the extended debate surrounding whether or not Elijah was considered a messianic forerunner by Jewish writers and audiences of the Second Temple period, which tends to read a later conception of "messianism" into earlier texts without questioning how the association developed.[5] Studies concerned with questions of the historical-psychological self-concept of Jesus and John the Baptist are equally unhelpful in tracing the development of this tradition.[6] The identification of a future returning prophet as Elijah assumes a figure whose roots lie in the Kings narrative, but the links between Kings and Malachi, where this expectation is introduced, remain insufficiently explored.

Second, the recent literary studies that have been done on Elijah in Kings have done his character, to my mind, a considerable injustice.[7] They have used various theories of narrative characterisation to suggest that Elijah in Kings is

---

4   See e.g. Brenda J. Shaver, "The Prophet Elijah in the Literature of the Second Temple Period: The Growth of a Tradition" (PhD diss., University of Chicago, 2001), 103; S.D. Snyman, "Malachi 4:4–6 (Heb 3:22–24) as a Point of Convergence in the Old Testament or Hebrew Bible: A Consideration of the Intra and Intertextual Relationships," *HTS Theological Studies* 68 (2012): 4–5; Lotta Valve, *Early Modes of Exegesis: Ideal Figures in Malachi as a Test Case* (Åbo: Åbo Akademi University Press, 2014), 90–126.

5   This debate can be followed via the interacting studies of Morris M. Faierstein ("Why Do the Scribes Say That Elijah Must Come First," *JBL* 100 [1981]: 75–86), Dale C. Allison, Jr. ("Elijah Must Come First," *JBL* 103 [1984]: 256–58), Joseph A. Fitzmyer ("More about Elijah Coming First," *JBL* 104 [1985]: 295–96), and Anthony Ferguson ("The Elijah Forerunner Concept as an Authentic Jewish Expectation," *JBL* 137 [2018]: 127–45), all of which are concerned with the interpretation of Elijah's role in the Second Temple period, but not with why it is Elijah who fills this role. While my methodology is based in a recognition of Second Temple scribal and exegetical practices, I would argue that the development and conception of Elijah's role in this period is best retraced by beginning with the oldest texts and working forward.

6   See e.g. the study of John A.T. Robinson, "Elijah, John, and Jesus: An Essay in Detection," *NTS* 4 (1958): 263–81.

7   Tchavdar S. Hadjiev has also noted this trend, commenting that "modern literary readings of prophetic narratives in the book of Kings have not been kind to poor Elijah" ("Elijah's Alleged

primarily a negative figure: a self-pitying prophetic failure who is decommissioned and replaced by Elisha. This perspective is concerned with the narrative presentation of the figure in Kings, but fails to consider the development of the Elijah tradition *after* Kings. It casts Elijah as a failed prophet without addressing the question of how such a failure came to be so thoroughly transformed into a national eschatological saviour.

The current study proposes to correct both of these imbalances. It analyses the Elijah texts in the Hebrew Bible, Second Temple literature, and the New Testament from a perspective sensitive to the literary composition and features of each unique text, while simultaneously recognising that these texts share references to a common figure. The New Testament epistles, for example, have rarely been treated as significant witnesses to this tradition in their own right, a deficiency which I will here try to correct. The purpose of the study overall is to determine how the later Elijah texts take up and use the literary figure developed in the earlier ones, beginning with Kings and moving through the development of the literary tradition.[8]

I propose that Elijah's recognised role as restorer and forerunner of Yhwh's restoration is based in a narrative characterisation that is already present in Kings, in which Elijah is portrayed simultaneously as a prophet like Moses and as a literary embodiment of Yhwh's preservation of a righteous remnant. This dual characterisation, in various forms and by various means, is clearly visible throughout the span of texts under analysis. Elijah is presented consistently as a single figure who is both a prophet to the community as a whole and a portrayal of a smaller remnant's preservation. As a prophet, he is persecuted for his words of judgement; as the remnant, he is in danger of extinction; yet he embodies life and survival at every turn. His ascension to heaven without death, cited by many as the obvious reason he particularly is expected to return, is indeed exactly that.[9] However, it is no literary afterthought. Elijah

---

Megalomania: Reading Strategies for Composite Texts with 1 Kings 19 as an Example," *JSOT* 39 [2015], 434).

8   The choice to limit my investigation to sources generally dated before the second century CE is due in part to space constraints, but also to my observation that these early texts lay the literary and traditional groundwork for later interpretation. An analysis of Elijah texts in the second century and beyond would also necessarily split into at least two branches to cover Jewish and Christian interpretation and would quickly become unmanageable for a single study. As noted by Ernst Axel Knauf, no doubt both somewhat ironically and fully accurately: "Eine halbwegs erschöpfende Behandlung [der Wirkungsgeschichte Elijas] erforderte mehrere Bände und die Kooperation von Experten aus mindestens 22 Fächern" (*1 Könige 15–22*, HThKAT [Freiburg: Herder, 2019], 229).

9   The observation itself is accurate, but it only succeeds in pushing the question back a step: namely, why is it Elijah, as opposed to any other prophet, who escapes death? Further, why does Malachi's epilogue find it necessary to reawaken a traditional prophet at all?

escapes death in the Kings narrative because, already there, he is an image of
the righteous remnant which cannot die. His character is developed and portrayed consistently throughout early Jewish and Christian texts as the prophet
who is simultaneously the righteous remnant people, and thereby, by his ongoing life, ensures their survival and restoration.

2   Overview of Analysis

As this study is specifically interested in the use of earlier Elijah texts by later
ones, a natural order of analysis falls into place. In this chapter (Chapter 1), I lay
the groundwork of relevant literature and methodological concerns. The literary analysis proper then begins in Chapter 2, with the narrative portrayal and
characterisation of Elijah in the Kings cycle, along with his singular mention in
2 Chron 21. The special interest of this chapter lies in tracing techniques of literary allusion by which analogies are drawn between Elijah and multiple other
Hebrew Bible figures, often at the same time. I argue that these analogies present Elijah as a prophet like Moses in line with Deut 18, who, from a post-exilic
perspective, must be seen to have failed. Simultaneously, these conflated literary analogies also portray Elijah as the embodiment of a righteous remnant.
From this angle, his survival and association with life provides an anchor point
of hope for the survival of the post-exilic community. I argue that these literary
techniques are recognised and understood by later interpreters, and that they,
in turn, take up a similar conflated presentation of Elijah in order to carry on
his identification as both a prophetic and a remnant figure.

   In Chapter 3, I turn to Elijah's abrupt appearance in the epilogue to the
book of Malachi. Scholarly consensus sees Malachi's last three verses, precisely
where Elijah is introduced, as a later addition, or multiple additions, to the rest
of the book. This epilogue may be demonstrated to represent a specific exegetical reading of the larger book, in which Malachi's four mentions of a "messenger" (מלאך) are taken to refer to a single figure and interpreted as applying to
Elijah. In this case, Elijah identifies not only the messenger(s) of Mal 3:1, but
also the priestly messenger of Mal 2:7 and the prophetic voice represented by
מלאכי in the superscript (1:1). As such, he represents the one who "fears" Yhwh,
acting both as the paradigmatic God-fearing prophet-priest (2:5) and as an
image of the God-fearers (3:16) who will be restored.

   Chapter 4 examines Elijah's appearance in Sir 48:1–11, 1 Macc 2:58, *Lives of the
Prophets*, the Apocalypse of Zephaniah, and the Qumran fragments 4Q558 and
4Q521. It argues that these texts demonstrate awareness, in some form, of the
development of the Elijah figure as initiated by Malachi's epilogue, and that

they both adopt and expand upon it. In this process, an association is made between Elijah and Deutero-Isaiah's servant figure, providing evidence that Elijah came to be associated with other literary designations applied to both a prophet and the people of Israel. While much of the context of the references in the Second Temple period is lost due to the fragmentary nature of many of the texts, Elijah's ongoing portrayal as both a prophet and an embodiment of the remnant continues to be supported.

In Chapter 5, I embark on a brief summary of Elijah references and imagery in the New Testament Gospels. Space does not permit an exhaustive study here; this has been undertaken by others.[10] My unique focus lies again on the Gospel writers' conflation of literary analogies in connection with the Elijah image, along the same lines as those observed in the earlier texts. The recognition and implementation of this strategy allows the writers to characterise both Jesus and John the Baptist with Elijah imagery, even within the confines of individual Gospel compositions, while portraying them simultaneously in light of other characters as well. The analogies drawn in these texts, if anything, only strengthen the depiction of the Elijah image as one of both the prophetic voice and the righteous people, arguing that the Gospel writers both recognised and extended this strategy.

Chapter 6 examines references and allusions to Elijah in the New Testament epistles. Paul, for example, explicitly cites the Elijah story in Rom 11 as an illustration of God's preservation of a remnant (11:2–4) and characterises himself as the quintessential example of that remnant (11:1, 5). Numerous scholars have suggested that Paul also identifies himself with Elijah in Gal 1, in references to his life both before and after conversion. I will argue for hints of a similar self-characterisation in 2 Cor 12 as well. This Pauline identification with Elijah underscores a motif also seen in the Gospels and Acts, in which Jesus' Elijah role is transferred onto his disciples. As a result, the Elijah image comes to characterise the early Christian community, both Jew and Gentile. It appears to be included in the portrayal of the faithful Israelite forerunners to the recipients of Heb 11, and Elijah's role as a model for the righteous community is central to his appearance in James 5. He is "a man like-natured to us," whose prayer for rain is analogous to the prayer of believers for restoration. Through prayer, then, they take on Elijah's prophetic role of preparation for the eschaton.

In the final chapter, I examine the presentation of the two witnesses in Rev 11, which have been largely recognised to allude to Moses and Elijah. I argue that the portrayal of these figures in relation to their surrounding context is best

10   As a primary example, see Markus Öhler, *Elia im Neuen Testament*, BZNW 88 (Berlin: de Gruyter, 1997).

understood, again, by recognising the function of conflated literary analogies in the rhetoric of Revelation. The literary vignette of the witnesses, in this case, is paralleled to several others that function as multiple facets of a singular gem, namely, Revelation's depiction of the people of God. The portrayal of the witnesses further displays unmistakable literary links to the endangered churches at the beginning of the book (Rev 1–3) and the restored holy city at the end (Rev 21–22). As such, I propose that the writer of Revelation chooses the Elijah image for the two witnesses with utmost intentionality, in order to portray the people of God in a single image as a prophetic voice, an endangered remnant, and finally a restored holy community.

3   Literature Review

3.1   *Comparable Studies*
As noted above, there exists a decided gap in Elijah scholarship in the area of comprehensive overviews. The majority of extant studies focus primarily on one to two of the contexts in which Elijah appears; very few claim to start at the beginning and methodically work their way forward.

There are a few exceptions that should be mentioned. Joachim Jeremias's article on Elijah in the 1935 *Theologisches Wörterbuch zum Neuen Testament* covers the Second Temple Elijah traditions leading up to the New Testament more adequately than do many longer, modern studies.[11] It offers an early answer to the question of "why Elijah," locating the prophet's later importance jointly in his ascension in Kings and the prophecy of his return in Malachi.[12] Jeremias also addresses the Elijah expectation in several other early Jewish texts,[13] before grounding the prophet's appearance in the New Testament thoroughly back in Hebrew tradition.[14] As a short article, of course, his treatment is inexhaustive, but it demonstrates the logic of an approach such as the one I endeavour to take.

Among modern works, the title of Henri Vallançon's *Le développement des traditions sur Élie et l'histoire de la formation de la Bible* presents this work as potentially comparable to the current study.[15] It indeed does offer an extended

---

11   Joachim Jeremias, "Ηλ(ε)ίας," *TWNT*, vol. 2, ed. Gerhard Kittel (Stuttgart: Kohlhammer, 1935): 930–43.
12   Jeremias, "Ηλ(ε)ίας," 932.
13   Jeremias, "Ηλ(ε)ίας," 933–35.
14   Jeremias, "Ηλ(ε)ίας," 936–43.
15   Henri Vallançon, *Le développement des traditions sur Élie et l'histoire de la formation de la Bible* (Leuven: Peeters, 2019).

analysis of roughly the same corpus of texts and traditions; however, the similarities go little further. Vallançon uses the development of the Elijah traditions as a source of insight into the development of a two-part biblical canon, attempting to reconstruct something of a timeline of the formulation of the Elijah traditions in relation to the standardisation of biblical texts.[16] Methodologically, this approach is completely unrelated to that of the current study, which is concerned with the fundamental literary relationships among the texts themselves. Rather than seek to determine the role of the Elijah traditions in the formation of a modern canon, I propose to look into the exegetical and literary processes by which these traditions took their current form.

Another potentially comparable study is presented by Brenda Shaver's University of Chicago dissertation, "The Prophet Elijah in the Literature of the Second Temple Period: The Growth of a Tradition." This project also examines a comparable body of texts, and Shaver even grounds her analysis in some similar questions: "Where do the novel elements in the [Elijah] tradition come from and what do they mean,"[17] and "why it was that the messenger [of Malachi] was identified as Elijah and given a new task to perform?"[18] In this case, she does offer a number of conclusions that support those of the current study. As a whole, however, Shaver's project reads largely like a summary and evaluation of previous historical and literary arguments, with regrettably little space allotted to original findings and numerous conclusions left insufficiently defended.[19] The reader is simply left with the sense that more could have been done. Shaver also deals with New Testament writings only in combination with rabbinic texts in a short epilogue,[20] leaving a gap in which the trajectory of the earlier Elijah tradition can be carried forward. On the one hand, I am only too

---

16   See Vallançon, *Le développement*, e.g. 3–5, 491.

17   Shaver, "The Prophet," 3.

18   Shaver, "The Prophet," 103.

19   For example, Shaver's answer in brief to the question of "why Elijah" in Malachi's epi-logue is dogged by absolute statements. She states that "the answer is fairly simple. He is absolutely the only figure who fits the profile of the מלאך no matter which way one wants to interpret Malachi's oracle. For Elijah is both a human messenger/prophet and a heavenly messenger/angel. Once he ascended into heaven, one has to presume that Elijah joined the rest of God's heavenly retinue – that is, that he became a member of the divine council. This fact coupled with an eschatological reading of YHWH's promise in Deut 18:18 to raise up in the future a 'prophet like Moses' makes the association of Elijah with the forerunner-messenger a surefire certainty" ("The Prophet," 108). While I agree that Elijah uniquely fits the portrait of a מלאך in the book of Malachi, as we will see, Shaver provides no arguments or secondary sources to back up these statements, nor does she acknowl-edge the multitude of debated issues she invokes by her choice of terminology.

20   Shaver, "The Prophet," 198–223.

aware of the impossibility of any exhaustive analysis of such a broad textual corpus. On the other, I remain convinced that significant gains in scholarly understanding of the Elijah traditions can be achieved through an approach that allows each unique text to speak for itself.

A recent commentary by Ernst Axel Knauf on 1 Kings 15–22 provides a refreshingly comprehensive examination not only of intertextual connections within the first half of the Elijah cycle, but also of its reception and interpretation in later tradition. He discusses Elijah's presentation in Ben Sira and in the New Testament figures of John the Baptist and Jesus, as well as his interpretation by other early Jewish, Christian, and Islamic traditions.[21] Curiously, Knauf has very little to say about Elijah's appearance in Malachi, which would appear to form a critical link between the Kings cycle and its later interpretation.[22] His investigation of the reception history of Elijah is also focused almost exclusively on the reception of 1 Kgs 17–18. As a commentary on the Kings narrative, Knauf's work does not pose the question of why Elijah in particular boasts such prolific later reception, but it does recognise the foundational character of Kings for the current shape of the later Elijah traditions.

If there is any research that has approached a similar cross-textual interest in Elijah with a similar methodology to mine, it is found in the work of Lotta Valve. Her monograph, *Early Modes of Exegesis: Ideal Figures in Malachi as a Test Case*, begins its section on Elijah with a very similar question, asking "why precisely Elijah was chosen" for Malachi's epilogue and noting past suggestions as insufficient.[23] It concludes that Elijah, as introduced in Malachi's epilogue, not only embodies the "messenger" of Mal 3, but that he was also exegetically associated by Ben Sira with the servant figure of Isa 61 and the priest Phinehas of Num 25.[24] The exegetical techniques on which Valve grounds these conclusions, described through the rubric of a midrashic approach and based in the work of James Kugel, are very similar to those which I have observed.[25] While this monograph is focused on Malachi and therefore only partially concerned with Elijah, Valve has also published multiple shorter articles that present portions of the Elijah and Elisha cycles in relation to their exegetical reception in

---

21   Knauf, *Könige*, 226–70; 339–41; 459–60.

22   See e.g. Knauf, *Könige*, 229.

23   Valve, *Early Modes*, 94.

24   Valve, *Early Modes*, 125–26. Sheree Lear argues that Elijah's association with Phinehas can already be derived from the text of Malachi, with which I agree and which I will also demonstrate below. See Sheree Lear, *Scribal Composition: Malachi as a Test Case*, FRLANT 270 (Göttingen: Vandenhoeck & Ruprecht, 2018), 121–46.

25   Valve, *Early Modes*, 23–27, 34–38; see also James L. Kugel, *In Potiphar's House: The Interpretive Life of Biblical Texts* (San Francisco: HarperCollins, 1990).

later Second Temple and New Testament texts.[26] My conclusions differ from
Valve's on a few points, and by definition the current study cannot reach nearly
the depth of analysis of Malachi as does her monograph.[27] On the other hand,
my approach employs a wider lens in both directions, basing the exegetical
techniques seen in Malachi more fundamentally in the character of Elijah as
developed in Kings, and expanding their reach more broadly into the New
Testament. Nevertheless, the span of Valve's published literature has provided
repeated positive confirmation that the approach and conclusions for which
I argue are logical and defensible.

Finally, Jeremy Otten's study entitled *I Alone Am Left: Elijah and the Remnant
in Luke-Acts* provides compelling support for the interlocked nature of the
character of Elijah and the remnant of the people of God.[28] Otten begins his
study with a brief survey of the same Hebrew Bible and Second Temple texts
that I examine. Though cursory, this survey observes that, already in these
texts, Elijah is connected with a "remnant theme."[29] Otten uses this theme as
the rubric for his analysis of Luke-Acts, concluding that Elijah is presented as a
"quintessential remnant figure,"[30] consistently associated with "(1) his removal
of the wicked through judgment, (2) the gathering of a righteous remainder,
and (3) the hope of renewal for the people of God."[31]

---

26   See Lotta Valve, "The Case of Messenger-Elijah: The Origins of the Final Appendix to
     Malachi (3:23–24)," in *'My Spirit at Rest in the North Country' (Zechariah 6.8): Collected
     Communications to the xxth Congress of the International Organization for the Study of
     the Old Testament, Helsinki 2010*, ed. Hermann Michael Niemann and Matthias Augustin
     (Frankfurt: Peter Lang, 2011), 93–103; idem, "Elijah, Elisha, and Other 'Prophets' in
     Hebrews 11:33–38," in *From Text to Persuasion: Festschrift in Honour of Professor Lauri
     Thurén on the Occasion of His 60th Birthday*, ed. Anssi Voitila, Niilo Lahti, Mikael Sundkvist,
     and Lotta Valve (Helsinki: Finnish Exegetical Society, 2021), 65–82; idem, "Elijah, the
     Servant, and Phinehas," in *Take Another Scroll and Write: Studies in the Interpretive
     Afterlife of Prophets and Prophecy in Judaism, Christianity and Islam*, ed. Pekka Lindqvist
     and Sven Grebenstein (Åbo: Åbo Akademi University Press, 2016), 1–30; idem, "Isaiah 61
     in Reception: Elijah and Elisha in Luke 4," in *Herald of Good Tidings: Essays on the Bible,
     Prophecy and the Hope of Israel in Honour of Antti Laato*, ed. Pekka Lindqvist and Lotta
     Valve (Sheffield: Sheffield Phoenix, 2021), 232–49; idem, "The Lord Elijah in the Temple
     as in Malachi 3.1: 'Overkilling' Elijah Traditions in Luke 2," in *Luke's Literary Creativity*, ed.
     Mogens Müller and Jesper Tang Nielsen (London: T&T Clark, 2016), 144–59.
27   For example, Valve argues for an identification of מלאך הברית in Mal 3:1 with האדון, "the
     Lord" (*Early Modes*, 57), while I remain convinced that this "messenger of the covenant"
     should be identified as one persona with the other occurrences of מלאך within the book
     and, therefore, with Elijah in the epilogue.
28   Jeremy D. Otten, *I Alone Am Left: Elijah and the Remnant in Luke-Acts* (Eugene: Pickwick,
     2021).
29   Otten, *I Alone*, e.g. 50, 61, 69–70.
30   Otten, *I Alone*, 162.
31   Otten, *I Alone*, 83.

To my view, Otten is absolutely correct to recognise the Elijah figure as linked to a righteous remnant. "New aspects" of a remnant concept present in the Elijah narratives were already recognised by Gerhard Hasel, both in the portrayal of Elijah himself as a righteous remnant within apostate Israel and in "the promise of a future remnant that constitutes the kernel of a new Israel."[32] However, Hasel locates Elijah's connection with this remnant only in a "religio-cultural threat" that is relevant to a ninth-century BCE context.[33] Otten, on the other hand, recognises the significance of this motif as a literary construct, and observes that a combination of Elijah-remnant imagery is present in the portrayal of John the Baptist, Jesus, and the disciples in the Gospel of Luke.[34] Here again, I believe that Otten is right to draw these connections. At the same time, I remain unconvinced that the character roles associated with Elijah at any given point can, or should, be differentiated as clearly as he has attempted. Part of the beauty of an artistic conflation of multiple literary analogies is found in its innate, nearly boundless, flexibility. Otten's three-fold framework for the "remnant concept" presents itself as somewhat of an artificial lens laid over the texts, rather than highlighting the conclusions arising from the composition of the texts themselves. His core observation of Elijah's presentation as based in the concept of a preserved remnant, however, recognises what I believe to be a key to Elijah's significance, and I will refer to his insights throughout this study.

3.2   *Text-Specific Studies*

3.2.1   Kings

In the realm of more text-specific works on Elijah, the Kings cycle has held continual fascination. The German tradition has given rise to a number of classic studies, including works by Hermann Gunkel,[35] Georg Fohrer,[36] Odil Hannes Steck,[37] Georg Hentschel,[38] and Ernst Würthwein,[39] as well as, more

---

32   Gerhard F. Hasel, *The Remnant: The History and Theology of the Remnant Idea from Genesis to Isaiah*, 2nd ed., AUMSR 5 (Berrien Springs: Andrews University Press, 1974), 164–65, 172.

33   Hasel, *Remnant*, 159–73; see Otten's similar critique in *I Alone*, 17.

34   See Otten, *I Alone*, chs. 5, 6, and 7 respectively.

35   Hermann Gunkel, *Elias, Jahwe und Baal* (Tübingen: J.C.B. Mohr, 1906).

36   Georg Fohrer, *Elia*, ATANT 31 (Zürich: Zwingli-Verlag, 1957).

37   Odil Hannes Steck, *Überlieferung und Zeitgeschichte in den Elia-Erzählungen* (Neukirchen-Vluyn: Neukirchener, 1968).

38   Georg Hentschel, *Die Elijaerzählungen: zum Verhältnis von historischem Geschehen und geschichtlicher Erfahrung*, ETS 33 (Leipzig: St Benno, 1977).

39   See his five collected articles on the Elijah narratives in Ernst Würthwein, *Studien zum Deuteronomistischen Geschichtswerk*, BZAW 227 (Berlin: de Gruyter, 1994). See also the shorter contributions of Eckhard von Nordheim ("Ein Prophet kündigt sein Amt auf

recently, a strong literary-critical analysis by Susanne Otto[40] and an accessible overview by Rainer Albertz.[41] The analysis of Erhard Blum on the composition of 1 Kgs 17–19 provides an intersection of diachronic and synchronic concerns that undergirds part of the methodology of the current study, as I will describe below.[42]

In the English-speaking world, much of Elijah scholarship has recently taken a fairly synchronic approach, analysing the presentation of the prophet as a literary character in the narrative cycle of Kings. With the notable exception of Dharamraj's study discussed below, the majority of these narrative analyses have concluded that Elijah is largely characterised as a failure. They have observed the jarring contrast between 1 Kgs 18 and 19, in which Elijah appears to morph from a fearless, unstoppable crusader for Yhwh on Carmel to a frightened, "whimpering defeatist" on Horeb.[43] Numerous scholars have chosen to reread chs. 17–18 with an eye toward this coming shift, arguing that the weakness that allows Elijah to buckle under pressure is established by the narrator's artful crafting of character flaws earlier in the story.[44] From such a perspective, Elijah becomes conceited,[45] self-pitying,[46] perfectionistic,[47] overly violent,[48] narcissistic,[49] unreliable,[50] victim to an overzealous "messianic

---

40   [Elia am Horeb]," *Bib* 59 [1978]: 153–73) and Rudolf Smend ("Das Wort Jahwes an Elia: Erwägungen zur Komposition von 1 Reg. XVII–XIX," *VT* 25 [1975]: 525–43).

40   Susanne Otto, *Jehu, Elia und Elisa*, BWANT 152 (Stuttgart: Kohlhammer, 2001).

41   Rainer Albertz, *Elia: Ein feuriger Kämpfer für Gott*, 4th ed. (Leipzig: Evangelische Verlagsanstalt, 2015).

42   Erhard Blum, "Der Prophet und das Verderben Israels: eine ganzheitliche, historisch-kritische Lektüre von 1 Reg XVII–XIX," *VT* 47 (1997): 277–92.

43   Alan J. Hauser, "Yahweh versus Death," in *From Carmel to Horeb: Elijah in Crisis*, JSOTSup 85 (Sheffield: Almond, 1990), 60.

44   E.g. Hauser, "Yahweh versus Death," 60; Paul J. Kissling, *Reliable Characters in the Primary History*, JSOTSup 224 (Sheffield: Sheffield Academic, 1996), 97; John W. Olley, "Yнwн and His Zealous Prophet: The Presentation of Elijah in 1 and 2 Kings," *JSOT* 80 (1998), 28.

45   Russell Gregory, "Irony and the Unmasking of Elijah," in *From Carmel to Horeb: Elijah in Crisis*, JSOTSup 85 (Sheffield: Almond, 1990), 152.

46   Hauser, "Yahweh versus Death," 60; Moshe Reiss, "Elijah the Zealot: A Foil to Moses," *JBQ* 32 (2004), 177.

47   Moshe Garsiel, *From Earth to Heaven: A Literary Study of Elijah Stories in the Book of Kings* (Bethesda: CDL Press, 2014), 19–21.

48   Frances Flannery, "'Go Back by the Way You Came:' An Internal Textual Critique of Elijah's Violence in 1 Kings 18–19," in *Writing and Reading War*, ed. Brad E. Kelle and Frank Ritchel Ames (Atlanta: SBL, 2008), 172–73.

49   Stuart Lasine, "Matters of Life and Death: The Story of Elijah and the Widow's Son in Comparative Perspective," *BibInt* 12 (2004), 130.

50   Kissling, *Reliable Characters*, 147–48.

complex,"[51] condemned by his own narrative,[52] and even a "tetchy and arrogant prima donna."[53] It notes that, where Moses intercedes for the life of Israel on Horeb (Exod 32–34), Elijah uses his parallel Horeb encounter merely to complain. Thus, the passing of prophetic authority to Elisha (1 Kgs 19:15–21) is read as Elijah's dishonourable decommissioning and replacement.[54]

That Elijah's character is portrayed in Kings as a narrative analogy to Moses has been universally recognised, and the contrast that these scholars observe is implicitly correct. All of them, however, fail to explain the successive Elijah traditions that portray him as a hero. If the Elijah cycle was indeed received and read only as an example of prophetic failure, it becomes very difficult to account for the development of the glowing figure seen in later texts. The alternative, espoused by Hadjiev, has been to abandon the search for underlying narrative characterisation altogether and fall back on a simple appeal to the remains of a redactional process.[55] While a redactional history is evident in the Kings cycle and a critical approach is needed, the present narrative displays too many overarching links between diverse literary segments to argue that these are not intended, at least at a late point in the process, to help define Elijah's story and character. The answer is not to ignore this larger characterisation, but rather to approach it, as closely as possible, through the lens of what early readers appear to have seen.

An exception to this trend of negative Elijah readings is found in the analysis of Havilah Dharamraj, in which she examines Elijah's character under the rubric of Deut 18's awaited "prophet like Moses."[56] She concludes that the contrasts noted by other scholars are literary devices that highlight Elijah's unique context, and that the Kings narrative does indeed portray Elijah as a Mosaic prophet.[57] I find her overall conclusion compelling in its recognition of the "prophet like Moses" image as critical to the background of Elijah's presentation and reception. At the same time, she may be somewhat too quick to

---

51   Olley, "Zealous Prophet," 48.

52   Neil Glover, "Elijah versus the Narrative of Elijah: The Contest between the Prophet and the Word," *JSOT* 30 (2006), 449–61.

53   Bernard P. Robinson, "Elijah at Horeb, 1 Kings 19:1–18: A Coherent Narrative?" *RB* 98 (1991), 535.

54   So already the commentary of Rashi (*Mikra'ot Gedolot*, "Haketer," vol. 4, ed. Menachem Cohen [Ramat Gan: Bar Ilan University Press, 1992], 134–36).

55   Hadjiev, "Megalomania," 449.

56   Havilah Dharamraj, *A Prophet Like Moses? A Narrative-Theological Reading of the Elijah Stories* (Milton Keynes: Paternoster, 2011).

57   Dharamraj, *A Prophet*, 218–25.

explain away purposeful contrasts.[58] Her study confines its scope quite legitimately to the Kings narrative, but fails to recognise that the strongest confirmation of her thesis comes from later texts.[59] I will argue that the contrasts evident between Elijah and Moses do, to an extent, demonstrate Elijah as a prophetic failure, but only with the recognition that Moses himself did not succeed, insofar as his mission was to establish a righteous community faithful to Yhwh.[60] The exegesis performed on the Kings cycle by Malachi's epilogue, as we will see, both confirms Elijah as a prophet like Moses and recognises that his mission ultimately remains to be fulfilled in the future.

3.2.2   Malachi

With notable exceptions like those of Valve mentioned above, studies of Elijah in Malachi's epilogue have been conducted primarily either in the immediate context of the book or in overarching reconstructions of the epilogue's redactional role in linking various parts of the Hebrew canon.[61] Neither of these approaches are insignificant to my interest in Elijah. Commentaries on Malachi overall, however, tend again to link the expectation of the prophet's return primarily to the continuation of this motif in later Second Temple texts and the New Testament, and not to a basis in Kings. The conclusion of scholars

---

58 Dharamraj notes the similarities between 1 Kgs 19 and Exod 33–34 (*A Prophet*, 135–36) but, rather than contrasting Moses' intercession with Elijah's failure to intercede, suggests that Elijah's death wish in the wilderness functions as a parallel to Exod 32:31, in which Moses offers his life for the nation (42–44).

59 She concludes that an extension of her analysis into the expectation of Elijah's return in Malachi would not "contribute to our particular study" (Dharamraj, *A Prophet*, 6).

60 I take the terminology and concept of the establishment of a righteous community as representative of the prophetic task from D. Andrew Teeter and Michael A. Lyons, to whom I will refer throughout this study ("The One and the Many, the Past and the Future, and the Dynamics of Prospective Analogy: The Servant[s] as the Vindication of Moses and the Prophets," in *Isaiah's Servants in Early Judaism and Christianity*, ed. Michael A. Lyons and Jacob Stromberg, WUNT II/554 [Tübingen: Mohr Siebeck, 2021], e.g. 16).

61 For exegetical studies of Malachi, see e.g. Beth Glazier-McDonald, *Malachi: The Divine Messenger* (Atlanta: Scholars, 1987); Jutta Noetzel, *Maleachi, ein Hermeneut* (Berlin: de Gruyter, 2015); Wilhelm Rudolph, *Haggai; Sacharja 1–8; Sacharja 9–14; Maleachi* (Gütersloh: Mohn, 1976); Valve, *Early Modes*. For the relationship between Malachi's epilogue and the prophetic corpus, see e.g. Stephen B. Chapman, "A Canonical Approach to Old Testament Theology? Deuteronomy 34:10–12 and Malachi 3:22–24 as Programmatic Conclusions," *HBT* 25 (2003): 121–45; Frank Crüsemann, *Elia – die Entdeckung der Einheit Gottes* (Gütersloh: Kaiser/Gütersloh, 1997), 149–52; Jakob Wöhrle, *Der Abschluss des Zwölfprophetenbuches*, BZAW 389 (Berlin: de Gruyter, 2008), 421–27; Yair Zakovitch, "Do the Last Verses of Malachi (Mal 3:22–24) Have a Canonical Function?" in *The Book of the Twelve – One Book or Many?: Metz Conference Proceedings, 5–7 November 2015*, ed. Elena Di Pede and Donatella Scaiola, FAT II/91 (Tübingen: Mohr Siebeck, 2016), 60–81.

such as Frank Crüsemann,[62] Jakob Wöhrle,[63] and Yair Zakovitch,[64] that the final verses in the present text of Malachi act as a cross-corporal link, highlights the significance of Elijah's appearance at this critical juncture but does not explain why he should receive a place at it. The fact that he does suggests a deeper connection to the Kings narrative than has normally been granted by Malachi studies.

Two further studies merit mention here. David Clark, a student of Joseph Blenkinsopp, produced a 1975 dissertation entitled "Elijah as Eschatological High Priest: An Examination of the Elijah Tradition in Mal. 3:23–24."[65] While Clark locates this motif in the context of pre- and post-exilic "priestly messianism" and the later Zealot tradition, he implicitly recognises a link between the character of Elijah and the priestly imagery in the body of the book of Malachi. This identification, I will argue, is critical to the prophet's appearance in the book's epilogue. Second, Sheree Lear's more recent monograph approaches the book of Malachi as a case study in scribal composition. A core chapter of her study concerns Elijah's identification with Phinehas in rabbinic tradition, which, she argues, is based in the text of Malachi itself.[66] In this way, she concurs with Clark's earlier conclusion that Elijah is considered by Malachi's epilogue to be a priestly figure, and supports the argument I will present for Elijah's identification with both the prophetic and priestly elements of Malachi's coming messenger.

3.2.3   Second Temple Literature

Studies of Elijah in later Second Temple literature have, ironically, lent themselves to a greater consideration of the narrative figure of Kings than have those in Malachi. This phenomenon is due in large part to the eleven verses dedicated to the prophet in Ben Sira 48, which unmistakably allude to both Kings and Malachi. This passage highlights both the importance of Malachi's epilogue as a linking text and the ease with which Second Temple writers combine multiple literary images. My brief foray into Ben Sira will be based largely in the work of Pancratius Beentjes, who has vastly expanded scholarly understanding of this text.[67]

---

62   Crüsemann, *Elia*, 149–52.
63   Wöhrle, *Abschluss*, 421–27.
64   Zakovitch, "Last Verses," 60–81.
65   David George Clark, "Elijah as Eschatological High Priest: An Examination of the Elijah Tradition in Mal. 3:23–24" (PhD diss., University of Notre Dame, 1975).
66   Lear, *Scribal Composition*, 121–46.
67   See, among others, Pancratius C. Beentjes, *The Book of Ben Sira in Hebrew*, VTSup 68 (Leiden: Brill, 1997); idem, "In Search of Parallels: Ben Sira and the Book of Kings," in

Works highlighting Elijah's appearance in Second Temple literature usually combine analyses of multiple texts, since outside of Ben Sira the prophet appears by name only in isolated or fragmented verses. Émile Puech's "L'attente du retour d'Élie dans l'Ancien Testament et les écrits péritestamentaires: 4Q558 et 4Q521," for example, begins with short summaries of Elijah in Kings and Malachi, and then offers a survey of his appearances in Second Temple and later literature far broader than its two titulary Qumran fragments.[68] Shaver's dissertation, already noted above, covers a similar collection of texts. Both of these works provide helpful surveys, but they also arrive quickly at conclusions that, I would argue, are not fully substantiated.[69] Further, it is not their purpose to discover why Elijah appears in these texts; they simply observe that he does and discuss the contemporary development of the reflected traditions.[70] My analysis works in the other direction, arguing that Elijah's presence in Second Temple texts can be grounded literarily in the exegetical reception and interpretation of earlier traditions and asking after the textual basis of Elijah's centrality in the traditions these other works observe.

3.2.4   New Testament Gospels

Recent interest in Elijah in the New Testament has been led by Markus Öhler's foundational work, published in 1997, at which point he noted that "niemand hat bisher einen Gesamtüberblick vorgelegt, wie ich ihn hier versuche."[71] Strictly speaking, to my knowledge, this statement remains true. Somewhat

---

Intertextual Studies in Ben Sira and Tobit: Essays in Honor of Alexander A. Di Lella, ed. Vincent Skemp and Jeremy Corley (Washington: Catholic Biblical Association of America, 2005), 118–31; idem, "Prophets and Prophecy in the Book of Ben Sira," in *Prophets, Prophecy, and Prophetic Texts in Second Temple Judaism*, ed. Robert D. Haak and Michael H. Floyd (New York: T&T Clark, 2006), 135–50. In a Festschrift honouring Beentjes, Bart J. Koet presents a short essay entitled "Elijah as Reconciler of Father and Son: From 1 Kings 16:34 and Malachi 3:22–24 to Ben Sira 48:1–11 and Luke 1:13–17" (in *Essays on Chronicles and Ben Sira in Honor of Pancratius C. Beentjes*, ed. Jeremy Corley and Harm van Grol [Berlin: de Gruyter, 2011], 173–90). It argues that Elijah's role as a reconciler of fathers and sons in Malachi is based in the text of Kings, and that this association is reflected in Ben Sira and Luke. While this essay is too brief to discuss any of the texts in detail, it does recognise the implicit progressive and literarily dependent development of the Elijah tradition.

68   Émile Puech, "L'attente du retour d'Élie dans l'Ancien Testament et les écrits péritestamentaires: 4Q558 et 4Q521," *RevQ* 30 (2018): 3–26.

69   Puech is eager to proclaim Elijah a messianic forerunner in 4Q521, an incredibly fragmented Qumran text about which very few absolute statements should be made ("L'attente," 18–19). See n. 19 above on Shaver's tendency to oversimplify issues via absolute statements.

70   As per Shaver's stated purpose: "to discuss the expansion of the tradition" ("The Prophet," 3).

71   Öhler, *Elia*, vii.

contrary to this purpose statement and to the title of the book, however, the vast majority of Öhler's work is focused on the New Testament Gospels, resulting in barely a tenth of the book dedicated to references and allusions to Elijah in Romans, Hebrews, James, and Revelation. Öhler rightly recognises that a basis in Jewish tradition is needed for an understanding of Elijah's role in the New Testament, and begins his study with a short chapter on Elijah in the Hebrew Bible and other Jewish literature.[72] Again, however, this chapter comprises only a fraction of the book overall, resulting in a work that reads much more like a study of Elijah in the Gospels with a prologue and an epilogue than one with an equal interest in all of the New Testament Elijah texts. While the current study is able to spend much less time in the Gospels, it could again be described as approaching a similar question from the opposite direction. Rather than preface a study on Elijah in the New Testament with a survey of the texts which lead to it, I build on the premise that Elijah in the New Testament is fundamentally based in an interpretation of those earlier texts. I further seek to introduce the Elijah references in the epistles in a way that highlights their unique contributions to this tradition as well.

Further studies on Elijah in the Gospels that should be mentioned include Thomas Brodie's *The Crucial Bridge*[73] and David Hoffeditz's dissertation entitled "A Prophet, a Kingdom, and a Messiah: The Portrayal of Elijah in the Gospels in Light of First-Century Judaism."[74] Brodie's proposal of the Elijah-Elisha narratives as a summary template of the Primeval History and a pattern template for the New Testament Gospels is fascinating in its recognition of the fundamental nature of these narratives to broader biblical literature. To the extent that they see the Kings cycle as a literary pattern for the characters within the Gospels, his observations are well grounded. Brodie instinctively recognises the similarities between the Elijah-Elisha stories and other significant Hebrew Bible narratives, some of which I will also highlight. His argument for specific one-to-one literary templates, however, arguably depends on too many subjective decisions to be substantiated. It seems to me that his observations would be better directed into the recognition of Elijah as a representative figure for the writing communities, a thesis which I hope to establish in this book.

Hoffeditz's dissertation offers abundant relevant insights. He purports to improve upon some of the weaknesses of Öhler's study, and indeed offers a more comprehensive chapter on Elijah in Second Temple literature. He also

---

72   Öhler, *Elia*, 1–30.
73   Thomas L. Brodie, *The Crucial Bridge* (Collegeville: Liturgical, 2000).
74   David M. Hoffeditz, "A Prophet, a Kingdom, and a Messiah: The Portrayal of Elijah in the Gospels in Light of First-Century Judaism" (PhD diss., University of Aberdeen, 2000).

argues for motifs that have been undervalued in other works, including, significantly, Elijah as an image of suffering.[75]

I disagree with Hoffeditz at two primary points. First, he claims to present a study of Elijah in light of first-century Judaism, but locates this Judaism's conception of the Elijah figure only back as far as Malachi, "the key text to later Jewish writings."[76] While Malachi's representation of Elijah unquestionably represents a turning point in the tradition, Hoffeditz overlooks the reality that this "key" took its conception of Elijah, to some degree or another, from the figure of Kings. Second, Hoffeditz's core emphasis on Elijah as a "messianic identifier" fails to define the slippery concept of "messianism" as present in the Second Temple and early Christian periods.[77] While some of my observations are similar to the ones that lead him to view Elijah as a messianic image, I find the messianic paradigm too debated in this case to be helpful. I argue, again, that exegetical deductions regarding Elijah's role as a restorer of Yhwh's people and a forerunner to Yhwh himself can be substantiated by the texts themselves, through a recognition of the various allusions present and the combined image they portray of the agent of Yhwh's restoration.

3.2.5   New Testament Epistles

Attention to the appearance of Elijah in the New Testament epistles has, historically, been rather isolated. Recent articles, however, have finally begun to draw attention to these texts as more than mere cursory illustrations. Eduardo de la Serna has argued specifically for Paul's identification with the figure of Elijah,[78] an observation also made to a somewhat less-developed extent in a well-known article by N.T. Wright.[79] De la Serna, significantly, bases Paul's identification with Elijah in the epilogue to Malachi, as does Osvaldo Vena in a separate article.[80] Both of these works provide an insightful cross-textual

---

75   Hoffeditz, "A Prophet," e.g. 96–101, 140–42.

76   Hoffeditz, "A Prophet," 13.

77   Hoffeditz's introductory chapter traces the debate of Elijah's connection to a messianic expectation, but fails to define what this link means for Elijah's own identity or for the identity of the one he precedes ("A Prophet," v, 1–12).

78   Eduardo de la Serna, "¿Pablo, el Precursor? Pablo y las tradiciones sobre Elías," *RevistB* 3/4 (2013): 161–80. See also František Ábel, "Elijah in the Message of Paul the Apostle: Typology of the Elijah Figure in Paul's Missionary Zeal for the Gospel," *StBiSl* 13 (2021): 266–95.

79   N.T. Wright, "Paul, Arabia, and Elijah (Galatians 1:17)," *JBL* 115 (1996): 683–92.

80   Osvaldo D. Vena, "Paul's Understanding of the Eschatological Prophet of Malachi 4:5–6," *BR* 44 (1999): 35–54.

perspective that is still too rare.[81] Levente Balázs Martos recognises the Elijah image both in Paul and in the remnant in Rom 11.[82] While the prophet's appearance in James has remained puzzling and often downplayed, Mariam Kamell Kovalishyn has argued that his depiction as an example of righteous prayer is intended to summarise the purpose and call of the entire letter.[83] Július Pavelčík further grounds Elijah's appearance in James in the author's purpose of calling readers to prepare for the eschaton.[84]

The most significant study for the current analysis, specifically regarding James, is an MA thesis by James Darlack entitled "Pray for Reign: The Eschatological Elijah in James 5:17–18," in which he argues that "Elijah's prayer for drought and rain functions to give the community of faith a prophetic role similar to that of the eschatological Elijah."[85] I suggest that this conclusion can be grounded even more fundamentally in the lexical and argument structure of the book of James itself, which is built around the prolific repetition of keywords. The significance of keywords in the structure and interpretation of James has been established previously by Daniel Eng[86] and by the broader analysis of Mark Taylor and George Guthrie.[87] I would argue that it is precisely this exquisite lexical arrangement that culminates in Elijah's pivotal role as an eschatological figure, in which he is presented as both a "man like-natured to us" and as an example of the power by which believers act as forerunners to the second coming of Jesus Christ.

3.2.6   Revelation

That Elijah appears in Rev 11, though not by name, has long been a traditional interpretation of the "two witnesses" that are there described. Theories differ regarding the role and purpose of these figures, but significant recent works,

---

81   Noteworthy for the same reason is Giovanni Claudio Bottini's "Continuity and Innovation in Biblical Tradition: Elijah from 1 Kgs 17–18 to Jas 5:17–18" (*StBiSl* 11 [2019]: 120–29), which presents a brief attempt to ground James's use of Elijah in "intermediate texts and traditions" (122).

82   Levente Balázs Martos, "Prophet and Remnant, Crisis and Renewal: Paul's Use of the Elijah Story in Romans 11," *StBiSl* 12 (2020): 252–65.

83   Mariam Kamell Kovalishyn, "The Prayer of Elijah in James 5: An Example of Intertextuality," *JBL* 137 (2018), 1028.

84   Július Pavelčík, "Eliáš v Jakubovom liste," *StBiSl* 12 (2020): 266–306.

85   James M. Darlack, "Pray for Reign: The Eschatological Elijah in James 5:17–18" (MA thesis, Gordon-Conwell Theological Seminary, 2007), 96.

86   Daniel K. Eng, *Eschatological Approval: The Structure and Unifying Motif of James* (Sheffield: Sheffield Phoenix, 2022); idem, "The Role of Semitic Catchwords in Interpreting the Epistle of James," *TynBul* 70 (2019): 245–67.

87   Mark E. Taylor and George H. Guthrie, "The Structure of James," *CBQ* 68 (2006): 681–705.

including the extensive commentary of G.K. Beale, have argued that the witnesses are in some way representative of the people of God.[88] If this is the case, then the presentation of the witnesses remains fully consistent with the image of Elijah as portrayed throughout biblical and Second Temple literature. I will again highlight the presence of this literary identification by means of intentional lexical connections within the book, as well as a broader range of literary features that portray the witnesses both as a prophetic voice and as the embodiment of the endangered remnant of God's people.

4 Methodology

4.1 *Literary Allusion*
The study of literary allusion in ancient Israelite and early Christian texts has grown increasingly sophisticated in the last several decades. Foundations in the definition and identification of allusions, laid by scholars such as Gérard Genette, Ziva Ben-Porat, Richard Hays, William Kynes, William Tooman, Michael Lyons, and many others, are now well established, and form the basis and methodological starting point for my approach to the Elijah texts.[89] I take

---

88   G.K. Beale, *The Book of Revelation*, NIGTC (Grand Rapids: Eerdmans, 1999).

89   For definitions of allusion, see e.g. Ziva Ben-Porat, "The Poetics of Literary Allusion," *PTL: A Journal for Descriptive Poetics and Theory of Literature* 1 (1976): 105–28; Gérard Genette, *Palimpsests: Literature in the Second Degree*, trans. Channa Newman and Claude Doubinsky (Lincoln: University of Nebraska Press, 1997), 1–3; Udo J. Hebel, "Towards a Descriptive Poetics of Allusion," in *Intertextuality*, Research in Text Theory 15, ed. Heinrich F. Plett (Berlin: de Gruyter, 1991), 135–64; Michael A. Lyons, "'I also could talk as you do' (Job 16:4): The Function of Intratextual Quotation and Allusion in Job," in *Reading Job Intertextually*, ed. Katharine J. Dell and William J. Kynes, LHBOTS 574 (New York: Bloomsbury T&T Clark, 2013), 169–77; Earl Miner, "Allusion," in *The New Princeton Handbook of Poetic Terms*, ed. T.V.F. Brogan (Princeton: Princeton University Press, 1994), 13–15; Wolfgang G. Müller, "Interfigurality: A Study on the Interdependence of Literary Figures," in *Intertextuality*, Research in Text Theory 15, ed. Heinrich F. Plett (Berlin: de Gruyter, 1991), 101–21. For guidelines in identifying the presence of allusion, see further Richard B. Hays, "'Who Has Believed Our Message?' Paul's Reading of Isaiah," in *The Conversion of the Imagination: Paul as Interpreter of Israel's Scripture* (Grand Rapids: Eerdmans, 2005), 25–49; David Katzin, "A Paradigm for Identifying the Use of Scriptural Allusion in Lemma-Based Exegesis Within the Qumran Library Using 4QpPsa (4Q171) as an Example," *HUCA* 87 (2016): 61–92; Joachim J. Krause, "Citations, Allusions, and Marking Them in the Hebrew Bible: A Theoretical Introduction with Some Examples," *BibInt* 31 (2023): 440–56; William J. Kynes, *My Psalm Has Turned into Weeping: Job's Dialogue with the Psalms*, BZAW 437 (Berlin: de Gruyter, 2012), 37–49; Jeffery M. Leonard, "Identifying Inner-Biblical Allusions: Psalm 78 as a Test Case," *JBL* 127 (2008): 241–265; idem, "Identifying Subtle Allusions," in *Subtle Citation, Allusion, and Translation in the Hebrew*

for granted that the writers of these texts allude to other texts at lexical, character, and plot levels. Further, I assume that the ancient writers expected their readers to understand these allusions and to interpret the texts and their plotlines, characters, and arguments in light of the "activated" referent texts.[90]

A less-explored interest within this field, represented largely by the work of Jonathan Grossman, is the observation that literary compositions are not bound to a single referent text at one time. Grossman presents, in a case study of the book of Esther, a compelling example of an ancient writer who shapes a single narrative around allusions to multiple other texts, reversing and mixing character roles at will.[91] His description of a Second Temple scribal strategy of "dynamic analogies" provides a framework for precisely the kind of conflated analogising that I have observed in the Elijah cycle of Kings. I would argue further that these "conflated" allusions or analogies, as I will refer to them, are also demonstrable in non-narrative texts, where a writer combines locutions from multiple referents in order to activate rhetoric or context from all of them at once.[92] Texts are thus creatively combined to make specific arguments. In the case of the Elijah texts, I will show that several key conflated allusions reveal intentional literary features within these texts that have not been observed before.

One of the primary challenges in determining the allusions present in a given text lies in establishing the direction of literary dependence.[93] This initial step becomes all the more critical when more than two texts are in question. In the current study, this question primarily affects the allusions I observe in the Kings cycle to Gen 21–22.[94] The function of Gen 21–22 as a redactional

---

Bible, ed. Ziony Zevit (Sheffield: Equinox, 2017), 91–113; Michael A. Lyons, From Law to Prophecy: Ezekiel's Use of the Holiness Code, LHBOTS 507 (New York: T&T Clark, 2009), 67–75, 80–109; Benjamin D. Sommer, A Prophet Reads Scripture: Allusion in Isaiah 40–66 (Stanford: Stanford University Press, 1998), 32–72; William A. Tooman, Gog of Magog: Reuse of Scripture and Compositional Technique in Ezekiel 38–39, FAT II/52 (Tübingen: Mohr Siebeck, 2011), 27–31.

90   I borrow this term from Ben-Porat's definition of literary allusion, though she would apply it both to the referent and the referring text ("Poetics," 107).

91   Jonathan Grossman, "'Dynamic Analogies' in the Book of Esther," VT 59 (2009): 394–414.

92   This strategy is evident in New Testament texts, as we will see, and I will argue that it is present in earlier texts as well.

93   On strategies for determining direction of dependence, see David M. Carr, "Method of Determination of Direction of Dependence: An Empirical Test of Criteria Applied to Exodus 34,11–26 and Its Parallels," in Gottes Volk am Sinai: Untersuchungen zu Ex 32–34 und Dtn 9–10, ed. Matthias Köckert and Erhard Blum (Gütersloh: Kaiser/Gütersloher, 2001), 107–40; Kynes, My Psalm, 49–59; Lyons, From Law, 59–67; Tooman, Gog, 31–35.

94   Georg Steins, for example, argues for the post-priestly nature of Gen 22 (Die "Bindung Isaaks" im Kanon [Gen 22], HBS 20 [Freiburg: Herder, 1999], 217–24). Christoph Levin does

unit is well established; the same holds true for 1 Kgs 17–19. Lyons has observed evidence of creative adaptation in the parallels between 1 Kgs 17–18 and Gen 22 that argue for the priority of Gen 22.[95] I am convinced that similar adaptation is evident in the use of Gen 21 by 1 Kgs 19. Further, the particular shaping of 1 Kgs 19 around the Hagar narrative of Gen 21 has been consistently and repeatedly noted, so that this configuration of the literary relationship should not quickly be overturned.[96] That the Elijah texts are, in general, the referring texts in these literary relationships will be taken throughout this study to be most plausible.

4.2   Developmental Model

The model of literary composition upon which this study is based further supports this direction of dependence. The classic view of the composition of the Elijah narratives largely held them to be an early source or sources adopted in the composition of the Deuteronomistic History (DtrH).[97] Already in 1977, however, Hentschel suggested that the Elijah narratives contained in 1 Kgs 17–19:21 were inserted into the text of Kings only at a late point in the

<hr>

the same for Gen 21 and would even see it as post-dating ch. 22 (*Der Jahwist*, FRLANT 157 [Göttingen: Vandenhoeck & Ruprecht, 1993], 173). Direction of dependence has also been called into question in the relationship of the Elijah cycle to various Moses narratives (see for comment Blum, "Der Prophet," 291 n. 45). I recognise that some of the Pentateuchal texts may well have been composed later than parts of the Elijah cycle; however, scholarship almost unanimously holds that the likelihood of the Elijah cycle drawing from the stories of Moses is much greater than the other way around (despite the rather singular assertion of Marvin A. Sweeney to the contrary [*I & II Kings*, OTL {Louisville: Westminster John Knox, 2007}, 222]). This direction of dependence will be assumed throughout this study.

95   Michael A. Lyons, "The Aqedah as 'Template'? Genesis 22 and 1 Kings 17–18," *JSOT* 46 (2021), 168–69.

96   See e.g. Glover, "Elijah," 458 n. 31; Gunkel, *Elias*, 22; Steven L. McKenzie, *1 Kings 16–2 Kings 16*, IECOT (Stuttgart: Kohlhammer, 2019), 148; John T. Noble, *A Place for Hagar's Son: Ishmael as a Case Study in the Priestly Tradition* (Minneapolis: Fortress, 2016), 35–36; Robinson, "Elijah at Horeb," 516. Steck sees the parallels as well, though he attributes them to potential descriptions of the same cult site, rather than to dependence on Gen 21 or any intended literary relationship between Hagar and Elijah (*Überlieferung*, 27–28 n. 3).

97   See e.g. Fohrer, *Elia*, 34–35; Martin Noth, *Überlieferungsgeschichtliche Studien*, 3rd ed. (Darmstadt: Wissenschaftliche Buchgesellschaft, 1967), 79; Odil Hannes Steck, *Israel und das gewaltsame Geschick der Propheten*, WMANT 23 [Neukirchen-Vluyn: Neukirchener, 1967], 197; idem, *Überlieferung*, 5; Winfried Thiel, "Deuteronomistische Redaktionsarbeit in den Elia-Erzählungen," in *Congress Volume: Leuven 1989*, ed. J.A. Emerton (Leiden: Brill, 1991), 148–71. For an extensive overview of various redactional models, see Otto, *Jehu*, 11–25.

development of DtrH.[98] Würthwein theorised individual pre-Deuteronomistic
(Dtr) Elijah traditions which were inserted into DtrH at various points during its composition.[99] Hermann-Josef Stipp, though investigating primarily
the Elisha cycle, also postulated pre- and post-Dtr layers within the Elijah
cycle.[100] More recently, Steven McKenzie has presented a detailed compositional model which sees the majority of the current Elijah cycle as the work of
a post-Dtr prophetic narrator.[101] He outlines a process in which a single narrator reworks earlier sources, including individual Elijah and Elisha stories, into
an overarching composition to be inserted into DtrH.[102] McKenzie draws upon
the observations of Blum which, on a smaller scale, are very similar.[103] Blum
argues that the Elijah cycle as a unit presupposes a literary Elisha cycle, as well
as literary forms of numerous Moses stories and the interconnected unit of
Gen 21–22.[104] This model, in turn, argues for a post-exilic date for the Elijah
cycle's completion.[105]

Such a late date in no way precludes the likelihood that individual stories
about Elijah and Elisha are older. Elijah's delivery of the judgement speech on
the house of Ahab in 1 Kgs 21 is likely Dtr in origin,[106] and some of the miracle
stories may even reach back into oral tradition.[107] It does, however, argue that
the Elijah cycle as it stands speaks to the concerns of a post-exilic audience.
When the texts are examined on their own merit, in light of their respective
intertexts, I am convinced that such concerns best explain the wholehearted
adoption of the Elijah figure by Second Temple communities. I will thus assume

---

98   Hentschel, *Elijaerzählungen*, 228–37, 332–33.
99   Ernst Würthwein, *Die Bücher der Könige: 1. Kön 17–2 Kön 25*, ATD 11/2 (Göttingen: Vanden-
       hoeck & Ruprecht, 1984), 269–72.
100   Hermann-Josef Stipp, *Elischa – Propheten – Gottesmänner*, ATSAT 24 (St Ottilien: EOS,
       1987), 477–78.
101   McKenzie, *Kings*, 37–45. McKenzie distinguishes this post-Dtr prophetic narrator from
       the one already proposed by Walter Dietrich, who recognised parts of the Elijah cycle as
       secondary to DtrH but still classified this narrator as Deuteronomistic (DtrP). See Walter
       Dietrich, *Prophetie und Geschichte: Eine redaktionsgeschichtliche Untersuchung zum deu-
       teronomistischen Geschichtswerk* (Göttingen: Vandenhoeck & Ruprecht, 1972), 122–27,
       134–39; McKenzie, *Kings*, 37–38.
102   McKenzie, *Kings*, 44–45.
103   Blum, "Der Prophet," e.g. 277–81, 288.
104   Blum, "Der Prophet," 286, 290–91.
105   Blum, "Der Prophet," 290–91; cf. McKenzie, *Kings*, 45. This conclusion holds, as Blum notes,
       "falls die diversen Anklänge nämlich auf eine zusammenhängende 'Pentateuch'-Erzählung
       rekurrieren (und nicht auf einzelne Traditionen)" (290).
106   See McKenzie, *Kings*, 178–79; cf. Otto, *Jehu*, 125, who posits its origin even earlier.
107   See especially the reconstruction of Alexander Rofé, *The Prophetical Stories* (Jerusalem:
       Magnes, 1988), 13–22, esp. 18; 132–35; also McKenzie, *Kings*, 37.

and refer primarily to McKenzie's compositional model as the diachronic basis for this study.[108]

4.3 Narrative Figures and Community Identity

Both McKenzie and Blum have argued that the Kings cycle, taken as a single post-exilic composition, presents "a paradigm in Elijah for judgement prophecy,"[109] "und zwar in der Rückschau."[110] A post-exilic writer looks back past the experience of exile and the voices of the classic judgement prophets to locate the beginnings of such prophecy already in a ninth-century context.[111] Blum notes the paradox that is produced by this image in the context of the larger narrative, in which both the failure and success of such a prophetic voice is highlighted and the people are portrayed, variously, as recipients either of judgement or salvation.[112] The combination of these images reveals an interpretive framework through which Elijah is depicted as a paradigmatic prophetic voice that is bound to the salvation of the people.

The legitimacy of such a framework for interpretation is supported by much recent research in the field of cultural memory.[113] Ben Zvi, for example, has compellingly shown that biblical figures were presented and received in the Judahite communities of the Persian period as "sites of memory," a term defined originally by the French historian Pierre Nora as "any significant entity, whether material or non-material in nature, which by dint of human will or the work of time has become a symbolic element of the memorial heritage of any community."[114] Ben Zvi argues that those biblical figures which take on far-reaching significance beyond the texts in which their stories appear do

---

108 McKenzie's commentary also includes extensive notes on the text-critical variants within the Elijah cycle, which may be recommended for reference. I am aware of the differences between the Masoretic and LXX versions of these texts, but have found that, to a large extent, the questions they raise are insignificant to the current analysis. I will note variants as relevant, but refer to the Masoretic versions of texts in the Hebrew Bible unless otherwise stated.

109 McKenzie, *Kings*, 44.

110 Blum, "Der Prophet," 288.

111 Blum, "Der Prophet," 288.

112 Blum, "Der Prophet," esp. 284–85; 288–90.

113 See e.g. the classic studies of Maurice Halbwachs (*La mémoire collective* [Paris: Presses Universitaires de France, 1950]) and Jan Assmann (*Das kulturelle Gedächtnis*, 8th ed. [Munich: C.H. Beck, 2018]), as well as the more recent work of Ehud Ben Zvi (*Social Memory among the Literati of Yehud* [Berlin: de Gruyter, 2019]).

114 Pierre Nora, "From *Lieux de mémoire* to Realms of Memory," in *Realms of Memory: The Construction of the French Past*, vol. 1, ed. Pierre Nora (New York: Columbia University Press, 1996), xvii.

so precisely because they have become such "sites of memory." These figures thereby "act as ciphers to be activated within a particular social discourse, and as places to be visited and revisited, even if only mentally, as part of a self-supportive mechanism of socialization and social reproduction."[115]

A similar line of thought is explored by David Carr, who has argued that the Israelite exilic and post-exilic communities found points of identification in ancestral narratives with which they could parallel their own experiences of displacement, endangerment, and suffering.[116] He proposes that this identification contributed to the development of the current shape of their texts.[117] In other words, when the people lacked the ability to describe their own experience, or felt the need to memorialise it against the passage of time, they found literary expression in the stories of ancient figures that embodied the communal hope of survival.[118] The figure of Moses provides one of the primary case studies for Carr's thesis. I have already noted Ben Zvi's description of the interlocked development of the Moses and Abraham traditions with the identity of the community. Given Elijah's clear portrayal on analogy with Moses, the possibility that a similar motivation lies behind the Elijah cycle in its current form should be seriously considered as well.

Indeed, significant precedent can be demonstrated in texts of the post-exilic period for figures holding both an individual and a community identity. Within the Hebrew Bible, such a figure is represented by the "servant of Yhwh" in Deutero-Isaiah. This figure is both part of Israel (e.g. Isa 44) and distinguished from Israel (e.g. Isa 53), and plays a significant role in the execution of Yhwh's judgement and salvation.[119] Further, Joel Willitts has shown that a very similar dual role can be demonstrated in the remnant theology of Qumran.[120]

---

115   Ehud Ben Zvi, "The Study of Forgetting and the Forgotten in Ancient Israelite Discourse/s: Observations and Test Cases," in *Cultural Memory in Biblical Exegesis*, ed. Pernille Carstens, Trine Bjørung Hasselbach, and Niels Peter Lemche, PHSC 17 (Piscataway: Gorgias, 2012), 141; see further idem, "Memory of Abraham," 5–6.

116   David M. Carr, *Holy Resilience: The Bible's Traumatic Origins* (New Haven: Yale University Press, 2014). See e.g. ch. 5, "Abraham and Exile," and ch. 6, "The Story of Moses."

117   Carr, *Holy Resilience*, 96; 102–9; 112–14; 117–20.

118   Carr, *Holy Resilience*, 95–96.

119   See e.g. Holly Beers, *The Followers of Jesus as the 'Servant': Luke's Model from Isaiah for the Disciples in Luke-Acts*, LNTS 535 (London: Bloomsbury T&T Clark, 2015), 31–48; Michael A. Lyons, "'He Will Call His Servants by Another Name': Concluding Reflections on Community Identity and the Exegesis of Isaiah," in *Isaiah's Servants in Early Judaism and Christianity*, ed. Michael A. Lyons and Jacob Stromberg, WUNT II/554 (Tübingen: Mohr Siebeck, 2021), 337–72; Peter Wilcox and David Paton-Williams, "The Servant Songs in Deutero-Isaiah," *JSOT* 42 (1988): 79–102.

120   Joel Willitts, "The Remnant of Israel in 4QpIsaiah[a] (4Q161) and the Dead Sea Scrolls," *JSJ* 57 (2006): 11–25.

The interpretation of Isaiah's remnant concept seen in 4QpIsaiah[a] and "solidi-fied" by several further texts reveals that the community considered itself to be God's righteous remnant people.[121] At the same time, further interpre-tive descriptions of this remnant concept also place it in a priestly role, by which the remnant acts as the agent of God's judgement.[122] "Thus," Willitts comments, "a fusion of two seemingly disparate ideas exists: simultaneously the remnant is both the recipient of eschatological salvation from judgement and God's agent of that eschatological judgement."[123] He further demonstrates that precisely this composite image of the remnant came to be associated with the expectation of a messiah, who both works on behalf of the remnant and comes from within the remnant; whose eschatological role of judgement is underscored by the same role held by the remnant.[124] It appears, then, that at least certain Second Temple communities had a conception of a righteous remnant that came to be merged with a figure who embodied Yhwh's judge-ment and salvation. The figure and role of an eschatological saviour was under-stood to function "interdependently" with the remnant; "collectively as well as individually."[125]

This is precisely the sort of function and role that I believe can be dem-onstrated of the figure of Elijah, who, as I have already noted, has repeatedly found his way into scholarly discussions on the messianic expectations of the Second Temple period. Elijah represents both a priestly and prophetic figure who is associated with eschatological judgement and restoration. He takes on imagery of both endangerment and life that is paralleled with that of the people. He is, I will argue, intentionally portrayed as the literary embodiment of the survival of Yhwh's remnant, and therefore functions as an image of hope for the survival of the post-exilic communities. I suggest further that this dual characterisation of Elijah as both the prophet and the people is the key to his undying significance in early Jewish and Christian tradition: Elijah cannot die because he embodies the remnant who lives.

To make this argument, I will utilise terminology of "remnant" that differs in referent somewhat from its usage in the work of Hasel or even Otten. Similarly to Willitts, I refer by this term to a subgroup within a larger group, which I will also assume broadly to represent the audience of each respective text

---

121   Willitts, "The Remnant," 19, 25.
122   Willitts, "The Remnant," 16–22.
123   Willitts, "The Remnant," 22.
124   Willitts, "The Remnant," 23–24.
125   Willitts, "The Remnant," 23–24.

I analyse.[126] This subgroup is considered to be righteous while the larger group is not, and it therefore hopes to be saved from, or through, the judgement that is expected, or experienced, to fall on the larger group. "Righteous community" will function as a synonymous term.[127] This group is further represented in both Jewish and Christian texts as the true people of God, in contrast to the larger group (whose identity shifts depending on text, context, and time period).[128] In reference to the historical "remnant" groups that resettled the Persian province of Yehud/Judah after the Babylonian exile, and whom I broadly consider to be the audience of the Elijah texts in Kings, Chronicles, and Malachi, I will use "post-exilic/Second Temple communit[ies]." In the context of these texts and their initial audiences, I would argue that the "remnant" and the "post-exilic communities," by the above definitions, at least largely overlap.[129] In the later texts, however, this remnant is repeatedly redefined.[130] By defining my own usage of these terms from the outset, I hope to avoid some measure of confusion and open the way for a recognition of the figure of Elijah as a prophetic voice to the larger group and the embodiment of the remnant within it, in all of the ways these groups are portrayed in each of the relevant texts.

5   Conclusion

The conclusion that Elijah holds this dual characterisation consistently throughout the span of literature approached by this study has, to my knowledge, never been explicitly described. His presence in the New Testament texts acts as a creative reimagining and conclusion to his character and role in Kings and Malachi, demonstrating the later writers' foundational recognition of his identity as both the paradigmatic Mosaic prophet and the embodiment of Yhwh's righteous people. It is this Elijanic role, representing God's people from without and from within, that connects the texts in which he appears, and that constitutes the primary contribution of this study to scholarship on Elijah and on early Jewish and Christian exegesis.

---

126   See Willitts, "The Remnant," 25.
127   See Teeter and Lyons, "The One and the Many."
128   Cf. Willitts, "The Remnant," 25.
129   See similarly Willitts on this perspective in Isa 10–11 via the uses of שׁוּב and שׁאר: "For Isaiah those who are the remnant of Israel *physically* are also those who are the remnant *theologically*; these are indistinguishable" ("The Remnant," 18).
130   Willitts notes such redefinition even within the various Second Temple Jewish groups ("The Remnant," 11).

CHAPTER 2

Elijah and the Endangered Son in Kings

1   Introduction

However great the change and development of Elijah's presentation and role throughout biblical and Second Temple texts, all of these texts draw in some way from the narrative figure of 1–2 Kings. This is where Elijah is portrayed as the main character in his own story. This is where his personality is depicted, if not explicitly described. These are the texts that introduce the reader of the Hebrew Bible to the prophet who will stand as a magnitudinous image well into the early Christian period, and in Jewish practice to the present.[1]

A literary reconstruction of the answer to the question "why Elijah?" would do well, therefore, also to have the Kings cycle as its foundation. It would seek to recognise what elements of Elijah's character and story in Kings are taken up and reapplied by the proponents of later tradition, by which he comes to be transformed into an idealised agent of national restoration. This is where I will begin my investigation.

One of the narrative elements which scholars have universally recognised in the Kings cycle is the unmistakable analogy to Moses which stands at the core of Elijah's character. This analogy offers both parallels and contrasts, and thus represents a significant point of departure both for those scholars who consider Elijah a prophetic exemplar and those who hold him to be an abject failure. In light of the weight of this analogy, and as others have also done, I will use the image of a "prophet like Moses" in the line of Deut 18 as the entry point and one of the standards of measure for my investigation of Elijah and the Kings cycle.[2]

---

1   For an overview of Elijah's traditional role in Late Antiquity and beyond, see e.g. Kristen H. Lindbeck, *Elijah and the Rabbis: Story and Theology* (New York: Columbia University Press, 2010); Daniel C. Matt, *Becoming Elijah: Prophet of Transformation* (New Haven: Yale University Press, 2022); Chana Shacham-Rosby, "Elijah the Prophet: The Guard Dog of Israel," *JH* 30 (2016): 165–82; Aharon Wiener, *The Prophet Elijah in the Development of Judaism* (London: Routledge & Kegan Paul, 1978), 132–35.

2   See specifically Dharamraj, *A Prophet*; Fohrer, *Elia*, 54–58; Reiss, "Elijah," 174–80. "In other words, Moses is the paradigm by which Elijah is to be measured" (Jerome T. Walsh, *1 Kings*, Berit Olam [Collegeville: Liturgical Press, 1996], 287).

2 The Prophet Like Moses

2.1 *Elijah as Like and Unlike Moses*

> A prophet like me from among you, from your brothers, Yhwh your God
> will raise up for you; to him you will listen. (Deut 18:15)[3]

The expectation of Deuteronomy that Yhwh would raise up a prophet like
Moses is of central concern to an evaluation of Elijah's characterisation in
Kings. On the one hand, Deut 18 contrasts this Mosaic prophet with a generic
image of false prophets (18:20–22), arguing that any Yahwistic prophet whose
word is fulfilled is a prophet like Moses.[4] On the other, Moses-like plot elements pervade the Elijah cycle to such a degree that he is arguably made to
look more like Moses than any other figure in DtrH.[5] Both characters receive
divine sustenance in the wilderness (1 Kgs 17:3–6; Exod 16:12). Both build an
altar symbolising the tribes of Israel at a mountain (1 Kgs 18:30–31; Exod 24:4).
Both experience theophanies at Horeb (1 Kgs 19:11–13; Exod 19:18–20; 33:18–23;
34:1–5) which are linked with a period of forty days and nights (1 Kgs 19:8;
Exod 24:18; 34:28). Both find their assignments too difficult and request that
Yhwh take their lives (1 Kgs 19:4, 7; Num 11:14–15). Both have an experience of
parting waters and crossing on dry ground (2 Kgs 2:8; Exod 14:21), both depart
the world mysteriously (2 Kgs 2:11; Deut 34:5–6), and both leave their successors
to cross the Jordan without them (2 Kgs 2:13–14; Josh 3:17; 4:22–23). Lexical similarities exist as well, in descriptions of Yhwh's "passing over" (עבר – 1 Kgs 19:11;

---

3 Unless otherwise noted, all translations of texts cited are my own. I have chosen at times to
   prefer a rougher English rendering in favour of the syntax of the original language.
4 See for discussion Christophe Nihan, "'Moses and the Prophets': Deuteronomy 18 and the
   Emergence of the Pentateuch as Torah," *SEÅ* 75 (2010), 22.
5 The prophets Samuel, Isaiah, Jeremiah, and Ezekiel have also been evaluated in light of
   comparisons to Moses, on the basis either of narrative elements or of their respective pro-
   phetic commissionings. See e.g. Georg Fischer, "Jeremiah – 'The Prophet like Moses'?" in
   The Book of Jeremiah: Composition, Reception, and Interpretation (Leiden: Brill, 2018): 45–66;
   Alphonso Groenewald, "Isaiah 1:2–3 and Isaiah 6: Isaiah 'a prophet like Moses' (Dt 18:18),"
   HTS Theological Studies 68 (2012): 1–7; Risa Levitt Kohn, "A Prophet Like Moses? Rethinking
   Ezekiel's Relationship to the Torah," *ZAW* 114 (2002): 236–54; Mark Leuchter, "Samuel: A
   Prophet Like Moses or a Priest Like Moses?" in *Israelite Prophecy and the Deuteronomistic
   History*, ed. Mignon R. Jacobs and Raymond F. Person, Jr. (Atlanta: SBL, 2013), 147–68; Henry
   McKeating, "Ezekiel the 'Prophet Like Moses'?" *JSOT* 61 (1994): 97–109; Benedetta Rossi,
   "Reshaping Jeremiah: Scribal Strategies and the *Prophet Like Moses*," *JSOT* 44 (2020): 575–93.
   However, Samuel's primary role is associated with the institution of the monarchy, and the
   highly conspicuous elements of wilderness and Horeb so present in Elijah's story are absent
   from Samuel's. Of the other three, Isaiah is the only one who plays any, and only a very secondary, role in the narrative of DtrH (2 Kgs 19–20).

Exod 33:19–22), references to zeal/jealousy (קנא – 1 Kgs 19:10, 14; Exod 20:5; 34:14), and real or promised intervention by Yhwh's מלאך (1 Kgs 19:7; Exod 23:20). Dharamraj concludes, "To the reader who responds to the richly nuanced resonance of this prophetic narrative with the Exodus stories, it appears that Kings recreates for a new generation ... a prophet like Moses."[6]

Her evaluation, however, is far from universal. On the basis of this same overarching analogy to Moses, other narrative critics have accorded Elijah harsh censure.[7] They have argued that, where Moses intercedes for Israel on Horeb (Exod 32:11–13, 31–32), Elijah accuses Israel and despairs only for himself (1 Kgs 19:9–14).[8] Insofar as intercession is considered a fundamental prophetic duty, he is considered to have failed the test of a true prophet.[9] This failure has then been taken as the basis for Yhwh's replacement of Elijah with Elisha.[10]

To conclude that Horeb represents Elijah's "decommissioning" is too harsh and applies the Moses-Elijah analogy only to one side of the argument. This view largely fails to account for the fact that Moses is explicitly rebuked for rebellion at Meribah and punished (Num 27:13–14), while Elijah is not rebuked at all. In the arrangement of the extant cycle, Elijah continues to minister as איש האלהים after his supposed failure on Horeb (2 Kgs 1:9–14),[11] and the narrator concludes the story with a glorious ascension, rather than a dishonourable discharge from duty.[12]

---

6   Dharamraj, *A Prophet*, 225.

7   See e.g. Gregory, "Irony," 145; von Nordheim, "Ein Prophet," 162; Olley, "Zealous Prophet," 41; Reiss, "Elijah," 178.

8   So e.g. Hauser, "Yahweh versus Death," 60–61.

9   For this view of prophetic intercession, see Teeter and Lyons, "The One and the Many," 16–18, 25–26; Lena-Sofia Tiemeyer, "God's Hidden Compassion," *TynBul* 57 (2006), 193–94; George W. Savran, *Encountering the Divine: Theophany in Biblical Narrative* (London: T&T Clark, 2005), 220. Contra Samuel E. Balentine, who has argued against the common understanding of intercession as a primary prophetic role ("The Prophet as Intercessor: A Reassessment," *JBL* 103 [1984]: 161–73).

10 See e.g. Gregory, "Irony," 102.

11 This title is, in all likelihood, evidence of the dependence of the Elijah cycle on the Elisha cycle, where it fits more consistently and logically as a generic term for a miracle-working prophet (2 Kgs 4–8; see e.g. Fohrer, *Elia*, 36; McKenzie, *Kings*, 102; Rofé, *Prophetical Stories*, 13–26, 133; Stipp, *Elischa*, 477; Walsh, *1 Kings*, 231). Nevertheless, it also reminds the reader of Moses, who was previously called by it (Deut 33:1; Josh 14:6; cf. 1 Chron 23:14; Ezra 3:2). See Knauf, *Könige*, 133). Even if this title does represent something of the remains of its formational process, the extant Elijah cycle would still have the reader encounter the stories in an order that sees him continue to function as a man of God after Horeb.

12 Those who argue that Elijah's continued ministry after Horeb represents his rebellion against Yhwh's punishment (e.g. Glover, "Elijah," 460; Kissling, *Reliable Characters*, 124–25) are reading their predetermined conclusions into the narrative.

At the same time, Elijah's journey through the wilderness to הר האלהים חרב (1 Kgs 19:8), the only biblical figure other than Moses to meet with Yhwh at this location, evokes such an overwhelming Mosaic memory that the reader cannot help but wait for his Moses-like intercession on the mountain.[13] Its absence rightly leads the reader to suspect that Elijah has not completed the mission of a Mosaic prophet. What this failure means for Elijah's prophetic persona, however, depends on what the reader of Deut 18 is led to expect in the first place.

2.2   *The Failure of Mosaic Prophets*

The promise of a prophet like Moses is set in the context of Moses' parting discourse before his death outside the land. He has been barred from entering Canaan (Num 27:12–14) and, in Deuteronomy, blames this failure squarely and repeatedly on the people (1:37; 3:26; 4:21). The accusation continues: "I spoke to you and you did not listen [לא שמעתם], but you rebelled against the mouth of Yhwh [פי יהוה]" (1:43). Contrary to their treatment of Moses, the people are told that they will "listen" (תשמעון) to a coming prophet like him (18:15), because "I [Yhwh] will put my words in his mouth [בפיו]" (18:18). In an immediate sense, then, the prophet like Moses can be any prophet who speaks the word of Yhwh and commands the ear of the people (Deut 18:9–22). Moses' words represented the mouth of Yhwh (1:43); those prophets who have Yhwh's word in their mouths (18:18) are therefore prophets like Moses.

The unfolding of prophetic tradition, however, reveals Israel's thorough-going failure to "listen" to any Yahwistic prophet in any lasting capacity, and demonstrates the continuing wistful hope for a successful Mosaic prophet well into the post-exilic period. Deuteronomy 34:9 describes Joshua's succession of Moses, including the hopeful note that "the children of Israel listened [וישמעו] to him and did just as Yhwh commanded Moses." The postscript introduced by 34:10, however, dashes any thought that Joshua might have been successful.[14] It is forced to clarify that "there has not arisen since a prophet in Israel like Moses, whom Yhwh knew face to face," and concede that Joshua failed to be

---

13   Michal Karnawalski has further noted the locution הר האלהים חרב appears only here and in Exod 3:1, in the context of Moses' encounter at the burning bush ("Proper Names in the Prophetic Narratives of the Hebrew Bible: Examples of Exodus and 1–2 Kings" [paper presented at the Annual Meeting of the European Association of Biblical Studies, Syracuse, 11 July 2023]).

14   Scholars are largely agreed on the late and secondary nature of Deut 34:10–12 in relation to the preceding context.

an adequate Mosaic successor, as did every prophet after him. According to Deut 34:10, to the time of writing, no prophet like Moses had come.[15]

If this postscript can be taken in some way as elaborating on the expectation of Deut 18, a fuller image takes shape.[16] Deuteronomy 34 acknowledges Moses as the greatest prophet to that time. Even if Deut 18 is interpreted simply as a line of Mosaic prophets who would follow in his footsteps, in the perspective of the post-exilic commentator who added 34:10, any potential successor to Moses had also failed. The specification in 18:15 that the people will listen to the coming prophet, then, becomes significant. The post-exilic community knows that the people did not listen to Moses. They also did not listen to any prophet after Moses; hence, to a Dtr perspective, the exile. However, this community still holds the promise of a prophetic voice that the people will indeed hear. There must, then, still be another prophet coming who will succeed where Moses failed; who will accomplish Moses' mission of persuading the people to heed Yhwh's voice and thereby establish a righteous community of Yhwh-worshippers with a permanence that Moses never achieved.

First Kings 17–19 (ch. 19 in particular), then, does depict Elijah as a Mosaic prophet who fails to live up to Moses' example – just as every other prophet had before him. The narrative itself highlights this conclusion when, after his flight from Jezebel, Elijah collapses under a bush and asks that Yhwh "take my life, for *I am no better than my fathers*" (19:4; emphasis added). With the larger prophetic task in view, this statement reads as a concession to the failure of all prophets to that point. Further, if one accepts a post-exilic composition of this scene, Elijah's words become a contemporary reflection on the unfulfilled prophetic mission, placed directly in the mouth of a Mosaic prophet.[17]

---

15   Joseph Blenkinsopp argues that Deut 34 represents a total denial that any prophet could reach the level of Moses, and that it should not be taken as an expectation that such a prophet might still appear in the future (*Prophecy and Canon* [Notre Dame: University of Notre Dame Press, 1977], 86). However, he also admits that this denial is curiously contrasted by the announcement of a coming Elijah in Mal 3 (121).

16   For one theory of the redactional relationship between the Pentateuch and the prophetic books in relation to the prophet like Moses, see Reinhard Achenbach, "'A Prophet Like Moses' (Deuteronomy 18:15) – 'No Prophet Like Moses' (Deuteronomy 34:10): Some Observations on the Relation between the Pentateuch and the Latter Prophets," in *The Pentateuch: International Perspectives on Current Research*, ed. Thomas B. Dozeman, Konrad Schmid, and Baruch J. Schwarz, FAT 78 (Tübingen: Mohr Siebeck, 2011), 435–58.

17   So also McKenzie, *Kings*, 144. See Knauf, *Könige*, 315 for the suggestion of a Persian-early Hellenistic context. Thiel notes the debate surrounding the identity of the "fathers" here, but concludes that, "im Zusammenhang des Textes, besonders im Spannungsbogen zwischen V.4b und 14, liegt es nahe, an prophetische Vorgänger zu denken" (Winfried Thiel, *Könige*, BKAT 9/2 [Göttingen: Vandenhoeck & Ruprecht, 2019], 253).

He speaks for the entirety of the failed prophetic office. When Elijah fails to intercede at Horeb, then, the narrative is only further demonstrating what the prophet himself has already spoken out loud: Elijah is not the prophet awaited by Deuteronomy. Given the trajectory of DtrH into which the cycle is placed, post-exilic readers know that he does not succeed in reforming the people, in spite of apparent initial success at Carmel.[18] They know the story ends in exile; thus, the Elijah story too must concede defeat. Ironically, it is precisely through this failure that the narrative leaves room for continued hope. If the promised Mosaic role was not fulfilled in the past, the post-exilic communities may continue to look for a prophet still coming in the future.

2.3   Elijah as Literary Image of Hope

On the one hand, then, Elijah is presented as a prophet like Moses who fails. At the same time, his character displays other intriguing elements which this rubric alone does not explain. Elijah repeatedly finds himself in a foreign land, both as a means of survival (1 Kgs 17) and in flight from a powerful threat (1 Kgs 19). He repeatedly claims to be left alone in his loyalty to Yhwh (18:22; 19:10, 14), even though the narrative cycle as a whole demonstrates otherwise (18:3–15; 19:18). He travels to Horeb, the traditional founding point of the nation, and is assured that, in spite of all appearances, a remnant of Israel will survive.

Carr's proposal of post-exilic communities' identification with traditional figures carries powerful weight here if applied to the figure of Elijah.[19] The communities' experience of displacement and suffering at the hands of oppressive powers finds reflection in Elijah's story of displacement and despair, as well as his fear that any righteous remnant within the nation will die out altogether. Even his name אליהו, "Yhwh is my God," is literally the confession of those who remain faithful. Yhwh's promise to this prophet that a remnant of Israel will survive is weighted by the narrative's portrayal of Elijah himself as this remnant, and by his consistent survival. This dual identification of Elijah as both a Mosaic prophet and the endangered remnant is consistently visible throughout his cycle. We will trace this thread, first of all, through an examination of the cycle's thematic presentation of various endangered entities, which, I will argue, work together to paint a picture of the survival of Israel's righteous remnant.

---

18   So also Blum, "Der Prophet," 290.
19   Carr, Holy Resilience, e.g. 95.

3 Endangered Entities in the Elijah Cycle

3.1 *1 Kings 17: the Prophet and the Son*

3.1.1 17A: the Endangered Prophet

The Elijah cycle begins in 1 Kgs 17:1 with the prophet's abrupt appearance before the northern king Ahab, pronouncing a drought that will only end at Elijah's word. For ease of reference, I will refer to this initial drought/wilderness story in 17:1–6 as pericope 17A. The reader of 17A is not given any information on Elijah or his background, other than the prophet's declaration that he stands in the service of Yhwh (17:1).[20] Whether it is the drought alone that poses a danger to Elijah's life, or whether he is threatened by Ahab's court and forced to flee, the reader is also not told. His summoning of a drought under the banner of Yhwh's authority is, however, "a direct challenge to the idea that Baal controls fertility, and thus to the faith of Jezebel and Ahab."[21] It further appears to be something of a judgement act, as it is subsequently revoked when the people return to Yhwh (1 Kgs 18).[22] In any case, Elijah hides himself at Yhwh's word at the wadi Cherith, where he is sustained by its water and by bread and meat brought to him by ravens (17:2–6). We will see in ch. 19 that an assault against Jezebel's cult again results in Elijah's flight to the wilderness – a motif which may very well be resumed from this verse.[23]

This introduction immediately sets up Elijah's story to be compared at multiple points with Moses and the wilderness narrative. It is a compact comparison, in which Elijah is at once paralleled to both Moses and Israel. He is Yhwh's prophet who presents himself before the king to announce calamity, as per Moses (e.g. Exod 5:1), while he is also sent out of the land to receive water in a waterless place and bread and meat from the heavens, as per Israel (e.g. Exod 16–17).[24] As he "stands before Yhwh" (1 Kgs 17:1) in this opening narrative, then, he is set up to stand in the position simultaneously of the prophet and of the people of Israel.

---

20 "... als wäre er vom Himmel gefallen (in den er am Ende zurückkehren wird)" (Knauf, *Könige*, 178).

21 McKenzie, *Kings*, 93.

22 So Thiel, *Könige*, 41–42.

23 The direct provocation in the context of 17:1, adopted as a link between the Elijah cycle and the narrative of DtrH surrounding it, is Ahab's wickedness as related at the end of ch. 16. See for discussion Koet, "Elijah as Reconciler."

24 Knauf recognises the significance of the wilderness motif for a post-exilic conception of the life and survival of the community: "Nur in der 'Wüste' ist die Tora (wieder) zu finden, ohne die Israels Existenz im Land keinen Bestand haben kann" (*Könige*, 182).

3.1.2   17B: the Endangered Son

When the wadi dries up, the next phase of the narrative is introduced. Elijah is directed to the care of a Sidonian widow in Zarephath (17:7–24; pericope 17B). She, in turn, is also on the verge of death by drought, depicted as preparing a last meal for herself and her son (17:12–14). Elijah appears to test her faith before facilitating a miraculous supply of flour and oil (17:8–16),[25] by which both the prophet and the foreigners survive. This demonstration of Yhwh's power outside of Israel – in the queen Jezebel's own country, no less (1 Kgs 16:31) – draws a clear contrast. Yhwh preserves the foreigners who believe, while his own nation, which should have believed, languishes under the curse of drought.[26] It raises, for the first time in the Elijah texts, the implicit question of just who will be saved through Yhwh's judgement.

As a result of Elijah's miracle, the widow and her son are initially preserved (1 Kgs 17:15–16). The rest of 17B, however, sees the son endangered again. He succumbs to a "very strong sickness, so that no breath remained in him" (17:17). Here Elijah steps in again. He takes the boy to an "upper room" (עליה – 17:19), performs a threefold physical sign of stretching himself out on the boy's body, and prays that the boy's נפש be returned (שוב) into him (17:21). The result: "Yhwh listened to the voice of Elijah and the life [נפש] of the boy returned [תשב] to his inward part and he lived" (17:22).

On the surface, this pericope tells of Elijah the prophet interceding for and reviving a foreign boy. Several significant narrative analogies are present in this account, however, which cast a much richer hue upon the story. First, the Zarephath pericope has been recognised to draw upon the Elisha narrative of 2 Kgs 4:8–37, in which the only son of a Shunammite woman is revived by Elisha.[27] In this story, the boy is revealed to be a miracle child, born to a mother

---

25   Garsiel has pointed out that the root of צרפת is צרף, meaning to "smelt, refine, test" (*From Earth*, 35).
26   Cf. Deut 28:24; 30:15. See Blum, "Der Prophet," 282; McKenzie, *Kings*, 94; Thiel, *Könige*, 42.
27   See e.g. Blum, "Der Prophet," 278–81; McKenzie, *Kings*, 101–2; Stipp, *Elischa*, 451–57; also Knauf, *Könige*, 91, who notes "Die 'Dachhütte' *ʿăliya* kommt aus Schunem (2 Kön 4,10) nach Sarepta." The story of the Shunammite also directly follows an account in which Elisha multiplies a supply of oil to save a widow and her sons (2 Kgs 4:1–7). This widow, however, is distinct from the Shunammite, who has a husband (4:9, 14, 22–23). The sudden designation of the poor widow of 1 Kgs 17 as בעלת הבית (17:17) poses no problems if it is recognised as a link to this wealthy Shunammite, who builds an upper room in her house for Elisha (2 Kgs 4:8–10) (so Blum, "Der Prophet," 279–80). Even if this rather odd formulation is a relic of the diachronic development of the Elijah cycle and its dependence on the Elisha stories, redactors at later stages evidently found the link unproblematic and left it intact, effectively activating both stories in the mind of the reader at once.

who had "no son, and her husband is old" (4:14).[28] Elisha's promise that "at this appointed time next year you will embrace a son" (חבקת את׳ חיה כעת הזה למועד בן – 4:16) is strikingly like the promise to Abraham and Sarah in Gen 18:14 that למועד... כעת חיה ולשׂרה בן.[29] The overlap of lexemes in these two promises is greater than in any other barrenness story, making a direct allusion to Genesis in the Elisha account highly probable.[30] The effect of such coordination, in turn, is to portray the son of the Shunammite as a child of promise, reminiscent of the son of Israel's patriarch Abraham. If the Elijah narrative indeed takes its shape directly from that of Elisha, the same image also lies in the background of 1 Kgs 17.

Further, Lyons has suggested that 1 Kgs 17 is also shaped around the pattern of the *Aqedah* in Gen 22. Both stories thematically concern "an only son whose life is threatened or lost and who is then restored to his parent,"[31] but Lyons argues specifically for a direct literary relationship between the two passages by highlighting the lexically similar fates of the two sons.[32] Abraham is commanded to "take" his son to "offer him up" "as a burnt offering" (קח־נא את־בנך ... והעלהו ... לעלה – Gen 22:2). Elijah "took" the son and "brought him up to the upper room" (ויקחהו ... ויעלהו אל־העליה – 1 Kgs 17:19).[33] The widow's son lies dead in the עליה; Abraham is commanded to kill his son as an עלה.

This analogy is strengthened by the links between Gen 22 and the Hagar/Ishmael narrative of Gen 21 that precedes it, upon recognition that Gen 21 also displays noteworthy parallels to 1 Kgs 17.[34] In this pericope, Hagar

---

28 See Jon D. Levenson, *The Death and Resurrection of the Beloved Son: The Transformation of Child Sacrifice in Judaism and Christianity* (New Haven: Yale University Press, 1993), 224; Lyons, "Aqedah," 167.

29 So also Levenson, *Beloved Son*, 224.

30 The terms מועד, עת, and בן are only found together in Gen 18:14 and 2 Kgs 4:16–17. See also McKenzie, *Kings*, 277.

31 Lyons, "Aqedah," 163.

32 Lyons, "Aqedah," 163–64.

33 Lyons, "Aqedah," 164–65. He further notes that both 1 Kgs 17 and 2 Kgs 4 contain what appear to be "independent allusions" to the *Aqedah*, indicating that 1 Kgs 17 is an intentional composition in its own right and not simply made up of "elements mechanically taken over from 2 Kgs 4" (167).

34 See Steins, *"Bindung Isaaks"*, 147–63. Both stories "culminate with a journey to a desolate place where the child's life is threatened but spared through divine intervention" (Scott Nikaido, "Hagar and Ishmael as Literary Figures: An Intertextual Study," *VT* 51 [2001], 223). See also the analyses of Levenson, *Beloved Son*, 89–110; Lyons, "Aqedah," 162; Hugh C. White, "The Initiation Legend of Ishmael," *ZAW* 87 (1975), 13–18; Yair Zakovitch, "Juxtaposition in the Abraham Cycle," in *Pomegranates and Golden Bells: Studies in Biblical, Jewish, and Near Eastern Ritual, Law, and Literature in Honor of Jacob Milgrom*, ed. D.P. Wright, D.N. Freedman, and A. Hurvitz (Winona Lake: Eisenbrauns, 1995), 519–20.

and Ishmael are sent from Abraham's house into the wilderness, where Ishmael nearly dies. Both stories concern poor, non-Israelite mothers with no husband, found in either a drought or a desert and told not to fear (Gen 21:17; 1 Kgs 17:13). Both mothers experience the provision of Yhwh in food or water (Gen 21:19; 1 Kgs 17:13–16). Both despair over sons about to die before experiencing their divine preservation.[35]

The fact that the widow's son is patterned on Isaac, the miracle child of the first patriarch, links him, like Elijah in 17A, with the larger entity of Israel. The fact that he is simultaneously patterned on Ishmael in Gen 21, on the other hand, might raise the objection that we see in 17B the survival not of an image of Israel, but of a foreign foil to Israel. This is not the case. Separate studies of Gen 21 have argued that Ishmael's character should be read as a "beloved son" in his own right, rather than simply as a rejected counterpart to Isaac. Already in a 1975 article, Hugh White proposed the Hagar/Ishmael cycle as an example of a larger ancient Near Eastern "endangered child" motif, in which the child of a hero is threatened and then miraculously rescued.[36] More recent narrative analyses have arrived at similar conclusions.[37] Here Grossman's work again proves significant, as he has produced two separate articles that argue specifically for the positive portrayal of Ishmael.[38] He notes that the narrator of Gen 21 avoids criticism of Ishmael by specifically stating God's presence with him, even in his rejection from Abraham's house (21:20).[39] When even Hagar herself casts Ishmael away (21:15), divine intervention saves him (21:17–18).[40] The larger narrative arc of Gen 21–22 thus argues for the paralleling of Isaac

---

35   Cf. Noble, *A Place*, 35. See also Gregory, "Irony," 141.
36   White argues for the "abundant" presence of this motif in ancient Greek mythology, showing from the birth narratives of various hero figures the frequency of "the separation of the mother and/or child from the father and the exposure of the mother and/or child to some kind of hazard" ("Initiation Legend," 267–71). His form-critical study proves overly speculative in its reconstructions, but it does observe the consistent portrayal in ancient literature of the endangered child in a heroic light.
37   See e.g. Noble's analysis of the characters of Hagar and Ishmael in *A Place*, 26–52.
38   Jonathan Grossman, "The Expulsion of Ishmael Narrative: Boundaries, Structure, and Meaning," in *Doubling and Duplicating in the Book of Genesis*, ed. Elizabeth R. Hayes and Karolien Vermeulen (University Park: Penn State University Press, 2021), 27–37; idem, "Hagar's Characterization in Genesis and the Explanation of Ishmael's Blessing," *Beit Mikra* (2018), 269–74.
39   Grossman, "Expulsion," 30.
40   Grossman, "Characterization," 269–71.

and Ishmael as two beloved sons of Abraham.[41] Scott Nikaido, along similar lines, notes a parallel drawn between Hagar in Gen 21 and Abraham in Gen 22, in that both parents are faced with the death of their beloved sons.[42] Thomas Dozeman further presents compelling analogies between Hagar and Moses which would, in turn, support the correlation of Ishmael with the people of Israel.[43]

These analyses highlight the narrative pattern present in Gen 21 as one of threat against beloved offspring, rather than one of the election of a specific line. This is precisely the pattern taken up by 1 Kgs 17.[44] Elijah intercedes for the threatened life of a foreign boy, who is portrayed via the pattern of a beloved son preserved from death. This boy is literarily paralleled with both Isaac and Ishmael, who in turn are linked to each other by means of the same pattern. When Elijah returns the child to his mother, she acknowledges, "Now I know this: that you are a man of God [עתה זה ידעתי כי איש האלהים אתה] and that the word of Yhwh in your mouth [דבר־יהוה בפיך] is truth" (17:24). Not only does her confession form another link to Gen 22, in which the beloved son also lives when the messenger of Yhwh announces "for now I know that you fear God [עתה ידעתי כי־ירא אלהים אתה]" (22:12),[45] but it also utilises the same verbiage as the Dtr expectation of a prophet like Moses, who will hold Yhwh's word in his mouth (דברי בפיו – Deut 18:18). These links serve, at the point of the text's final composition, to depict Elijah as the Mosaic prophet who ensures the life of a foreign boy portrayed, surprisingly, on analogy to Israel.

That the writer of 1 Kgs 17 exploits ironic contrasts between Israelites and foreigners to highlight the unfaithfulness of Israel, and the preservation of an unexpected remnant, was already evident in 17A. In 17B again, the beloved son who is linked with Israel's patriarchal identity is, quite intentionally, *not* an Israelite. This detail is picked up by the broader Elijah cycle via the creation

---

41   Grossman, "Expulsion," 28–31. This conclusion is supported by Gen 21:10–11, in which Abraham is distressed by Sarah's demand that he send Hagar and Ishmael away. See also Zakovitch, "Juxtaposition," 519–20.

42   Nikaido, "Literary Figures," 223. See also Noble, *A Place*, 37–39.

43   Thomas B. Dozeman, "The Wilderness and Salvation History in the Hagar Story," *JBL* 117 (1998), 29–32.

44   Knauf notes the command to the widow not to fear (1 Kgs 17:13) is one frequently found in salvation oracles directed towards Israel or its leaders. He also notes its presence in Gen 21:17 (*Könige*, 88).

45   Lyons has pointed out that the locution עתה ידעתי כי ... אתה appears only in these two texts ("Aqedah," 164). See also Knauf, *Könige*, 93.

of an inclusio with the judgement narrative against Ahaziah in 2 Kgs 1.[46] Both accounts utilise the עלה/עליה motif noted earlier, as well as Elijah's title as איש האלהים.[47] Together, the two pericopes establish a structural framework around the larger cycle that highlights Elijah's relationship to the downfall of Ahab's house and simultaneously parallels a foreign beloved son ironically to the Israelite king:

1 Kings 17:17–24	2 Kings 1
deathly illness (חלה – 17:17)	deathly illness (חלה – 1:2)
boy is taken up (עלה) to an upper room (עליה – 17:19)	Ahaziah falls from an upper room (עליה) and goes up (עלה) to his bed (1:2, 4)
Elijah addressed as איש האלהים, first in doubt then faith (17:18, 24)	Elijah addressed as איש האלהים, first in doubt then faith (1:9, 11, 13)[48]
Elijah brings life with three movements (17:21)	Ahaziah seeks life with three delegations (1:9–13)
boy is brought down (ירד) alive (17:23)	Ahaziah will not come down (ירד) but will die (1:6, 16)

This framework argues that pericope 17B intentionally plays off Ahaziah's judgement oracle. It leads the reader to observe that, while the Israelite king falls down from an upper room and dies, the beloved son of a foreigner is brought down from an upper room and lives. In other words, where the larger institution of Israel fails, an unexpected remnant is preserved. In the pericopes of 1 Kgs 17, this remnant is personified both by the single prophet Elijah and by the widow's son. Elijah is a Mosaic prophet who also survives like Israel in the wilderness; the boy survives like Ishmael in the desert and Isaac on the altar. The resulting composite image embeds within the Elijah cycle, at its outset, the surety of Yhwh's preservation of a remnant in the midst of broader judgement. It further implies that those who make up this remnant are the weak

---

46   McKenzie's model sees 2 Kgs 1:1–18 as including some of the oldest material in the Elijah cycle (*Kings*, 225–26). See also Otto, *Jehu*, 249.

47   Though both of these locutions likely come from the Elisha material (see McKenzie, *Kings*, 102), I would argue that the Elijah cycle uses them to produce an intentional parallel here. McKenzie states that "Elijah's transport of the boy to the upper room serves no clear purpose and becomes a blind motif" (*Kings*, 101), but I believe its purpose to be clear at the structural and rhetorical levels.

48   So Walsh, *1 Kings*, 231.

and the endangered; those who may have even found themselves, for a time, outside the land of Israel.

3.2 *1 Kings 18: the Prophets and the Nation*
3.2.1 18A: the Endangered Prophets

First Kings 18 opens and closes with the status of the drought (18:1, 41–46). The intervening narrative, like that of the previous chapter, can be divided into two distinct but connected pericopes: first, Elijah's encounters with Obadiah and Ahab (18:2–19; pericope 18A), and second, the confrontation on Carmel (18:20–40; pericope 18B). Both pericopes, again, are concerned with two distinct endangered entities.

First, on his way to announce to Ahab the end of the drought, Elijah encounters Obadiah, who serves as the head of Ahab's household (18:3). This character, whose name "servant of Yhwh" (עבדיהו) is also appropriate, is revealed to have hidden and covertly provided bread and water to 100 Yahwistic prophets in the face of Jezebel's killing crusade (18:3–4). Lexically, this pericope (18A) parallels 17A.[49] Obadiah "sustains" (כלכל – Pilp. כול) the prophets of Yhwh (18:4, 13) in the same way that Elijah was "sustained" (כלכל) in the drought (17:4, 9).[50] Elijah hides at the wadi כרית (17:3), while Jezebel carries out a "cutting off" (הכרית) of Yhwh's prophets (18:4).[51] Both units concern prophets who are endangered and preserved, but the stakes have escalated. In 17A, the endangered entity was a single prophet. In 18A, it is 100 prophets and Obadiah, the servant of Yhwh.

Meanwhile, 18A is also linked to 17B just preceding it. Both Obadiah and the widow connect the calamity facing them with their own iniquity or sin (עון – 17:18; חטא – 18:9). The widow is resentful of the death of her son; Obadiah is fearful of his own. The juxtaposition of all three units reveals the writer's ability to manipulate the relevant character roles. Elijah, the endangered prophet in 17A, becomes the preserver in 17B. The preserver of prophets in 18A, however, Obadiah, is simultaneously the most endangered of them all.

---

49 Blum has noted that Obadiah is the faithful counterpart to Ahab that the widow was to Jezebel, and agrees that the Obadiah pericope "erweist sich ... Zug um Zug aus dem Stoff der Sareptastücke gewoben" ("Der Prophet," 283).

50 See e.g. McKenzie, *Kings*, 116; Walsh, *1 Kings*, 228.

51 So Walsh, *1 Kings*, 228. Carlson and McKenzie, on the other hand, both take כרית to be a derivative of כרה, meaning "to give a feast" (R.A. Carlson, "Élie à l'Horeb," *VT* 19 [1969], 421; McKenzie, *Kings*, 86). McKenzie notes that this term occurs elsewhere only in the Elisha cycle (2 Kgs 6:23) and even suggests that the name "may have been coined" specifically for the story of Elijah at the wadi (*Kings*, 86, 98).

The interrelated nature of these three pericopes is supported by the structural bracket formed by Elijah's Yahwistic invocation in 18:15 (18A), paralleling 17:1 (17A): חי־יהוה ... אשר עמדתי לפניו.[52] Just as he proclaimed the drought by the authority of Yhwh's name, he now faces Ahab to end it by the authority of Yhwh's name. The result is that all three of the initial pericopes of the cycle reiterate and mutually extend the themes of the others. All three concern endangered entities who require preservation. The first two are individuals (Elijah and the widow's son); the third is a group (the prophets). The first two are characterised with imagery of Israel. In the third, this identification becomes more explicit as the danger now very obviously concerns a group within Israel: specifically, those who hold to the word of Yhwh. This progression effectively sets the context for the Carmel confrontation that follows, in which the battle for life and death concerns nothing less than the status of Israel itself.[53]

3.2.2 18B: the Endangered Nation

When Elijah ascends Carmel to challenge the prophets of Baal, it is on the understanding that he is the sole defender of Yhwh (אני נותרתי נביא ליהוה – 18:22). On the one hand, scholars have implied that Obadiah's preservation of 100 prophets in 18A renders Elijah's statement inaccurate.[54] On the contrary, McKenzie argues that the prophetic narrator included this statement precisely to coordinate the Carmel account with the rest of the story, "which show[s] that the other prophets of Yhwh are either dead or in hiding."[55] Pericope 18B, therefore, presents a juxtaposition of Elijah both with the prophets of Baal and with the people. Not only is he one prophet against 450 (18:22), but, when the people refuse to choose a side, he is also positioned as "the only

---

52   Yhwh's title in 18:15 includes צבאות, while in 17:1 it is often supplemented with אלהי ישראל (missing from the Lucianic recension – see McKenzie, *Kings*, 86). Knauf notes that the Yahwistic oath formula is otherwise spoken in the Elijah cycle only by the widow and Obadiah (חי יהוה אלהיך – 1 Kgs 17:12; 18:10) (*Könige*, 200).

53   Blum sees the motif of "Schuld, Tod und Prophet" evident in the Zarephath and Obadiah pericopes cast onto a national level through Ahab and Elijah's mutual accusations of "troubling Israel" (18:17–18) ("Der Prophet," 283–84).

54   As argued by Lissa M. Wray Beal, *1 & 2 Kings*, ApOTC (Downers Grove: InterVarsity Press, 2014), 253; Mordechai Cogan, *1 Kings*, AB 10 (New York: Doubleday, 2001), 440; Robert L. Cohn, "The Literary Logic of 1 Kings 17–19," *JBL* 101 (1982), 342; Garsiel, *From Earth*, 72; Gregory, "Irony," 105–6. Glover argues that the repetition of כלכל in 17:4, 9 and 18:4, 13 serves to compare Elijah with Obadiah's Yahwistic prophets and thereby disprove his claim to being alone ("Elijah," 458–59). However, this is only one possible explanation for the parallel and depends on a negative reading of the story overall.

55   McKenzie, *Kings*, 130.

remaining Israelite still faithful to Yahweh."[56] By this reading, the showdown at Carmel represents nothing less than a contest for Israel's existence as a nation under Yhwh.[57]

The prophets of Baal fail to bring down fire from heaven in response to Elijah's challenge (18:26–29), and Elijah has a chance to win the people to his side. At this point, his role as the solitary faithful remnant of Israel takes on a priestly character.[58] Elijah repairs (lit. "healed" – וירפא) the altar of Yhwh "that had been torn down [ההרוס]," with a stone for each tribe to enact a prophetic representation of the nation (18:30–31).[59] The memory of Moses' similar altar of twelve pillars at the foot of Sinai, on which were offered "burnt offerings" (עלת) and the sacrifice of bulls (פרים – Exod 24:4–5), is clearly visible here. Elijah likewise prepares his bull (פר – cf. פרים in 1 Kgs 18:23) at the time of "offering up [עלות] of the sacrifice" (18:36; cf. 18:29).[60] He then performs a symbolic action in a set of three, reminiscent of his three movements to resurrect the son of the widow (17:21), here thrice commanding that water be poured over the offering, the wood, and the altar (18:34).

Strikingly, in another link to 17B, it is in front of this altar, at the עלות, that Elijah offers his second prayer of the cycle (18:36–37). The first was for the beloved son in the עליה (17:19–21). The two prayers exhibit numerous similarities, either via direct lexical correspondence or by the use of synonymous terms:

---

56   Otten, *I Alone*, 31.

57   See Blum, "Der Prophet," 284.

58   See e.g. Knauf, *Könige*, 173–76; Marvin A. Sweeney, "Prophets and Priests in the Deuteronomistic History: Elijah and Elisha," in *Israelite Prophecy and the Deuteronomistic History*, ed. Mignon R. Jacobs and Raymond F. Person, Jr. (Atlanta: SBL, 2013), 35–49, who sees a priestly function in Elijah and Elisha throughout their narrative cycle. Cf. also Willitts, who has noted the priestly character of the Second Temple remnant conception at Qumran ("The Remnant," 21).

59   This detail, as McKenzie has noted, supports the post-Dtr origin of the narrative in its current form, since it has been "widely acknowledged as a flagrant violation of the doctrine of cultic centralization" (Steven L. McKenzie, "My God Is Yhwh," in *Congress Volume 21: Munich 2013*, ed. Christl M. Maier [Leiden: Brill, 2014], 103–104). The emphasis on the restoration of a twelve-stone construction and the specific mention of the naming of Israel (18:31) in relation to twelve tribes is also striking.

60   See Otten, *I Alone*, 31 n. 15 for these and further parallels. Knauf further sees in Elijah's instructions regarding laying the sacrifice with wood upon an altar another allusion to Gen 22 (v. 9) (*Könige*, 146), which would strengthen a reading of the Carmel episode as an intensified endangerment story in relation to 1 Kgs 17.

1 Kgs 17:19, 21, 24

And he brought him up [ויעלהו] to the upper room [עליה] ... and he cried out to Yhwh and said, 'Yhwh my God, please cause to return [תשב] the life [נפש] of this young man into his inner being' ... And the woman said to Elijah, 'Now I know [ידעתי] this: that you are a man of God [כי איש אלהים אתה] and that the word of Yhwh [דבר־יהוה] in your mouth is truth.

1 Kgs 18:36–37

And it happened in the offering up [עלות] of the sacrifice that Elijah the prophet drew near and said, 'Yhwh, God of Abraham, Isaac, and Jacob, let it be known [יודע] this day that you are God in Israel and I am your servant, and I have done all these things by your word [דבריך]. Answer me, Yhwh, answer me – and this people will know [וידעו] that you, Yhwh, are God [כי־אתה יהוה האלהים] and that you have caused their heart [לב] to turn back [הסבת].

Elijah's request in the first case is that a life be returned, and the result is knowledge of Yhwh's word and of Elijah as a man of God. His request in the second case is for the knowledge of Yhwh as God, of his power to turn back hearts, and of Elijah as working by his word. Both prayers concern the turn or return (שוב, סבב) of an essence of life (לב, נפש). The widow, upon reception of her miracle, exhibits a knowledge of truth, which is essentially what Elijah prays will come to Israel.[61]

When fire falls from heaven in response to Elijah's prayer, the priestly nature of his role is highlighted again. This account is very similar in verbiage and imagery to Yhwh's validation of the true priesthood in Lev 9:24.[62] In both cases, the fire of Yhwh confirms his chosen servant, with the same response of awe and recognition from the people:

1 Kings 18:38–39

And the fire of Yhwh [אש־יהוה] fell and consumed [ותאכל] the burnt offering [העלה] and the wood pieces and the stones and the dust, and licked up the water that was in the trench. And all the people saw it [וירא כל־העם] and fell upon their faces [ויפלו על־פניהם] and said, 'Yhwh, he is God! Yhwh, he is God!'

Leviticus 9:24

And fire [אש] went out from before Yhwh [יהוה] and consumed [ותאכל] upon the altar the burnt offering [העלה] and the fat, and all the people saw it [וירא כל־העם] and shouted and fell upon their faces [ויפלו על־פניהם].

---

61   So also McKenzie, *Kings*, 123.

62   See Knauf, *Könige*, 115, 146.

Diachronically, the direct literary dependence of 1 Kgs 18:38–39 on Lev 9 is difficult to confirm, especially if, as McKenzie's model proposes, Elijah's summoning of fire in 1 Kgs 18 is part of an earlier source.[63] Nevertheless, the noticeable (and unique) similarities between the current forms of both texts, at the very least, support the unequivocal conclusion of later interpreters that Elijah represents a very specific, chosen priestly figure. In the Leviticus text, supernatural fire follows Aaron's sin offerings on behalf of the nation (9:1–21), upon which they are blessed as Yhwh's people (9:22–23). Elijah's offering appears to have a similar effect after the fact, as the people reject their indecision and declare Yhwh as God. Elijah then embarks on a slaughter of the prophets of Baal (18:40) that is frequently associated with the priest Phinehas's zealous cleansing of the camp of Israel in Num 25.[64] The combination of these elements with Elijah's restoration of Yhwh's altar appears intentionally to portray Elijah as a priestly figure, which lays the groundwork for future creative interpretation, as we shall see.

The breaking of the curse of drought at the end of the chapter acts as confirmation of the nation's restoration (18:41–46). Elijah ascends Carmel a second time,[65] crouching down with his head between his knees to wait for the return of rain (18:42). The verb utilised here for Elijah's position (גהר) appears elsewhere in the Hebrew Bible only in 2 Kgs 4:34–35, where Elisha crouches upon the dead son of the Shunammite woman and raises him back to life.[66] Both

---

63   McKenzie, *Kings*, 129. McKenzie notes the motif of supernatural fire in the Leviticus text as well, but argues that its purpose in Kings to reveal Yhwh as God should not be conflated with the sanctification of the altar in Lev 9 (135). Nevertheless, both texts are concerned not only with the fire itself, but with the confirmation of Yhwh's true (priestly) servants. In support of this connection, see Knauf, who locates the motif of fire from heaven in the Persian period and therefore has no trouble recognising the similarities between 1 Kgs 18 and Lev 9 (*Könige*, 170–71; cf. 219–20).

64   While the root קנא ("to be jealous, zealous") is used frequently of human jealousy and ambition, as well as depicting a defining characteristic of Yhwh (e.g. Exod 20:5), its only human subjects in the sense of cultic zeal are Elijah (1 Kgs 19:10, 14), Phinehas (Num 25:11), and Jehu (2 Kgs 10:16). See Benjamin J. Lappenga, *Paul's Language of Ζῆλος: Monosemy and the Rhetoric of Identity and Practice* (Leiden: Brill, 2015), 171. For a contrasting view that again sees Elijah as the negative counterpart to Phinehas, see Micha Roi, "Phinehas Is Not Elijah: The Zeal at Shittim (Num 25:6–15) in Light of the Zeal at Horeb (1 Kgs 19), and the Altar at Gilgal (Josh 22:9–34) in Light of the Altar at Mount Carmel (1 Kgs 18)," *RB* 127 (2020): 487–93.

65   McKenzie's diachronic model attributes these verses to a separate source underlying the prophetic redaction, which was only linked with the primary Carmel episode upon compilation of the larger cycle. This reconstruction would explain the second mention of Carmel (18:42) without reference to the preceding narrative.

66   See Peter J. Leithart, *1 & 2 Kings*, BTC (Grand Rapids: Brazos, 2006), 136; McKenzie, *Kings*, 295. Elijah's position has frequently been interpreted as one of prayer (see e.g. Leithart, *1 & 2 Kings*, 136; Sweeney, *I & II Kings*, 229–30); an interpretation which may be influenced

events occur in the context of Carmel (cf. 2 Kgs 4:25).[67] The Elisha narrative, in which a miracle child is resurrected by a crouching prophet coming off Carmel, thus acts as a single source for two Elijah stories. In 17B, Elijah resurrects the beloved son. Here, he assumes the same prophetic position on a mountain and waits for the reinstatement of Israel's blessing as Yhwh's people; in a sense, "resurrecting" the nation. When the rain comes, the reversal of Israel's death curse is complete, and the endangered nation appears to have been saved.

3.3   Summary: 1 Kings 17–18

In the literary unit formed by 1 Kgs 17–18, Elijah is portrayed as a prophetic figure who simultaneously plays the role of an endangered righteous remnant. He is the endangered entity preserved in the drought; he is the faithful remnant on Carmel. Both cases further reveal that the remnant image is to be identified as a group within the people of Israel. This image is developed with progressively higher stakes, moving from the preservation of an individual to that of the nation and culminating with the repentance of Israel and the reinstatement of rain. As such, the first two chapters of the Elijah cycle, in their current arrangement, form a self-contained unit with a highly satisfactory ending.[68]

From a post-exilic viewpoint that looks onto the larger history of Kings, however, this ending is one that cannot and will not be sustained. Readers of DtrH know that no repentance under any prophet was permanent or successful in preventing exile. To a post-DtrH redactor, then, on the other side of exile, the narrative must be shaped in such a way as to leave space for the continuation of the story; namely, what happens if the nation does not repent. This, I would argue, is the primary purpose of 1 Kgs 19.

3.4   1 Kings 19: the Son, the Prophet, and the People

3.4.1   Introduction

The shift in Elijah's characterisation from 1 Kgs 18 to 1 Kgs 19 has proven to be one of the most vexing of the entire cycle. The chapters are linked via Ahab's

---

by the connection of Elijah with prayer in James 5. It is not specified as a position of prayer in 1 Kgs 18, but the link to 2 Kgs 4, in which Elisha intercedes for the life of the boy just prior to assuming this position (4:33–34) renders the deduction likely legitimate.

67   McKenzie argues that the naming of Carmel in the Elisha narrative is a late addition, potentially inserted to tie it to the Elijah story (*Kings*, 293–94). In either case, an intentional connection is made between the texts, at least at a late point in the redactional process.

68   So also Blum: "womit alle Spannungsbögen an ihrem Ziel angelangt erscheinen" ("Der Prophet," 277; cf. 285–86).

report to Jezebel in 19:1 of Elijah's killing of the prophets of Baal (18:40), and by Jezebel's oath to kill Elijah in revenge (19:2).[69] The rest of ch. 19, however, shows no trace of national revival. Indeed, these first two verses provide the only transition between the victorious prophet of 1 Kgs 18 and a very different, very defeated Elijah, running from a nation that has "forsaken [עָזַב] your covenant, torn down [הָרַס] your altars, and killed [הָרַג] your prophets with a sword" (19:10, 14).[70]

It is at this point that synchronic literary critics locate Elijah's fatal failure, arguing that the chapter ultimately represents his dishonourable decommissioning and replacement by Elisha. I have noted in Chapter 1 that arguments for Elijah's overall "unreliability" based on 1 Kgs 19 are weak.[71] On the other hand, the prophetic transition from Elijah to Elisha is indeed critical to the progression of the cycle and to its integration in the larger narrative of Kings. This transition unit (1 Kgs 19:19–21) was likely already part of the earlier Elisha stories.[72] After 1 Kgs 19, Elijah appears next in the extant cycle in the judgement oracle of 1 Kgs 21:21–24, which is an earlier DtrH unit that forms the necessary context for the judgement on Ahab's house.[73] This unit is connected via the Naboth story (21:1–20) to 1 Kgs 18, but not to the Horeb pericope.[74] On the other side of 1 Kgs 21, the storyline remains consistent, as Elijah's pronouncement of judgement on Ahab's house is carried out in 2 Kgs 1, before he ascends to heaven and makes way for Elisha in 2 Kgs 2.

In other words, if Elijah's flight to the wilderness and Horeb encounter (1 Kgs 19:1–18) were removed from the narrative, the rest of the cycle could stand on its own. The reader would be left with an unwaveringly strong and

---

69   For discussion of the longer reading of LXX 1 Kgs 19:2 that includes Εἰ σὺ εἶ Ηλιου καὶ ἐγὼ Ιεζαβελ, see Otto Eissfeldt, "'Bist du Elia, so bin ich Isebel' (1 Kön. xix 2)," in *Hebräische Wortforschung: Festschrift zum 80. Geburtstag von Walter Baumgartner*, VTSup 16 (Leiden: Brill, 1967), 65–70. Eissfeldt concludes, followed by McKenzie, that this phrase is lost in the MT version to haplography ("Bist du Elia," 67; cf. McKenzie, *Kings*, 139).

70   For the later addition and relationship of 1 Kgs 19 to the cycle in relation to chs. 17–18, see already Hentschel, *Elijaerzählungen*, 332. McKenzie notes that the chapter "at once presupposes and is in tension with the previous chapters" (*Kings*, 147).

71   The term utilised by Kissling, *Reliable Characters*.

72   See e.g. McKenzie, *Kings*, 138, 151–52.

73   McKenzie, *Kings*, 40, 178–79.

74   The narrative of 1 Kgs 18 leaves Elijah in Jezreel (18:46), which is mentioned next as Naboth's city of origin and the context for his story (21:1). Ahab's ironic greeting of Elijah and Elijah's responding rebuke in 21:20 is reflected in their similar encounter in 18:17–18. So also Stipp: "Die Dürreeinheit setzt in ihrem Schluß (1 18,45–56) die Naboteinheit als nächstfolgende Elijaerzählung voraus" (*Elischa*, 478).

relatively consistent Elijah figure, who passes prophetic authority to his disciple of his own accord. If the wilderness and Horeb accounts, then, are *not* intended to describe the failure that leads to Elijah's replacement by Elisha, another explanation must be offered.

I would argue that the addition of the wilderness/Horeb units into the cycle had its own separate, unique purpose. The combined unit of 1 Kgs 17–18 depicts a prophetic paradigm in which the prophet brings about the life of the endangered entity of Israel through repentance and faith. The unit of 19:1–18 provides the perspective of the post-exilic community, which knows that that repentance did not last.[75] If any part of Israel is still to be preserved, it must be by a means other than the repentance of the majority. This unit is linked to chs. 17–18, therefore, to present a direct contrast; "der komplementäre Gegensatz zweier Paradigmata."[76] Where Elijah has been an image of preservation, he now becomes the embodiment of endangerment and fear. It can be no coincidence that it is this second facet of Elijah's character, placed in a context in which greater Israel does not repent, that receives Yhwh's explicit promise of a remnant.

3.4.2   19A: Elijah as Mother and Son

The most immediately noticeable feature of Elijah's wilderness journey (1 Kgs 19:1–8; pericope 19A) is its comparison and contrast of Elijah with Moses, as noted previously. At the same time, 19A also displays internal links with earlier parts of the Kings cycle. Elijah has already once found himself displaced and alone in a waterless environment (17A).[77] More specifically, his request of the widow in 17A was for an עגה (17:13) and a "little water" (מעט־מים) in a vessel (17:10), before promising that her "jar of oil" (צפחת השמן) would not run out (17:14, 16).[78] In 19A, he is revived by a "bread cake" (עגה) and a "jar of water" (צפחת מים – 19:6) in a parallel provision of supernatural sustenance.[79]

Elijah's death wish is also structured to look distinctly like a contrast to the death and revivification of the widow's son in 17B. The prophet "lies down" (שכב) under a bush (19:5) of his own volition; the boy is "laid" (שכב) on his bed (17:19) because he is already dead. Elijah prays that the boy's "life" (נפש) be "returned" (שוב) to him (17:21), while he prays that his own "life" (נפש) be

---

75   So also Blum, "Der Prophet," 290.

76   Blum, "Der Prophet," 290.

77   Also noted by Blum, "Der Prophet," 286; Thiel, *Könige*, 21.

78   So also McKenzie, *Kings*, 144.

79   עגה is a rare term, with only seven occurrences in the Hebrew Bible including these. See also Gen 18:6; Exod 12:39; Num 11:8; Ezek 4:12; Hos 7:8.

"taken" (לקח – 19:4). In 17B, Elijah is the agent of life. In 19A, he is so sure of death that he enacts it symbolically while still alive.[80]

The connection between these two pericopes becomes undeniable upon recognition that 19A, like 17B, is also patterned upon the narratives of Gen 21–22. Genesis 21, like 1 Kgs 19, sees its protagonist driven into the wilderness by a figure in power (Gen 21:9–14). Both stories connect that wilderness with Beersheba (Gen 21:14; 1 Kgs 19:3–4).[81] Elijah is afraid (1 Kgs 19:3), and Hagar is commanded not to fear (Gen 21:17).[82] Elijah leaves his "young man" (נער) at Beersheba (1 Kgs 19:3), and Hagar casts down her child, who is later called a נער (Gen 21:17–20), in the same wilderness (21:15).[83] Elijah sits down under a

---

80 McKenzie has commented that Elijah's sleep under the bush is "a symbol of the death he has requested" (*Kings*, 144). The overly modern psychologising that has, at times, been used to interpret Elijah's sudden "depression" is, as Kissling has rightly commented, an "anachronistic" attempt to "impose a modern reader's idea of psychological coherence on our reader" (*Reliable Characters*, 101 n. 11). Wiener, for example, takes the psychologising of Elijah's story to an extreme, arguing that Horeb represents a sort of spiritual self-actualising experience (*The Prophet*, 23, 26–27). See also Ronald Barclay Allen, "Elijah the Broken Prophet," *JETS* 22 (1979), 198; Garsiel, *From Earth*, 17–21; Paul M. Joyce, "The Prophets and Psychological Interpretation," in *Prophecy and the Prophets in Ancient Israel: Proceedings of the Oxford Old Testament Seminar*, ed. John Day, LHBOTS 531 (New York: T&T Clark, 2010), 133; Manfred Oeming, "Das Alte Testament als Buch der Kirche?: Exegetische und hermeneutische Erwägungen am Beispiel der Erzählung von Elija am Horeb (1 Kön 19), alttestamentlicher Predigttext am Sonntag Okuli," *TZ* 52 (1996), 311–325.

81 Knauf connects Elijah's flight to the wilderness here with 1 Kgs 17 and Beersheba with Gen 21, effectively supporting the three-way link between these texts for which I am arguing (*Könige*, 313).

82 Here the textual witnesses to 1 Kgs 19:3 reveal a significant variant. LXX, Vulgate, Syriac, and several Hebrew witnesses read "and he was afraid" (root ירא) while B19a and other manuscripts read "and he saw" (root ראה). The consonantal 3ms *waw consecutive* forms of both verbs are identical. The latter is difficult because of the lack of direct object, while the former seems inconsistent with the bold presentation of Elijah in the previous chapter. If, however, 1 Kgs 19 is intended not to carry on the victorious image of ch. 18, but rather be seen as a contrast, then ירא becomes the more logical and better-supported choice. The Masoretic reading could have been introduced by a misunderstanding of this intended contrast and an attempt, as McKenzie also notes, "to guard the character of Elijah" (*Kings*, 139). Interestingly, the Hagar allusion remains intact in either case, as her story contains intentional wordplay between "fear" and "seeing" (Gen 21:16, 17, 19; cf. 16:13–14). It is even possible that the Hebrew text of 1 Kgs 19:3 was intentionally left ambiguous to account for this allusion.

83 This נער has already appeared, rather out of nowhere, as Elijah's assistant in the anticipation of rain on Carmel (1 Kgs 18:43–44). Scholars have suggested that Elijah's abandonment of this servant in the Beersheba wilderness seems to indicate his abdication of prophetic responsibility (so e.g. Simon J. DeVries, *1 Kings*, 2nd ed., WBC 12 [Dallas: Word, 2003], 235). This may well be the case; Grossman has argued that Hagar's "casting away" (שלך) of Ishmael in the same wilderness also indicates purposeful abandonment ("Characterization," 269–74). However, Elijah's abandonment of his commission, to my

broom tree (1 Kgs 19:4), while Hagar leaves Ishmael under a bush (Gen 21:15) and sits down a distance away (21:16). Both stories involve a supply of bread and water (Gen 21:14; 1 Kgs 19:6), a motif of supernatural provision (Gen 21:19; 1 Kgs 19:5–6), and the intervention of a מלאך (Gen 21:17; 1 Kgs 19:5–7).

All of these elements in 1 Kgs 19 have the effect of mapping Elijah's character directly onto that of Hagar. Closely intertwined, however, are simultaneous analogies that place him in the role of Ishmael. We have already observed the conflated analogy in 1 Kgs 17 that places Elijah simultaneously in the roles of Moses and Israel, and a similar strategy can be demonstrated here. Hagar, upon casting away her child, leaves him under "one of the bushes" (אחד השיחם – Gen 21:15). The parallel in 1 Kings is the "one broom tree" (רתם אחד) which Elijah finds in the wilderness (19:4), an enigmatic notation which supports a reworking of Genesis by Kings, rather than the other way around.[84] Further, it is not Elijah's נער who takes his place under this very specific shrub, but rather Elijah himself! Even as he fills the narrative slot of a mother grieving the impending death of her child, he takes on the role of the child: he himself lies under a bush, barely alive. The Elijah image in 19A thus takes up the separate images of Hagar's parental grief and Ishmael's critical endangerment and applies them both to the prophet.

Given the well-established links between Gen 21 and 22, as well as their appearance together in the backdrop of 1 Kgs 17, it should not be surprising that pericope 19A reveals allusions to Gen 22 as well.[85] Both Abraham and Elijah move towards divine encounters on a mountain. Abraham undertakes a journey with two "young men" (נערים) and eventually leaves them behind (Gen 22:5). It is later revealed that these נערים go with Abraham to Beersheba (22:19; cf. 1 Kgs 19:3). Abraham is addressed twice by the מלאך יהוה, who first stops him from killing his son and then promises a blessing (22:11–12, 15–18). Elijah also is addressed twice by a מלאך (1 Kgs 19:5, 7) who, in the second instance, is revealed to be the מלאך יהוה.[86]

─────────

view, is not a case of the petulant self-pity that others have seen. Instead, it supports the function of 1 Kgs 19 as a contrast to the previous two chapters. The leaving behind of a נער also triggers an intentional connection with Gen 22 (see below). Knauf suggests that this נער needs to be out of the way to make room for the appointment of Elisha at the end of the chapter (*Könige*, 312–13). However, this explanation does not address why the נער appears in 1 Kgs 19 at all, which an intentional connection to Gen 21–22 does.

84   Knauf notes the similarity between locutions here but sees it as a contrast – where Elijah's shrub is specific, Hagar's is simply "(irgend)einen" (*Könige*, 278).

85   See Garsiel, *From Earth*, 87. For the broader links between 1 Kgs 17–19 and Gen 21–22, see Lyons, "Aqedah," 2–7.

86   LXX 1 Kgs 19 does not name the entity touching Elijah as an ἄγγελος until v. 7. 19:5 simply states καὶ ἰδού τις ἥψατο αὐτοῦ. McKenzie argues that the introduction of the מלאך in 19:5 "is a gloss from v. 7" (*Kings*, 140).

In the allusion to Gen 22 in 1 Kgs 19, Elijah primarily follows the pattern of Abraham. The one exception, again, lies in the fact that Elijah himself is the endangered entity. In that sense, he assumes the combined roles of bereaved parent and endangered child in both Gen 21 and 22.[87] He wanders in the wilderness like Hagar, before placing himself under a bush near death. He leaves his servant in Beersheba and climbs a mountain like Abraham, while his own life is the one to be lost barring supernatural intervention.

It seems, then, that 1 Kgs 19 intentionally uses the same source narratives that shaped 1 Kgs 17 to produce an intentionally comparable, and unmistakably contrasting, effect. The dying child who was paralleled to Israel in 1 Kgs 17 is now replaced by a dying prophet who fills the same role.[88] In 1 Kgs 17, the

---

[87] Lyons argues that Gen 21, rather than 22, should be considered primary to the background of 1 Kgs 19, because its parallels to Gen 22 are also found, along with others, in 21 (2 n. 10). I agree with this assessment, but would add that, if 1 Kgs 19 is indeed a late composition and knows the Gen 21–22 unit, then the author may well have had the images of Abraham and Isaac in mind, as well as those of Hagar and Ishmael, in his characterisation of Elijah.

[88] Even White observes the image of an endangered child in the shape of Elijah in the wilderness in 1 Kgs 19 ("Initiation Legend," 294–95). While he sees little significance in these narrative parallels in their own right, viewing them as evidence for a larger genre of cult legend, his conclusion does suggest that the portrayal of Elijah somehow evokes the familiar image of a child about to die (304–305). Grossman comes so close as to note the similarities between Hagar in Gen 21 and Elijah in 1 Kgs 19, but stops short of identifying an allusion ("Characterization," 253 n. 14).

[89] Numerous scholars have noted at this point the unmistakable allusion to 1 Kgs 19 in Jon 4. In Jon 4:3, Jonah prays "and now, Yhwh, please take my life, for my death is better than my life" (4:3). Two verses later, he is sitting on the ground under a "plant" (קיקיון) that Yhwh has caused to grow (4:5–6). When Yhwh sends a wind to wither the plant and it dies, Jonah's response is taken verbatim from 1 Kgs 19:4: וישאל את־נפשו למות (Jon 4:8). To Elijah's critics, this allusion in Jonah to Elijah's character is a confirmation that he is petulant and self-absorbed, caring only for his own comfort without thought for the fate of others (as a primary example, see Robinson, "Elijah at Horeb," 529, 533–34). However, this conclusion represents a misinterpretation of Jonah, as well as of Elijah in Kings. The character of Jonah is well recognised to be patterned on numerous scriptural figures (see e.g. Yitzhak Berger, *Jonah in the Shadows of Eden* [Bloomington: Indiana University Press, 2016]), but generally as a negative contrast to the positive figures. In other words, he is portrayed as something of a composite anti-prophet, who highlights exactly what a prophet should not do. The overly ironic and almost humorous language of the book supports this assessment. In this case, Jonah's use of the Elijah cycle is simply another facet of this pattern: he looks like Elijah because he is an anti-Elijah. Jonah is angry that Yhwh will allow a foreign nation to repent; the Elijah cycle, on the other hand, uses foreign figures as part of an image of a righteous Israel, or at least as recipients of blessing from Israel's God. It presents Elijah as wishing for death precisely because he has failed to bring Israel to repentance (so also Thiel, *Könige*, 250). The motivations behind these characters are opposite. Thus, the allusion to the Kings cycle in Jonah should be seen as one of contrast rather than correspondence, supporting rather than undermining the positive portrayal of Elijah in the Kings cycle overall. See similarly McKenzie, et al.: "The

dying child was saved by the prophet's intercession. Now that same prophet intercedes for his own death,[89] crying רב – "it is too much!" (19:4).[90]

At the same time, Elijah is also the prophetic parent – represented by Hagar and Abraham – of the endangered child, who, in his case, is Israel. This is the opposite conclusion to that reached repeatedly by 1 Kgs 17–18, where the endangered child and the endangered nation both appear to have been saved. Here, that nation is also represented by the dying child under the bush, effectively reversing the repentance portrayed in the previous chapter. Therefore, Elijah grieves that he is no better than his fathers (19:4). He has failed at the prophetic task. 19A thus reuses thematic, contextual, and lexical elements introduced in 17A to lead the reader to re-examine earlier conclusions. The people who appeared to have been saved are in fact still endangered. Their repentance did not last; a deeply personal and obvious conclusion to a post-exilic composer. Therefore, in the unfolding of the story, both the prophet and the people require supernatural intervention if they are to survive.

3.4.3   19B: Horeb as Inverse of Carmel

From a wilderness unit that forms a counterpart to ch. 17, the narrative of 1 Kgs 19 moves to a mountain unit corresponding to ch. 18. Elijah's Horeb encounter (19:9–18; pericope 19B) utilises vocabulary and images from both the Obadiah encounter in 18A and the Carmel episode in 18B. Lexical links to 18A are present already in 19A,[91] but the parallels between the two chapters increase when Elijah reaches Horeb. The cave in which he stays on the mountain is described via the same term as that in which Obadiah hid Yhwh's prophets (מערה – 18:4,

---

allusions to the Elijah story in 1 Kings 19 in Jonah's repeated request to die (4:3, 8–9) suggest that this revision was intended as a parody of judgement prophecy in contrast, as the reviser perceived it, to divine mercy" (Steven L. McKenzie, Rhiannon Graybill, and John Kaltner, "Underwater Archaeology: The Compositional Layers of the Book of Jonah," *VT* 70 [2020], 103). For a discussion of the parallel death wishes of Jonah and Elijah, see Hanne Løland Levinson, *The Death Wish in the Hebrew Bible: Rhetorical Strategies for Survival*, SOTSMS (Cambridge: Cambridge University Press, 2021), 57–88. For the book of Jonah as "metaprophetic" reflection, see Ehud Ben Zvi, "Jonah 4:11 and the Metaprophetic Character of the Book of Jonah," *JHebS* 9 (2009).

90   Elijah's assessment is acknowledged by the heavenly messenger in 19:7: רב ממך הדרך – "the journey is too much for you" (see McKenzie, *Kings*, 145).

91   Ahab's report of Elijah's "slaughter" (הרג) of the prophets (19:1) utilises the same term as Obadiah's fear of death at the hand of Ahab, as does his protection of prophets from Jezebel's "slaughter" (18:12–14). The motif of sustenance by bread and water, used in Elijah's wilderness journey, is also central to the story of Obadiah (18:4, 13).

13; cf. 19:9).[92] Obadiah repeats the same fear that Ahab will kill him (18:9–14); Elijah repeats the same complaint that the children of Israel seek his life (19:10, 14). Both present themselves as a solitary remnant of righteousness in an apostate land.[93] However, where in 18:13 it is Jezebel who has slaughtered (הרג) the prophets of Yhwh, in 19:10, 14 it is the people of Israel who have done the same. In 18:18, Ahab has forsaken (עזב) Yhwh; in ch. 19, so has Israel (19:10, 14). The allusions in 19B to 18A present the nation not as reformed, but as having fallen to the level of its wicked leaders.

Pericope 19B also directly recollects the Carmel pericope from 18B. The setting of both is a mountain on which Elijah encounters Yhwh. On both mountains he declares that he is the "only one left" (אני נותרתי – 18:22; אותר אני לבדי – 19:10, 14). Here too, both the thematic and lexical links occur largely as contrasts. On Carmel, Elijah is portrayed as a remnant who is confident of victory. On Horeb, he is a remnant resigned to defeat. On Carmel, he rebuilds the altar of Yhwh that had been "torn down" (הרס – 18:30) with twelve stones to represent the tribes of a single Israel (18:31); on Horeb, he laments that the "sons of Israel" themselves have "torn down" (הרס) Yhwh's altars (19:10, 14). On Carmel, Yhwh's supremacy is demonstrated by fire falling from heaven to consume the wood, the stones, the dust, and the water around Elijah's altar (18:38). The "sound" (קול) of a heavy shower heralds the reversal of the curse (18:41). On Horeb, there is a fire, an earthquake, and a wind that breaks the rocks to pieces

---

92   This cave also forms a thematic parallel to the cleft in which Moses was hidden in Exod 33:22 (see Knauf, *Könige*, 317–18), but the term used there is נקרה, rendering the verbal parallel to 1 Kgs 18 the stronger link. The cave also appears at the point of a potentially significant textual discrepancy between Masoretic and LXX renderings, in which the Hebrew active participle of Yhwh's "passing over" (עבר) is rendered by the Greek in the future tense (παρελεύσεται) (19:11). Where many modern translations have rendered the Hebrew participle in the past (i.e. "Yhwh passed by"), the NRSV chooses the future ("the LORD is about to pass by"). Max Rogland suggests that this rendering would solve the conundrum of why Elijah otherwise appears only to exit the cave after Yhwh has passed (cf. 19:13) and thereby to miss the very appearance of Yhwh that he was commanded to experience in v. 11: "Go out and stand on the mountain before Yhwh." A future rendering, as noted by Rogland, is supported by the reading of Josephus (Max Rogland, "Elijah and the 'Voice' at Horeb [1 Kings 19]: Narrative Sequence in the Masoretic Text and Josephus," *VT* 62 [2012]: 88–94).

93   Scholars who see these parallels have primarily used them to argue that Obadiah is the positive counterpart to Elijah's failure (e.g. Glover, "Elijah," 458–59; Gregory, "Irony," 112–13; Olley, "Elijah," 36–39, 47), and that Elijah misrepresents reality (e.g. Cohn, "Literary Logic," 342; Hauser, "Yahweh versus Death," 68). For the purpose of 1 Kgs 18–19, however, Elijah must be portrayed as the solitary righteous remnant, even if Obadiah's 100 prophets are still alive (cf. comments on 18:22 above), because he holds the narrative position of a single figure that represents the remnant community.

(19:11–12), but Yhwh's presence is not in any of them. What follows, instead, is the diametrically opposing "sound of a thin whisper" (קול דממה דקה – 19:12).[94] Where on Carmel the people respond in faith (18:39), on Horeb, Elijah grieves their apostasy (19:10, 14). On Carmel, Elijah acts with Phinehas-like fervour in eradicating the prophets of Baal (18:40). It would therefore be expected that, like Phinehas, he would succeed in restoring the community to Yhwh and turning away Yhwh's curse (Num 25:7–13). While the restoration of rain in 1 Kgs 18 might initially indicate this to be the case, by 1 Kgs 19 Elijah laments that his zeal (קנא) has accomplished nothing (19:10, 14). In other words, the scenario described on the second mountain is the complete inverse of that on the first.

First Kings 19, then, takes the motifs and images introduced in the previous two chapters and turns them on their heads. Chapters 17 and 18 have built to a climax: the character placed in the narrative slot of Israel always survives. Yhwh's preservation is applied to increasingly larger entities until, at the point of crisis on Carmel, Yhwh emerges victorious and the endangered nation is restored. However, as we have noted, the Dtr storyline into which the cycle is placed entirely disallows any permanent change. I would therefore argue that the dissonance felt between 1 Kgs 19 and the previous two chapters is precisely the point. In 1 Kgs 19, the nation is no longer presented as restored. Yhwh does not correct Elijah's assessment of Israel's unfaithfulness. He does not remind the prophet that the people have repented, or that the representative altar has been rebuilt. Instead, with the command to anoint Hazael and Jehu as instruments of judgement (19:15–17), Yhwh confirms everything Elijah has said to be true.[95] The people have been unfaithful, and Elijah has been no better than his fathers in establishing and preserving Yhwh's righteous community.

From the perspective of a post-exilic redactor, then, 1 Kgs 19 is needed in order to wrestle with a very personal and pressing question: what does Elijah's role as the prophet of Yhwh's preservation mean if the people do not repent, or if repentance proves only temporary? Does it continue to apply? The tidy

---

94   Scholars have debated the nature of this קול; whether it should be understood as a voice (as per e.g. Thiel, *Könige*, 269–70) or as an anti-voice: "'hörbare Stille'" (Würthwein, *Könige*, 230), "the sound of silence" (Knauf, *Könige*, 323), or simply "a gentle little breeze" (DeVries, *1 Kings*, 236). Nelson's assessment is more determined, interpreting קול דממה דקה as "nothing more than a signal that the theophanic excitement is over" (Richard D. Nelson, *First and Second Kings*, IBC [Louisville: Westminster John Knox, 1987], 125). That it is best interpreted as Yhwh's voice, however, is demonstrated by the introduction of Yhwh's question in the following verse via והנה אליו קול (19:13), which is paralleled to the והנה דבר־יהוה אליו of the first question in 19:9. So also McKenzie, *Kings*, 150; Thiel, *Könige*, 270.

95   So also Blum, "Der Prophet," 289.

conclusion offered by 1 Kgs 17–18 is negated by the post-exilic communities' lived experience, and must therefore also be reframed by the larger story.[96] At this point, the dual characterisation that we have observed of Elijah in 1 Kgs 19 becomes critical. He is no longer cast as the agent of Yhwh's preservation. The prophetic voice, at this point, can speak only judgement (19:10, 14). However, if that voice is also the voice of a grieving mother, lamenting the imminent death of her child; if the prophet weeps with the voice of the dying people themselves, wasting away in the wilderness, then Yhwh himself can step in and preserve the endangered remnant. This is the image of Elijah presented in 1 Kgs 19, which introduces the only outcome on which the post-exilic communities can hang their hope: that Yhwh himself will preserve a righteous remnant in Israel (19:18).

3.4.4 The Promise of a Remnant

When Elijah is commanded to anoint Hazael and Jehu, he is also told to anoint Elisha to succeed him as prophet. These three figures together, representing a foreign enemy, an internal ruler, and a prophetic voice, will be responsible for bringing judgement on Israel (19:16–17). If Yhwh's command to anoint Elisha here were meant to be interpreted as his punitive removal of Elijah, such a sentiment would have been much better communicated by placing this command, together with Elisha's commissioning account (19:19–21), near the end of the cycle to avoid the awkward continuation of Elijah's ministry as איש האלהים in the meantime (2 Kgs 1). Instead, it is linked strategically with Elijah's Horeb encounter and tied to the preservation of a righteous remnant. In other words, even in the wake of judgement, Yhwh "will leave [השארתי] in Israel seven thousand, all the knees which have not knelt before Baal and every mouth which has not kissed him" (19:18).

As noted, the pericope of Elisha's appointment likely originally belonged to an older Elisha collection, but it has been thoroughly integrated into the narrative structure of 1 Kgs 17–19.[97] Elisha receives Elijah's mantle, symbolising his prophetic authority, and responds by offering a sacrifice of his ploughing oxen and providing a feast for the people (19:21). The inclusion of this detail appears completely enigmatic in its immediate context, unless it is recognised as intentionally located to reawaken motifs from 1 Kgs 18. Carmel was the

---

96　"[Die Rezipienten] 'wissen' ja, daß die Umkehr des Volkes auf dem Karmel keineswegs von nachhaltiger Dauer war. Mehr noch, in ihrer Perspektive *kann* die Erzählung nach dem 'Happy-End' von Kap. xviii gar nicht ausklingen; erst mit dem Umschlag in xix gewinnt sie 'geschichtliche' Plausibilität" (Blum, "Der Prophet," 290).

97　See McKenzie, *Kings*, 151–52.

last point at which a sacrifice was offered. Elijah laid his sacrifice on twelve stones (18:31–32); Elisha, with parallel symbolism, offers the twelfth pair of oxen (19:19, 21).[98] The Carmel account also represents the last use of the collective עַם (18:39). The "people" have last been seen declaring that Yhwh is God after Elijah's sacrifice. Now, after Elisha's, they receive food, linked repeatedly in the cycle to survival.[99] Prophetic succession is ensured through the calling of Elisha, and the survival of the people is symbolised in his feast. Again, both the prophetic voice and the people are preserved. In a sense, the account of Elisha's sacrifice reinstates the restoration seen on Carmel on a smaller scale, and thereby answers the fundamental question raised by 1 Kgs 19: even though "the children of Israel have forsaken your covenant, torn down your altars, and killed your prophets with a sword," a remnant will survive.

Throughout 1 Kgs 17–19, then, Elijah is portrayed as a prophet who simultaneously embodies the fate of the righteous community within Israel. If, as I argue, this figure functions specifically as a point of identification and hope for the post-exilic communities, then this hope must be grounded in something other than pre-exilic national repentance such as that portrayed on Carmel. If Elijah's embodiment of Israel in 1 Kgs 17–18 is one of preservation and victory, the image in ch. 19 is one of endangerment and despair. Elijah's prophetic persona in chs. 17–18 is one that rebukes the nation but leads it to repentance, while the prophet of ch. 19 unabashedly condemns the unfaithfulness that ultimately led to exile and fears that all of Israel will be lost. That Yhwh's promise of a remnant is given to this second version of Elijah, rather than the first, assures his post-exilic readers that the promise of preservation is, indeed, also for them. If this Elijah survives, then so can they.

3.4.5   The Prophet Like Moses in 1 Kings 19

This reading also offers a compelling explanation for the failure of Elijah in 1 Kgs 19 to meet the standard of Mosaic intercession. If 1 Kgs 19 is structured to highlight Yhwh's preservation of a remnant in spite of judgement, then prophetic intercession cannot be allowed to prevent that judgement. Lena-Sofia

---

98   "The number twelve is symbolic for the twelve tribes of Israel that Elisha is about to lead (cf. 18:31)" (McKenzie, *Kings*, 147).

99   See Lissa M. Wray Beal, "Setting the Table for Christ in the Elisha Narratives in 1 and 2 Kings," in *Interpreting the Old Testament Theologically: Essays in Honor of Willem A. VanGemeren*, ed. Andrew T. Abernethy (Grand Rapids: Zondervan, 2018), 165–70; cf. Winfried Thiel, "Essen und Trinken in der Elia- und Elisa-Tradition," in *Diasynchron: Beiträge zur Exegese, Theologie und Rezeption der hebräischen Bibel*, ed. Thomas Naumann and Regine Hunziker-Rodewald (Stuttgart: Kohlhammer, 2009), 378.

Tiemeyer has argued that intercession is portrayed in the Hebrew Bible as central to Yhwh's actions with respect to his people.[100] Biblical writers portray Yhwh as restricting the intercession of prophets so that he can hold back his own compassion and judge his people.[101] In the case of Elijah, the narrator of the cycle may employ a similar strategy. It is clear that Elijah *can* intercede; he does so in the case of the widow's son (1 Kgs 17:21) and, arguably, at the altar on Carmel (18:36–37). He further is portrayed unmistakably throughout the narrative as a prophet like Moses. If the awaited prophet like Moses, more powerful than Moses himself in bringing the people to listen (Deut 18:15), had come in the form of Elijah and had interceded, then Yhwh would not have been able to condemn Israel to exile. Elijah's failure, therefore, is required to account for the exilic experience.

The intercession analogy between Elijah and Moses is primarily based in the narrative of Moses on Horeb in Exod 32–34. There is, however, another theophany earlier in the Moses cycle that also takes place at Horeb, and that exhibits equally strong parallels to Elijah in 1 Kgs 19. I have already noted Exod 3:1 as the only direct reference to הר האלהים חרב outside of 1 Kgs 19:8. In the larger unit of Exod 2–4, Moses is threatened by a hostile ruler (2:15), flees in fear (2:14–15), and has an encounter with the מלאך יהוה at a bush (3:2). This Moses narrative is already linked internally with Exod 32–34,[102] but, in similar form to the conflated allusions observed to this point, 1 Kgs 19 clearly draws elements from both. The particular brilliance of an allusion in 1 Kgs 19 to Exod 2–4 is seen in Yhwh's commission to Moses in Exod 4:

> [19] Go, return [לך שוב] to Egypt, for all the men who sought your life [כל־האנשים המבקשים את־נפשך] are dead ...
> [22] And you shall say to Pharaoh, "Thus says Yhwh, '*Israel is my firstborn son*.' [23] And I said to you, 'Send out my son that he may serve me,' but you refused to send him out. Behold, I am the one who slaughters your firstborn son. (Exod 4:19, 22–23; emphasis added)

Elijah's parallel commission, also introduced by שוב לך and following a complaint that his life is being sought, is accompanied by the promise that Yhwh will preserve a righteous remnant in Israel:

100   Tiemeyer, "Hidden Compassion," 194–95.
101   Tiemeyer, "Hidden Compassion," 197–213.
102   Savran (*Encountering*, 205) notes the interconnected nature of Moses' several theophanies in Exod 3, 19–20, 24, and 33–34.

^{14–15} The children of Israel ... seek my life [יבקשו את־נפשי] to take it ...
¹⁸ Go, return [לך שוב] on your way to the wilderness of Damascus ... and I will leave in Israel seven thousand, all the knees which have not knelt before Baal and every mouth which has not kissed him. (1 Kgs 19:14–15, 18)

An allusion to Exod 4 in 1 Kgs 19 would both strengthen the image of Israel as an endangered son in 1 Kgs 19 and reinforce the narrative's identification of this beloved son with the remnant of 7000. In Exodus, Yhwh's son Israel is endangered. In Kings, a beloved son is endangered and a remnant of Israel will be preserved. While the allusion to Exod 32–34 identifies Elijah's failure, the simultaneous analogy to Exod 2–4 confirms what the shape of the Elijah cycle has indicated from the beginning: Israel is the endangered beloved son. The existence of Yhwh's people is the entity that hovers near death, from which only a righteous remnant will be preserved. Elijah, in his role as both the prophetic parent and the dying child, simultaneously laments over this remnant and embodies it, even as his prophetic voice must indict the larger group. His fate in the narrative mirrors the remnant's in reality, with which the post-exilic communities identified themselves. His survival, therefore, stands as a symbol of the post-exilic remnant's ongoing preservation.

4   The Rest of the Cycle: Judgement, Remnant, and Survival

4.1   *Introduction*

After 1 Kgs 19, Elijah's wilderness experience and Horeb encounter play no further explicit role in the cycle. The chapter appears to have been placed in its current position both to link it to the preceding chapters and to introduce the previously existing stories about political conflict and the downfall of Ahab's house that follow.[103] The cycle overall that includes these stories, however, demonstrates logical coherence, and consistently underscores the image of a small righteous remnant that is contrasted with an apostate nation and royal house.

4.2   *The Slaughter of the Righteous: 1 Kings 21*

The Naboth narrative of 1 Kgs 21 forms the context for the judgement of Ahab's house, which is described in 21:17–29 and begun to be carried out in 2 Kgs 1. Theories regarding its compositional history are complex, but McKenzie assigns

---

103   See McKenzie, *Kings*, 151.

the Naboth story itself to the post-Dtr prophetic narrator, who joined it to a DtrH judgement oracle against Ahab's house (21:20b–22, 24, 27–29).[104] This reconstruction fits the overall tenor of the Elijah cycle, as the Naboth narrative becomes a worst-case study in the fate of Yhwh's people and the reason for the nation's downfall. It also displays lexical links to 1 Kgs 17–19.[105] Naboth is portrayed as an exemplary Israelite (21:3) who is condemned by false witnesses and put to death by the established royal house (21:11–16). This atrocity is given as the reason for Ahab's judgement (21:19), consistent with the escalating distinction drawn in 1 Kgs 17–19 between those who remain faithful in Israel and the established house that will be judged. In this case, however, the power of the unit's rhetoric is found in the fact that the endangered righteous figure does *not* survive. Unlike Elijah, Naboth is not to be identified with the post-exilic righteous community, but rather with the snuffing out of all but a remnant of Israel pre-exile, highlighting just how critical its status became. Jezebel's treachery in slaughtering Yahwistic prophets, described in the Obadiah pericope, is now heightened to include the slaughter of righteous Israelites as well. The narrative demonstrates indisputably why the indictment of Ahab's house is justified, it sets the scene for the re-entry of Elijah as judgement prophet in 21:17,[106] and it functions for the post-exilic prophetic narrator as one more piece of evidence – one more reminder to his readers – of just why the exile ultimately occurred.

4.3 Judgement on the Second Generation: 2 Chronicles 21[107]

The judgement on Ahab's house that is introduced in 1 Kgs 21 provides the interpretive key to another scene in which Elijah appears; one which has raised significant scholarly discussion. The letter of judgement which is said to come from Elijah to Jehoram, king of Judah, in 2 Chron 21:12–15 is perplexing for several reasons. First of all, Elijah appears nowhere else in Chronicles.

---

104   See McKenzie, *Kings*, 178–79; also Knauf, *Könige*, 427. For alternative extensive investigations of the compositional history of 1 Kgs 21, see Patrick T. Cronauer, *The Stories about Naboth the Jezreelite*, LHBOTS 424 (New York: T&T Clark, 2005); Otto, *Jehu*, 120–43.

105   These parallels include the mention of Jezreel and the meetings between Ahab and Elijah mentioned in n. 74 of this chapter. Further, Jezebel in 1 Kgs 21 appears to take on a role ironically parallel to the divine agent in 1 Kgs 19. When Elijah lies (שכב) under a bush despondent, the מלאך יהוה commands him, קום אכול (19:5, 7). When Ahab lies (שכב) on his bed depressed (21:4), Jezebel tells him, קום אכל־לחם (21:7).

106   See Blum, "Der Prophet," 288; McKenzie, *Kings*, 44.

107   Portions of this section in significantly expanded form are to appear in Alicia R. Hein, "Rhetoric through Allusion: A Literary Solution to the Letter from Elijah in 2 Chronicles 21," in *Citations and Allusions in the Former Prophets*, BN, ed. Walter Bührer, Friedrich-Emanuel Focken, and Joachim J. Krause (Freiburg: Herder, forthcoming 2026).

Second, nowhere in Kings does he have contact with a southern king.[108] Third,
the timelines of the two books are very difficult to harmonise at this point,
as the Masoretic regnal chronology of Kings places Jehoram's accession to the
throne of Judah six chapters after Elijah's ascension and well into the ministry
of Elisha.[109] This discrepancy has proved to be the primary point of discussion
for commentators of this passage, leading to numerous theories with varying
degrees of plausibility which all fail to answer the question of why precisely
Elijah is named as the source of Jehoram's letter.[110]

---

108   Jacob Myers and Wilhelm Rudolph both make the argument that, if Elijah had had con-
       tact with Jehoram, DtrH would surely have included it (Jacob M. Myers, *II Chronicles*,
       AB 13 [Garden City: Doubleday, 1965], 121–22; Wilhelm Rudolph, *Chronikbücher*, HAT
       1/21 [Tübingen: Mohr Siebeck, 1955], 267). The lack of any reference to this letter in
       Kings, according to this argument, demonstrates its fictional character in Chronicles (so
       Rudolph, *Chronikbücher*, 267). If, however, we take the insertion of the Elijah cycle into
       Kings to be post-DtrH, then this objection is eliminated and both texts become post-exilic
       reflections on the figure of Elijah.

109   Elijah's ascension is placed, in the arrangement of Kings, near the beginning of the reign of
       Joram of Israel (also called Jehoram, to add to the literary tangle). Joram is the son of Ahab
       and the brother of Ahaziah who preceded him. Ahaziah reigned near the end of the min-
       istry of Elijah (1 Kgs 22:51; 2 Kgs 3:1). According to 2 Kgs 3:1, Joram's accession corresponds
       to the eighteenth year of Jehoshaphat of Judah. Jehoshaphat's son, Jehoram of Judah and
       the recipient of Elijah's letter in Chronicles, does not ascend the throne until 2 Kgs 8, in
       the fifth year of Joram of Israel (8:16). It is true that a chronological note preserved in MT
       2 Kgs 1:17 would allow for the possibility of overlap between Elijah and Jehoram, since it
       describes, contrary to 2 Kgs 8, Jehoram of Judah already on the throne for two years when
       Joram of Israel ascends. However, as McKenzie has argued, a good text-critical case can be
       made that this note is secondary and does not reflect the primitive Masoretic chronology
       (*Kings*, 20, 228; idem, "The Priority of the MT Chronology in Kings," in *Biblical and Ancient
       Near Eastern Studies in Honor of P. Kyle McCarter, Jr.*, ed. Chris A. Rollston, Neal H. Walls,
       and Susanna Garfein, ANEM 27 [Atlanta: SBL, 2022], 185–89. See also Ronald S. Hendel,
       "The Two Editions of the Royal Chronology in Kings," in *Textual Criticism and Dead Sea
       Scrolls Studies in Honour of Julio Trebolle Barrera*, ed. Andrés Piquer Otero and Pablo A.
       Torijano Morales, JSJSup 158 [Leiden: Brill, 2012], 99–114). If this conclusion is correct, and
       2 Kgs 8:16 is to be followed, Jehoram's reign begins well after Elijah is no longer on earth.

110   See for discussion e.g. Sara Japhet, *I & II Chronicles*, OTL (London: SCM, 1993), 812;
       Rudolph, *Chronikbücher*, 267. Suggestions have included a prophetic letter, written before
       Elijah's ascension (Carl Friedrich Keil, *Biblischer Commentar über die nachexilischen
       Geschichtsbücher: Chronik, Esra, Nehemia und Esther*, BCAT 5 [Leipzig: Dörfling und
       Franke, 1870], 297–99), a letter thought to have been sent from heaven itself (an older
       suggestion which Samuel Oettli already calls "eine abenteuerliche Vorstellung, die jeder
       Analogie innerhalb der heiligen Schrift entbehrt" ("Die Bücher der Chronik, Esra und
       Nehemia," in *Die geschichtlichen Hagiographen und das Buch Daniel*, KKAT 8 [Nördlingen:
       C.H. Beck, 1889], 115), or that Elijah did not actually ascend to heaven but was simply
       picked up and deposited somewhere else (J. Edward Wright, "Whither Elijah? the
       Ascension of Elijah in Biblical and Extrabiblical Traditions," in *Things Revealed: Studies*

That the Chronicler knows a form of Kings in which the cycle is present is undisputed.[111] It must therefore be concluded that he was compelled to include Elijah's name in his historiography of the southern kingdom for a specific purpose, and it is precisely this question of literary rhetoric that has been largely neglected by those scholars focused on a chronological harmonisation with Kings. When 2 Chron 21 is approached literarily in light of 1 Kgs 21, the purpose of a letter from Elijah becomes clear.[112] The judgement pronounced by this letter explicitly applies to Jehoram of Judah the same status and fate as that given to Ahab of Israel: "You have walked in the way of the kings of Israel and have caused Judah and the inhabitants of Jerusalem to prostitute themselves like the prostitutions of the house of Ahab" (2 Chron 21:13). Jehoram has joined himself to Ahab's house by marrying Ahab's daughter and has adopted the northern king's cult loyalties. His judgement, appropriately, is placed by the Chronicler into the mouth of the same prophet who indicted Ahab.

Elijah's indictment of Ahab in 1 Kgs 21 follows upon a specific accusation. First, Ahab has "killed and also taken possession" (21:19); then he is told that "you have sold yourself to do evil in the eyes of Yhwh" (21:20) and "you have caused Israel to sin" (21:22). As a result, Yhwh will bring disaster (רעה)

---

in *Early Jewish and Christian Literature in Honor of Michael E. Stone*, ed. Esther G. Chazon, David Satran, and Ruth Clements, JSJSup 89 [Leiden: Brill, 2004], 123–38; Roy E. Knuteson, "Elijah's Little-Known Letter in 2 Chronicles 21:12-15," *BSac* 162 [2005]: 23–32). Thomas Willi proposed that Elijah left the letter to be delivered after his lifetime (*Die Chronik als Auslegung*, FRLANT 106 [Göttingen: Vandenhoek & Ruprecht, 1972], 230). Edward L. Curtis and Albert A. Madsen conclude that the letter represents "a pure product of the imagination, since Elijah had nothing to do with the S. kingdom, and clearly was not living at this time" (*The Books of Chronicles*, ICC [Edinburgh: T&T Clark, 1952], 415–16).

111 The introduction of Jehoram in 2 Chron 21:5–7 is taken almost verbatim from 2 Kgs 8, currently in the middle of the Elisha cycle, while the ill-fated offensive battle of Ahab of Israel and Jehoshaphat of Judah against Ramoth-Gilead in 2 Chron 18, a few chapters earlier, comes directly from 1 Kgs 22, which is situated in the middle of the Elijah cycle. The fact that the Chronicler names Elijah specifically as the author of this letter demonstrates that he knows a version of Kings in which Elijah is present.

112 A similar conclusion was reached in a little-known article by Bernd Jørg Diebner in 1986 entitled simply "Überlegungen zum 'Brief des Elia' (2 Chr 21,12–15)" (*DBAT* 23 [1986], 66–97). In it, Diebner was well ahead of his time in providing a detailed argument for a very specific and intentional literary purpose for this letter. He argued that its entire context is "kunstvoll und bewusst konzipiert" – that is, artfully and intentionally designed (95). As such, the function of the letter is revealed precisely *not* through a harmonisation with Kings, but rather through a recognition of the polemical purpose of the tensions and contrasts that it raises (69–70). Diebner ultimately sees every use of so-called "historically reliable" materials in this segment as serving a greater theological purpose, which is presented in condensed form in Elijah's letter (92).

upon Ahab and cut off every male from his household (21:21). The similarities between this judgement and that against Jehoram in Chronicles are noticeable. Jehoram has also "done evil in the eyes of Yhwh" (2 Chron 21:6, 20), has "caused Judah to go astray" (21:11), and "slaughtered" those who were "better than" he was (21:13). Therefore, Yhwh will bring down "a great affliction" (מגפה) on Jehoram's entire household and all of his possessions (21:14). The Chronicler presumes his readers to know that it was Elijah who pronounced Ahab's judgement, so he now summons the same prophet *in absentia* to pronounce judgement on Jehoram.[113] He makes the parallel between the two unmistakable and thereby applies to Jehoram of Judah the same status and ultimate fate as that given to Ahab of Israel.

Jehoram's marriage into Ahab's family carries further significance. At Elijah's word of judgement in 1 Kgs 21, Ahab, surprisingly, responds in abject humility and repentance (21:27). Yhwh takes note, and postpones the promised disaster by a generation to the reign of Ahab's son (21:28–29). This is precisely the generation to which Jehoram of Judah has joined himself by marrying Ahab's daughter. Unlike Ahab, Jehoram shows no hint of repentance, and therefore suffers a sickness and death parallel to that of Ahab's son Ahaziah in Kings (2 Kgs 1:2, 15–17; 2 Chron 21:14–15, 18–19).[114] Thus, the chronological discrepancy that has been the subject of so many harmonisation attempts becomes precisely the point of Elijah's letter: Jehoram represents the second generation of Ahab's family, and he must bear the weight of Elijah's judgement.

4.4   *Judgement in Contrast to the Remnant: 2 Kings 1*

We have already observed the narrative bracket that is formed between the death of Ahab's son Ahaziah in 2 Kgs 1 and the revival of the widow's son in 1 Kgs 17. A foreign boy acts as an image of the remnant of Israel who survives, while the king of Israel, who should have ensured the life of the nation, dies. Elijah, meanwhile, functions after Horeb with unabated power to call down fire from heaven (2 Kgs 1:9–12), resuming, in the cycle's extant arrangement, the motif of 1 Kgs 18. The fact that 2 Kgs 1 is linked structurally with 1 Kgs 17

---

113   Japhet's assessment that "the choice of Elijah for the task of warning is almost self-evident" (*Chronicles*, 812) is somewhat optimistic, since interpreters have not universally reflected this conclusion!

114   Jehoram's gruesome sickness in Chronicles (חליים רבים – 2 Chron 21:15, 19) finds no precedent in the account of his death in Kings (2 Kgs 18:16–24) and is likely a part of the Chronicler's literary strategy. Either the Chronicler knew of a tradition not included in Kings in which Jehoram did indeed die of sickness and chose to highlight this tradition, in contrast to Kings (cf. 2 Kgs 8:24), or he introduces it himself, intentionally, to worsen Jehoram's image and highlight the parallel to Ahaziah.

and thematically with 1 Kgs 18, showing a consistency in Elijah's power and function, supports the proposal that 1 Kgs 19 was not composed to describe a disqualification of his prophetic status. The cycle as a whole artfully portrays Elijah as a powerful prophetic authority even as he is an image of the remnant, who therefore ensures the rightful judgement of the apostate larger group even as he guarantees the preservation of the remnant.

4.5   *The Remnant's Perpetual Existence: 2 Kings 2*

Elijah's embodiment of the remnant's survival is underscored in magnificent form in the account of his heavenly ascent in 2 Kgs 2. Here again, Mosaic elements pervade the narrative. Elijah parts the Jordan river with his mantle and crosses over with Elisha, ending his prophetic assignment outside the land as Moses did (2:7–8). Even this detail may support an underlying sense of prophetic failure, as Elijah mimics Moses' inability to see the righteous community of Israel established in the land (cf. Num 20:12; Deut 1:37; 3:23–28; 32:52; 34:4–5).

The setting of Elijah's ascent east of the Jordan nevertheless allows Elisha to re-cross the river as something of a new Joshua figure and Elijah's rightful successor.[115] Elisha's legitimacy is demonstrated in his determination to follow Elijah (2:2–6), his request for a double portion of Elijah's spirit (2:9–10), his "seeing" of Elijah's ascension (2:10–12), and his successful use of Elijah's mantle to split the Jordan a second time (2:13–14). Literarily, these elements connect the two prophetic cycles into a single story. They promise that, even though Elijah is taken to heaven, the prophetic voice on earth will continue. The two prophets together are thus able to embody survival in two realms. The one survives in heaven, superseding death; the other continues alive on earth to demonstrate that the voice of Yhwh in Israel will not die out.

A particularly intriguing element of this account is the exclamation uttered by Elisha as Elijah ascends in the whirlwind. He calls out אבי אבי רכב ישׂראל ופרשׁיו (2:12), a cry which has been translated along the lines of "My father, my father, the chariot(s) of Israel and its horsemen." Numerous interpretations have been offered towards the significance of this phrase,[116] including

---

115   See Joel S. Burnett, "'Going Down' to Bethel: Elijah and Elisha in the Theological Geography of the Deuteronomistic History," *JBL* 129 (2010): 281–97; Leithart, *1 & 2 Kings*, 172.

116   Kristin Weingart argues that the phrase belongs in the Elisha material, here as well as in its parallel in 2 Kgs 13:14, and that the purpose for its inclusion was initially to demonstrate Elijah as the legitimate predecessor to Elisha, rather than vice versa ("My Father, My Father! Chariot of Israel and Its Horses!" [2 Kings 2:12//13:14]: Elisha's or Elijah's Title?" *JBL* 137 [2018], 257–70). Gene Rice connects the title with 2 Kgs 6:17, in which fiery chariots and horsemen are associated with spiritual sight, and argues that Elisha's use

a curiously compelling suggestion by Matthieu Richelle. He proposes, based on a shorter *Vetus Latina* reading and evidence of its ancient Greek *Vorlage*, that the formulation in 2 Kgs 2:12 originally read only "My father, my father, the charioteer of Israel!"[117] This shorter text was harmonised to the longer version attested in all witnesses to 2 Kgs 13:14, where Joash utters the same cry at Elisha's deathbed.[118]

Richelle argues that "charioteer of Israel" is a military designation of leadership that is, remarkably, applied by these verses to Elijah and Elisha.[119] If רכב here indeed refers to a leader who fights for the nation in battle, as suggested by Richelle, then the title is not only an honorific but also supports the thesis that Elijah acts on behalf of Israel, both as an authority figure and as its representative. As its leader, his life is critical to Israel's survival. When Elijah is taken to heaven, then, Elisha laments that the nation's warrior is gone. Elisha's later reception of the same title would subsequently confirm that he has successfully carried on Elijah's leadership role.

This rendering of רכב may shed light on another puzzling notation earlier in the Elijah cycle, and in turn be supported by it. When rain falls on Carmel after the drought, 1 Kgs 18:45 states that Ahab "rode [וירכב] and went to Jezreel." This is the point at which Yhwh's hand comes upon Elijah and "he ran before Ahab" (18:46). The image here is of the leader of Israel riding in his chariot; yet Elijah, by the hand of Yhwh, surpasses him. Neither the nominal nor the verbal form of רכב is found in the Elijah narratives again until the description of his ascension in 2 Kgs 2:11.[120] At this point, Elijah no longer needs to run ahead of the charioteer of Israel; he is recognised in his own right as the nation's true leader, following his fiery chariots (רכב) and horses towards the heavens (2:11) while the house of Ahab faces ruin.

---

of it demonstrates that he had received the "spiritual sight" required by Elijah ("Elijah's Requirement for Prophetic Leadership [2 Kings 2:1–18]," *JRT* 59/60 [2006/2007]: 1–12). A similar connection between the Elijah image and spiritual sight indeed comes into play in the Gospel of John, as we shall see.

117   Matthieu Richelle, "Élie et Élisée, Auriges en Israël: Une Métaphore Militaire Oubliée en 2 R 2,12 et 13,14," *RB* 117 (2010), 329–31. Richelle's proposal is also integrated by McKenzie (*Kings*, 240).

118   Richelle, "Auriges," 333.

119   Richelle, "Auriges," 331–34. Evidence that רכב can indeed have a human referent is found in Ezek 39:20, which reads ושבעתם על־שלחני סוס ורכב. Here רכב cannot refer to a chariot since the "birds and the beasts" of 39:17, which form the subject of this clause, do not satiate themselves (שבע) on inanimate objects, but rather on human flesh.

120   The term is otherwise found in the battle narratives of 1 Kgs 20 and 22.

The ascension account itself likely belongs to the early stories about Elijah.[121] To a post-exilic compilation, however, such an end offers the perfect climax to the literary life of a prophet who personifies Yhwh's preservation of a remnant. If Elijah does not die, he can continue to embody the ongoing existence of a righteous remnant in Israel. The remnant survives because Elijah survives, and vice versa. The immortal prophet, by his ascension to heaven, thus ensures the perpetual continuation of the community whose life is incarnate in his.

5   Conclusion: Elijah as Prophet and People

Within the completed narrative cycle in Kings, Elijah is presented both as the paradigmatic prophetic voice in Israel and as the embodiment of the endangered righteous remnant of the nation. Literary allusions are strategically employed to depict Israel as an endangered beloved son, and Elijah simultaneously as that child and its grieving mother. The life of just such a literal son is vividly revived and assured in 1 Kgs 17, as is that of his analogical counterpart, Israel, in 1 Kgs 18. In 1 Kgs 19, this outcome is turned on its head by an intensified description of endangerment, portrayed through the near death of Elijah himself. This chapter reverses the victorious image of Elijah that is present in the rest of the cycle to demonstrate that, even at its points of greatest weakness, Israel may know that Yhwh yet preserves a remnant. Elijah's very existence is turned into a promise that the beloved son will survive.

Elijah is also portrayed as representative of the collective failure of Mosaic prophets. His character is shaped around allusions to Moses, yet he fails to intercede and prevent judgement. Therefore, it is granted by the post-exilic writers that the prophet like Moses has not yet come, which is precisely what allows them to hope for a prophet still in the future. This is the perspective of the epilogue to Malachi, to which we turn in the following chapter. This epilogue sees in the rest of the book of Malachi an expectation of Elijah's return; a return with a prophetic mission expected to succeed where it failed the first time. In the meantime, Elijah lives on to ensure that the righteous remnant he embodies cannot and will not die.

---

121   McKenzie, *Kings*, 238, 250–52.

CHAPTER 3

Elijah and the Messenger in Malachi

1   Introduction

If the Elijah of Kings had been left alone, perhaps his unique representation as a prophet like Moses and the righteous remnant of Israel could have been forgotten. His story, together with the Elisha cycle, forms a self-contained unit. Neither figure is mentioned in Kings after Elisha's death (2 Kgs 13), and the interpolation of the cycle into the books' regnal progression has comparatively little effect on the other narratives in its literary context. Elijah's prophetic image, however, seems to have been too dynamic to remain untouched. In a notation that would change the reception of his character throughout the rest of the Second Temple period, he reappears in the conclusion to the book of Malachi.[1]

The Elijah of Malachi's epilogue, while recognised as the same figure that appears in Kings, has largely been treated as a thematically distinct portrait.[2] Indeed, the eschatological figure awaited by an epilogue reflecting the Persian period appears to have little in common with the miracle worker described in a ninth-century BCE context in Kings. If again, however, the completed Elijah cycle is recognised as a post-exilic addition into a form of DtrH, then all three of Elijah's appearances in the Hebrew Bible (Kings, Chronicles, Malachi) become relatively contemporary compositions in their current form. In this case, rather than asking why Elijah reappears in Malachi after centuries of absence, the reader should instead investigate the significance of this figure to the post-exilic communities and their texts. While Kings and Chronicles locate Elijah back in an earlier time, the book of Malachi introduces a unique innovation: a second appearance of Elijah, projected into the future.[3]

---

1   I use the versification of the Hebrew text that numbers this epilogue as Mal 3:22–24; it is found in 4:4–6 of English translations.

2   See e.g. Dharamraj's comment above (ch. 1 n. 59) that consideration of Malachi's epilogue would not "contribute" to her investigation of Kings (*A Prophet*, 6).

3   Rudolph observes, "Hier taucht zum erstenmal Elia in dieser Rolle auf, ohne daß wir erfahren, was ihn zu diesem Vorläufer gemacht hat" (*Maleachi*, 291–92). The other Second Temple texts that utilise the image of a returning Elijah almost certainly draw on Malachi, as I will demonstrate in the next chapter.

Malachi 3:22–24 almost unquestionably represent a later epilogue to the body of the book.[4] Far from diminishing the significance of these verses, a recognition of their secondary character offers a glimpse into an early reader's interpretation and application of the rest of the book. It argues that these final verses are intended to stand as something of a summary of what comes before. With this in mind, the epilogue states:

> [22] Remember the Torah of Moses my servant, which I commanded him at Horeb together with all Israel; statutes and judgements.
>
> [23] Behold, I am sending to you Elijah the prophet before the coming of the great and fearful day of Yhwh.
>
> [24] And he will turn back the heart of fathers together with sons, and the heart of sons together with their fathers, lest I come and strike the land with a curse. (Mal 3:22–24)[5]

Neither Moses nor Elijah is mentioned in the body of the book of Malachi, raising the question of how they come to represent its conclusion. Moses receives only one other mention in the Book of the Twelve (Mic 6:4) and Elijah none at all, so their significance cannot be explained solely on the basis of this corpus either. While numerous suggestions have been offered for why Elijah particularly is chosen by Malachi to return, few are compelling on their own.[6] Closest

---

4 So Noetzel: "Heute werden Mal 3,22–24 in der historisch-kritischen Forschung nahezu unumstritten als ein oder zwei Anhänge verstanden" (*Maleachi*, 240–41, also 243) and Petersen: "universally recognized" (David L. Petersen, *Late Israelite Prophecy* [Missoula: Scholars, 1977], 44). See also Rudolph, *Maleachi*, 291–92; John M.P. Smith, *A Critical and Exegetical Commentary on the Book of Malachi*, ICC (Edinburgh: T&T Clark, 1912), 81–85; Ralph L. Smith, *Micah–Malachi*, WBC 32 (Dallas: Word, 1984), 340–41; Odil Hannes Steck, *Der Abschluß der Prophetie im Alten Testament*, BiThSt 17 (Neukirchen-Vluyn: Neukirchener, 1991), 128; Wöhrle, *Abschluss*, 251–53; Zakovitch, "Last Verses," 61. For scholars allowing for the possibility of single composition, see e.g. Joyce G. Baldwin, *Haggai, Zechariah and Malachi*, TOTC 28 (Nottingham: Inter-Varsity Press, 1972), 275; Jonathan Gibson, *Covenant Continuity and Fidelity: A Study of Inner-Biblical Allusion and Exegesis in Malachi* (London: Bloomsbury T&T Clark, 2016), 219–35; Glazier-McDonald, *Malachi*, 243–45; Pieter A. Verhoef, *The Books of Haggai and Malachi*, NICOT (Grand Rapids: Eerdmans, 1987), 337–38.

5 The LXX epilogue places the reference to Moses after Elijah, which has led to the conclusion that the respective references represent two separate addenda that were subsequently merged together (see e.g. Arndt Meinhold, *Maleachi*, BKAT 14/8 [Neukirchen-Vluyn: Neukirchener, 2006], 411; Wöhrle, *Abschluss*, 421). Zakovitch, in contrast, argues for the preference of the Masoretic ordering, even maintaining that there is no reason to assume the two were added separately ("Last Verses," 61. See n. 3 and also pp. 77–80).

6 Theories as to Elijah's enduring significance have included his association with Horeb in Kings, which is reintroduced with Moses in Mal 3:22 (e.g. Andrew E. Hill, *Malachi*, AB [New York:

comes the frequent emphasis on Elijah's heavenly ascent: that, because he was taken up to heaven alive, he remains available to return.[7] Even this observation, however, fails to explain why the epilogue feels the need for a prophet to return at all.[8] The argument that Elijah returns because he is the only figure in the Hebrew Bible to have had a divine encounter on Horeb like Moses also fails at this point – why not then predict the return of Moses himself?[9] We have seen that the popular arguments for Elijah's entirely negative portrayal in Kings offer no compelling explanation for the shift in favour that would see a disgraced prophet return to effect Yhwh's restoration, as in Malachi.[10] If, on the other hand, Elijah's failure in 1 Kgs 19 represents the failure of all Mosaic prophets, and if his character is intentionally shaped in such a way as to offer

---

Doubleday, 1998], 368), his character-level connection to Moses (Marvin A. Sweeney, *The Twelve Prophets* [Collegeville: Liturgical, 2000] 2:749), and his defence of Yahwism (Rex Mason, *The Books of Haggai, Zechariah and Malachi*, CBC [Cambridge: Cambridge University Press, 1977], 160). David DeJong suggests that the choice of Elijah reflects a "compromise" between "the traditions of Dtr and 'classical' prophecy" (David N. DeJong, *A Prophet Like Moses* [*Deut 18:15, 18*]: *The Origin, History, and Influence of the Mosaic Prophetic Succession*, JSJSup 205 [Leiden: Brill, 2022], 163). Baldwin argues that "Elijah served as a moral catalyst to the nation. No other prophet so dramatically changed the attitude of his contemporaries, nor so influenced the destiny of the nation" (*Haggai*, 276). As we have seen, however, this is only true in a temporary sense in 1 Kgs 18, and does not translate to any lasting effect on the downfall progression described by DtrH.

7   See e.g. Robert C. Dentan and William L. Sperry, "Malachi," in *IB*, vol. 6 (New York: Abingdon, 1956), 1143; Glazier-McDonald, *Malachi*, 267; Meinhold, *Maleachi*, 420; Sigmund Mowinckel, *He That Cometh*, trans. G.W. Anderson (New York: Abingdon Press, 1954), 299; Henning Graf Reventlow, *Die Propheten Haggai, Sacharja und Maleachi*, 9th ed., ATD 25/2 (Göttingen: Vandenhoeck & Ruprecht, 1993), 161; Rudolph, *Maleachi*, 292; Wöhrle, *Abschluss*, 423; Zakovitch, "Last Verses," 66–67; Arie W. Zwiep, *The Ascension of the Messiah in Lukan Christology*, NovTSup 87 (Leiden: Brill, 1997), 60.

8   Valve poses the same question: "Who says that a past-time figure had to be chosen at all?" (*Early Modes*, 94).

9   Moses is also considered by several midrashic traditions not to have died, and even to have ascended to heaven alive (see for discussion Samuel E. Loewenstamm, "The Death of Moses," in *Studies on the Testament of Abraham*, ed. George W.E. Nickelsburg, SBLSCS 6 [Missoula: Scholars, 1976]: 185–211). Zakovitch argues that this tradition is actually older than that of Moses' death as described in Deuteronomy, and that the former was intentionally silenced ("Last Verses," 79). See also Loewenstamm's argument that "the texts of the Torah should be interpreted on the same lines as the post-biblical texts describing Moses' mysterious disappearance, i.e., as a toning down of a tradition relating Moses' ascent to heaven" ("Death of Moses," 198).

10   Zakovitch, who also argues that Elijah's "second Moses" image in Kings is one of contrast, opposition, and dismissal ("Last Verses," 77–79), rather unsatisfactorily concludes simply that, in Malachi, Elijah "is no longer the opposite of Moses" and "no longer seeks vengeance" (79).

the hope of survival to the remnant, then his reappearance in Malachi represents a thrilling continuation of this saga. Moses himself does not return, but a prophet like Moses does, just as Deuteronomy expects. The embodiment of Israel's righteous remnant, who is supernaturally preserved in Kings and whisked away to heaven, now returns from heaven to complete the Mosaic mission which he failed to accomplish the first time.

This chapter is not concerned primarily with an exegesis of the book of Malachi, or with establishing the relationship of Malachi's epilogue to the rest of the book and the prophetic corpus. Though both of these pursuits will come into play, they have been much more thoroughly engaged by other scholars. The specific interest of this study lies in the question of Elijah's role in Malachi's epilogue, and of how the prophet of Kings comes to represent the hope of restoration that summarises the book of Malachi. I will propose an exegetical progression by which a later reader of Malachi, like the writer of the epilogue, might have deduced from the book's general expectation of a coming messenger that this role could only be fulfilled by the return of the prophet Elijah.

2   Malachi's Messenger

2.1   *The Messenger as Priest and Prophet*

2.1.1   מלאכי ,האדון, and מלאך הברית

Malachi's expectation of a coming messenger of Yhwh is explicitly introduced in 3:1, which is without doubt one of the interpretive keys to the book. This verse represents Yhwh's ironic response to the cynicism of the people at the end of ch. 2, where they conclude that Yhwh loves evil and delights in evildoers, and that the God of justice is nowhere to be found (2:17).[11] In response to their accusation of his absence, Yhwh responds that he is indeed coming (3:1), and so is a forerunner who will prepare his way:

> "Behold, I am sending my messenger [מלאכי], and he will prepare a way before me,
> and suddenly the Lord [האדון] whom [אשר] you are seeking will come [יבוא] to his temple,
> and the messenger of the covenant [מלאך הברית] in which [אשר] you are delighting,
> behold, he is coming [בא]," says Yhwh of hosts. (Mal 3:1)

---

11   See e.g. Wöhrle, *Abschluss*, 240.

The precise interpretation and redactional history of this verse has, unsurprisingly, been widely contested.[12] Many scholars have understood the second half of the verse to be part of a redactional addition (3:1b–4) that is marked primarily by the switch from a first to third-person presentation of Yhwh's speech.[13] Others have argued that the logic of the passage is consistent as it stands.[14] I lean towards the presence of redactional activity because I believe it adds to, rather than diminishes, the integrated nature of the passage with the rest of the book, in which a secondary author employs specific exegetical techniques to tie various earlier passages together.

In the case of Mal 3:1, the presence of a secondary redaction helps to explain what is likely the most contentious issue surrounding this verse, namely, the question of precisely how many figures are represented.[15] Four personas are technically in question: Yhwh the speaker, מלאכי, האדון, and מלאך הברית. Representative scholars can be listed for nearly any configuration of mutual identification and differentiation between these personas.[16] The majority, however, have identified "the Lord" as Yhwh and distinguished between this

---

12   For an overview of redactional theories and interpretations, see Richard M. Blaylock, "My Messenger, the LORD, and the Messenger of the Covenant: Malachi 3:1 Revisited," *SBJT* 20 (2016), 70–74. See also discussion in Adam Simon van der Woude, "Der Engel des Bundes: Bemerkungen zu Maleachi 3,1c und seinem Kontext," in *Die Botschaft und die Boten: Festschrift für Hans Walter Wolff zum 70. Geburtstag* (Neukirchen-Vluyn: Neukirchener, 1981), 290–93.

13   E.g. Bruce V. Malchow, "The Messenger of the Covenant in Mal. 3:1," *JBL* 103 (1984), 253; Mason, *Haggai*, 152; Meinhold, *Maleachi*, 245–46; David L. Petersen, *Zechariah 9–14 & Malachi*, OTL (London: SCM, 1995), 209–12. See also Wöhrle, who argues that 3:2 remains part of the earlier layer with 3:1a (*Abschluss*, 240–44).

14   See e.g. Glazier-McDonald, *Malachi*, 129 n. 16; Hill, *Malachi*, 260; Verhoef, *Haggai*, 176–77, 293 (also 183 n. 4 for a list of scholars on both sides of the debate); Karl William Weyde, *Prophecy and Teaching: Prophetic Authority, Form Problems, and the Use of Traditions in the Book of Malachi*, BZAW 288 (Berlin: de Gruyter, 2000), 290. Rainer Kessler, while remaining somewhat uncommitted, suggests that the same creativity granted a redactor should also be allowed of an "authentic" author (*Maleachi*, HThKAT [Freiburg: Herder, 2011], 223–24).

15   The extent of this debate, and its lack of any unanimity, is reflected in such scholarly titles as S.D. Snyman's "Once Again: Investigating the Identity of the Three Figures Mentioned in Malachi 3:1" (*VEccl* 27 [2006]: 1031–44).

16   For scholars preferring a single individual in addition to Yhwh, see e.g. William J. Dumbrell, "Malachi and the Ezra-Nehemiah Reforms," *RTR* 35 (1976), 48; Charles D. Isbell, *Malachi: A Study Guide Commentary* (Grand Rapids: Zondervan, 1980), 59; Petersen, *Zechariah*, 211–12; van der Woude, "Der Engel," 293–99. For scholars positing three distinct individuals, see Baldwin, *Haggai*, 242–43; Malchow, "Messenger," 253. Hill remains undecided, but identifies both האדון and מלאך הברית as divine beings (*Malachi*, 289).

figure and "my messenger," resulting in a discussion centred around the identity of מלאך הברית.[17]

The argument for identifying מלאך הברית with האדון, and thereby with
Yhwh, is relatively strong when it is based in the structure of the segment
itself. Gibson, for example, identifies the chiastic parallelism in 3:1b framed by
the "coming" (בוא) of both figures, both of which are introduced by a relative
clause (אשר).[18] Others have argued similarly.[19] Within the context of the larger
book, however, this position is more difficult to maintain.[20] The term מלאך is
found only four times in the extant arrangement of Malachi: in its superscript,
identifying the message of the book as coming ביד מלאכי (1:1); in 2:7, identifying the ideal priestly figure as מלאך יהוה־צבאות, and in 3:1, via מלאכי and מלאך
הברית. Scholars have noted that אדון appears only four other times in Malachi,
and in each case refers either directly or analogously to Yhwh (1:6 [×2], 12, 14).[21]
The same consistency granted to the book's use of מלאך would result in the
identification of מלאך הברית with מלאכי, rather than with האדון.[22]

Support for this configuration becomes clearer if 3:1b–4 is indeed taken as
a redactional expansion. If this segment is removed, 3:5 follows directly on the
heels of 3:1a and provides a unified answer to 2:17. Meinhold has noted this

---

17   Contra Isbell, who argues that אדון here "is merely a common noun referring to a per-
      son of noble station socially" (*Malachi*, 59). For scholars associating מלאך הברית with
      האדון/Yhwh, see e.g. Gibson, *Covenant Continuity*, 169; Glazier-McDonald, *Malachi*, 130–32;
      Snyman, "Once Again," 1041; Verhoef, *Haggai*, 289. For a link between this figure and
      מלאכי, separate from האדון, see Meinhold, *Maleachi*, 261; James D. Nogalski, *The Book of
      the Twelve: Micah–Malachi*, SHBC (Macon: Smyth & Helwys, 2011), 1049; Weyde, *Prophecy*,
      288–90; Wöhrle, *Abschluss*, 240–41.
18   Gibson, *Covenant Continuity*, 168–69.
19   See e.g. Blaylock, "My Messenger," 83; Andrew S. Malone, "Is the Messiah Announced
      in Malachi 3:1?" *TynBul* 7 (2006), 219; Snyman, "Once Again," 1040. Van der Woude also
      argues that this parallelism functions to mutually identify the two figures, but he does not
      consider האדון to refer to Yhwh ("Der Engel," 294).
20   And see also Meinhold, who argues that the parallelism between these clauses is not as
      strong as some have made it seem. "Auch die beiden Langzeilen von V.1b sind ihrerseits
      durch ein vergleichbares Anschlußprinzip sowohl aufeinander bezogen als auch vonein-
      ander unterschieden worden ... Wird für das Kommen des einen Plötzlichkeit hervorge-
      hoben, so für den anderen Faktizität" (*Maleachi*, 245–46).
21   See Gibson, *Covenant Continuity*, 168; Snyman, "Once Again," 1038–39.
22   See Jeremias, "Ηλ(ε)ίας," 932. Blaylock argues for a human identification of מלאכי in 3:1
      based on the occurrences of מלאך in 1:1 and 2:7 ("My Messenger," 80–81). Inexplicably, he
      does not extend this argument to מלאך הברית, as would be required by a consistent read-
      ing of the term. Further, his argument for מלאכי as a priestly figure is based on the priestly
      identification of the messenger who receives the covenant of Levi, and even recognises
      the reference of מלאך הברית to this passage (84). Yet he insists that מלאך הברית cannot
      refer to the same figure as מלאכי (82–83).

direct correlation: Yhwh responds to the accusation "Where is the God of justice [מִשְׁפָּט]" (2:17) by announcing first that he is sending a messenger to prepare his way (3:1a), and then that he himself is indeed coming in judgement (מִשְׁפָּט – 3:5).[23]

The redactional interpolation likewise describes the coming of two figures: also a Lord (הָאָדוֹן) and a messenger (מַלְאַךְ הַבְּרִית). I would thus argue that it offers an exegetical expansion of the two figures expected in 3:1a and 5, with the purpose of connecting them more explicitly with the rest of the book. The reference to Yhwh as הָאָדוֹן in 3:1b links this segment to ch. 1, in which the priests despise the table of אֲדֹנָי and offer him blemished sacrifices (1:12, 14). In 3:1b, this Lord will "suddenly come" to his temple. The coming מַלְאַךְ הַבְּרִית not only expands upon מַלְאָכִי in 3:1a (and, by extension, 1:1, as discussed below), but the combination of "messenger" and "covenant" succinctly encompasses the only other occurrence of מַלְאָךְ in Malachi: that of the priestly messenger who receives the covenant of Levi in 2:4–7.[24] In other words, the author of 3:1b–4 sees the expectation of Yhwh's coming preceded by his messenger (3:1a) and poetically expands it with a description that assumes the book's messenger figures are one and the same.[25]

---

23 Meinhold, *Maleachi*, 245, 255. See also Petersen, *Zechariah*, 208–209.

24 This is the only other point at which Malachi's messenger figure and covenant theme overlap. Corinna Körting notes that "it becomes clear that the insertion of מַלְאַךְ הַבְּרִית 'the messenger of the covenant' refers back to the Levi covenant of Mal. 2.4" ("Days of Old and the Day to Come: Malachi between Protology and Eschatology," in *Herald of Good Tidings: Essays on the Bible, Prophecy, and the Hope of Israel in Honour of Antti Laato*, ed. Pekka Lindqvist and Lotta Valve [Sheffield: Sheffield Phoenix, 2021], 97). See similarly Mason, *Haggai*, 153; Snyman, "Once Again," 1041. Malchow also identifies the two, arguing that the text expects a coming priestly messenger in addition to the prophetic or angelic מַלְאָכִי ("Messenger," 253). Contra Verhoef, who insists that the messengers of 3:1 and 2:7 cannot be mutually identified (*Haggai*, 288), and Glazier-McDonald (*Malachi*, 132 n. 23), who argues that Mason's connection of this covenant with that of Levi in ch. 2 "does not take into account either the dependence of 3:1 on Exod 23:20f or the pervasive Yôm Yahweh imagery" (*Malachi*, 132 n. 23). This conclusion imposes a false dichotomy on Mal 3, however, which is clearly concerned with the priesthood in the context of a coming day of Yhwh. The allusion to Exod 23 also poses no problem to this identification, as I will demonstrate.

25 So also Meinhold: "Strukturell fällt dabei auf, daß die ersten beiden Langzeilen (V.1b) auf die beiden vorhergehenden Langzeilen in derselben Reihenfolge kommentierend Bezug nehmen" (*Maleachi*, 245). See also Wöhrle: "Die Begriffe הָאָדוֹן und מַלְאַךְ הַבְּרִית sind deshalb nicht, wie häufig angenommen, als zwei parallel gebrauchte Begriffe für ein und dieselbe Größe bezeichnet. Aus demselben Grund ist nebenbei auch die weitere Alternative, dass mit מַלְאַךְ הַבְּרִית neben dem in 3,1a genannten מַלְאָךְ und dem in 3,1b genannten אָדוֹן eine dritte Größe gemeint sei ... doch ausgesprochen unwahrscheinlich. Dagegen spricht ebenfalls die Tatsache, dass sowohl in Mal 3,1a als auch in Mal 3,1b von

Simultaneously, this expansion contributes a further angle to the larger passage's response to 2:17, even as the chiastic structure evident in 3:1b reflects the segment's own innate compositional creativity. The first of the two parallel relative clauses ("whom you are seeking") provides another reference to Yhwh's accused absence. The second ("in which/whom you are delighting" [חפץ]) has been argued by Anthony Petterson to represent an inversion of the people's accusation that Yhwh "delights" (חפץ) in evildoers (2:17).[26] If אשר here is taken to refer to the covenant, rather than the messenger, this statement becomes an ironic accusation of exactly what, according to the rest of the book, the people have failed to do.[27] They have claimed that Yhwh is absent; hence, "the Lord whom you are seeking" will appear. They have accused Yhwh of delighting in evildoers; hence, equally ironically, the covenant in which *they* claim to delight is about to be enforced by Yhwh's coming messenger.[28] "But who can endure the day of his coming?" (3:2).

2.1.2 The Prophet-Priest

The portrayal of Yhwh's coming messenger as מלאך הברית in 3:1b–4 further places upon this figure the primary role of purifying the "sons of Levi" (3:2–4). To some who would associate מלאך הברית with האדון, this is a role that Yhwh himself must carry out.[29] However, we have already seen that the redactor who composed 3:1b appears to link the coming forerunner with the priestly messenger of 2:4–7. Since this messenger is the ideal priest who stands in contrast

---

einem מלאך die Rede ist und dass diese beiden Gestalten nicht explizit gegeneinander abgegrenzt werden" (*Abschluss*, 241 n. 71).

26   Anthony R. Petterson, "The Identity of 'The Messenger of the Covenant' in Malachi 3:1 – Lexical and Rhetorical Analyses," *BBR* 29 (2019), 285–86. The same term (חפץ) appears in 1:10, where Yhwh declares that he has no "delight" in the priests or their offerings (see Snyman, "Once Again," 1038), which is the "state of affairs [that] will be righted when Yahweh comes" (Glazier-McDonald, *Malachi*, 154).

27   While most translations of 3:1 identify the messenger as the object of the relative clause, it may be read syntactically either way. Malchow recognises this possibility as well, though preferring to read the messenger as the object ("Messenger," 254).

28   Petersen suggests that the role of מלאכי is that of "covenant enforcer" (*Prophecy*, 43) which, according to the identification I have laid out, would apply to מלאך הברית as well.

29   Glazier-McDonald notes an allusion to Ps 12:7, in which the words of Yhwh himself are described as "pure [טהרות] words, silver smelted [כסף צרוף] in the furnace to the ground, refined [מזקק] seven times," in Mal 3:3, in which מלאך הברית comes as מצרף ומטהר כסף to "refine" (זקק) the sons of Levi (*Malachi*, 151). This link can hardly be coincidental. Contrary to her argument, however, it is Yhwh's words, not Yhwh himself, that are described as pure, refined silver. These are precisely the words, in the form of Yhwh's Torah, which Malachi's ideal priestly messenger carries in his mouth (2:6–7).

with the corrupted priesthood denounced in the rest of the book,[30] that he should be given the task of purifying that same priesthood is logically consistent. Where Mal 2 describes how the priesthood has corrupted the "covenant of Levi" and failed to live up to the messenger's example (2:8), in Mal 3 the "messenger of the covenant" comes to purify the "sons of Levi" (3:3). The fact that these contexts represent the only three mentions of Levi in the book of Malachi underscores their connection.

No "covenant of Levi" is named elsewhere in the Hebrew Bible. However, its description as a covenant of "life and peace" (Mal 2:4–5), as well as the messenger's portrayal as one who "turned many back [השיב] from iniquity" (2:6–7), has evoked general association with the figure of Phinehas in Num 25, whom we have already noted as an exemplar of zeal in relation to 1 Kgs 18. Phinehas receives "my covenant of peace" (בריתי שלום) for having "turned back [השיב] my wrath from the children of Israel" (Num 25:11–13).[31] The interpretation of the Tg Ps-J of Num 25:11–12 unequivocally links Phinehas to Malachi, describing Phinehas's reception of "my covenant of peace" and promising to make him "the messenger of the covenant, and he will live forever to bring tidings of redemption at the end of days."[32] The portrayal of Malachi's messenger as a priestly figure who comes to bring about purification before the appearance of Yhwh is therefore supported by later interpretation.

At the same time, this priest also holds "the Torah of truth in his mouth" (Mal 2:6). If he is to be associated with מלאכי in 3:1a, then the description of מלאכי in the book's superscript also becomes relevant.[33] Here, the messenger

---

30 See Lear's description of Malachi's "Ideal Levite" (*Scribal Composition*, 126ff).

31 See e.g. Glazier-McDonald, *Malachi*, 79–80; Lear, *Scribal Composition*, 128–30; Karl William Weyde, "The Priests and the Descendants of Levi in the Book of Malachi," *AcT* 35 (2015), 242–45; Jakob Wöhrle, "Jacob, Moses, Levi: Pentateuchal Figures in the Book of the Twelve," in *The Formation of the Pentateuch*, ed. Jan C. Gertz, Bernard M. Levinson, Dalit Rom-Shiloni, and Konrad Schmid, FAT 111 (Tübingen: Mohr Siebeck, 2016), 1012; Alexander Zeron, "The Martyrdom of Phineas-Elijah," *JBL* 98 (1979), 99. Alternatively, the "covenant of Levi" has also been connected with Lev 2:13, Num 18:19, Deut 33:8–10, Jer 33:20–26, and Neh 13:29. For an overview, see Steven L. McKenzie and Howard N. Wallace, "Covenant Themes in Malachi," *CBQ* 45 (1983), 550–51, though they dispute the relevance of all of these passages, including Num 25, as background for Malachi's Levitical covenant.

32 ואעבדיניה מלאך קיים ויחי לעלם למבשרא גאולתא בסוף יומיא, as per the edition of Alexandro Diez Macho, *Targum Palaestinense in Pentateuchum*, vol. 4: Numeri, Biblia Polyglotta Matritensia IV (Madrid: 1977), 247. See Lear, *Scribal Composition*, 143–44.

33 The designation in the superscript almost certainly refers to an anonymous agent of Yhwh rather than to the proper name of a prophet. So e.g. Wöhrle, *Abschluss*, 254–55, noting that the term is unique to these two contexts in the entire Hebrew Bible: "Dass aber ein solcher, dann zumindest nur recht selten belegter Name ausgerechnet am Beginn eines Prophetenbuches steht, in dem ein Bote Jhwhs genannt wird, dürfte doch kaum

carries the message of the book in his hand (1:1), and it is only with the addition of this superscript, and its mutual interpretation with 3:1, that the messenger of 3:1a is identified as a prophet.[34] When this figure is combined with the prophetic role already given to the priest of 2:6, and at the level of the book overall, the messenger of Malachi becomes both priestly and prophetic. His predicted return implies that Israel's restoration, when it comes, must take place at a level that is both cultic and prophetic; both among the priests and the people. This is the mission required of the one who prepares the way for Yhwh's coming.

2.2 The Messenger as Restorer of the People: Exodus 23:20 and Isaiah 40:3

This conclusion, that מלאכי is both prophetic and priestly, therefore arises from the text of Malachi itself. The book's portrayal of this priestly-prophetic messenger is then further articulated by literary analogies to other Hebrew Bible texts, such as that seen, for example, in the use of Num 25 to colour the priestly figure of Mal 2. Malachi 3:1a has also been widely recognised to allude to two primary intertexts in its depiction of the messenger, namely, Exod 23:20 and Isa 40:3.[35]

First, Exod 23:20 presents Yhwh's promise of a מלאך who will guard the people of Israel on their way into the land of Canaan:

> Behold, I am sending a messenger before you to guard you in the way and to cause you to come to the place which I established.[36]

Zufall sein. Und deshalb ist eben die Annahme berechtigt, dass dieser Name von Mal 3,1a her gebildet wurde" (254). Weyde also argues that Malachi's use of the messenger image argues for the mutual interpretation of all of its occurrences, and that מלאך הברית should both be identified with מלאכי and interpreted as a priestly figure (*Prophecy*, 288–90).

34 So Wöhrle, *Abschluss*, 254.

35 Many scholars have cited both allusions, though some remain unconvinced of either or both. For scholars acknowledging significance in both allusions, see e.g. Blaylock, "My Messenger," 77–79; Kessler, *Maleachi*, 228–29; Weyde, *Prophecy*, 288. Recognising only Isa 40 is e.g. Mason, *Haggai*, 152; Verhoef, *Haggai*, 287. Recognising only Exod 23 is e.g. Mignon R. Jacobs, *The Books of Haggai and Malachi*, NICOT (Grand Rapids: Eerdmans, 2017), 272; Puech, "L'attente," 7.

36 I am aware of recent discussion on the compositional history of the Covenant Code (Exod 20:23–23:19) that would see it potentially dated into the exilic period. However, the book of Malachi as a Second Temple text is still almost unquestionably later, thereby allowing for the possibility of access to the Covenant Code in textual form. Further, David P. Wright has argued that the so-called "Covenant Code Appendix" (Exod 23:20–33) was central to the development of the Covenant Code proper ("The Covenant Code Appendix [Exodus 23:20–33], Neo-Assyrian Sources, and Implications for Pentateuchal

While some scholars would downplay their significance,[37] the lexical similarities between this promise of a messenger and that of Mal 3:1a are undeniable.[38] The two figures are introduced via almost identical announcements, and their roles both involve acting upon the "way" (דרך) of another entity:

Malachi 3:1a
Behold, I am sending my messenger [הנני שלח מלאכי], and he will prepare a way before me [פנה־דרך לפני]

Exodus 23:20
Behold, I am sending a messenger before you [הנה אנכי שלח מלאך לפניך] to guard you in the way [לשמרך בדרך]

This connection is somewhat obscured in most English translations by their renderings of מלאך in the Exodus text as "angel" and in Malachi as "messenger," but neither Hebrew nor Greek know any lexical difference.[39] The variation that does exist is found in the recipient of the messenger's work. In Exodus, this figure is sent before the people (לפניך) to guard them in their way (לשמרך בדרך). In Malachi, he is sent to prepare Yhwh's way (פנה־דרך לפני). This latter image recalls Isa 40:3, which introduces a voice calling in the wilderness: פנו דרך יהוה. The fact that scholars have long noticed both of these allusions seems to indicate that both are present, and that the author of Mal 3:1a has intentionally merged them.[40] This conflation results in the image of a single coming figure who prepares the way for Yhwh's arrival in the future, while simultaneously guarding the people in a manner reminiscent of a new exodus.[41]

Study," in *The Formation of the Pentateuch*, ed. Jan C. Gertz, Bernard M. Levinson, Dalit Rom Shiloni, and Konrad Schmid, FAT 111 [Tübingen: Mohr Siebeck, 2016], 47, 53), which would render it part of an earlier stage of composition. For extensive discussion and likely dating of the Covenant Code in the neo-Assyrian period, see Bernard M. Levinson, *"The Right Chorale": Studies in Biblical Law and Interpretation*, FAT 54 (Tübingen: Mohr Siebeck, 2008), 276–330.

37 See e.g. Snyman, who concludes that it is "unlikely that this Exodus-verse plays a role in the understanding of the messenger" ("Once Again," 1042).

38 So Petersen, *Prophecy*, 43; Weyde, *Prophecy*, 288.

39 The German Zürcher Bibel is the only modern translation of which I am aware that renders מלאך in the Old Testament almost universally as "Bote."

40 For further discussion on both of these allusions, see Gibson, *Covenant Continuity*, 170–77. Gibson notes that the LXX appears not to have seen the link, since פנה is translated in Mal 3:1 as ἐπιβλέψεται rather than the ἑτοιμάσατε of Isa 40:3. This is quite possible, since the Greek of Mal 3:1 also renders שלח as ἐξαποστέλλω, rather than the ἀποστέλλω of Exod 23:20. However, Gibson argues for the legitimacy of the allusion in the Hebrew based on the unique appearance between these two texts of the Piel form of פנה with דרך as direct object (176). See also Lear, *Scribal Composition*, 77 n. 8.

41 So similarly Gibson: "The themes of exodus and covenant, subtly introduced here with the allusion to Exod 23.20, are brought into sharper focus with an allusion to Isa 40.3"

Fascinatingly, Jacob Stromberg has observed a similar phenomenon already present in the composite book of Isaiah itself. He demonstrates compelling evidence for a post-exilic interpretation of Isa 40:3 in Isa 57:14, which anticipates a saying in the future: "Prepare a way [פנו־דרך], remove a stumbling block [מכשול] from the way of my people [מדרך עמי]."[42] Stromberg argues that post-exilic reworkings of earlier texts reveal the writing communities' creative application of these texts to their contemporary situations.[43] Where Isa 40 anticipates a future unconditional restoration of the nation when Yhwh appears, Isa 57, post-exile, recognises that this restoration has not come and thus describes an obstacle (מכשול) in its way.[44] To this perspective, "preparing the way" implies removing the obstacle hindering the people's restoration; in other words, preparing the way for them. Stromberg argues that this obstacle, in the view of Trito-Isaiah, is the iniquity of the people (cf. 57:17).[45] "In its new post-exilic configuration, then, the imperative to 'prepare the way' has become moral preparation."[46] The community has "gone, turning away in the way of his heart [שובב בדרך לבו]" (57:17). In response, Yhwh states "I have seen his ways [דרכיו] and I will heal [רפא] him ... and I will restore comfort [נחם] to him" (57:18). Here it is the people's ways which need healing in order for them to experience the comfort (נחם) promised by Isa 40 (40:1).[47]

The use of Isa 40 in the book of Malachi reveals an uncannily similar interpretive strategy, down to the level of word choice. Malachi 3:1a invokes a recognisable figure whose role is to guard the people on their way (Exod 23:20). It then gives that figure the additional role of preparing the way for Yhwh's

---

(*Covenant Continuity*, 174, and further on 175). See also Rikki E. Watts, *Isaiah's New Exodus and Mark*, WUNT II/88 (Tübingen: Mohr Siebeck, 1997), 61–84.

42 Jacob Stromberg, "Isaiah's Interpretive Revolution: How Isaiah's Formation Influenced Early Jewish and Christian Interpretation," in *The Book of Isaiah: Enduring Questions Answered Anew*, ed. Richard J. Bautch and J. Todd Hibbard (Grand Rapids: Eerdmans, 2014), 227. He notes that the "interpretive transformation" of Isa 40:3 by 57:14 has been consistently observed, as seen in e.g. Joseph Blenkinsopp, *Isaiah 56–66*, AB 19B (New York: Doubleday, 2003), 168–70; Wolfgang Lau, *Schriftgelehrte Prophetie in Jes 56–66*, BZAW 225 (Berlin: de Gruyter, 1994), 118–20; Walther Zimmerli, "Zur Sprache Tritojesajas," in *Gottes Offenbarung: Gesammelte Aufsätze* (Munich: Kaiser, 1969), 223–24. See also Meinhold, *Maleachi*, 256.

43 Stromberg, "Interpretive Revolution," 226–27. He observes a similar interpretation in the Qumran *Community Rule* (1QS), in which members are called to prepare Yhwh's way by withdrawing into the wilderness for purification themselves (230–31).

44 So also Lau: "מכשול ist etwas, was zwischen Jahwe und dem Volk steht und ins Verderben führt" (*Prophetie*, 119).

45 Stromberg, "Interpretive Revolution," 228.

46 Stromberg, "Interpretive Revolution," 228.

47 Stromberg, "Interpretive Revolution," 229.

coming, as per Isa 40. The verses immediately following, however, whether one includes the redactional insertion or not, make abundantly clear that this is no unconditional promise of restoration. In Mal 3:5, Yhwh declares that he is drawing near for judgement against all who do not fear him, envisioning a purging of the rebellious from among the people. In 3:2–4, the writer insists on a fiery purification of the priesthood. Both the priesthood and the people, like the community of Isa 57, can only experience restoration when the obstacle of their own iniquity is removed.[48] This, to Malachi, is what is entailed in keeping the way of the people. They will only be "kept" when they are returned to a conduct of life that renders them ready for the appearance of Yhwh.[49]

The same outcome observed by Stromberg in the post-exilic reworking of Isa 40 by Isa 57, then, is seen in Malachi's conflation of Isa 40 with Exod 23. Those who will experience the comfort promised by Isa 40:1 are those whose way has been kept and cleared of iniquity. Where Isa 57 leaves this task anonymous, Mal 3 assigns it to a specific individual by reawakening the promised messenger of Exod 23. Both texts insist on the fundamental differentiation between those who have been purified and those who have not, and both reserve Yhwh's restoration for the former. It is the purified who will make up the righteous community; the second iteration of the nation entering the promised land.

The messenger's restoration of the people along the lines of Exod 23 and Isa 57 provides a point of convergence for themes already introduced throughout the rest of the book of Malachi. Malachi 2:15–16 commands the people to "take heed" (נשמרתם) to their "spirit" (רוח) in regard to covenant faithfulness.[50] Isaiah 57 also speaks of the people's "heart" (לב) and "spirit" (רוח) in the context of Yhwh's coming to bring "healing" (רפא) to their ways (57:15–18). Malachi, in turn, also features an image of healing (מרפא) in 3:20, which occurs only after a distinction has been made between the righteous and the wicked (3:18). From the perspective of Isa 57's later reading of Isa 40, it is the way of the heart, consistently turned away, which needs this healing (57:17). A later reader of Mal 3, which also begins with a basis in Isa 40, sees that the same type of healing is

---

48   Van der Woude also notes Isa 57:14 in the background of the redactional insertion in Mal 3 ("Der Engel," 294). See also Jacobs, *Haggai*, 272. Precedent for the image of "keeping" (שמר) the way of the people as one of moral restoration is also provided by the use of the same metaphor in 1 Kgs 8:25 and 2 Chron 6:16 to command Israel's kings to "take heed" (שמר) to their own "way" (דרך) as they walk with Yhwh.

49   See similarly Gibson, *Covenant Continuity*, 176.

50   Malachi 2:10–16 is undoubtedly the most exegetically difficult passage of the entire book, and any just analysis of it is beyond the scope of this chapter. The fact that it addresses guarding one's behaviour in the context of a covenant is sufficient to make the point here.

needed (3:20). This is just the kind of later reading that is reflected in the book's epilogue (3:22–24), where the writer assigns the turning of Israel's hearts (לב – 3:24) to the same person he has deduced to be the coming messenger: Elijah, the one who turns back hearts to prevent Yhwh's curse before the day of his coming (3:23–24).

3 Elijah as Malachi's Messenger

3.1 Introduction

That the epilogue to the book of Malachi intentionally identifies Elijah as the coming messenger of 3:1 is virtually undisputed.[51] He is introduced in almost identical terms, awaited, like the messenger, before Yhwh's own appearance:

(Mal 3:1) הנני שלח מלאכי ופנה־דרך לפני ופתאם יבוא אל־היכלו האדון

(Mal 3:23)[52] הנה אנכי שלח לכם את אליה הנביא לפני בוא יום יהוה הגדול והנורא

The decision to identify the anonymous messenger of 3:1 as a specific prophet with a story set in Israel's history is a very intentional one. No justification is given as to why Elijah should be the one to return and fill this role; the connection seems to be assumed. While it is true that Elijah is uniquely available because he did not die, the question of why Malachi's messenger needed to be associated with a prophet of Israel's past tradition remains. Further, Enoch also did not die (Gen 5:24), and neither, according to some traditions, did Moses.[53] Elijah's identification with Malachi's messenger, over against any other figure, must therefore have an underlying basis in the available texts themselves.

Several scholars have argued for thematic similarities between the Elijah figure in Kings and the role of Elijah and the messenger in Malachi.[54] His presence in the context of covenant descriptions is not unique; covenant imagery is

---

51   Silvia Pellegrini (*Elija – Wegbereiter des Gottessohnes* [Freiburg: Herder, 2000], 197) and Reventlow (*Die Propheten*, 161) represent exceptions to this consensus, while Weyde remains uncommitted (*Prophecy*, 392–93).

52   The Greek ἀποστέλλω in LXX 3:22 reflects the locution of Exod 23:20, rather than the ἐξαποστέλλω of Mal 3:1.

53   See Loewenstamm, "Death of Moses."

54   See e.g. Brevard S. Childs, *Introduction to the Old Testament as Scripture* (London: SCM, 1979), 495–96; Glazier-McDonald, *Malachi*, 257. Gibson critiques this approach by noting that it is focused on parallels to Carmel, while Malachi's composite epilogue places Elijah's return in the context of a mention of Horeb (*Covenant Continuity*, 245).

certainly present in the Kings narrative.[55] His association with Moses through the linking of Mal 3:23–24 with 3:22 also is not surprising, given his Mosaic characterisation in Kings. His rebuke of the people on Carmel (1 Kgs 18:21) could be argued to highlight a similar sort of cultic apathy to that decried in Malachi.[56] The Elijah of Malachi turns back hearts (3:24); the Elijah of Carmel prays for the people's recognition that Yhwh turns back their hearts (1 Kgs 18:37). We have noted that the expected messenger in the larger book of Malachi is both priestly and prophetic. Elijah in Kings is unquestionably a prophetic figure, but, as noted in the previous chapter, priestly elements are evident as well, specifically in his sacrifice on Carmel and his zeal in the pattern of Phinehas.

These thematic similarities are not insignificant, but, on their own, they form a weak case for Elijah's unique suitability for the role of Malachi's messenger. I would argue that the fundamental reason for the epilogue's use of Elijah has still been missed. If the writer of the epilogue assumed that the messenger figures of the book were to be taken as a single individual, this writer would have held these texts to be mutually elucidating. We have already observed this kind of exegetical conflation in the coordinated expansion of Mal 3:1–5 and its depiction of the מלאך in light of the other occurrences of the term within the book. To go one step further, if exegetical strategies such as that shown by Stromberg in Isaiah are indeed demonstrable in the book of Malachi, as I have argued, then any writer undertaking a summary of the book would also need to consider the impact of its source texts on the underlying message. I suggest that this is precisely what the writer of Mal 3:23–24 did, and that the interpretive progression which led him to an Elijanic messenger can be reconstructed with at least a measure of confidence.

3.2 Elijah in the Reading of Malachi 2–3

First, we have seen that the introduction of Elijah in Mal 3:23 is based on the sending of מלאכי in Mal 3:1a, who is to be identified with מלאך הברית and with the priestly messenger of 2:4–7. This messenger is said to have the "Torah of truth in his mouth [בפיהו]" (2:6), and others "will seek Torah from his mouth [מפיהו]" (2:7). The fact that Malachi's composite epilogue includes an injunction to "remember the Torah of Moses" (3:22) supports a thematic correlation between this Torah and the introduction of Elijah as the messenger that follows.

Malachi 3:23 also displays syntactic similarities to the description of Yhwh's judgement on the priesthood in 2:3. "Behold, I am rebuking your seed" is

---

55 E.g. Elijah's altar of twelve stones (1 Kgs 18:31), his appeal to "the God of Abraham, Isaac, and Israel" (18:36), and his lament that Israel has forsaken the covenant (19:10, 14).
56 See Childs, *Introduction*, 495.

formulated similarly to "behold, I am sending my messenger" in 3:1a, both introduced by הנני and an active participle followed by the object. The introduction of Elijah, argued to reflect the structure of 3:1a, is syntactically even closer to 2:3. It shares the verb and theme of 3:1a while reflecting the clause structure of 2:3:

Malachi 2:3	Malachi 3:1a	Malachi 3:23
הנני גער לכם את־הזרע	הנני שלח מלאכי	הנה אנכי שלח לכם את אליה הנביא

Of course, no argument can be built on the basis of syntactical correlation alone. Nevertheless, in view of the book's overall rhetoric, it is possible that the writer of the epilogue not only intends to name Elijah as the anonymous coming messenger, but also to portray his coming as a contrast to the rebuke of corrupt priests levelled by 2:3. Such an identification would follow a similar exegetical strategy to that leading to the identification of מלאכי as מלאך הברית, for which I have argued above.

Elijah's identity as an ideal priest is also supported by later witnesses. Jewish interpretation, as we have seen, names the priest Phinehas as the "messenger of the covenant" who will "live forever to bring tidings of redemption at the end of days" (Tg Ps-J Num 25:11–12). The same Targum on Exod 6:18 further identifies "Phinehas, who is Elijah" as "the great priest, the one being sent to the captivity of Israel at the end of days."[57] Later readers evidently recognised the inclusion of Elijah in Malachi's epilogue as an identification not only of מלאכי in 3:1a, but also of מלאך הברית in 3:1b and of the Phinehas-like messenger of 2:7, who, in turn, is described by the Targum as "living forever."[58] An interpretation that identifies Elijah as this composite messenger figure can therefore take shape, again, based on the text of Malachi, rather than on thematic correlations alone.

---

57 פנחס הוא אליהו כהנא רבא דעתיד למשתלחא לגלוותא דישראל בסוף יומייא, as per Alexandro Diaz Macho, *Targum Palaestinense in Pentateuchum*, vol. 2: Exodus, Biblia Polyglotta Matritensia IV (Madrid: 1980), 35.

58 Lear's extensive study on the relationship between Phinehas and Elijah ultimately argues that this conflation is based in the text of Malachi, rather than arising from later rabbinic tradition (*Scribal Composition*, 121–46). See also Alexander Zeron, "Einige Bemerkungen zu M.F. Collins 'The Hidden Vessels in Samaritan Traditions,'" *JSJ* 4 (1973): 165–68; idem, "Martyrdom," 99. Lear is explicitly indebted to Zeron and builds her conclusion on his earlier work ("Scribal Composition," 123). Contra others like Clark, who sees Elijah's priestly identification as a later result of the Hasmonean identification of Phinehas with Elijah ("Eschatological High Priest," 238).

Once this textual relationship has been established, however, those same thematic correlations begin to bear weight. The priestly messenger holds the "Torah of truth in his mouth [תורת אמת היתה בפיהו]" and "turned back [השיב] many from iniquity" (2:6). With Elijah already in mind, readers may now remember the words of the widow of Zarephath in 1 Kgs 17:24: "Now I know this: that you are a man of God and that the word of Yhwh in your mouth is truth [בפיך אמת]." They may observe Elijah's identification with the prophet like Moses, who has Yhwh's words "in his mouth" (בפיו – Deut 18:18). His "sustenance" (כלכל) at the wadi Cherith in 1 Kgs 17:4, as well as Obadiah's "sustaining" (כלכל) of Yhwh's prophets (18:4, 13) may be linked to Mal 3:2: while Elijah sustained and was sustained when he appeared the first time, no impure person will "endure" (כלכל) when he comes again.[59] Elijah's "healing" (רפא) of the altar of Yhwh in 1 Kgs 18:30 could also be reflected in Malachi's use of "healing" (מרפא) for those who fear Yhwh's name (3:20). In 1 Kgs 18:37, Elijah's prayer is that "this people will know that you, Yhwh, are God and that you have caused their heart to turn back." While the verb used for "turn back" in Kings is סבב, it is easy to pick up a further link to Elijah in the שוב of Mal 2:6 once the association has already been made. The priest who "turns back" many from iniquity and the prophet who prays for Yhwh to turn hearts converge in a single description of a messenger-Elijah who turns back the hearts of the people before the coming of Yhwh (Mal 3:24).[60]

Perhaps the most compelling link of all is found in a reading of Mal 3:1 against the backdrop of its allusion to Exod 23. This latter text, as we have seen, speaks of a guiding figure who "keeps" the people on their way to the promised land. Malachi gives this figure a future restorative role by conflating it with Isa 40's preparation of the way of Yhwh, implying that the people must be kept on the way of obedience. Significantly, Exod 23 itself calls the people to obedience, commanding them to "keep yourselves before [the messenger] [השמר מפניו]"

---

59   See Valve, "Messenger-Elijah," 100–101. Glazier-McDonald notes the use of this verb in Mal 3:2, but does not connect it with Kings (*Malachi*, 143). Cf. also the parallel description of the day of Yhwh in Joel 2:11.

60   It is even possible that the substitution in LXX Mal 3:22 of Ηλιαν τὸν Θεσβίτην for the MT's אליה הנביא (3:23) stems from a play on words between Elijah's role and the single statement made about his origin in 1 Kgs 17. He is התשבי (1 Kgs 17:1), the one who "causes to turn" (השיב – Mal 2:6; 3:24). Interestingly, this variant is the opposite of that between the Hebrew and Greek texts of 1 Kgs 17:1. The MT here simply reads אליהו התשבי, while the LXX includes Elijah's prophetic status (Ηλιου ὁ προφήτης ὁ Θεσβίτης). Alternatively, as suggested by Meinhold, the LXX clarification in Malachi could be meant to ensure a clear connection to the Elijah of Kings (*Maleachi*, 403).

and listen (שמע) to his voice (23:21). If they do not listen, the messenger will not pardon them (23:21). If they do, however, a series of blessings will follow:

> [22] For if you surely listen to his voice and you do all which I will say, then I will oppose your opponents and I will antagonise your antagonists ...
> [24] You shall not bow down to their gods and you shall not serve them, and you shall not do according to their deeds, for you shall surely destroy them and you shall surely shatter their sacred pillars.
> [25] But you shall serve Yhwh your God, and he will bless your bread and your water, and I will remove sickness from your midst.
> [26] There will not be one miscarrying or barren in your land; I will fulfil the number of your days. (Exod 23:22, 24–26)

If the coming messenger of Mal 3:1 is based on that of Exod 23, then this is a figure to whom Israel is commanded to listen – just like they will "listen" (שמע) to the coming prophet like Moses (Deut 18:15).[61] The rewards of obedience in Exod 23, exemplified in the destruction of idolaters and their sacred spaces, include blessing on bread and water, removal of sickness, removal of barrenness, and a full lifespan. To an interpreter of the book of Malachi who already has the priestly-prophetic character of Elijah in mind as a result of the other links we have noted, this description provides the linchpin for his identification. There is no other figure in the Israelite scriptures who embodies all of these images like Elijah. He is a zealous fighter for Yhwh who seeks to overthrow Baal worship and lead the people to do the same. He is Yhwh's channel for the blessing of bread and water in 1 Kgs 17–18, while also receiving that blessing himself in chs. 17 and 19. He is the healer of a widow's sick and dying son. His authority over the span of life is displayed in the linked and contrasting images of the widow's son (1 Kgs 17) and Ahaziah (2 Kgs 1). When his story cycle is combined with that of Elisha, both the curses of barrenness and of miscarriage are revoked as well. We have seen that Elisha's promise of a son to the Shunammite woman alludes directly to the barrenness motif in Gen 18 (2 Kgs 4:14). Elisha's cleansing of a spring in 2 Kgs 2:21 also represents the blessing of waters and, astonishingly, the removal of miscarriage (also rendered "unfruitfulness") via the same root (שכל) utilised in Exod 23:26! The Elisha narratives may well be subsumed by the author of Malachi's epilogue under the umbrella of Elijah's spirit and prophetic role (cf. 2 Kgs 2:9–10, 15).

---

61   See also Petersen: "If one uses Ex. 23:20–22 as an interpretive backdrop, 'my messenger' is supposed to enable the people to do something. In both Exodus 23 and Mal 3:1b, 5, that 'something' is obeying the stipulations of the covenant" (*Zechariah*, 210).

If this is the case, Elijah remains the only figure in Hebrew tradition who can be associated with all of the blessing images of Exod 23 at once. Best of all, he never died and so is able to return! In short, to the author of Malachi's epilogue, the book's awaited figure – who is a priest like Phinehas and also the promised messenger of Exodus – must and can only be Elijah.

3.3   *Elijah in the Epilogue*

In this way, the identification of Elijah in Malachi's epilogue as the book's composite coming messenger can be clearly established through a reconstructed reading of the book within the context of Second Temple interpretive and exegetical practices. This Elijah's mission, linked to Mal 2:6 and to his prayer in 1 Kgs 18:37, consists of an appearance before the day of Yhwh to "turn back" the hearts of fathers and sons (השיב לב־אבות על־בנים ולב בנים על־אבותם – Mal 3:24).

Precisely what sort of "turning" is in view here, however, has been a further object of extensive discussion. Some scholars have posited a reconciliation of literal human relationships with the goal of restoring familial and social harmony.[62] Others have suggested that אבות and בנים refer to Israel's founding generation and the subsequent generations of their children,[63] or that they represent a metaphor for nationwide eschatological renewal.[64] Still others, notably Elie Assis, have argued that Israel's relationship with Yhwh specifically is in view, where he represents the fathers and Israel the sons.[65]

All of these interpretations, on their own, contain elements of weakness. Reading Elijah's mission purely in terms of familial harmony minimises its direct relationship to חרם, a term with cultic and military connotations that

---

62   An older proposed context for this domestic strain was the tension of a new Hellenistic mindset being embraced by the younger generation and resisted by the older (so Rudolph, *Maleachi*, 292–93; Ernst Sellin, *Das Zwölfprophetenbuch*, KAT 12 [Leipzig: Deichert, 1930], 2:618; J.M.P. Smith, *Malachi*, 83). However, even Reventlow notes that this "ist wohl eine zu moderne Vorstellung" (*Die Propheten*, 161). A better justification for a familial interpretation of Elijah's "turning" could be drawn from Mic 7:6, where members of the same household treat each other with contempt (so Pierre Grelot, "Michée 7,6 dans les évangiles et dans la littérature rabbinique," *Bib* 67 [1986], 375). Glazier-McDonald (*Malachi*, 254–55) and Verhoef (*Haggai*, 342) tie the presupposition of familial conflict to Malachi's own treatment of apparent intermarriage and divorce in 2:10–16.

63   See e.g. Jacobs, *Haggai*, 334. Gibson proposes an alternate interpretation of this reading, which locates both sides of this restoration in the future: "that is, Yhwh will send Elijah the prophet to ensure *generational covenant fidelity* in the future" (*Covenant Continuity*, 254; original emphasis).

64   So Caryn A. Reeder, "Malachi 3:24 and the Eschatological Restoration of the 'Family,'" *CBQ* 69 (2007), 707.

65   Elie Assis, "Moses, Elijah and the Messianic Hope: A New Reading of Malachi 3,22–24," *ZAW* 123 (2011), 212–14.

refers to utter destruction.[66] Further, the LXX epilogue does not reflect the MT's couplet, but rather renders the second stich an interpretive parallel to the first: καὶ καρδίαν ἀνθρώπου πρὸς τὸν πλησίον αὐτοῦ (LXX Mal 3:23). Its inclusion of "the heart of a man to his neighbour" would seem to eliminate any exclusively familial understanding. The generational interpretation is similarly problematised by the second stich of the LXX, while it simultaneously makes little sense of the first stich in the MT (אבות על־בנים), in which a past generation must have its heart turned by a future prophet.[67] A recognition that Elijah's mission must concern Israel's relationship to Yhwh hits closer to the mark, but Assis's reading is forced to twist itself around the usage of the plural אבות in reference to Yhwh, which, if true, would represent an extraordinary aberration in the Hebrew Bible.[68]

A potential solution, I would argue, may be found in the translation adopted by Glazier-McDonald, who renders the preposition על in Mal 3:24 as "together with" instead of "toward."[69] By this reading, fathers are turned back "together with" sons, and sons "together with" their fathers. This is a defensible translation of the preposition, and comparable interpretations have been proposed by rabbinic commentaries.[70] Zakovitch comes to a similar conclusion, translating

---

66   See Jackie A. Naudé, "חרם," *NIDOTTE*, vol. 2, ed. Willem A. VanGemeren (Grand Rapids: Zondervan, 1997), 276–77.

67   Keil and Delitzsch suggest that "to" could also be understood as "in," rendering the hearts of the faithful fathers restored within the sons, while the sons have their hearts turned back to the faithfulness of the fathers. Rudolph counters, however, that the hearts of the Israelite fathers were hardly models of faithfulness! See Carl Friedrich Keil and Franz Delitzsch, *Commentary on the Old Testament*, vol. 10 (Peabody: Hendrickson, 1996), 664–65; Rudolph, *Maleachi*, 292. Cf. Gibson, *Covenant Continuity*, 254–55.

68   So Reeder, "Eschatological Restoration," 703; S.D. Snyman, "Malachi's Controversial Conclusion: Problems and Prospects," *AcT* 40 (2020), 132. While Assis maintains אדונים in Mal 1:6 as a precedent for referring to Yhwh in the plural ("Messianic Hope," 214), this parallel is difficult to sustain. אדני appears regularly in the plural in references to Yhwh in the Hebrew Bible, while אבות is never used.

69   Glazier-McDonald, *Malachi*, 256.

70   Assis cites Rashi's "by means of" and Ibn Ezra's "and" ("Messianic Hope," 212). See definition of על as "bei" in Wilhelm Gesenius, *Hebräisches und Aramäisches Handwörterbuch*, 18th ed. (Heidelberg: Springer, 2013), 962, and "with" in *The Enhanced Brown-Driver-Briggs Hebrew and English Lexicon* (Oxford: Clarendon, 1959), 755. The latter cites Exod 35:22 as an example: האנשים על־הנשים should be rendered "men *and* women," or "men *with* women," rather than "men *to* women," which is nonsensical in context. Zakovitch notes Rabbi Kimchi's comment that "'and he shall return the hearts of the fathers *on* the sons' is like '*with* the sons,'" and raises the precedent of Deut 22:6, which commands that a mother bird not be taken "with" (על) her young ("Last Verses," 64). Reventlow acknowledges the possibility of this translation as well (*Die Propheten*, 161). Sellin notes a suggested emending of על to עם but argues against it (*Zwölfprophetenbuch*, 2:617).

עַל literally as "on," but reading the entire phrase as a merism denoting repentance: "He shall cause fathers and sons to repent, sons and fathers."[71] This reading bases the "turning" firmly in Israel's relationship with Yhwh, while avoiding the grammatical and hermeneutical difficulties raised by Assis's interpretation. It renders Elijah's mission one of bringing about the repentance of the entire community, which simultaneously encompasses both the "guarding" and "preparing" task of the messenger of 3:1, as well as the "turning" role of the priest of 2:6. As the prophetic מלאכי and the priestly מלאך הברית, Elijah's roles function together to prevent Yhwh's curse upon the land (3:24). The role of Phinehas in zealously turning back Yhwh's anger from Israel (Num 25:11), then, may be considered to be fulfilled by Elijah, not in his first appearance, but in his second.

Interestingly, there is one instance in the Hebrew Bible in which a known prophetic figure is explicitly called a messenger, and it also appears in the Book of the Twelve. The prophet Haggai is called מלאך יהוה (Hag 1:13) and said to be "sent" (שלח) by Yhwh (1:12).[72] He prophesies against the sin of the people and declares that a drought has come on the land because of them (1:10–11). When the "remnant of the people" (שארית העם) heed (שמע) the words of this drought-pronouncing messenger-prophet, they are said to have "feared before Yhwh" (וייראו העם מפני יהוה – 1:12).

In the book of Malachi, it is the idealised messenger-priest who "feared me and was dismayed before my name" (וייראני ומפני שמי נחת הוא – 2:5), in contrast to the rest of the priests who have no "fear" (מורא) of Yhwh (1:6) and refuse to "listen" (שמע – 2:2).[73] In Mal 3, salvation from judgement is given to those who "fear Yhwh and esteem his name" (ליראי יהוה ולחשבי שמו – 3:16). Those who follow the example of the messenger-priest of Malachi are thus described in the same way as those who heed the prophetic drought-pronouncing messenger of Yhwh in Haggai. The writer of Malachi's epilogue likely knows the larger corpus, and knows Elijah as the paradigmatic prophet who pronounces drought. Therefore, it is no exegetical stretch for this writer to conclude that Elijah is also Malachi's messenger and priest, who fears Yhwh as an example of the righteous remnant among the people.

---

71   Zakovitch, "Last Verses," 64. Contra J.M.P. Smith, who argues that such a reading produces "an intolerable tautology" (*Malachi*, 83).

72   See Glazier-McDonald, *Malachi*, 264; Petersen, *Prophecy*, 43; Sellin, *Zwölfprophetenbuch*, 616. R.L. Smith notes regarding Haggai that "מלאך 'angel' is frequently used for the 'angel of Yahweh' but only here of a prophet," and calls it a "strange and enigmatic expression" (*Micah*, 154–55).

73   Israel's priests here are portrayed as even worse than the other nations by the comment in Mal 1:14 that, in contrast, Yhwh's "name is feared in the nations [שמי נורא בגוים]."

4   Elijah's Coming as Conclusion to the Law and the Prophets

The exegetical progression described above, executed on the book of Malachi by its epilogue, confirms the importance of these final verses for the interpretation of the book in its current form. The epilogue affords modern interpreters quite possibly the earliest recorded reading and application of the book overall, and it pins its audience's hopes of restoration on a single figure with whom, as demonstrated by the Kings narrative, they already associated their survival as Israel's remnant.

Scholarship in recent years has been fascinated by the compelling editorial links that exist between corpora in the canonical Hebrew Bible. Lexical and thematic ties appear at corporal seams to connect the Torah to the Prophets, the Prophets to the Writings, and the Writings back to the Torah, by means of linking passages in Deut 34, Josh 1, Ps 1, 2 Chron 36, and Mal 3:22–24.[74] A significant question with respect to Malachi's epilogue, then, is whether it was primarily intended as a conclusion to the book of Malachi, the Book of the Twelve, or the larger prophetic corpus. In the end, it shows evidence of composition toward all of these ends.[75] We have observed the epilogue's elaboration of the expectation of a coming messenger within the confines of the book, which practically assigns the problem of delayed restoration to the people's sin, as in Isa 57. It further effectively promises that this problem will be solved when the purifying messenger comes, who therefore becomes the people's hope of restoration. The epilogue assigns this role to the only prophet who fits it: Elijah, the one who remains alive and whose presentation in Kings already embodied the survival of a remnant.

At the same time, links can be seen in Mal 3:22–24 specifically to both Deut 34 and Josh 1, on either side of the seam between the Torah and the Former Prophets.[76] The epilogue enjoins readers to "remember the Torah of Moses my servant" (Mal 3:22), recalling Josh 1:7's command to "be careful to do

---

74   See already Blenkinsopp, *Prophecy*, 80–95, 120–23 for Deut 34 and Mal 3; further e.g. Crüsemann, *Elia*, 149–52; Zakovitch, "Last Verses," 60–81. For a helpful visual diagram, see Wöhrle, *Abschluss*, 426.

75   For the relationship of Malachi's epilogue specifically to the Book of the Twelve, see Wöhrle, *Abschluss*, 421–23.

76   See Crüsemann, *Elia*, 149–52; Rudolph, *Maleachi*, 291; Steck, *Abschluß*, 127–36; Wöhrle, *Abschluss*, 424–27; Zakovitch, "Last Verses," 67–68; Erich Zenger and Christian Frevel, *Einleitung in das Alte Testament*, 9th ed., ed. Christian Frevel (Stuttgart: Kohlhammer, 2016), 27.

according to all the Torah which Moses my servant commanded you."[77] When Mal 3:22 is taken as a unit with 3:23–24, it also reveals significant lexical overlap with Deut 34:10–12:[78]

Deuteronomy 34:10–12	Malachi 3:22–23
And there has not arisen since a prophet [נביא] in Israel like Moses [משה], whom Yhwh knew face to face, for all the signs and the wonders which Yhwh sent him [שלחו] to do in the land of Egypt ... and for all the strong hand and for all the great fear [המורא הגדול] which Moses [משה] did before the eyes of all Israel [לעיני כל־ישראל].	Remember the Torah of Moses [משה] my servant, which I commanded him at Horeb together with all Israel [על־כל־ישראל]; statutes and judgements. Behold, I am sending [שלח] to you Elijah the prophet [נביא] before the coming of the great and fearful [הגדול והנורא] day of Yhwh.

Both passages direct the reader to a memory of Moses and to Yhwh's work through him in the context of "all Israel."[79] In Deut 34, Moses is called a "prophet" who was "sent," while in Mal 3 "Elijah the prophet" is promised to be "sent" in the future. Moses' past signs in Deuteronomy are described as "great fear," while Malachi's still-future day of Yhwh is "great and fearful." Deuteronomy 34 further perpetuates the expectation that Mal 3 purports to fulfil: that of a coming prophet like Moses. Where the Pentateuchal corpus ends by stating that the prophet like Moses has not come, the colophon to the prophets announces that he still will.

This conclusion is supported further by the observation that the messenger passages in both Mal 2 and 3 are also linked to Deut 18.[80] Malachi 2 rebukes the priests for refusing to listen (שמע) and give honour to Yhwh's name (שם) (2:2),

---

77   Contra Chapman, who argues that the function of Josh 1 is primarily within the book and DtrH, rather than functioning as a "programmatic conclusion" like Deut 34 and Mal 3 ("Canonical Approach," 139–40).

78   See Glazier-McDonald, *Malachi*, 265. The probability of an intentional connection between these passages is supported by the status of both as redactional conclusions in their own right to their respective books and larger corpora. See Crüsemann, *Elia*, 151.

79   See also כל־בני ישראל in 1 Kgs 18:20, as per Childs (*Introduction*, 495).

80   DeJong also argues that "the earliest articulations of the eschatological Elijah tradition, present in Mal 3:24 and Sir 48:10, reflect a Hellenistic-era scribal interpretation of Deut 18:15, 18, which asserts that the Mosaic prophetic succession has been provisionally closed in the present, and is therefore deferred to the eschatological future" (*A Prophet*, 156).

in contrast, as we have seen, to the priestly messenger who reveres Yhwh's name (שׁם) and holds the Torah in his mouth (תורת אמת היתה בפיהו – 2:5–6). The prophet like Moses of Deut 18 appears with a statement that Israel will "listen" (שׁמע) to him (18:15, 19), because Yhwh's words are in his mouth (דברי בפיו – 18:18) and "he will speak in my name" (ידבר בשׁמי – 18:19). The context of this passage draws on Yhwh's appearance on Horeb as related in Deut 5, but the same story is told in Exod 20:18–21, the context in which the messenger of Exod 23 appears. Exodus 23, in turn, is cited by Mal 3:1. It is possible that a reader of Malachi with the entire Pentateuch at hand could have exegetically combined the messenger of Exodus and the prophet of Deuteronomy into a single individual.[81] Both are promised, both are coming, and both are figures to whom Israel must listen. The author of Malachi's epilogue, in any case, seems to have recognised and clarified the simultaneous embodiment of all of these images in the single figure of the prophet Elijah.

When these lexical links are combined with Elijah's Mosaic image in Kings, the reader discovers that Malachi's epilogue is giving Elijah another chance. A returning Elijah means a returning prophet like Moses, who will succeed where he failed the first time.[82] This returning Elijah is expected to complete what no prophet had previously been able to do: turn the entirety of Israel back to Yhwh and establish his righteous community. From this reading, the question of whether Mal 3:22–24 was added primarily as a conclusion to the book or to the prophetic corpus becomes relatively irrelevant. It functions as both at once.

Even the corpus of the Writings may secondarily underscore the restoration embodied by Malachi's messenger.[83] Apart from Hag 1 noted above, 2 Chron 36:15–16 is the only passage in the Hebrew Bible in which the term מלאך is explicitly a prophetic designation.[84] It is also the only text outside of Mal 1:1 in which Yhwh is said to send his own word ביד מלאך:[85]

---

81   The plausibility of such a connection is supported by Isa 42:19 and 44:26 in which Yhwh's "servant" (עבד – cf. Moses as עבדי in Mal 3:22) is placed in apposition to his messenger(s). See Glazier-McDonald, *Malachi*, 264. Second Temple interpretation will increasingly conflate Elijah with this servant figure, as we shall see.

82   Even Blenkinsopp cautiously allowed for this possibility: "Given the close thematic links between the Moses and Elijah of Jewish tradition, it is not impossible that the eschatological messenger identified in Mal. 3:23–24 with Elijah was thought to be the Mosaic prophet, though this cannot be proved" (*Prophecy*, 87).

83   See Zakovitch, "Last Verses," 63.

84   Cf. also Isa 44:26. Petersen also notes the Chronicler's use of מלאך in a prophetic capacity (*Prophecy*, 43).

85   Outside of these texts, formulations of שׁלח ביד מלאך appear only in the context of a human being sending "by the hand of" another human messenger (1 Sam 11:7;

¹⁵ And Yhwh, the God of their fathers, sent [שלח] to them by the hand of his messengers [ביד מלאכיו] repeatedly, because he had compassion [חמל] on his people and on his dwelling place.
¹⁶ But they were continually making fun of the messengers of God [מלאכי האלהים] and despising [בזה] his words and mocking his prophets, until the hot anger of Yhwh arose against his people until there was no healing [מרפא]. (2 Chron 36:15–16)

While it would be difficult to confirm a direct literary relationship between two such late texts, the similarities between them may speak of a developing conception of the role of prophets as messengers and the need for a success-ful prophet still to come. In Chronicles, Yhwh is depicted as sending word by his prophetic "messengers" repeatedly, only for them to be rejected by the people. He "has compassion" (חמל), until the people's stubbornness and "despising" (בזה) of his words extends to such a degree that "there was no more healing" (עד־לאין מרפא – 36:16). When there is no more healing – that is, no more possible restoration of the people – to the Chronicler, exile is the only option (36:17–21).

In Malachi, Yhwh also sends a message ביד מלאכי (Mal 1:1). The people are now on the other side of exile, but their rebellion, including "despising" (בזה) Yhwh's offerings (1:12), is such that they risk judgement again. Those who listen, first to the message of the book via מלאכי and then to מלאכי who is still to come, are the ones upon whom Yhwh will "have compassion" (חמל) as a man has on his son (3:17). Those who fear Yhwh are the ones preserved, just as in Kings, in contrast to the cultic establishment that is rebuked. It is the Yhwh-fearers on whom the sun of righteousness will rise with "healing" (מרפא) in its wings, "'on the day when I act,' says Yhwh of hosts" (3:20–21); the great and fearful day preceded by the second coming of Elijah.

5   Conclusion: Elijah as Past and Future

To the author of Malachi's epilogue, Elijah represents both the past and future of God's people. In his role as the messenger, in the sense of Exod 23 and that reflected in Chronicles, he evokes both the people's journey to the promised land and the rebellion that forced them to leave it. With his promised return as a prophet like Moses, he encompasses both the story of Israel and its hope

---

Jer 27:3). Haggai 1 overlaps here as well, as the word of Yhwh is said to come ביד־חגי הנביא (1:1, 3), who is later described as sent (שלח) by Yhwh (1:12) and called מלאך יהוה (1:13).

for restoration. Not only does the writer of the epilogue draw directly on the Kings narrative and the traditions surrounding it in identifying Elijah as Malachi's messenger, but he also portrays Elijah as representative of those who fear Yhwh among the people. The exegetical reconstruction I have suggested offers a demonstrable rationale for the choice of Elijah for Malachi's epilogue. His adoption into Jewish, and even Christian, tradition goes far beyond textual data, however, to the much deeper level of personified hope. In the following chapters, we will see this hope progress and develop, reflected in texts that creatively merge the portraits of Kings and Malachi into an ever-growing composite image of a prophet who is enlivened by the traditions, identities, and expectations of the Second Temple communities.

CHAPTER 4

Elijah and the Hope of Second Temple Texts

1   Introduction to the Texts

That the expectation of a returning prophetic figure struck a deep and resound-
ing chord within Second Temple Jewish communities can hardly be disputed.
We have seen in Malachi that the connection between Elijah and an earlier
image of a coming messenger/prophet like Moses is the result of organic exegetical conclusions drawn by the writer of the epilogue from the rest of the
book. However, similar images, some of them citing Malachi directly, quickly
begin to appear in other texts as well.[1] Whether these writings explicitly mention Elijah or not, they undoubtedly reflect the growing contemporary conflation of various eschatological themes with the kind of priestly-prophetic figure
that Malachi's epilogue names Elijah.[2]

For the sake of space, I have chosen here to analyse only those texts generally dated within the Second Temple period which name Elijah, or Malachi's
epilogue, and reveal something of the contemporary understanding of his
role. As such, the texts in view are Sir 48:1–11, 1 Macc 2:58, *LivProph* 21, the
Apocalypse of Zephaniah, 4Q558, and 4Q521.[3] I will present a brief summary

---

1   See Puech: "En effet, à l'époque hellénistique, un rappel du retour d'Élie dans une sorte de
    paraphrase de Ml 3,23 paraît assuré" ("L'attente," 14–15).
2   Puech's study of "the return of Elijah in the Old Testament and the intertestamental writ-
    ings" includes numerous Second Temple texts which do not explicitly mention Elijah, but
    which can be, and likely were, exegetically connected (Dan 9:24–25, 1 En 89–90, 4Q175, 1QS
    [Community Rule], the Damascus Document, 4Q252, 4Q174 and 4Q253a [Pesher Malachi])
    ("L'attente," 12–26). However, Elijah's connection with these texts results from a combination
    of later tradition and continued exegetical inferences, and space prevents further discussion
    of them here.
3   Ben Sira can be dated to the second century BCE, both in its original Hebrew version and
    its Greek translation a few decades later (see Patrick W. Skehan and Alexander A. Di Lella,
    The Wisdom of Ben Sira, AB 39 [New York: Doubleday, 1987], 8–10). First Maccabees is dated
    to the late second century BCE (Daniel R. Schwartz, *1 Maccabees*, AYB 41B [New Haven:
    Yale University Press, 2022], 8), while *Lives of the Prophets* is traditionally dated to the first
    century CE (D.R.A. Hare, "The Lives of the Prophets," in *The Old Testament Pseudepigrapha*,
    vol. 2, ed. James H. Charlesworth [Garden City: Doubleday, 1985], 380–81). The Apocalypse
    of Zephaniah is dated by Wintermute between the first century BCE and the first century CE
    (O.S. Wintermute, "The Apocalypse of Zephaniah," in *The Old Testament Pseudepigrapha*,
    vol. 1, ed. James H. Charlesworth [Garden City: Doubleday, 1983], 500–501). Puech dates
    4Q558 to the second–first century BCE and the extant 4Q521 to the early first century CE,

of the role these texts play as links between the Elijah images of Kings and Malachi and those reflected in the New Testament, highlighting those elements which reveal their dependence on Kings and Malachi and those which may represent conceptual innovations.[4] We will see that all of these texts, to a greater or lesser extent, underscore the image of Elijah as representing both the paradigmatic Mosaic prophetic voice and the embodiment of Israel's ongoing preservation.

2   Elijah in Ben Sira/Sirach

2.1   *Dependence*

The use of Elijah in Ben Sira 48 provides the most indisputable example of a Second Temple conception of the prophet drawn from both Kings and

---

though its content is older ("L'attente," 14–15). The most significant additional texts of similar provenance are likely 1 En 89:51–53 and 90:31–32 (a portion of the Animal Apocalypse) and Josephus in *Ant.* 8.319–362; 9.18–28. The Animal Apocalypse, dated by Nickelsburg to the mid-second century BCE, by nature does not mention Elijah by name, though he is generally associated with one of the figures dressed in white (90:31) (see George W.E. Nickelsburg, *1 Enoch 1*, Hermeneia [Minneapolis: Fortress, 2001], 384, 405; Daniel C. Olson, *A New Reading of the Animal Apocalypse of 1 Enoch* [Leiden: Brill, 2013], 7, 58–59, 92, 130–31, 226). Josephus also presents a retelling of the Elijah cycle of Kings, but his *Antiquities* dates post-70 CE. Further texts include Philo's *Quaestiones et Solutiones in Genesin* 1.86, which mentions Elijah's ascension to heaven alongside its discussion of Enoch but goes into little further detail (see edition of C.D. Yonge, *The Works of Philo* [Peabody: Hendrickson, 1993], 809). Fourth Ezra 6:26 connects an eschatological vision of "the men who were taken up, who from their birth have not tasted death" with the changing of hearts of the earth's inhabitants (translation by B.M. Metzger, "The Fourth Book of Ezra," in *The Old Testament Pseudepigrapha*, vol. 1, ed. James H. Charlesworth [Garden City: Doubleday, 1983], 535), but it is also generally dated post-Second Temple (Metzger, "Fourth Ezra," 520). Shaver's analysis includes the *Sibylline Oracles* (book 2, lines 187–89) which promises Elijah's return on a heavenly chariot, and the *Apocalypse of Elijah*, in which Elijah is martyred with Enoch and returns to earth to annihilate the paradigmatic eschatological adversary ("The Prophet," 204–206). While *Sib Or 2* may originally have been a Second Temple text, it contains significant Christian redaction (John J. Collins, *Sibylline Oracles*, in *The Old Testament Pseudepigrapha*: vol. 1, ed. James H. Charlesworth [Garden City, NY: Doubleday, 1983], 330–32). The *Apocalypse of Elijah* is also dated post-70 CE (see O.S. Wintermute, "Apocalypse of Elijah," in *The Old Testament Pseudepigrapha*: vol. 1, ed. James H. Charlesworth [Garden City, NY: Doubleday, 1983], 729–30; David Frankfurter, *Elijah in Upper Egypt: The Apocalypse of Elijah and Early Egyptian Christianity* [Minneapolis: Fortress, 1993], 17–20). Its imagery draws on the two witnesses of Rev 11, which will be discussed in the final chapter of this book.

4   The value of this approach is seen in its use by Pancratius C. Beentjes's analysis in "Ben Sira's Portrayal of Aaron and Phinehas (Sir 45:6–25): An Interaction between Tradition and Innovation," in *Ben Sira in Conversation with Traditions* (Berlin: de Gruyter, 2022), 51–63.

Malachi. He appears in a literary unit formed of Sir 44–50 (the "Praise of the Ancient Fathers" [שֶׁבַח אָבוֹת עוֹלָם]), which presents annotated commemorations of Israel's ancestral heroes in a sort of narrative chronology.[5] Textual issues abound, of course, as the original Hebrew text is incomplete, the Greek translation applies considerable interpretive licence, and the Syriac version is late with likely Christian influence.[6] Nevertheless, both the Greek and the Syriac are helpful for reconstruction where the Hebrew is fragmented, and they equally display both past and future prophetic characteristics of the returning Elijah.

Elijah's introduction into the pattern of Sir 44–50 is unique in that it is framed, both before and after, by recollections of the exile that break the chronological pattern (47:24; 48:15).[7] The exile is depicted first as the result of the nation's sin (47:24–25), which continues in spite of the ministries of Elijah and Elisha (48:1–14). As a result, the exile is recalled again (48:15). Between these two indictments, however, Elijah's appearance is assigned something of a halting influence over the wickedness of the nation:

> [47:25] Its sinfulness grew exceedingly great,
>   and [they gave themselves over] to every evil
> [48:1] *Until* (עַד) there arose a prophet like fire
>   and his words like a burning oven.
> [2] And he shattered for them a staff of bread,
>   and in his zeal he diminished them;
> [3] By the word of God [he shut] heavens
>   [and three times thus brought down] fires.
> [4] How fearful are you, Elijah!
>   And who like [you] can glorify himself?
> [5] The one raising a corpse from death
>   and from Sheol by the will of Yhwh.
> [6] The one causing kings to descend to the pit,
>   and honoured ones [to] their places of lying.

---

5   I take the Hebrew text of Ben Sira from the edition of Beentjes, *Ben Sira in Hebrew*. For the superscript cited here, see p. 77.

6   For an overview of the dating and context of Ben Sira, see Skehan and Di Lella, *Ben Sira*, 8–16. See also Robert J. Owens, "Christian Features in the Peshitta Text of Ben Sira: The Question of Dependency on the Syriac New Testament," in *The Texts and Versions of the Book of Ben Sira*, JSJSup 150, ed. Jean-Sébastien Rey and Jan Joosten (Leiden: Brill, 2011), 177–96.

7   See Beentjes, "Parallels," 194; Koet, "Elijah as Reconciler," 181; Skehan and Di Lella, *Ben Sira*, 534.

⁸ The one anointing the fulfilment of recompenses
    and a prophet to succeed you in your place.
⁷ He also announced reproofs at Sinai;
    and at Horeb, judgements of [vengeance].
⁹ The one being taken on high in a whirlwind,
    and by troops of [fire].
¹⁰ The one about whom is written, as one established for a time
    "To turn back wrath before [fury],
    To turn back the heart of fathers with sons,
    and to restore [the tribes of Israel[8]]."
¹¹ [Blessed is he who shall have seen you *and died//having been established in love*]
    [*and blessed are you, for you will surely live//for we will also live in life//for he does not die but will surely live*].[9]

While Greek Sirach introduces Elijah by name immediately (48:1), Hebrew Ben Sira withholds the prophet's identification until v. 4. This delay retains something of the mystery surrounding his character that is present in Kings and Malachi.[10] The descriptions present in 48:1–3, however, can leave no doubt that readers are about to re-encounter the prophet of Kings. He is described as a "prophet like fire" (נביא כאש) who shatters the "staff of bread" (מטה־לחם), displays great zeal (קנאה), and shuts up heavens (48:1–3).[11] The end of the second line of v. 3 is missing in the Hebrew manuscript, but the Greek text provides κατήγαγεν οὕτως τρὶς πῦρ, resulting in a second mention of fire and an inclusio formed with v. 1.[12] When Elijah finally is named in 48:4, of course, this description proves perfectly fitting.

---

8   The Greek here reads καταστῆσαι φυλὰς Ιακωβ, but it is likely that the Hebrew originally read ישראל, since the corrupted line ends with a ל. See Shaver, "The Prophet," 145.

9   My own translation, based on Beentjes' Hebrew text edition, Rahlfs' Greek edition where the Hebrew is missing, and with insight and adaptations from the New American Bible (Revised Edition), Corley, Shaver, and Skehan and Di Lella. Italics represent various options within the Greek and Syriac where the Hebrew is missing. Bold is my own emphasis. See Beentjes, *Ben Sira in Hebrew*, 85–86; Jeremy Corley, "Elijah Among the Former Prophets in Hebrew Ben Sira 48:1–12," *StBiSl* 12 (2020), 201–17; Shaver, "The Prophet," 129–49; Skehan and Di Lella, *Ben Sira*, 529–30. Versification as per Hebrew.

10   See Koet, "Elijah as Reconciler," 181; Shaver, "The Prophet," 131.

11   The phrase שבר מטה־לחם is used in the Hebrew Bible to denote famine "within the context of divine punishment" (Shaver, "The Prophet," 132). See Lev 26:26; Ezek 4:16, 5:16, 14:13; Ps 105:16.

12   The "three times" (τρὶς) Elijah brought down fire likely refer to Carmel and the two judgements against Ahaziah's delegations (2 Kgs 1:10, 12). The Greek text fills in a further

Ben Sira continues to colour his portrait of Elijah with references to Kings, describing the prophet's power over life and death, the Horeb theophany, and the ascension in a whirlwind (48:5–9). He also seems to recognise Elijah's Mosaic role, relating how he "announced reproofs at Sinai; and at Horeb, judgements of [vengeance]" (48:7). Whether one accepts the Hebrew השמיע (Hiph. "caused to hear," i.e. "announced") or the Greek ἀκούων ("hearing"), the image of a voice speaking from Horeb remains fundamentally Mosaic, even as it reflects the Elijah narrative.[13] Further, Elijah's introduction begins, as noted, with עד אשר קם נביא; "until there arose a prophet" (48:1). On the one hand, this introduction is structured as a syntactic parallel to that of Jeroboam in Sir 47:23 (ירבעם בן נבט ... עד אשר קם), positioning Elijah's ministry in contrast to the corrupting effect of Israel's king.[14] At the same time, the combination of קום and נביא is rare in the Hebrew Bible and evokes, again, the unmistakable memory of Deut 18.[15] Israel's one light in the looming face of exile appeared when there arose a prophet like Moses. Ben Sira's description of Elijah thus indicates an awareness not only of the explicit Mosaic descriptions in Kings, but also of the larger conceptual framework behind them.[16]

Ben Sira also utilises unmistakable allusions to Malachi, placing them at the beginning and end of the Elijah section to encompass the intervening material from Kings.[17] In 48:1, the נביא כאש of the first stich is paralleled with the prophetic words "like a burning oven" (כתנור בוער) of the second. This image, in turn, provides an exact "inverted quotation" of Mal 3:19's description of the coming day of judgement (בער כתנור).[18] The referent, appropriately, is inverted

occurrence of fire in the description of Elijah's ascension in v. 9, reiterating the memory of the prophet of Kings as the one who wields fire.

13   The Hebrew and Greek renderings may reflect allusions to 1 Kgs 19:10, 14 (Elijah's lament on Horeb) and 19:18 (Yhwh's response), respectively.

14   Here MS B avoids the use of Jeroboam's name, replacing it with אל יהי לו זכר (see Skehan and Di Lella, *Ben Sira*, 530–31; Beentjes, *Ben Sira in Hebrew*, 84–85).

15   Outside of Deut 18, the use of קום with reference to a נביא is found only in Deut 13:2 and 34:10; Jer 29:15; and Amos 2:11.

16   A similar apparent memory of Deut 18 is preserved in 1 Macc 14:41, which assigns Simon a perpetual high priesthood ἕως τοῦ ἀναστῆναι προφήτην πιστόν (cf. ἀνίστημι also as the translation of קום in LXX Deut 18:15, 18), and further indicates an understanding in the Second Temple period of the prophet like Moses as a future figure. See for discussion Ferguson, "Elijah Forerunner," 130–31.

17   See already Solomon Schechter and Charles Taylor, *The Wisdom of Ben Sira* (Cambridge: Cambridge University Press, 1899), 23.

18   Beentjes, "Parallels," 194. For further examples of this phenomenon, see idem, "Inverted Quotations in the Bible: A Neglected Stylistic Pattern," *Bib* 63 (1982): 506–23. The parallel to Mal 3:19 is not picked up by the Greek Sir 48:1, which renders the Hebrew's תנור as λαμπάς rather than the κλίβανος of LXX Mal 3:19. Shaver argues that the Greek rendering

by Ben Sira as well: the תנור בוער describes not a future day, as in Malachi, but the past words of Elijah.[19] Ben Sira's use of Malachian vocabulary is creative, assigning the power of Malachi's day of judgement to the words of the prophet of Kings.

The second half of this Malachian bracket is formed by Sir 48:10, which appears to have its basis in Elijah's recorded mission in Mal 3:24. The verse is introduced by the definite passive participle הכתוב, "the one about whom it is written."[20] According to Beentjes, this locution represents the most formal announcement anywhere in Ben Sira of a scriptural quotation to follow,[21] even though what follows is not a direct quote of any extant text. What it is, however, is an effective strategy to endow Elijah's mission to turn back wrath (להש־ בית אף לפנ [ ] – 48:10) with scriptural authority. The terminus before which he is to accomplish this task is, unfortunately, obscured by the fragmented Hebrew text. The Greek "to cause wrath to cease before fury" (κοπάσαι ὀργὴν πρὸ θυμοῦ), however, likely refers to a motif similar to Malachi's day of Yhwh, along the lines of the times of wrath connected to Yhwh's day of judgement in Lam 1–2 and Zeph 2:2–3.[22]

---

should be considered original because of the similarity to Torah interpreters described as "flaming torches" in various rabbinic sources. However, the rabbinic sources she cites are in themselves not consistent (see Shaver, "The Prophet," 131). Much more conclusive evidence would be needed to prioritise the Greek rendering which is generally known to be later. See Shaver, "The Prophet," 131–32; Naphtali Wieder, "The 'Law-Interpreter' of the Sect of the Dead Sea Scrolls: The Second Moses," *JJS* 4 (1953), 163–65.

19　Beentjes, "Prophets," 215. The connection of this Malachian description with Elijah's "words" may further assume his identification with the Torah-speaking priestly messenger of Mal 2:6–7.

20　While some argue that the Qal passive participle should be translated "being destined" or "being established" in order to remain consistent with the participial form of the previous verses, the Greek translation καταγραφείς seems to confirm that a written text is being referenced. See Shaver, "The Prophet," 141–42; Benjamin G. Wright, *No Small Difference*, SCS 26 (Atlanta: Scholars, 1989), 210.

21　Pancratius C. Beentjes, "Canon and Scripture in the Book of Ben Sira," in *"Happy the One who Meditates on Wisdom"* (Leuven: Peeters, 2006), 172–75.

22　So Shaver, "The Prophet," 143. The Syriac renders the object of the preposition explicitly as the day of Yhwh, though this interpretation is more likely based on an explicit attempt to harmonise with Mal 3 than on the original Hebrew, since the lacuna in MS B appears to be too small to support this reading (*Facsimiles of the Fragments Hitherto Recovered of the Book of Ecclesiasticus in Hebrew* [London: Oxford University Press and Cambridge University Press, 1901]). So Pancratius C. Beentjes, *Jesus Sirach en Tenach*, PhD diss., Catholic Theological University Amsterdam (1946), 40 n. 58; Shaver, "The Prophet," 139. See also Owens, "Christian Features," 192–93. Émile Puech, however, accepts "day of Yhwh" as the correct translation ("Ben Sira and Qumran," in *The Wisdom of Ben Sira*, ed. Angelo Passaro and Giuseppe Bellia [Berlin: de Gruyter, 2008], 101). A further connection

Ben Sira's direct dependence on Mal 3 is confirmed by the quotation that does follow in the Greek version of 48:10b. In addition to turning back wrath, Elijah will come "to turn back the heart of a father to/with [πρός] a son,[23] and to establish the tribes of Jacob [καταστῆσαι φυλὰς Ιακωβ]." At least by the time of the Greek translation, then, the Malachian background introduced in 48:1 is clearly bookended in 48:10.[24] Sirach encompasses the description of the prophet of Kings with the identity of the returning forerunner of Malachi, effectively merging the two portraits into a single image of a past heroic prophet, significant to Israel's experience of exile, who will return in the future to restore the community.[25]

2.2   *Innovation*

2.2.1   The Isaian Servant

At the same time, the way in which Ben Sira uses Kings and Malachi is also marked by his own innovation. In the rendering of 48:10 just discussed, Greek Sirach quotes Mal 3:24, but not verbatim. We have seen that the Hebrew text of Malachi's epilogue expresses Elijah's mission in terms of an inverted couplet, while the Greek renders the second clause as καὶ καρδίαν ἀνθρώπου πρὸς τὸν πλησίον αὐτοῦ (LXX Mal 3:23). Sirach departs still further, replacing the second stich with καταστῆσαι φυλὰς Ιακωβ.[26] This clause appears to reflect a similar interpretive trajectory to that of LXX Mal 3:23 in rendering the second line an explanation of the first, but it moves away from the metaphor of interpersonal turning altogether. To Sirach, השיב לב־אבות על־בנים means "to establish the tribes of Jacob."[27]

---

may be seen in Ben Sira's earlier description of Elijah as נורא (48:4), the same term used in Mal 3:23 of the day of Yhwh.

23   The semantic range of πρός allows it to be translated as "with" as well as "to" with an accusative object, similar to על in Mal 3:24. See Frederick William Danker, ed., *A Greek-English Lexicon of the New Testament and other Early Christian Literature*, 3rd ed. (BDAG) (Chicago: University of Chicago Press, 2000), 874–75.

24   See Puech, "L'attente," 14–15.

25   Beentjes assumes the intentionality of this parallel, and contends that "it is precisely these two [Malachian] quotations that identify Elijah as the subject of the Ben Sira passage" ("Parallels," 194). See also Corley, "Elijah," 216.

26   Cf. Syriac "to announce good news to the tribes of Jacob"; so Owens, "Christian Features," 192.

27   This rendering conceptually begins to look very much like Malachi's conflation of Isa 40 with Exod 23 in its communication of the conditions for restoration. Even as he uses and expands on Mal 3:24, Ben Sira's rendering supports the underlying sense of the source text, understanding Elijah's mission of turning hearts to imply a turning back of the entire people to Yhwh.

This rendering also introduces a new scriptural allusion that is not found in Malachi. The Hebrew retroversion of φυλὰς Ιακωβ is שבטי יעקב, a locution which appears in the extant Hebrew Ben Sira only in 36:11. In this context, it is used in a grouping of scriptural allusions presented as a prayer for Israel's restoration.[28] This particular locution alludes to Isa 49:6, its only occurrence in the Hebrew Bible.[29] There, it describes the role of Yhwh's servant: "to raise up the tribes of Jacob [להקים את־שבטי יעקב; LXX στῆσαι τὰς φυλὰς Ιακωβ] and turn back the preserved ones [LXX διασποράν – "dispersion"] of Israel."[30] The Hebrew of Sir 48:10 likely originally read "Israel" rather than "Jacob," as reflected in my translation above. Both Sir 36 and Isa 49, however, utilise both titles as synonyms in parallel lines, so the integrity of the allusion is retained either way.[31] Either term in Sir 48:10 results in a resumption of the prayer for restoration in Sir 36:11 and, by implication, its allusion to Isa 49.[32]

The effect of this allusion in Sir 48:10 is to link Elijah to the Isaian servant.[33] Teeter and Lyons have presented this figure as something of a paradigm for the fulfilment of the Mosaic mission;[34] a mission which is reawakened in Malachi by the expectation of Elijah's return. Ben Sira also appears to recognise the identity of Elijah as a prophet like Moses, as we have noted, indicated by his description of Elijah as a prophet "arisen" (Sir 48:1; cf. Deut 18:15). Further, the

---

28   See Pancratius C. Beentjes, "Relations between Ben Sira and the Book of Isaiah," in *"Happy the One who Meditates on Wisdom"* (Leuven: Peeters, 2006), 205 n. 24; John G. Snaith, "Biblical Quotations in the Hebrew of Ecclesiasticus," *JTS* 18 (1967), 9.

29   Interestingly, its closest parallel occurs in 1 Kgs 18:31, where Elijah chooses twelve stones for his altar according to the number of the שבטי בני־יעקב. Cf. Knauf, *Könige*, 111.

30   See Shaver, "The Prophet," 145–49; Skehan and Di Lella, *Ben Sira*, 534; Snaith, "Biblical Quotations," 9. Beentjes notes this as one of only ten "unique word combinations" between Ben Sira and the Hebrew Bible, which act as confirmation of direct quotation and always appear in passages significant to the book's theology (Pancratius C. Beentjes, "Some Major Topics in Ben Sira Research," in *"Happy the One who Meditates on Wisdom"* [Leuven: Peeters, 2006], 15).

31   Beentjes, "Relations," 205. While Benjamin G. Wright does not mention an allusion to Isaiah, he acknowledges that Ben Sira 48:10 "reprises a theme from chapter 36" ("Eschatology without a Messiah in the Wisdom of Ben Sira," in *The Septuagint and Messianism*, ed. Michael A. Knibb [Leuven: Leuven University Press, 2006], 320).

32   Hebrew Ben Sira may have even switched the title intentionally to highlight the connection between Elijah and the northern kingdom, and to imply that even the most rebellious will be restored when the prophet comes again (so Beentjes, "Prophets," 216). The Greek likely sought to make the allusion more explicit by replacing "Israel" with "Jacob."

33   See Beers, *Followers*, 74–75; Jeremias, "'Ηλ(ε)ίας," 933; Shaver, "The Prophet," 144–48; Valve, "Lord Elijah," 149–51. Contra Richard Bauckham, who denies any allusion to Isa 49:6 and argues that "an identification of Elijah with the Servant of Isaiah 49 would be unparalleled, as well as odd" ("The Restoration of Israel in Luke-Acts," in *Restoration: Old Testament, Jewish, and Christian Perspectives*, ed. James M. Scott [Leiden: Brill, 2001], 441).

34   Teeter and Lyons, "The One and the Many," 32–35.

title of "servant" in Isaiah is used in reference both to the nation and to an individual; an individual who is "one like Moses."[35] This presentation parallels that which we have seen at work in the portrayal of Elijah in Kings, in which the roles of the Mosaic prophet and the righteous remnant are represented by a single figure. Ben Sira's conflation of Isa 49:6 with Mal 3:24 speaks to an implicit awareness of the returning Elijah as suitable to fill the roles of Isaiah's servant figure(s). Ben Sira takes the image of Elijah from Kings, frames it with references to Malachi, and adjusts the Malachian mission just enough to highlight Elijah's simultaneous identification with Israel, in parallel fashion to Isaiah's servant. While this particular conflation may represent an innovation by Ben Sira over against the texts of Kings and Malachi,[36] it reflects a recognition of Elijah's function as a single figure who both works on behalf of the larger community and embodies the righteous remnant.

2.2.2 Elijah and Life

The final verse of Ben Sira's praise of Elijah is perhaps the most tantalising of all in its glimpse of the author's interpretive innovation. Unfortunately, the Hebrew text of Sir 48:11 is almost entirely lost, and the Greek is unhelpfully enigmatic.[37] The best chance at a plausible reconstruction draws on both the Greek and Syriac versions, but any results must remain speculative. Corley renders some of the major reconstructive and interpretive options as follows:[38]

> 48:11 (Heb): Happy is the one who saw you and died.
>   But happy are you, because you will indeed live.
> 48:11 (Gr):   Happy are those seeing you
>   And those having been established in love,
>   For we also will live in life.
> 48:11 (Syr):   Happy is the one who saw you and died,
>   Yet he does not die but will indeed live.

---

35   Dale C. Allison, Jr., *The New Moses: A Matthean Typology* (Eugene: Wipf & Stock, 1993), 142.
36   It is possible that this association began to appear in other traditions around the same time. See Shaver, "The Prophet," 147; Valve, *Early Modes*, 103–105.
37   See Skehan and Di Lella, *Ben Sira*, 531 n. 11.
38   Corley, "Elijah," 217. Here he follows the reconstruction of Rudolf Smend for the Hebrew, Joseph Ziegler for the Greek, and Moshe Segal for the Syriac. For a fuller discussion of the texts of various translations, see Conleth Kearns, *The Expanded Text of Ecclesiasticus*, ed. Pancratius C. Beentjes (Berlin: de Gruyter, 2011), 205–209; Émile Puech, "Ben Sira 48:11 et la résurrection," in *Of Scribes and Scrolls: Studies on the Hebrew Bible, Intertestamental Judaism, and Christian Origins*, ed. Harold W. Attridge, John J. Collins, and Thomas H. Tobin, s.j. (Lanham: University Press of America, 1990), 81–90; Jean-Sébastien Rey and Jan Joosten, eds., *The Texts and Versions of the Book of Ben Sira* (Leiden: Brill, 2011); Skehan and Di Lella, *Ben Sira*, 532–31 n. 11.

What remains of this verse suggests that Ben Sira had some conception of life as the result of Elijah's mission.[39] The fragmented text allows for no definitive conclusion, however, on whether this life actually represents an early conception of eschatological resurrection or an afterlife, as the Syriac would seem to allow.[40] On the other hand, Ben Sira clearly acknowledges the possibility of the revivification of the dead (e.g. 48:5).[41] An association of Elijah with life, even supernatural life, is consistent with his narrative presentation in Kings, and we have already seen that Ben Sira's use of Kings and Malachi reflects a recognition of this character pattern.[42] At the very least, if no more can be definitively said, Ben Sira associates Elijah with life and also with the restoration of Israel, and further reveals a conception of resurrection that provides the hope of life even to those, like the widow's son (Sir 48:5), who have already died.

2.3   *Summary*

Ben Sira's conception of Elijah represents a conflation of images from both Kings and Malachi, and also incorporates new links with Isaiah and Deuteronomy. It skilfully blends the source traditions into a single image of a prophet like Moses who brandishes fire, overpowers death, and must return before the appearance of Yhwh. Though the fragmented Hebrew text leaves

---

39   Corley notes the Origenic rendering in Ziegler's edition of κεκοιμημένοι ("fallen asleep"), rather than κεκοσμημένοι ("established"), which would indeed be more consistent with the theme of life reflected in other versions ("Elijah," 271 n. 72).

40   Jean-Sébastien Rey argues that there is no reason to believe that the concept of future resurrection was unknown at the time of Hebrew Ben Sira ("L'espérance post-mortem dans les différentes versions du Siracide," in *The Texts and Versions of the Book of Ben Sira*, ed. Jean-Sébastien Rey and Jan Joosten [Leiden: Brill, 2011], 263). Puech also contends for an early conception of the afterlife already present in Hebrew Ben Sira, which is then expanded and elaborated by the Greek ("Ben Sira 48:11," 89; idem, *La croyance des Esséniens en la vie future: immortalité, résurrection, vie éternelle?*, vol. 1 [Paris: Gabalda, 1993], 74–75). Shaver, on the other hand, examines his proposal and disagrees ("The Prophet," 152–59). John J. Collins argues that "a differentiated afterlife" "first appears in Jewish tradition in the apocalypses of Enoch and Daniel" ("The Afterlife in Apocalyptic Literature," in *Judaism in Late Antiquity 4: Death, Life-After-Death, Resurrection and The World-to-Come in the Judaisms of Antiquity*, ed. Alan Avery-Peck and Jacob Neusner, HdO [Leiden: Brill, 2000], 119). Skehan and Di Lella see a concept of Davidic messianism in Sir 47:22, but cannot grant Ben Sira's belief in a final resurrection (*Ben Sira*, 528, 532, 534). Wright, on the other hand, sees no indication of a messianic conception in 48:11, even by the Greek. He does not, however, dismiss the possibility of "some kind of resurrection connected with Elijah" ("Eschatology," 321–23). Corley grants it to the Greek and Syriac versions, but not to the Hebrew *Vorlage* ("Elijah," 220–21), while Wright also argues that the Greek Sirach rarely alters the basic theology of the Hebrew in any significant way ("Eschatology," 314).

41   Puech, "Ben Sira and Qumran," 101.

42   Also noted by Puech, *La croyance*, 75.

Ben Sira's own conception of life after death unclear, it opens the possibility of Elijah's association with eschatological resurrection. In any case, any ambiguity that remains in Malachi about the national scope of Elijah's mission is thoroughly removed by Ben Sira. He draws together the prophet like Moses, the firebrand of Kings, the servant of Isaiah, and the messenger of Malachi to converge in a single figure who will return in the future to "restore the tribes" of Israel.

3   Elijah in Other Second Temple Texts

3.1   *1 Maccabees 2:58*
The smaller Second Temple texts significant to the development of the Elijah tradition also demonstrably draw on the image portrayed in Kings and Malachi. First Maccabees 2 presents a list of exemplary figures (2:51–60) reminiscent, in miniature, of that of Ben Sira 44–50.[43] Elijah is named in this list as the one who, "in the zealousness of zeal [ἐν τῷ ζηλῶσαι ζῆλον] for the law was taken up into heaven [εἰς τὸν οὐρανόν]" (2:58). Similar to Ben Sira, the primary source of this description is Kings, not Malachi. It alludes to Elijah's assumption as related in 2 Kgs 2:11 (LXX εἰς τὸν οὐρανόν), while the intensified construction ζηλῶσαι ζῆλον recalls the prophet's plea on Horeb in 1 Kgs 19:10, 14 (קנאתי קנא; LXX ζηλῶν ἐζήλωκα). Rather than citing zeal for Yhwh himself, however, as Elijah does in Kings, 1 Macc 2:58 describes the prophet's zeal as being for the law. This formulation undergirds an explicit parallel to Phinehas in the same chapter, who is also described as acting ἐν τῷ ζηλῶσαι ζῆλον (2:54). Elijah and Phinehas are the only two figures in this list praised for their zeal, providing additional support for the argument that the conflation of Elijah and Phinehas seen in later rabbinic writings was already being deduced much earlier.[44] This dual characteri-

---

43   Christian M.M. Brady acknowledges the similarities of these accounts but argues that Ben Sira, in contrast to 1 Macc 2 and also to Heb 11, is "a true encomium, praising the individuals without explicitly offering them as examples to be emulated" ("What Shall We Remember, the Deeds or the Faith of Our Ancestors? A Comparison of 1 Maccabees 2 and Hebrews 11," in *Earliest Christianity within the Boundaries of Judaism: Essays in Honor of Bruce Chilton*, ed. Alan Avery-Peck, Craig A. Evans, and Jacob Neusner [Boston: Brill, 2016], 108). Pamela Michelle Eisenbaum, conversely, sees similarities between Ben Sira 44–50 and Heb 11 not shared by 1 Macc 2 (*The Jewish Heroes of Christian History: Hebrews 11 in Literary Context*, SBLDS 156 [Atlanta: Scholars, 1996], 35–43).

44   As per Lear, *Scribal Composition*, 121–46. Phinehas is also praised for his zeal in Sir 45, which notes his διαθήκη εἰρήνης (45:24); cf. the διαθήκην ἱερωσύνης αἰωνίας in 1 Macc 2:54. For further comment, see Anna Maria Schwemer, "Die Elijagestalt im Wandel der Zeiten," *BK* 66 (2011), 229–30.

sation is used here to spur the sons of Mattathias on to similar zeal for the law, likely in hopes of gaining a reward similar to that of Elijah (2:61–64).

3.2   *Lives of the Prophets*

Lives of the Prophets is traditionally viewed as a text of Jewish origin, stemming from the first century CE.[45] Its earliest manuscripts are Greek, though many have posited a Semitic *Vorlage*, and it dedicates a chapter to a retelling of the life of Elijah.[46] The longer version of this text recounts the prophet's miracles relatively directly from Kings, including the drought, Zarephath, Carmel, the judgement against Ahaziah and his men, and the prophet's fiery ascension (*LivProph* 21:4–15).[47] It is likely, however, that the earliest version was much shorter, containing only the first three verses.[48] This segment is made up entirely of non-biblical material, offering a hagiographic infancy narrative that identifies Elijah as "of Aaron's tribe" (*LivProph* 21:1).[49] His birth is greeted by "men of shining white appearance" who wrap him in fire and give him fire to eat (21:2), upon which his father is reassured, "Do not be afraid, for his dwelling will be light and his word judgement, and he will judge Israel" (21:3).[50]

---

[45]   While David Satran has argued, on the basis of Christian influence, that this text should be dated to the fourth–fifth century CE (*Biblical Prophets in Byzantine Palestine: Reassessing the* Lives of the Prophets [Leiden: Brill, 1995], 118), Géza G. Xeravits maintains that the traditional view of a Jewish author in the first century CE is still weighty (*From Qumran to the Synagogues* [Berlin: de Gruyter, 2019], 141 with n. 1; also 132). See also Hare, "The Lives," 380–81.

[46]   See Hare, "The Lives," 379–80; Charles Cutler Torrey, *The Lives of the Prophets: Greek Text and Translation*, JBLMS 1 (Philadelphia: SBL, 1946), 7–12.

[47]   See for discussion Xeravits, *From Qumran*, 143–47. Interestingly, the events recorded skip from 1 Kgs 18 (Carmel) to 2 Kgs 1 (Ahaziah) (*LivProph* 21:10–11). The omission of any reference to 1 Kgs 19 here (also noted by Knauf, *Könige*, 340) is noteworthy and may support a recognition of the chapter's differing purpose, or suggest that early interpreters were already struggling with its relationship to the surrounding material. Elijah is also mentioned, fascinatingly, in *LivProph* 10:5–7 on Jonah, which may well recognise the link between the two figures that is produced by allusions to 1 Kgs 19 in Jon 4 (see ch. 2 n. 89 above). Jonah and Elijah are portrayed as contemporaries, and the text appears to "assume familiarity with the widespread tradition that Jonah was the son of the widow of Zarephath," which some versions explicitly state (Hare, "The Lives," 392, n. 10d.). See also Schwemer, "Elijagestalt," 231; Torrey, *The Lives*, 16.

[48]   See Hare, "The Lives," 396 n. 21g.; Torrey, *The Lives*, 8–9, 32, 47.

[49]   See Torrey, *The Lives*, 8; Xeravits, *From Qumran*, 131–39. All quotations taken from the translation of Hare, "The Lives" (here 396). See Jeremias, "Ηλ(ε)ίας," 932 for theories regarding Elijah's origin.

[50]   Xeravits compares this act to the consecration of Isaiah's lips for prophetic ministry in Isa 6:6–7 (*From Qumran*, 135). Some manuscripts here add "with sword and fire" (see Hare, "The Lives," 396 n. 21f.; Torrey, *The Lives*, 32, 47).

The combination of images of fire with Elijah's word of judgement is reminiscent of Ben Sira's description of the prophet's "words like a burning oven" (48:1), as well as Elijah's connection to the refinement of the priesthood and to Yhwh's fiery judgement in Malachi (3:2, 19).[51] *Lives of the Prophets* describes Elijah as both priest and prophet, drawing on traditions that were evidently extant even before the passage was harmonised to the Kings account.[52] Xeravits further suggests that the description of the men who attend his birth, as well as the fire imagery that frames the longer version of the passage (21:2, 15), is intended to portray Elijah with angelic imagery.[53] A similar conception of Elijah as a supra-natural heavenly being may lie behind some of the descriptions that appear in the New Testament Gospels as well, as we shall see.

3.3   *Apocalypse of Zephaniah*

The Apocalypse of Zephaniah is a fragmented Coptic text, preserved in a Greek quotation and incomplete Sahidic and Akhmimic manuscripts.[54] A compilation of the fragments reveals various apocalyptic visionary vignettes, highlighting the distinction between the fates of the righteous and the wicked. In contrast to the other Second Temple Elijah texts, the Apocalypse of Zephaniah does not particularly highlight the elements that distinguish Elijah from other traditional figures. He is named as one of a list of paradigmatic "righteous ones," along with the patriarchs, Enoch, and David (ApZeph 9:4–5). On the other hand, this text may indeed hint at a developing association of Elijah with an afterlife. The protagonist visionary is assured of escape from death because his "name is written in the Book of the Living" (9:2).[55] This notation reflects a conception that will also be seen in the New Testament book of Revelation,[56] in which Elijah-like figures are indeed resurrected from death (Rev 11:11).[57]

---

51   See Xeravits, *From Qumran*, 138.

52   Noteworthy, however, is that this harmonisation includes one of the few witnesses to a tradition in which Elijah prays for rain to end the drought after Carmel, a detail not made explicit in Kings: "Elijah prayed, and it did not rain for three years, and after three years he prayed again and abundant rain came" (*LivProph* 21:5). The same tradition is attested in the New Testament letter of James, where the linking of both prayer and rain with the figure of Elijah becomes a key part of its argument, as we shall see. Because of the uncertainty surrounding the dating of both *Lives of the Prophets* and James, it is impossible to confirm dependence in either direction.

53   Xeravits, *From Qumran*, 134–35.

54   Wintermute, "Zephaniah," 497–500.

55   Translation by Wintermute, "Zephaniah," 514.

56   Cf. Rev 3:5; 13:8; 17:8; 20:12, 15; 21:27.

57   The conception of a divine book in which the righteous are recorded, however, appears already in Malachi (3:16) and Exodus (32:32–33).

The immortalised visionary is then introduced to Elijah and his righteous companions, implying that they too were thought to have continued to exist, in some state, after death.[58] While it cannot confirm a mature Second Temple conception of a merit-based afterlife, this text does present Elijah as something of a paradigm of those who are righteous and escape death, which will be developed further in the texts of the New Testament.

3.4   4Q558

4Q558 (4QVision[b] ar), the only other Second Temple text in which Elijah is mentioned by name, is extant only in small fragments.[59] The first fragment preserves the Aramaic אשלח לאליה, followed by a description of lightning and what appears to be some sort of cosmic event (1.11.4–5). Though little more can be gleaned, this fragment would indicate an awareness of the Elijah expectation and its connection with a phenomenon resembling the day of Yhwh.[60] Like the other texts we have surveyed, it demonstrates dependence on an image of Elijah derived from earlier scriptural texts, further supporting the fundamental role of the Kings cycle and Malachi's epilogue in shaping Second Temple tradition.[61]

3.5   4Q521

A most fascinating text with regard both to its use of sources and its role as a link to the traditions that follow is 4Q521, the so-called Messianic Apocalypse. While much has been written on this extensively fragmented text, largely because of its use of the term משיח, very little can be stated beyond conjecture.[62]

---

58   See Wintermute, "Zephaniah," 514 n. 9a.

59   For the Qumran fragments I primarily follow the edition of Florentino García Martínez and Eibert J.C. Tigchelaar (*The Dead Sea Scrolls Study Edition*, 2 vols [Leiden: Brill, and Grand Rapids: Eerdmans, 1997–98]), with a few of my own adaptations in translation.

60   See John J. Collins, *The Scepter and the Star* (New York: Doubleday, 1995), 116. Jean Starcky interprets this fragment as specifically presenting Elijah as a forerunner to Yhwh's "Chosen One" ("Les quatre étapes du messianisme à Qumran," *RB* 70 [1963], 498), though this is likely too heavy an interpretation to hang on a fragmentary text, as many have noted since (see e.g. Alex P. Jassen, *Mediating the Divine: Prophecy and Revelation in the Dead Sea Scrolls and Second Temple Judaism* [Leiden: Brill, 2007] 143–44; Shaver, "The Prophet," 165–67).

61   So also Jassen: "Based on the extant text, this one line seems to assume for Elijah the preparatory role first located in the scriptural tradition found in Malachi" (*Mediating*, 143).

62   See for discussion e.g. Michael Becker, "'4Q521' und die Gesalbten," *RevQ* 18 (1997): 73–96; Jassen, *Mediating*, 144–48; Émile Puech, "Une apocalypse messianique (4Q521)," *RevQ* 15 (1992): 475–522. The description that is given of the משיח is that "the heavens and the earth will listen [שמע] to" him (2.11.1). Deuteronomy 30:19 (cf. 4:26) calls upon heaven and earth as witnesses against the people in Yhwh's covenant with them, which may also

It is significant to our discussion because of a near-direct quote of Mal 3:24 in frag. 2, which states that "fathers are coming with sons [באים אבות על בנים]" (2.III.2).[63] The earlier parts of this fragment describe a scene of restoration in which Yhwh's "spirit hovers" (רוחו תרחף) upon the poor and he "renews" (יחליף) the faithful "with his strength" (בכחו – 2.II.5–6). In this scene, "he will free prisoners [מתיר אסורים] and give sight to the blind [פוקח עורים]" (2.II.8). A similar image is reiterated a few lines later, where "he will heal the pierced" (ירפא חללים), "he will give life to the dead" (מתים יחיה), and "he will proclaim good news to the poor" (ענוים יבשר – 2.II.12). Following a few more gaps in the text, "he will enrich the hungry" (רעבים יעשר – 2.II.13). The quotation from Mal 3 appears in the much smaller following column (2.III.2), surrounded by broken descriptions of favour and blessing for which no definite context can be reconstructed. The fragment is incomplete on either side of the Malachi quotation, separating it from any of the text's references to a messianic figure (or figures).[64] 4Q521 therefore cannot be used, as some have attempted, to confirm Elijah's role as a messiah or messianic forerunner.[65]

What does remain of this fragment is a collage of allusions to a broad range of scriptural texts.[66] The image of Yhwh's spirit "hovering" appears in the Hebrew Bible only in Gen 1:2 (רוח אלהים מרחפת), in a scene of wholeness about to come

---

be in mind here (cf. Ps 50:4). Becker notes that Moses in Deut 32:1 calls upon heaven and earth to listen to him, while in Isa 1:2 the heavens and earth are commanded to listen when Yhwh speaks ("4Q521," 84). These descriptions again bring to mind the image of Deuteronomy's awaited prophet to whom the people will listen. The figure of 4Q521, however, captures the ears not only of the people, but of the entire cosmos!

63   García Martínez and Tigchelaar highlight the Malachi allusion here with the translation "The fathers will return towards the sons" (1045), but this rendering unhelpfully glosses over the choice of בוא rather than Malachi's שוב. Bauckham suggests a "literal spatial movement" indicated by בוא that suggests fathers returning to their sons from the realm of the dead. He also admits that "the very fragmentary context of these words makes it impossible to be sure of their significance" ("Restoration," 443 n. 20).

64   The term משיחו in frag. 2 could theoretically be either singular or defective plural, especially since a plural form is found in frag. 8; the context remains ambiguous (see Puech, "L'attente," 16). Becker notes a likely third occurrence of משיח in frag. 9, but admits that it is too fragmentary to be definitive ("4Q521," 77).

65   See e.g. Collins, Scepter, 120; John C. Poirier, "The Endtime Return of Elijah and Moses at Qumran," DSD 10 (2003), 227; Puech, "Une apocalypse," 497; Starcky, "Les quatre étapes," 498.

66   See also Becker's representation of a selected list of allusions in "4Q521," 93. For the observation of the "juxtaposition of scriptural texts" in the Dead Sea Scrolls, see Susan Docherty, "Israel's Scriptures in the Dead Sea Scrolls," in Israel's Scriptures in Early Christian Writings: The Use of the Old Testament in the New, ed. Matthias Henze and David Lincicum (Grand Rapids: Eerdmans, 2023), 154–55.

from disorder.[67] The combination of "renewal" and "strength" recalls Isa 40:31, in which the righteous will "renew strength" (יחליפו כח). The freeing of prisoners, restoring of sight, and feeding of the hungry quotes almost directly from Ps 146:7–8 (נתן לחם לרעבים יהוה מתיר אסורים: יהוה פקח עורים...), though a similar release of prisoners is also reflected in Isa 61:1 (לאסורים פקח־קוח) which, in turn, is behind the reference of proclamation to the poor (לבשׂר ענוים).[68] A similar "herald" (מבשׂר) of good news, announcing salvation to Yhwh's people, also appears in Isa 52:7. Descriptions of resurrection are rare in the Hebrew Bible, but an exception which may offer further background to 4Q521 is Isa 26, in which the nation fails to accomplish its own deliverance (26:18) but the "dead" of Yhwh's people "will live" (יחיו מתיך – 26:19).[69] The reference to Mal 3:24 furthers this pattern of scriptural allusions concerned with Israel's renewal, even if its exact connection to the preceding material is unclear. What remains is a relatively small text that feels the need to bring all of these images together to describe a coming restoration, in which Yhwh "will honour the faithful upon the throne of an enduring kingdom" (2.11.7).

Perhaps most intriguing for the present study is the ambiguity in 4Q521 concerning who is to facilitate this restoration. Though Elijah's mission is quoted, it is left unassigned.[70] Lines 4–8 of 2.11, where the spirit hovers over the poor, the prisoners are freed, and blind eyes are opened, identify their acting subject as אדני (2.11.4–5). The same is likely the case for line 12 and the healing of the pierced, raising of the dead, and proclamation to the poor.[71] Line 13,

---

67   See Shaver, "The Prophet," 174 as well as a brief mention in Puech, "Une apocalypse," 488.

68   See Shaver, "The Prophet," 178. Similar images are present in Isa 58:6, in the form of loosing bonds and yoke straps, and in 42:7 ("to open the eyes of the blind [לפקח עינים עורות]; to bring out the prisoner [אסיר] from the dungeon").

69   This statement contrasts Yhwh's people to the lords of other nations, who are "dead; they will not live" (26:14). See further scriptural images of resurrection in Ezek 37:12 and Hos 13:14.

70   A similar apparent allusion to Mal 3:24 may be seen in *LAB* 23:13, which states in the context of Yhwh's address to Joshua, "At the end the lot of each one of you will be in eternal life, for you and your seed, and I will take your souls and store them in peace until the time allotted the world be complete. I will restore you to your fathers and your fathers to you, and they will know through you that I have not chosen you to no purpose" (translation of Howard Jacobson, *A Commentary on Pseudo-Philo's* Liber Antiquitatum Biblicarum [Leiden: Brill, 1996], 1:131; see 2:729 for the potential allusion to Malachi). This text, the dating of which into the Second Temple period is debated but possible (1:199), assigns Elijah's mission of restoration directly to Yhwh. For this parallel, see Bauckham, "Restoration," 443 n. 20.

71   Beers conflates Yhwh with his agent here, inadvertently making a similar point to mine: "Though grammatically Yahweh is the subject of the works, his work is often carried out through human agents" (*Followers*, 70).

where the hungry are enriched, is too fragmented to identify the subject with certainty. In column III, the subject changes at least once to the first person (2.III.1), while in the Mal 3 allusion the "fathers" themselves are the subject of the participle. The cause of their "coming" is either obscured by the fragmented text or intentionally left unstated.

While the actions described in the entire passage have been assigned by some to the משיח, and even directly to Elijah, such a concrete conclusion is ultimately pure conjecture.[72] Fascinating, however, is the variation in the subjects performing these works in the texts cited by 4Q521. In Ps 146:7–8, the miracles are performed by Yhwh himself. In Isa 61:1, on the other hand, many of those same miracles are assigned to an anointed (משח) agent. In Isa 26:19, it is the earth that will allow the dead to rise. The combination of חלל ("pierce") and רפא ("heal") is found in the Hebrew Bible only in Isa 53:5, but there it is the agent of Yhwh himself who is "pierced" in order to bring about the "healing" of the people. In Malachi's epilogue, Elijah is the messenger who turns back fathers and sons to Yhwh, while 4Q521 obscures this messenger altogether.

The picture allowed by this fragmented text – that is, the result of its collage of allusions – is one of a future restoration that is sure because it is ultimately Yhwh's doing. Whether Yhwh himself performs the work or whether it is assigned to his agents appears to be secondary to the reality of the restoration itself.[73] The extant 4Q521 offers no hint of a forerunner to this restoration; it is preoccupied with the ultimate result. As such, even the designation "Messianic Apocalypse" may be something of a misnomer.[74] The anointed figure(s), like the messenger of Malachi who receives no mention here, is not the focus.[75] At the same time, the observation that many of the cited texts emphasise a secondary agent is not irrelevant. These figures, including Elijah, become part of the expanded vision of restoration that is conceptualised by the writer. The fact that Elijah is so clearly in the background of the Malachi quotation

---

72   Puech acknowledges that it is impossible to tell whether one or multiple (i.e., a priestly and a Davidic) figures are at work in this passage, but then claims that, "il ne devrait pas s'agir d'un simple consacré, tel un prophète ou prêtre, étant donné la suite du passage, mais bien du messie" ("Une apocalypse," 488). He suggests elsewhere that the messiah of 4Q521 is Yhwh's messenger, who is, in turn, Elijah ("L'attente," 17).

73   Precedent for such flexibility in acting subject may be found in Ezek 34, in which Yhwh initially refers to himself as the shepherd (רעה) who will tend (רעה) his sheep (34:15–16), before announcing that he will raise up over them a Davidic shepherd (רעה) who will tend (רעה) them (34:23). The same restoration is described, whether Yhwh accomplishes the work by his own hand or by the hand of an agent.

74   So also Becker, "4Q521," 74.

75   Contra Puech's conflation of the two ("L'attente," 17).

reminds readers of one of Yhwh's agents who is able to heal the sick, raise the dead, and feed the hungry, just as the text expects.[76] The ambiguity seemingly embraced by 4Q521 allows readers to look for Yhwh's restoration in any number of its textually-suggested figures and forms.

What remains of 4Q521, then, provides an example of a Second Temple scribal impulse to create a more comprehensive image of restoration out of earlier texts: in this case, a remarkable conflation that spans the Hebrew Bible. The reference to Elijah, already a figure with multiple roles himself, argues for literary conflation as a scribal strategy on multiple levels. Looking forward, the ambiguity of agency left by this text provides a further strategic hook for the writers of the New Testament Gospels. The deliberate ways in which they both preserve and exploit this feature in their presentations of John the Baptist and Jesus will be explored in the following chapter, where we will see that a conflated Elijah image is given a pivotal role that is remarkably consistent with its appearance in 4Q521. Elijah is simultaneously identified with both John and Jesus. His role can be one of forerunner or agent, the latter of which will also consistently be identified with the righteous people. 4Q521, even in its fragmented form, thus offers another link between Elijah in the Hebrew Bible and Elijah in the Gospels, furthering the tradition of a prophet who is more than a prophet: one who exists in these texts as the embodiment of a larger reality.

4   Conclusion: a Conflated Expectation

After the epilogue to Malachi, references to Elijah in Jewish literature display the continued ability to take up earlier traditions and conflate them with further traditional texts and images. Ben Sira provides the clearest presentation of Elijah as a composite figure based in both Kings and Malachi. He further clarifies Elijah's role to be one, unequivocally, of restoring all of Israel. First Maccabees 2 describes the Elijah of Kings, but also represents an early understanding of his conflation with Phinehas, again, as understood by the epilogue to Malachi. *Lives of the Prophets* 21 describes Elijah as both prophet and priest even before its addition of a recounting of the Kings narrative, thus attesting to traditions seen in Malachi and Ben Sira even in its earliest form.

---

76   Contra Becker, who dismisses in passing both the reference to Mal 3:24 and any potential allusions to the Kings cycle in Yhwh's miracles of resurrection, healing, and care for the poor. He argues in a footnote that the allusion to Malachi in 4Q521 is too short to carry much weight, especially considering the different verb used (89–90 n. 79), and that the raising of the dead is not connected to the expectation of Elijah (92 n. 91).

The Apocalypse of Zephaniah hints at a growing association of Elijah with an immortal life, while 4Q558 knows him as forerunner to the day of Yhwh. 4Q521 cites Elijah's mission from Malachi but leaves its agent ambiguous, allowing this role to be absorbed into a larger, encompassing image of restoration.

The expectation of Elijah in the Second Temple period, then, is a shape-shifting one. The prophet's return is awaited, but his role evolves even from one text to another. Such variability, by this point, should come as no surprise. Elijah is the prophet who can shift from mother to child in the same story, who can represent both prophet and people. The ability of this image to encompass multiple characters and roles at once becomes critical to an understanding of Elijah in the New Testament Gospels, to which we now turn.

Elijah, John, and Jesus in the Gospels

1   Introduction

In the combined early Jewish and Christian tradition, the tendency of the Elijah figure to take on a variety of shapes and forms is far more than an interesting result of the gradual merging of various traditions. To the writers of the New Testament Gospels, it is a critical piece of the logic with which they present the story of Jesus. The multiple character facets we have observed as transmitted through Second Temple tradition – Elijah as a forerunner and coming restorer in his own right, while at the same time only a part of something greater – are reflected in the various emphases of the Gospels. The Synoptics, for example, unquestionably reveal their writers' understanding of John the Baptist as Malachi's Elijah (e.g. Matt 11:14; Luke 1:17). On the other hand, the Baptist of the Fourth Gospel directly denies this identity (John 1:21). Jesus himself, meanwhile, appears in all four accounts as a distinctly Elijah-like miracle worker, and is repeatedly characterised by other allusions to the Elijah/Elisha cycle as well. The question of identity surrounding both John and Jesus consumes all four Gospels, demonstrating not only the writers' purpose of establishing who Jesus is, but also the discontinuity between what the people are portrayed as expecting and what they get. They are expecting the physical return of Elijah.[1] Instead, they get John and Jesus, who both look like Elijah, but bring with this image some profoundly unexpected characteristics.

Complicating matters further is that both John and Jesus are portrayed on analogy with multiple other figures as well. The same literary strategies that map John and Jesus onto the image of Elijah also portray them in light of Moses, Elisha, various patriarchs, Esther, and the servant of Isaiah, to name only a few. These conflated character analogies work together with structural features and extended plotlines to produce multifaceted and tightly knit images that resist any attempt at simple one-to-one correlation.[2]

---

1   See e.g. Matt 11:14; 16:14; 17:10; Mark 6:15; 9:11; Luke 9:8; John 1:21.

2   An example of such an attempt is the conclusion of Walter Wink, who argues that Luke intentionally does not portray John the Baptist as Elijah in order to leave open "the exegetical analogy between Elijah and Jesus" (*John the Baptist in the Gospel Tradition* [Cambridge: Cambridge University Press, 1968], 44–45). See also Hoffeditz on Mark and Matthew ("A Prophet," 127, 138). A similar observation regarding the insufficiency of the "one-to-one correlation that has dominated the scholarly debate for so long" is made by Otten, though he

Based on our observations of the characterisation of Elijah thus far, I suggest that this conflation of character analogies, bound up in the identity of a single person or persons, functions as a very intentional medium for the Gospel writers. The figure of Jesus emerges from the various Gospel accounts portrayed as the fulfilment of a multiplicity of Israelite traditions. In order to shape this portrait, the writers work within those traditions and their literary conventions to describe a single figure by means of various traditional images merged together. If the Gospel writers are granted the same compositional intentionality and awareness as that which we have begun to observe of other Second Temple writers, then not only is it possible for John the Baptist and Jesus both to be portrayed in light of Elijah, but their literary significance only increases with each additional image worked into their portraits.[3] Jesus and John are both simultaneously Elijah and non-Elijah, because each image represents a different facet of their roles and of the larger narrative of God's people. Further, both similarity and dissimilarity in analogies may be accounted for by the use of various facets of an image for varying purposes. In this case, the literary creativity of the writers ceases to be a problem to be harmonised away; it rather becomes a most efficient and beautiful means of communicating the overarching identities of key figures.[4]

---

does not describe the alternative specifically in terms of conflated literary allusions (*I Alone*, 139, cf. 165). Allison recognises the targeted use of just such conflated allusions in the characterisation of Jesus in Matt 2, and reacts against overly "wooden" readings: "Where is the tittle of evidence that Matthew did not construe Jesus' status as the new Israel and his identity as another Moses as correlative conceptions? Was his thought really so constricted and wooden as to prohibit such?" (*New Moses*, 142).

3   See for discussion Gerhard Dautzenberg, "Elija im Markusevangelium," in *The Four Gospels 1992: Festschrift Frans Neirynck* (Leuven: Leuven University Press, 1992), 1083.

4   Thomas R. Hatina expresses a similar observation regarding the Gospel of Mark: "If Mark is taken seriously as narrative art, a search for *the* meaning, and hence *the* echo, is reductionistic because it potentially excludes the other layers of meaning which would have been open to the earliest audiences (and should remain open to the modern literary critic)" ("Embedded Scripture Texts and the Plurality of Meaning: The Announcement of the 'Voice from Heaven' in Mark 1.11 as a Case Study," in *Biblical Interpretation in Early Christian Gospels*, vol. 1: *The Gospel of Mark*, ed. Thomas R. Hatina [London: T&T Clark, 2006], 82). So also Jeffrey W. Aernie's similar comments: "Likewise, as with John the Baptist, comparing the shape and function of Jesus' ministry with a single prophetic figure (e.g. Elijah) would likely result in an oversimplification of the extant evidence. Rather, it seems that the material in the Gospels points more readily to the idea that the prophetic shape of Jesus' ministry is to be understood as part of the larger development of Israel's prophetic history" (*Is Paul Also Among the Prophets? An Examination of the Relationship between Paul and the Old Testament Prophetic Tradition in 2 Corinthians*, LNTS 467 [London: T&T Clark, 2012], 66).

A comprehensive analysis of all the references and allusions to Elijah in the Gospels would require a book of its own.[5] In this chapter I will highlight select case studies that outline the picture of Elijah's character and role that emerges when it is read in the context of its conflation with other representative images. I will argue that the Gospel writers' use of this technique continues the trajectory begun in earlier Jewish literature, and provides further evidence that the drawing of creative conflated analogies represented a significant means by which writers of this period read and responded to earlier texts and traditions. The result of this strategy in the Gospels is that John the Baptist is portrayed in light of a number of scriptural images, including the expectation of Elijah. Jesus, however, is portrayed in an overarching role that encompasses *all* of the images to which he is compared, cohering in an Elijah-like identity as both the paradigmatic prophet and the ideal personification of the righteous community.

2   The Synoptics

2.1   *Conflated Roles in the Introductory Narratives*
2.1.1   Mark 1
The opening verses of the Gospel of Mark provide immediate and compelling evidence toward this thesis. The text begins:

> [1] The beginning of the gospel of Jesus Christ, the son of God.[6]
>
> [2] Just as it stands written in Isaiah the prophet: "Behold I am sending my messenger before your face, who will prepare your way.
>
> [3] A voice of one crying out in the wilderness, 'Make ready the way of the Lord; make straight his paths.'"
>
> [4] John appeared, [the one] baptising in the wilderness and preaching a baptism of repentance for the forgiveness of sins.
>
> [5] And all the region of Judea went out to him, and all the Jerusalemites, and they were being baptised by him in the Jordan River, confessing their sins.

---

5   For a more comprehensive study along these lines, see Öhler, *Elia*.

6   For a text-critical overview of υἱοῦ θεοῦ in Mark 1:1, see Eve-Marie Becker, *Das Markus-Evangelium im Rahmen antiker Historiographie*, WUNT 194 (Tübingen: Mohr Siebeck, 2006), 103 n. 139; Max Botner, "The Role of Transcriptional Probability in the Text-Critical Debate on Mark 1:1," *CBQ* 77 (2015): 467–80.

⁶ And John was dressed in camel's hair with a leather belt around his waist, and ate locusts and wild honey.

⁷ And he was preaching, saying, "One greater than I is coming after me, of whom I am not worthy, stooping, to loose the straps of his sandals.

⁸ I baptised you with water, but he will baptise you with the Holy Spirit."

⁹ And it appeared in those days: Jesus came from Nazareth of Galilee and was baptised in the Jordan by John.

¹⁰ And immediately, coming up from the water, he saw the heavens split and the spirit coming down onto him like a dove.

¹¹ And a voice appeared out of the heavens: "You are my beloved son; in you I am well pleased."

¹² And immediately the spirit cast him out into the wilderness.

¹³ And he was in the wilderness forty days being tested by the adversary, and he was with the wild beasts, and the angels/messengers were ministering to him.

¹⁴ And after the arrest of John, Jesus went into Galilee, preaching the gospel of God

¹⁵ and saying, "The time has been fulfilled and the kingdom of God has drawn near; repent and believe in the gospel." (Mark 1:1–15)

While Mark 1:1 promises the "beginning of the gospel of Jesus Christ," the first figure to be introduced is not Jesus but John the Baptist (1:4).[7] Between the two introductions is placed a weighty scriptural allusion that effectively defines the roles of both.[8] We have already observed the initial conflation of Exod 23:20 and Isa 40:3 in the text of Mal 3:1. Mark appears to take advantage of and extend this strategy. Where Malachi turned the "before you" of Exod 23:20 into "before me" to match the preparation of Yhwh's way in Isa 40, Mark quotes both the Isaiah and the conflated Malachi text but reintroduces the second-person pronoun of Exodus (Mark 1:2).[9] He goes on to introduce John as

---

7   Becker presents literary-critical options that either see Mark 1:1–3 as a later addition to the introduction of the Baptist starting in 1:4 or posit a lost original introduction, in place of which Mark 1:1 was later added (*Markus-Evangelium*, 103). While either of these options is possible, neither is necessary if Mark uses the intervening conflated quotation to introduce John on one side and Jesus simultaneously on the other.

8   So Becker: "Mk 1,1 und die darauf folgende Zitatkombination (1,2f.) thematisieren und definieren in grundsätzlicher Weise das für das Markus-Evangelium wichtige Verhältnis des Täufers zu Jesus" (*Markus-Evangelium*, 109; cf. 241). See also Robert A. Guelich, *Mark 1–8:26*, WBC 34A (Dallas: Word, 1989), 12; Pellegrini, *Elija*, 182–87.

9   Guelich observes the same exegetical progression in his commentary on Mark 1: "Thus the angel of Exod 23:20 becomes Elijah, the eschatological messenger promised for the age of

baptising "in the wilderness" (ἐν τῇ ἐρήμῳ – 1:4), unmistakably identifying the Baptist as the voice crying ἐν τῇ ἐρήμῳ (1:3) and therefore as the preparatory Malachian/Isaian messenger of the previous verse.[10]

If John is the messenger, then Jesus is left as the referent of Mark's "you" (1:2).[11] The reader familiar with Mal 3:1 will recall that the referent of the pronoun in that text was Yhwh himself: from Yhwh's first-person perspective, the messenger will "prepare the way before me" (3:1a). Mark replaces Malachi's first-person reference to Yhwh (LXX μου) with a second-person pronoun referring to Jesus (σου).[12] This interpretation is confirmed by the addition of Isa 40:3 in Mark 1:3. Its "make ready the way of the Lord" is arranged as a parallel with "prepare your way," just as the messenger and the voice are paralleled to each other. Jesus Christ (1:1) is the Lord whose way is being prepared;[13] John the Baptist (1:4) is the messenger and the voice, preaching the way of repentance.[14]

At the same time, both the positions of John and Jesus in this conflated quotation are multifaceted in themselves. John's preparatory role picks up the blurred lines between a heavenly or an earthly origin of the מלאך/ἄγγελος already present in Exodus and Malachi.[15] He simply "appears" (ἐγένετο – 1:4) without birth story or origin,[16] similar to Elijah in Kings, and some have

---

salvation in Mal 3:1; 4:5" (*Mark*, 11). Contra Öhler, who argues that the original Markan quotation is based on Mal 3 and that the Exodus wording is a Christian reworking to present the quote as messianic (*Elia*, 34–35). Öhler also draws a distinction between John's role as "Vorläufer Jesu" and the "Elia-Rolle" (36). For discussion, see R.T. France, *The Gospel of Mark*, NIGTC (Grand Rapids: Eerdmans, 2002), 63–64; Watts, *New Exodus*, 53–90. For further comment on composite quotation and textual juxtaposition in the Second Temple period, see Docherty, "Israel's Scriptures," 146, 154–55.

10 So also Becker, *Markus-Evangelium*, 240. Where some translations of Isa 40 have located Yhwh's way in the wilderness, Mark makes the wilderness the location of the voice. This interpretation is consistent with the LXX rendering of the ambiguous syntactic position of במדבר in the Hebrew Isa 40:3.

11 See Guelich, *Mark*, 11; Pellegrini, *Elija*, 201; Larry Perkins, "Kingdom, Messianic Authority and the Re-constituting of God's People – Tracing the Function of Exodus Material in Mark's Narrative," in *Biblical Interpretation in Early Christian Gospels*, vol. 1: The Gospel of Mark, ed. Thomas R. Hatina (London: T&T Clark, 2006), 103.

12 See Becker, *Markus-Evangelium*, 241; Guelich, *Mark*, 11.

13 "Dass der 'Kyrios' auf Jesus zu deuten ist, ergibt sich aus dem Kontext" (Thomas Söding, *Das Evangelium nach Markus*, THKNT 2 [Leipzig: Evangelische Verlagsanstalt, 2022], 24).

14 This message of repentance via the voice of Isa 40:3 could well be carrying on the interpretive tradition observed by Stromberg in Isa 57, in which the preparation of Yhwh's way is accomplished by the repentance of the people ("Interpretive Revolution," 226–30).

15 See discussion in Christine E. Joynes, "The returned Elijah? John the Baptist's angelic identity in the Gospel of Mark," *SJT* 58 (2005), 463–65.

16 "Abruptly," as per Guelich (*Mark*, 16).

argued that Mark presents John as a heavenly figure in his own right.[17] Not only does Mark attest to an accepted identification of Elijah as the messenger of Mal 3:1, but he may also be capitalising on the perception of Elijah as one alive in heaven to hint at the heavenly authority carried by John.[18] On the other hand, he is also described as wearing camel's hair with a leather belt around his waist (1:6), a note which unmistakably references the description of Elijah in 2 Kgs 1:8: "a man of much hair with a girdle of leather girding his waist."[19] John's baptism, therefore, is presented as the preparatory work of the messenger-Elijah of Malachi, while his location in the wilderness recalls the people of Israel in Exodus, the voice of Isa 40, and Elijah in 1 Kgs 19.

Mark's presentation of Jesus reflects the characteristics of both the divine and human recipients of the Malachian messenger's work. Through the lens of the Baptist's role as the messenger, Jesus' divine characteristics begin to unfold: he is the one who is "greater than I … of whom I am not worthy, stooping, to loose the straps of his sandals" (1:7). He is the one who is to baptise "with the Holy Spirit" (1:8). Concurrently, however, Jesus receives the baptismal/ preparatory ministry of John in the same way that the people do (1:9). His heavenly designation as "my beloved son" (1:11) recalls the title also used by Yhwh of Israel (Exod 4:22), as we have seen.[20] Upon his baptism, Jesus is cast into the wilderness for a forty-day period of testing (1:12–13), which recalls the similar forty-year period of Israel.

This dual characterisation of Jesus immediately calls to mind the strategy used to characterise Elijah in Kings, even though the figure initially associated

---

17   Joynes has argued that Mark intends John the Baptist to be interpreted as the returned Elijah himself, rather than as a fulfilment of "Elijah typology." From this perspective, she suggests that John came to be considered something of an angelic identity ("Returned Elijah," 462–67). The ambiguity between the heavenly and earthly identity of the Elijah figure will also be exploited by the Gospel of Luke, as we shall see.

18   Cf. Mark 11:30.

19   Allison expresses this similarity succinctly: "The text might just as well say: John was like Elijah" (*New Moses*, 19). See also Pellegrini, *Elija*, 207–208; Eduard Schweizer, *Das Evangelium nach Markus*, 17th ed., NTD 1 (Göttingen: Vandenhoeck & Ruprecht, 1989), 11; Adam Winn, *Mark and the Elijah-Elisha Narrative* (Eugene: Pickwick, 2010), 70–71; contra Guelich, *Mark*, 21. Cf. also the prophetic attire described in Zech 13:4; see de la Serna, "Pablo," 162.

20   James R. Edwards observes this connection as supportive of an identification of Jesus as Isaiah's servant, as per Isa 49:3: "You are my servant Israel in whom I will show my glory" ("The Servant of the Lord and the Gospel of Mark," in *Biblical Interpretation in Early Christian Gospels*, vol. 1: The Gospel of Mark, ed. Thomas R. Hatina [London: T&T Clark, 2006], 52). Hatina also notes the proposal of an allusion to Gen 22 in this title for Jesus ("Embedded Scripture," 88–93), the significance of which we have already observed in its connection to the representation of a righteous remnant of Israel in the Elijah narrative.

with Elijah in this passage is John. Similar to the conflated analogies in Kings which portray Elijah as filling the roles of both the prophet and the righteous remnant, here the presentation of the narrative, in light of its intertexts, portrays Jesus from opposite but concurrent poles as both Yhwh's agent and the paradigmatic Israelite. As the narrative continues, Jesus' assumption of the Elijah role initially applied to John becomes more and more explicit. John appears ἐν τῇ ἐρήμῳ at the start of the passage, "preaching [κηρύσσων] a baptism of repentance [μετανοίας]" (1:4). Jesus receives this baptism and then is sent into the wilderness (εἰς τὴν ἔρημον) himself (1:12–13), where his forty-day period is also reminiscent of Elijah (1 Kgs 19:8).[21] The next thing the reader hears is that John has been arrested (1:14), and that "Jesus went into Galilee, preaching [κηρύσσων] the gospel of God and saying, '... repent [μετανοεῖτε] and believe in the gospel'" (1:14–15).[22] He explicitly takes over John's ministry, thereby stepping fully into the sandals of Elijah. Jesus identifies with the people by receiving the baptismal ministry of the Elijah figure like they do,[23] before going into the wilderness and assuming the Elijah role himself.

Mark's opening portrait of the identities of John and Jesus, then, is formed from such a rich conflation of scriptural texts that no single analogy can be isolated from its effect on the others.[24] John is Elijah, based on the images of both Kings and Malachi, and Jesus is the agent of Yhwh. Simultaneously, Jesus also takes the shape of the people of Israel, before taking over the Elijah role himself. These effortless shifts of character roles present a compelling argument that early Jewish and Christian literary practice continued in the vein of

---

21   The note that "the ἄγγελοι were ministering to him" (1:13) has been suggested as an anecdotal reference to the angelic provision Elijah received in the wilderness (1 Kgs 19:5–8). See S. Anthony Cummins, "Integrated Scripture, Embedded Empire: The Ironic Interplay of 'King' Herod, John and Jesus in Mark 6.1–44," in *Biblical Interpretation in Early Christian Gospels*, vol. 1: The Gospel of Mark, ed. Thomas R. Hatina (London: T&T Clark, 2006), 42; Heike Omerzu, "Geschichte durch Geschichten: Zur Bedeutung jüdischer Traditionen für die Jesusdarstellung des Markusevangeliums," EC 2 (2011), 85. Contra Schweizer, who comments, "Daß auch Elia in der Wüste weilte ... spielt wahrscheinlich keine Rolle" (*Markus*, 12).

22   These parallels are observed by Guelich, who argues that both Mark's introduction and the descriptions of John's and Jesus' ministries that follow fall under an Isaian rubric that explains the quotation attributed to Isaiah in Mark 1:2 (*Mark*, 10). Winn argues that Mark 1:12–20 is based on a pattern of 1 Kgs 19:4–21 (*Mark*, 71–76).

23   This reversal of roles is also highlighted by Matthew's addition to the baptism narrative, which sees John hesitate to baptise Jesus (Matt 3:14). Jesus, however, responds that "in this way it is fitting for us to fulfil all righteousness" (3:15).

24   Omerzu argues that, with this opening conflated quotation, Mark has simultaneously introduced the "stories" of Elijah, Moses, and Isaiah, which merge throughout the Gospel to further, in the portrait of Jesus, the larger story of Israel ("Geschichte," 83).

Second Temple conventions as we have observed them, and also that Elijah's association with a paradigmatic righteous community was taken for granted. If the Elijah figure was already recognised to bear the characteristics of multiple character patterns at once, then the extension of those patterns to apply to John and Jesus interchangeably is entirely unproblematic. Such conflation is part of their Elijanic shape. Both John and Jesus bear roles that are at least prophetic, if not heavenly, and both stand in the position of the people. Both are presented as simultaneously within and representative of the righteous people of God, even as both use the prophetic voice to call the broader community to repent.

2.1.2 Luke 1

A similar character role conflation, by means of different analogies, introduces the Baptist's character in Luke. In contrast to his sudden appearance in Mark, John's coming in Luke is described by means of an extended annunciation and birth narrative, shaped according to the classic barrenness/miracle child motif (1:7). Luke alludes here specifically to both the promise of Isaac to Abraham and Sarah in Gen 11–18 and to the promise of Samson's birth in Judg 13, thereby placing John the Baptist, even from before his conception, in the tradition of both the patriarchs and the deliverers of Israel.[25] At the same time, John is to bear the "spirit and power of Elijah" (Luke 1:17), further merging the patriarch and deliverer images with that of Malachi's awaited prophet. The depiction of an Elijah role within a patriarchal framework both recalls Elijah's association with the barrenness motif in Kings via allusions to Exod 23 and 2 Kgs 4, and lends support to the idea that his image was held and passed on in a similar way to those of the patriarchs: that is, as a paradigm for the self-identification of the post-exilic communities.[26]

---

25   Both accounts highlight a "barren" (עקרה – Gen 11:30; Judg 13:2; LXX στεῖρα – cf. Luke 1:7) wife who conceives a son after an encounter with Yhwh or his מלאך (Gen 18:1–15; Judg 13:3, 13–21). While the motif of reversed barrenness is found in numerous other Hebrew Bible narratives, Gen 18:11 specifically states that Abraham and Sarah were "of advanced age" (באים בימים; LXX προβεβηκότες ἡμερῶν – cf. προβεβηκότες ἐν ταῖς ἡμέραις in Luke 1:7). Both the promises to Abraham and to Zechariah are initially prefaced by a command not to fear (Gen 15:1; Luke 1:7, 18), and both are accompanied by a response of unbelief (Gen 18:11–15; Luke 1:18–20). Judges 13:4–5 contains a Nazirite commissioning, paralleled in Luke 1:15 (contra I. Howard Marshall, who downplays this connection [*The Gospel of Luke*, NIGTC {Exeter: Paternoster, 1978}, 57]). Joel B. Green observes Luke's use here of precisely what I have called "conflated allusions": "[Luke] can move easily from character to character in his employment of the Genesis story – thus, for example, Zechariah is like Abraham, but so is Mary; Zechariah is like Sarah, but so is Elizabeth; John is like Isaac and Ishmael; and so on" (*The Gospel of Luke*, NICNT [Grand Rapids: Eerdmans, 1997], 56).
26   Cf. Carr, *Holy Resilience*, 91–109.

Gabriel's prediction of the awaited John as an Elijah-like prophet reveals Luke's reworking of Elijah's Malachian mission in a similar way to that of Ben Sira 48:10.[27] Like Ben Sira, Luke replaces the second line of Malachi's reciprocal turning of fathers and sons with a broader image that explicitly concerns the community as a whole (1:17).[28] Uniquely, however, Luke introduces another parallel line at the front end of the quotation which confirms his interpretation of Malachi's prophecy as a turning of the people back to Yhwh:

> [16] And many of the sons of Israel he will turn back [ἐπιστρέφω] to the Lord their God.
> [17] And he will go forth before him in the spirit and power of Elijah,
> To turn back [ἐπιστρέφω] the hearts of fathers toward [ἐπί] children
> And the disobedient unto [ἐν] the wisdom of the righteous,
> To prepare for the Lord a people made ready. (1:16–17)[29]

Luke bookends his naming of Elijah with two references to a mission of "turning" that expand and clarify his interpretation of Mal 3:24. He reworks the second line of Malachi's couplet to parallel the turning of fathers and sons with the turning of "the disobedient unto the wisdom of the righteous" (1:17).[30] Both lines together are already anticipated by the broad expectation of the turning of "many of the sons of Israel to the Lord their God" (1:16), which is chiastically paralleled to the turning of fathers and sons.[31] The explicit naming of Elijah, together with a mission to turn the entire nation back to Yhwh, communicates

---

27   Valve notes that "the line between the books of Kings and the Gospel of Luke ... also goes via intertestamental exegetical currents, most notably those reflected in Ben Sira 48" ("Lord Elijah," 148). She goes on to see a continuation of the Elijah image in Luke 2, this time in the person of Jesus (151–58).

28   So also Otten, *I Alone*, 73.

29   Luke's rendering of Malachi's preposition as ἐπί, on its own, is difficult to translate as "with." However, the function accomplished by עַל as "with" in Malachi is equally accomplished by Luke's bookending of the quotation with two references to the moral turning of Israel. As such, he demonstrates the same understanding of Elijah's mission for which I have argued in Malachi. Luke's quotation further demonstrates flexibility in his use of prepositions (ἐπί, ἐν) that correspond to the semantic range of עַל.

30   Otten sees in this line potential allusions to Mal 2:6 and 3:18, in which the priestly messenger "turned many back from unrighteousness" and the "righteous" and "wicked" are distinguished at the day of Yhwh (*I Alone*, 73 n. 9).

31   While Luke uses different terms for offspring (υἱοί in 1:16 and τέκνα in 1:17), the common use of "turning" (ἐπιστρέφω) places both lines under the scope of the same mission. The parallel nature of vv. 16–17 is also noted by Green (*Luke*, 76). He is somewhat preoccupied with positing a negative view of the fathers due to their structural paralleling with the disobedient. However, Luke's quote performs the double function of referring back to Malachi while simultaneously explaining that Malachi's turning of fathers and sons is an

the same conception of broad communal restoration as that seen in Ben Sira's reworking of Malachi.

Luke's expansion thus places him squarely within a previous interpretive tradition, in which Malachi's couplet is creatively reworked into a clarifying extension and explanation. To Luke, to turn back the hearts of fathers and sons is to turn back the disobedient to a righteous life, which is encompassed in the broader image of turning back Israel to Yhwh. This mission, in turn, is to be accomplished by one acting in the "spirit and power of Elijah," who enters the world miraculously like Isaac and is expected to deliver Israel like Samson (cf. Luke 1:71, 74). Luke therefore combines the Elijanic mission of "turning" with the miracle child motif that evokes memories of the patriarchal identity of the righteous community. He endows the yet unborn John with a role that encompasses both the prophetic voice and the identity of the people of Israel; in other words, he presents John as Elijah.[32]

At the same time, the annunciation of Jesus that immediately follows (Luke 1:26–38) also bears elements of this pattern. The two announcements of Gabriel are literarily paralleled,[33] and both are questioned by the recipient, though for opposite reasons: Zechariah and Elisabeth are too old (1:18); Mary is a virgin (1:34). While Mary's account is less obviously connected to the patriarchal narratives, it completes a critical part of the patriarchal promise that was omitted in Zechariah's. Gabriel concludes his announcement to Mary with the statement ὅτι οὐκ ἀδυνατήσει παρὰ τοῦ θεοῦ πᾶν ῥῆμα – "for no matter will be impossible for God" (1:37). The announcement of the angels to Abraham in Gen 18 concludes with virtually the identical statement: μὴ ἀδυνατεῖ παρὰ τῷ θεῷ ῥῆμα (LXX Gen 18:14). The miraculous nature of the conception of Jesus is therefore also connected to the miraculous existence of Israel as a community, in that both can be brought about only by the lifegiving power of God.

Both John the Baptist and Jesus, then, are located in the framework of the same patriarchal narrative in which they parallel the miraculous existence of Israel. John is further cast as a prophet and deliverer; Jesus is to go one step

---

image of turning Israel back to Yhwh. As such, an over-exegeted negative reading of the fathers is not necessary.

32   Contra Walter Grundmann, who argues that the purpose of 1:16 is to clarify that John is *not* the coming Elijah, but merely comes in his spirit and power (*Das Evangelium nach Lukas*, 9th ed., THKNT 3 [Berlin: Evangelische Verlagsanstalt, 1981], 51). So similarly Marshall (*Luke*, 59) and Wink (*John*, 42–45).

33   In both cases, Gabriel gives the command not to fear, calling the recipient by name (μὴ φοβοῦ, Ζαχαρία/ Μαριάμ – Luke 1:13, 30). Both announcements dictate the names to be given to the awaited sons (1:13, 31), and both allude to Hebrew Bible texts and figures in their descriptions of the roles these sons will fulfil (1:14–17, 32–33).

further still: "The Lord God will give to him the throne of David his father, and he will reign over the house of Jacob forever" (Luke 1:32–33). Thus, John and Jesus are simultaneously alike and different.[34] The specific identities of both John the Baptist and Jesus, and the roles they play within this larger framework, become a focal point for all three synoptic writers in the continuation of their story.

2.2   *The Question of Identity*
2.2.1   Mark 6
These conflated presentations of the Elijah image, as well as their application to both John and Jesus within a prophetic and patriarchal framework, allow the Gospel writers to capitalise on the question of Jesus' identity that is repeatedly posed by onlookers. In Mark's account, the next direct mention of John after the opening chapter comes after his beheading, in the context of just such a question of identity:[35]

> [14] They were saying, "John the Baptist has been raised from the dead, and for this reason these powers are working in him."
> [15] But others were saying "he is Elijah"; and others were saying "a prophet, like one of the prophets."
> [16] But Herod, hearing [this], was saying, "John, whom I beheaded – he has been raised." (Mark 6:14–16)

Curiously, the presentation of this pericope reflects a close literary relationship to the story of Esther.[36] Mark tells of a young woman who enters the royal court, in the context of a feast, and pleases the king so much that he swears, "Whatever you ask me I will give you, up to half of my kingdom [ἕως ἡμίσους τῆς βασιλείας μου]" (6:23). This last phrase is a near-verbatim quote of the words of Ahasuerus to Esther in the Greek text of Est 5:3 and 7:2,[37] a recognition which triggers the perception of further plot-level parallels.[38] In Esther, the young

---

34   Intentional parallels between John and Jesus continue in Luke's infancy account. Luke 1:80, for example, states of John that "the child grew and became strong" (τὸ δὲ παιδίον ηὔξανεν καὶ ἐκραταιοῦτο), which is the same phrase used of Jesus in 2:40.

35   So also the introduction to Pellegrini's discussion (*Elija*, 239).

36   See Roger Aus, *Water into Wine and the Beheading of John the Baptist* (Atlanta: Scholars, 1988), 41–66; also Cummins, "Integrated Scripture," 31–48; Joynes, "Returned Elijah," 461–62; Pellegrini, *Elija*, 265–66.

37   There, ἕως τοῦ ἡμίσους τῆς βασιλείας μου.

38   Aus's study draws ten such parallels (*Water into Wine*, 41–66), to which Robert H. Gundry, in turn, has objected (*Mark: A Commentary on His Apology for the Cross* [Grand Rapids:

woman in question petitions for the life of her people (Est 7:3–4). In Mark, her inverted analogue petitions for the death of the prophet (Mark 6:24–25).[39] Other scholars have noted a further parallel with 1 Kgs 19 in this account, in which both Elijah and John are threatened with death by a royal figure after confronting kings who are controlled and manipulated by their wives.[40]

In both the Kings and Esther analogies, the threatened entity survives. Israel survives the threat of Haman; Elijah escapes the clutches of Jezebel. On the basis of these analogies, the reader of Mark's account is set up to expect that John the Baptist will survive too; that the prophet who stands in the role of Elijah, and therefore of the endangered remnant of Israel, cannot possibly die.[41] In a grim inversion, John's severed head is placed on a platter and given to the girl who should have saved it (Mark 6:28).[42] His disciples then collect his body and "laid it in a tomb" (ἔθηκαν αὐτὸ ἐν μνημείῳ – 6:29).

When John, as the semi-immortal Elijah figure, is killed, his slot in the story of Israel's restoration is reopened. This is precisely when Jesus takes his disciples, who have just returned from a crusade of miracles (Mark 6:7–13, 30), to a "desert place" (ἔρημος τόπος) to rest, because "they did not even have time

---

Eerdmans, 1993], 313). These objections are largely based on a search for direct correlation, however, rather than allowing for literary reshaping. I agree with Aus's assessment that the similarities between the two accounts "may be questioned individually. Cumulatively, however, they simply provide too many exact word and motif similarities for the latter to be dismissed as mere 'reminiscences' of the former" (*Water into Wine*, 67).

39   Pellegrini draws the parallel between Esther and Herodias, rather than Herodias's daughter, to highlight the contrast between the good and evil queens (*Elija*, 266).

40   See Cummins, "Integrated Scripture," 42–43; Pellegrini, *Elija*, 280–81; Johannes Schreiber, *Der Kreuzigungsbericht des Markusevangeliums* (Berlin: de Gruyter, 1986), 185; Schweizer, *Markus*, 70; Michael Tilly, *Johannes der Täufer und die Biographie der Propheten* (Stuttgart: Kohlhammer, 1994), 60–61. Joynes notes that "these parallels indicate that [the] Mark 6:17–29 story can be interpreted in terms of more than one typological narrative, combining references from both the books of Kings and Esther" ("Returned Elijah," 462). Contra Öhler, who sees similarities to the Esther story and thereby discounts the parallel to Elijah (*Elia*, 37). Hoffeditz is persuaded in the opposite direction, arguing that, "while the story of Queen Esther remains doubtful, the story of Elijah in 1 Kings should not be so quickly dismissed" ("A Prophet," 92).

41   Hoffeditz recognises this strategy in the parallels between Kings and Mark 6, noting that "the story is to shock the reader, who would naturally expect the story to end like the victorious account of Elijah over the Omri dynasty" ("A Prophet," 92). It is curious that he does not allow for similar contrasts in his hesitation to grant the allusion to Esther.

42   Far from discounting the allusion, as it does for Öhler (*Elia*, 37), this inversion should be seen as an intentional literary strategy. See Aus on *Midr. Esther* re: a tradition of Vashti's head on a platter (*Water into Wine*, 59–64).

to eat" (6:31).[43] He responds to the death of the Elijah figure by once again taking it on himself, playing out with his disciples something of a reenactment of the story of Kings.[44] This story further anticipates the moment when this second, greater Elijah will also be "laid in a tomb" (ἔθηκεν αὐτὸν ἐν μνημείῳ – Mark 15:46) in apparent defeat, only to be raised back to life and succeed in saving his people.[45]

2.2.2 Matthew 11

2.2.2.1 The Coming One

The identification of John the Baptist as Elijah is nowhere made more explicit than in Matt 11, where it is confirmed unequivocally by Jesus himself. Here the imprisoned John, not yet beheaded, sends a delegation to Jesus to ask "are you the coming one [ὁ ἐρχόμενος] or do we expect another?" (11:3). Jesus does not answer the question explicitly; he replies instead: "Go and report to John what you hear and see: blind receive sight, lepers are cleansed and deaf hear, dead are raised up, and poor have the good news preached to them" (11:4–5).

Several scholars have noted the similarities between this quotation and the miracles listed in 4Q521.[46] It does seem likely that an awareness of this text, or at least of a tradition behind it, lies in the background of Matt 11's nearly identical selection of images. While lepers and the deaf do not appear in the extant 4Q521, they could easily have existed in one of the missing fragments; even if not, Matthew would simply be taking an already-conflated text and conflating

---

43   Cummins notes the similarity in this passage both to "John the Baptist's earlier ministry and also Jesus' initial victory of Satan's wilderness temptation" ("Integrated Scripture," 40), which, as we have seen, both unmistakably allude to Elijah in the wilderness.

44   For this connection, see also Howard Clark Kee, *Community of the New Age*, NTL (London: Bloomsbury, 1977), 169. In 1 Kgs 19:1–8, Elijah retreats to the wilderness after a miracle-filled ministry that is followed by the shadow of death. His sleeping under a bush demonstrates exhaustion, and his weakness from lack of food is indicated by the heavenly messenger's repeated urgings to eat. Jesus' retreat with his disciples, further, occurs immediately before the feeding of the 5000, one of the miracles which has been associated with the Elijah/Elisha cycle (see e.g. Guelich, *Mark*, 337; Schweizer, *Markus*, 74).

45   This particular locution (roots τίθημι + μνημα/μνημειον) is used in the Gospels only here of John the Baptist (Mark 6:29), and elsewhere only of Jesus himself (Matt 27:60; Mark 15:46; Luke 23:53, 55). As such, Mark foreshadows that Jesus' assumption and extension of John's Elijah role will continue to the end. See Gundry, *Mark*, 312. It is also used in Rev 11 in the context of the two witnesses who die for their testimony, who are evidently associated with Moses and Elijah, but who do not even receive the dignity of being laid in a tomb (11:9).

46   So e.g. Lidija Novakovic, *Messiah, the Healer of the Sick*, WUNT II/170 (Tübingen: Mohr Siebeck, 2003), 177; Puech, "L'attente," 25–26.

it further with additional scriptural allusions.[47] His mention of the deaf hearing (κωφοὶ ἀκούουσιν) most likely alludes to Isa 35:4–5, which supports the image presented by the extant 4Q521 of Yhwh's own hand acting in salvation: "Behold, your God will come with vengeance; the recompense of God – he himself will come and save you. Then the eyes of the blind will be opened, and the ears of the deaf will be opened [אזני חרשים תפתחנה; LXX ὦτα κωφῶν ἀκούσονται]."[48] Yhwh's "coming" here is particularly important to the Hebrew, if not the Greek, text of Isa 35:4–5.[49] These miracles will occur when Yhwh himself comes. An argument for Matthew's awareness of the Hebrew rendering can be made from the relationship of the Baptist's question to Jesus' response.[50] John has asked if Jesus is the one who is coming, and Jesus has responded that the blind see and the deaf hear. This statement is far more than a simple challenge to John to evaluate the miracles being performed. It is an answer in the affirmative that Jesus is "the coming one," as per Isa 35; that is, he claims the role of the God of Israel who will himself ensure the completion of his salvific work.

2.2.2.2   *The Greatest and the Least*

As Jesus begins to speak to the crowds about John, Matthew further introduces an allusion to Mal 3:1 (Matt 11:10). Both this scene and its direct parallel in Luke 7 identify John as "the one about whom it stands written: 'Behold, I am sending my messenger before you, who will prepare your way in front of you'" (Matt 11:10; cf. Luke 7:27). Both accounts here utilise a second-person indirect object, along the same lines as the conflation of Mal 3 and Isa 40 in Mark 1. However, while Mark 1 directs the second-person pronoun at "the Lord" (1:2–3;

---

47   W.D. Davies and Dale C. Allison, Jr. identify allusions to Isa 26:19; 29:18; 35:5–6; 42:7, 18; 61:1 in this passage (*The Gospel According to St Matthew*, ICC [Edinburgh: T&T Clark, 1991], 2:242). See also R.T. France, *The Gospel of Matthew*, NICNT (Grand Rapids: Eerdmans, 2007), 424. Both of these commentaries have noted a potential allusion to Elisha's healing of the leper Naaman in 2 Kgs 5, as there are no instances of leprosy recorded in Isaiah (see Davies and Allison, *Matthew*, 2:243; France, *Matthew*, 424). See also Wolfgang Wiefel, *Das Evangelium nach Matthäus*, THKNT 1 (Leipzig: Evangelische Verlagsanstalt, 1998), 210.

48   See e.g. Francis Wright Beare, *The Gospel According to Matthew* (Oxford: Blackwell, 1981), 257; France, *Matthew*, 424.

49   The LXX of this segment of v. 4 reads ἰδοὺ ὁ θεὸς ἡμῶν κρίσιν ἀνταποδίδωσιν καὶ ἀνταποδώσει, αὐτὸς ἥξει καὶ σώσει ἡμᾶς. Ἐρχόμαι does not appear, and a synonym, ἥκω, is used only once. The Greek appears to emphasise Yhwh's recompense of judgement, rather than his coming, and renders the recipient of this recompense in the first-person plural, rather than the second person.

50   Davies and Allison also assume that the author of Matthew would have had access to "the Hebrew OT" (*Matthew*, 1:80). See e.g. their comment on Matt 11:10, for which they prefer MT Mal 3:1 over the LXX as a source (2:249).

cf. Luke 1:76), in Matt 11 and Luke 7, "you" is directed at the people. Like Mark, Matthew also follows the Malachian exegesis of Isa 40 and Exod 23: the way of the Lord is prepared when the way of the people is kept in repentance. Further, the image of the people going into the wilderness to encounter a prophet who will prepare their way (Matt 11:6–10; Luke 7:24–27) presents a close thematic parallel to the original context of Exod 23:20, where the people in the wilderness are promised Yhwh's messenger to go before them. Jesus' description of John in this chapter thus not only identifies him as Malachi's messenger, but reaches back even further to the source context of Exodus and the people's journey of deliverance.

What follows in Matthew's account is one of the book's more exegetically problematic passages, and one for which I will not claim a definitive solution.[51] It is striking, however, that Jesus appears to be laying out something of a progressive timeline of prophetic revelation:

> [11] Truly I say to you: among those born of women there has not arisen one greater than John the Baptist, but the one who is least in the kingdom of heaven is greater than he.
> [12] But from the days of John the Baptist until now the kingdom of heaven is treated violently and violent people seize it.
> [13] For all the prophets and the law prophesied until John;
> [14] And if you are willing to accept it, he is Elijah, the one who is to come. (Matt 11:11–14)

The figure of Elijah, in the person of John the Baptist, appears here at the seam between the old and the new.[52] If no one who came before John was greater than John (Matt 11:11), then this statement includes the law and the prophets who ministered until his arrival (11:13). This hierarchy is consistent with Jesus' previous statement that John is "more than a prophet" (11:9). If John is Elijah (11:14), then Elijah is here identified as greater than all the other pre-Johannine prophets. As much as Jesus was the "coming one" (ὁ ἐρχόμενος) awaited by John (11:2–6), John himself is a "coming one" in his role as Malachi's returning Elijah (Ἠλίας ὁ μέλλων ἔρχεσθαι – 11:14).[53]

---

51 "Without a doubt, one of the NT's great conundrums" (Davies and Allison, *Matthew*, 2:254); "a grotesque jumble," as per Wink (*John*, 29).
52 So also France, who notes that "the contrast is between two eras" (*Matthew*, 428).
53 "Der Nachsatz ὁ μέλλων ἔρχεσθαι spielt pauschal auf die Verheißung in Mal 3,23 und weiterführende Traditionen an" (Öhler, *Elia*, 72).

On the other hand, as per the Malachi quotation, John remains a forerunner and not the culmination of prophetic history. Even the person who is "least in the kingdom of heaven" is to be considered greater than this greatest of prophets (11:11).[54] From this second, juxtaposed perspective, the messenger of Malachi is only a forerunner to the righteous community envisioned by "the kingdom of heaven"; thus, it is he who will "prepare *your* way" (11:10; emphasis added). To add even a third element of complexity, Jesus has just identified his own miraculous works with the awaited coming of God (11:4–5; cf. Isa 35:4–6), which places him unquestionably on a higher level than John. The role of Malachi's forerunner was known to be one of preparing the way for Yhwh's own coming. It is possible that Matthew alters the pronoun of Malachi's prophecy specifically to allow for this dual meaning: the forerunner prepares the way for the least in the kingdom of heaven, even as he also prepares the way for Jesus and the coming of Israel's God.

2.2.3   A Suffering Prophet

This logical progression may offer some insight into the enigma that immediately follows: "But from the days of John the Baptist until now the kingdom of heaven is treated violently and violent people seize it" (11:12). Lexically, the "kingdom of heaven" (βασιλεία τῶν οὐρανῶν) should immediately recall "the least in the kingdom of heaven" (ὁ μικρότερος ἐν τῇ βασιλείᾳ τῶν οὐρανῶν) from the previous verse. As such, it would seem that the violence towards the kingdom of heaven is personal; that is, it is inflicted on those who inherit it.[55] The context of this passage is John's imprisonment, which is literarily linked in Matthew to the account of his death.[56] The reference to violence against those "greater than" John, even as John, their forerunner, sits in prison, seems to predict the type of suffering that will be experienced by those in the kingdom of

---

54   See Davies and Allison for a summary of views on this statement (*Matthew*, 2:251–52).

55   It is possible to argue for a positive reading of this verse based on a middle, rather than passive, translation of βιάζεται, in which case the "kingdom" is the entity applying the violence or force. However, as France has noted, "there is nothing in Matthew to suggest any other meaning for these strongly pejorative terms, and the concentration of negative language demands [a negative] interpretation" (*Matthew*, 430). For an extensive overview, see Peter Scott Cameron, *Violence and the Kingdom: The Interpretation of Matthew 11:12*, ANTJ 5 (Frankfurt: Peter Lang, 1984); also Davies and Allison, *Matthew*, 2:254–56; Donald A. Hagner, *Matthew 1–13*, WBC 33A (Dallas: Word, 1993), 306–307; Hoffeditz, "A Prophet," 146–48; Barbara E. Reid, "Violent Endings in Matthew's Parables and Christian Nonviolence," *CBQ* 66 (2004), 239–40.

56   Jesus' blessing of those who do not "take offence" (σκανδαλίζω – Matt 11:6) at him is resumed in 13:57 when the people indeed "took offence" (ἐσκανδαλίζοντο) at him just prior to John's death.

heaven.[57] In other words, John, the imprisoned Elijah, becomes something of a paradigm for the suffering righteous community.[58] He is arrested and killed, even as he is depicted as standing on the shoulders of earlier prophets who similarly suffered.[59] Those in the kingdom of heaven, in turn, stand on his shoulders and should expect to suffer in the same way.

This pericope provides a ranking of the roles of Israel's traditional figures in relation to Jesus and John the Baptist. John is Elijah, who is greater than the prophets and the law, but who is less than Jesus and, astonishingly, less than those who will make up Jesus' community. While to argue that this progression intends to parallel "the least in the kingdom of heaven" with Jesus himself may go a step too far,[60] it does indicate once again that both John and Jesus are seen as paradigmatic figures for the remnant community, even – perhaps especially – in its experience of suffering. John embodies and extends the ministry and the suffering of the prophets, and he prepares the way for the people who, collectively, are greater than he. Jesus mirrors yet goes beyond John. When Jesus begins to predict his own suffering, then (e.g. Matt 16:21), the literary effect is that he takes over John's role in a manner similar to that already seen in Mark.[61] Jesus becomes the paradigmatic sufferer, who suffers at the hands of the people and on behalf of the people, and who in turn becomes the pattern for the righteous community that will surpass John in both ministry and suffering.[62]

2.3   The Suffering Elijah at the Transfiguration

This motif of Elijah as a paradigmatic sufferer becomes one half of a dual purpose for his presence at the transfiguration. His appearance on the mountain with Moses has traditionally been explained as an embodiment of Israelite

---

57   So Davies and Allison, *Matthew*, 2:256; France, *Matthew*, 429.

58   So similarly Michael Knowles, *Jeremiah in Matthew's Gospel: The Rejected-Prophet Motif in Matthaean Redaction*, JSNTSup 68 (Sheffield: Sheffield Academic, 1993), 231. He becomes "a prototype of the persecuted" (Robert H. Gundry, *Matthew: A Commentary on His Literary and Theological Art* [Grand Rapids: Eerdmans, 1982], 209).

59   Matthew's Jesus laments the killing of these prophets as well, in his later woe against the Pharisees (23:29–39).

60   On the other hand, just such a parallel between Jesus and his disciples is brought out by e.g. Mark 10:38–45, where he himself provides the example of how the greatest must become the slave.

61   So also Hoffeditz: "John the Baptist's ultimate suffering provides the template for the life of Jesus" ("A Prophet," 100–101).

62   This role is underscored by his later warnings that those who follow him will drink the same cup that he drinks (Matt 20:22–23; 26:42).

prophecy, even as Moses represents the law.[63] This categorisation has too often been made without sufficient grounding, and has therefore been variously protested.[64] However, it can be legitimately established via the exegesis we have observed in Malachi's epilogue, which concludes that the returning Elijah will be the paradigmatic prophet like Moses.[65] Matthew 11:13, as we have seen, also recognises John, identified as Elijah, as the culmination of Israelite prophecy.[66] As such, the reader's conclusion that Elijah represents the Hebrew prophetic tradition is thoroughly justified, and the two figures who appear with Jesus on the mountain can indeed be seen, in this context, to embody the law and the prophets.

In all three Synoptics, Moses and Elijah appear next to Jesus as he is gloriously transfigured (Mark 9:2–4; Matt 17:1–3; Luke 9:29–31). It cannot be coincidental that, in addition to encompassing Israelite tradition, these two figures are also the ones who previously experienced Yhwh's glory on a mountain.[67] To the Gospel writers, Jesus therefore assumes the position of Yhwh's self-revelation encountered by Moses and Elijah. Through the appearance of precisely these two figures at the transfiguration, the Gospel writers effectively bring the entirety of Israelite identity face to face with one whose glory is unambiguously placed above both the prophets and the law.

This image of glory, however, is bound inextricably to one of suffering. In Mark and Matthew, the transfiguration is bookended by Jesus' foretelling of his upcoming death and resurrection. This prediction appears before the transfiguration in the context of Jesus' mistaken identity as John the Baptist, Elijah, or

---

63 See Hoffeditz, "A Prophet," 158; Pellegrini, *Elija*, 317, though she opposes this conclusion. For discussion, see Jeremias, "Ἠλ(ε)ίας," 940–41; John Nolland, *Luke 9:21–18:34*, WBC 35B (Dallas: Word, 1993), 499. Hoffeditz argues "prophetic representation" to be one of the primary characteristics of Elijah developed by Matthew and Luke ("A Prophet," 156–62; 204–12).

64 See e.g. Gundry, *Mark*, 478; Margaret Pamment, "Moses and Elijah in the Story of the Transfiguration," *ExpTim* 92 (1981), 338; Nolland, *Luke 9*, 499, who has difficulty with Elijah's representation of the "writing prophets," and J.A. Ziesler, "The Transfiguration Story and the Markan Soteriology," *ExpTim* 81 (1970), who argues that Moses "indeed is a more likely candidate than Elijah for the role of representative prophet" (266).

65 Omerzu observes Jesus' characterisation as the prophet like Moses in Mark's transfiguration account (9:7; see also Matt 17:5; Luke 9:35) ("Geschichte," 88), as does de la Serna ("Pablo," 165). Blum's ("Der Prophet," 288) and McKenzie's (*Kings*, 44) presentation of Elijah in 1 Kgs 17–19 as a paradigmatic judgement prophet also supports this conclusion.

66 Jacob J. Scholtz proposes a chiastic structure of Matt 11:2–17:13 which parallels Jesus' discourse with and about John in Matt 11 with the transfiguration account ("One Messiah, Two Advents, Three Forerunners: The Chiastic Structure of Matthew 11:2–17:13," *IDS* 50 [2016]: 1–10).

67 See Otten, *I Alone*, 125.

"one of the prophets" (Mark 8:28; Matt 16:14), upon which Peter identifies him as the Christ (Mark 8:29; Matt 16:16). On the other side of the transfiguration, the dialogue of suffering is taken up again, when Jesus commands the disciples to keep their vision of Elijah on the mountain a secret until after he has risen from the dead (Mark 9:9; Matt 17:9).[68]

The reaction of the disciples to this command to secrecy must be interpreted in light of both Peter's confession and the transfiguration they have just witnessed. They immediately respond with the question, "Why then do the scribes say that Elijah must come first?" (Matt 17:10; cf. Mark 9:11). "First" here presumably refers to Elijah's role as forerunner to Yhwh's day of judgement and restoration.[69] If Jesus indeed is the Christ, as Peter has confessed, and if his resurrection will mean the eschaton they have envisioned, then Elijah's appearance on the mountain means that the forerunner has arrived.[70] His coming should be announced to the world and not kept a secret![71] In both accounts, however, Jesus responds that Elijah has already come (Mark 9:12–13; Matt 17:11–12). This reply looks back further than the prophet's appearance on the mountain they have just descended. Elijah's coming had already been visible to the world in the person of John the Baptist, but it was evidenced in suffering rather than in the glory they had expected. It is not to be announced a

---

68   Because Luke does not include this dialogue, Hoffeditz argues that he omits the "suffering Elijah motif" that is seen in Mark and Matthew ("A Prophet," 198). However, as we shall see, Luke utilises other narrative references to the passion that may be connected with Elijah.

69   Faierstein argues that the reference to the scribes here, rather than to scripture directly, prohibits a direct understanding of Malachi as predicting Elijah as a forerunner figure ("Why Do the Scribes Say," 77–78). However, he assumes that the forerunner image must be messianic, thereby reading later interpretation back into the text of Malachi to argue that Malachi does not fit later interpretation! Further, to place a quotation of scripture at odds with a scribal quotation assumes that the scribes would not have been understood as mediators of the scriptures, which also does not follow.

70   Here I must disagree strongly with Öhler's conclusion that "die Verklärung ... geht nicht auf die Eliaerwartung zurück, sondern auf die Überzeugung, daß Elia als einer der Himmlischen gilt und damit Zeichen für die Herabkunft der βασιλεία ist" (Elia, 247 n. 671). I would argue that the association of Elijah with a restoration coming from heaven is precisely the result of the Malachian expectation of his return!

71   Contra Gary Yamasaki, who argues that the disciples' question does not relate to Jesus' command to secrecy (John the Baptist in Life and Death, JSNTSup 167 [Sheffield: Sheffield Academic, 1998], 134), I find a direct correspondence the best explanation for both the command and the question, both of which are enigmatic otherwise. Hoffeditz argues that the presence of Elijah and Moses at the transfiguration, specifically in Mark's account, represents an allusion to Malachi's epilogue, indicating that the eschaton has arrived ("A Prophet," 109).

second time. "Elijah has already come," but the people "did not recognise him, but did to him whatever they wished" (Matt 17:12).[72]

According to Mark, this suffering of Elijah was "just as it stands written about him" (9:13). Scholars have stumbled over the fact that no scriptural text explicitly describes Elijah, specifically Malachi's returning Elijah, as "suffering."[73] To the Gospel writers, however, the fact that Elijah is a paradigmatic sufferer appears self-evident.[74] All of the figures for whom Jesus is mistaken by the crowds (John the Baptist, the prophets, Jeremiah in Matthew's account) are recognisable by their suffering (Mark 8:27–30; Matt 16:13–20; Luke 9:18–21).[75] The inclusion of Elijah in this list would indicate that he is another example of the same. Further, if Elijah is understood to be the paradigmatic prophet, then this role is one of suffering by definition.[76] Elijah suffers because he is a

---

72   See Pellegrini's conclusion: "Zusammenfassend: Die Jünger haben Elija gesehen, aber dürfen davon nicht erzählen. Die Schriftgelehrten möchten ihn sehen, doch werden sie auf ihn vergeblich warten. Dabei verstehen beide nicht, daß Elija, als Figur der Wiederherstellung, vom Schicksal des Leidens nicht zu trennen ist" (*Elija*, 344).

73   This point is noted vehemently by Wink, who argues that "this passage teems with confusion" (*John*, 13). He attempts to solve the issue by offering a re-translation of Mark 9:12–13 that presents the "Son of Man" as referring to Elijah (14)! Hoffeditz notes that "there are no existing pieces of Jewish literature which speak of a suffering Elijah" ("A Prophet," 98), and attempts to tie the suffering of John the Baptist to the curse of Mal 3:24, resulting from the larger community's rejection of Elijah (108 n. 124, 149). This link does not follow, however, because the curse predicted by Malachi's epilogue is to fall on the land, not on the prophet who is rejected. Hoffeditz further suggests that the image of a suffering Elijah is an innovation of Mark and Matthew (vii), which, as we will see, is unnecessary and does not account for earlier literature from which this connection can be deduced.

74   Even as scholars have struggled with the image of a suffering Elijah, they have repeatedly observed that it exists. Knowles simply comments that, "as Elijah's antitype, John the Baptist is not only the forerunner of the messiah, but also one who suffers" (*Jeremiah*, 231), without elaborating on how Elijah came to be understood as a suffering figure. Schweizer argues that "für Markus ist aber das Schicksal Elias als Vorbild für das Leiden des Menschensohns wichtiger als die bloße Tatsache seines Gekommenseins" (*Markus*, 100). Wink (*John*, 16) refers to this suffering as an "Elijianic [*sic*] secret." Steck notes support for a suffering prophet motif in general, among other passages, in 1 Kgs 18:4, 13 and 1 Kgs 19:10, 14 (*Israel*, 60).

75   So Knowles: "The popular opinions of Jesus' similarity to John, Elijah and 'the prophets' become, in the Matthaean redaction, not erroneous alternatives raised only for the sake of rejection, but intimations or approximations of the messiah's true identity as one who suffers" (*Jeremiah*, 91).

76   The image of prophets as suffering figures already arises out of the Moses narratives (e.g. Exod 16:2–3; 17:2–4; Num 14:1–5; 16:1–35; 20:2–13). It is also supported by the Kings cycle, via the repeated hostility and endangerment Elijah experiences at the hands of the royal house (1 Kgs 18:17; 19:2; 2 Kgs 1:9–13; see e.g. Gundry, *Mark*, 465; Pamment, "Moses and

Mosaic prophet; as the paradigmatic Mosaic prophet, he becomes the paradigmatic sufferer.

We have observed Mark's use of the Elijah image as a conflation of scriptural prophetic descriptions from the start (1:2–3), and seen that this image
absorbs characteristics of the prophetic tradition as a whole. In view of the
overarching tradition, the summary of Israel's relationship with her prophets
in 2 Chron 36:15–16, a text which we have already observed for its similarity to
Malachi's messenger image, again becomes significant:

> 15 And Yhwh the God of their fathers sent to them by the hand of his mes-
> sengers repeatedly, because he had compassion on his people and on his
> dwelling place.
> 16 But they were continually making fun [מלעבים – LXX ἐξουδενοῦντες] of
> the messengers of God and despising his words and mocking his proph-
> ets, until the hot anger of Yhwh arose against his people until there was
> no healing.

In addition to the commonalities between this passage and the book of
Malachi, it may also contribute to the background of Mark's suffering Elijah.[77]
The term used in 2 Chron 36:16 for "making fun" (לעב) is a Hebrew *hapax lego-
menon*, and its Greek translation, ἐξουδενέω, is found in only five LXX passages.[78]
In the New Testament, ἐξουδενέω occurs only twice including here in
Mark 9:12–13 (cf. 2 Cor 10:10), which places Jesus' coming suffering in the con-
text of the Son of Man and the suffering "written of" Elijah:

> 12 Elijah indeed came first to restore all things. But what stands written
> concerning the Son of Man, that he would suffer many things and be
> mocked [ἐξουδενηθῇ]?
> 13 But I say to you that Elijah also has come, and they did to him whatever
> they wished, just as it stands written about him.

Mark's reference to a textual tradition of Elijah's suffering places both Jesus
and John into the broader written landscape of prophets who suffer at the

---

Elijah," 338–39; Wink, *John*, 14 n. 2). For a suffering motif as central to the prophetic image,
see Steck, *Israel*; Teeter and Lyons, "The One and the Many," 15–38.

77 Hoffeditz notes 2 Chron 36 in passing in his discussion of Elijah as a suffering prophet
("A Prophet," 99), as does Serge Ruzer in his description of the suffering prophet motif in
Luke (*Mapping the New Testament: Early Christian Writings as a Witness for Jewish Exegesis*
[Leiden: Brill, 2007], 182–84).

78 2 Kgs 19:21; 2 Chron 36:16; Job 30:1; Ezek 21:10; 22:8.

hands of their own people, especially those prophets characterised as God's "messengers" as per 2 Chron 36. Here Omerzu observes that Mark 9:13 is "nicht als Zitat oder Anspielung, sondern als ein exegetischer Schluss anzusehen."[79] While I would argue that v. 12 does intend to allude specifically to 2 Chron 36, the passage as a whole represents an interpretation of prophetic tradition that was already known. The Gospel of Luke seems to attest to a similar tradition, either textual or familiar, when the writer records Jesus saying "For this reason also the wisdom of God said: 'I will send [ἀποστελῶ] to them prophets and apostles [ἀποστόλους], and some of them they will kill and persecute'" (11:49).[80] Elijah's status as the messenger of Malachi, specifically sent (LXX ἀποστέλλω – Mal 3:22) by Yhwh, places him at the head of the company of those about whom sufferings and mockings are written (2 Chron 36:16). Mark 9:13 not only states that John the Baptist has already experienced this suffering, but it also identifies the "Son of Man" as the messenger-prophet who is mocked, as per Chronicles. In a single verse, Mark has once again applied the Elijanic prophetic image to both John and Jesus, presenting them both as fulfilling prophecy precisely in their suffering.[81]

In Luke's transfiguration account, Moses and Elijah are said to speak with Jesus of "his exodus [ἔξοδος] which he was about to fulfil in Jerusalem" (9:31). This term has been broadly taken as a Mosaic allusion that refers to Jesus' passion.[82] Later in the same chapter, Luke's metaphor shifts to become "ascension" (ἀναλήμψις – 9:51), which "immediately call[s] to mind Elijah's spectacular ascent into heaven" (cf. LXX 2 Kgs 2:11).[83] These two descriptions present a

---

79   Omerzu, "Geschichte," 87. So similarly Öhler, who places the background to this statement in the scriptural motif of prophetic persecution (*Elia*, 46).

80   See e.g. Wilfried Eckey, *Das Lukasevangelium* (Neukirchen-Vluyn: Neukirchener, 2004), 2:556–57. Contra Nolland, who suggests that "we are probably to understand not that some written or traditional source is being appealed to by Jesus but rather that he has personally been informed by Wisdom" (*Luke*, 2:668).

81   The fact that Elijah appears at the transfiguration after the death of John the Baptist further indicates that a part of his mission remains to be fulfilled in the suffering of Jesus.

82   So e.g. Marshall, *Luke*, 384; Nolland, *Luke 9*, 499–500; Otten, *I Alone*, 118 n. 96; Zwiep, *Ascension*, 86.

83   Arie W. Zwiep, *Christ, the Spirit and the Community of God*, WUNT II/293 (Tübingen: Mohr Siebeck, 2010), 60. The use of ἀναλήμψις here is consistent with an Elijanic tenor that is present in the narratives before and after. In Luke 9:37–43, Jesus heals a boy with an unclean spirit, in which Otten points out "unmistakable similarities to Elijah and Elisha's healing miracles" (*I Alone*, 117). In 9:52, on the other side, Jesus himself "sent messengers ahead of him" (ἀπέστειλεν ἀγγέλους πρὸ προσώπου αὐτοῦ) to "prepare for him" (ἑτοιμάσαι αὐτῷ) (see also Otten, 139–40). James and John, perhaps still in awe of the figure they have just witnessed at the transfiguration, ask to call down fire, like Elijah in 2 Kgs 1, to consume the Samaritans who refuse to receive Jesus (9:53–54). Jesus, however, rebukes them,

vivid analogical summary of the dual image of Moses and Elijah at the transfiguration: that of glory and of suffering. Their appearance ἐν δόξῃ on a mountain, as well as the recollection of Elijah's spectacular ascension, highlights the glory of the one who stands before them in the position of Yhwh's self-revelation, and prefigures Jesus' own glorious ascension to heaven. The exodus, on the other hand, is an image of deliverance in the context of suffering, and recalls the figure to whom all subsequent suffering prophets would be compared.[84] Jesus' mission and his triumph, his suffering and his glory, are thus highlighted at the transfiguration in equal and opposite measure by the appearances of Moses and Elijah. Simultaneously, this tension of suffering and glory is innate in the image of Elijah himself. He is awaited as a glorious restorer, yet has been received in the person of a suffering John the Baptist. This tension will continue to be transferred onto Jesus as he continues his journey to the cross.

2.4 *The Crucifixion*
2.4.1 The Chosen One
Luke's transfiguration is linked lexically to the crucifixion in a way that further highlights an Elijah image in the background of Jesus' suffering. This is the only transfiguration account in which the voice from heaven calls Jesus "the chosen one" (ὁ ἐκλελεγμένος – 9:35),[85] a title used in the Hebrew Bible (in adjectival rather than verbal form) of Moses (Ps 106:23), the people of Israel (Ps 105:6, 43; 106:5; Isa 45:4; 65:9, 15, 22), and the servant of Yhwh (Isa 42:1; cf. 49:7). It is resumed by Luke at the crucifixion. The same adjective is placed into the mouth of the crowd at the cross, which mocks the very identity established at the transfiguration: "He saved others; let him save himself if this is the Christ of God, the chosen one [ὁ ἐκλεκτός]" (Luke 23:35).[86]

---

and continues with a dialogue on the cost of discipleship that echoes the calling of Elisha in 1 Kgs 19 (9:57–62). The sending of his own messengers portrays Jesus in the role of Yhwh in Mal 3, and he expects his followers to fill the preparatory role of Malachi's Elijah (9:52). Their response, however, alludes instead to the Elijah of Kings, and Jesus' rebuke indicates that they have misunderstood how Malachi's forerunner role is to be worked out. See for discussion Otten, *I Alone*, 119–21.

84 See Teeter and Lyons, "The One and the Many." Hoffeditz downplays the Mosaic tenor of ἔξοδος here, connecting it instead to Mic 5:1–5 ("A Prophet," 205–208). Its combination with ἀνάλημψις in the same chapter as the transfiguration, however, seems to constitute a clear combined reference to Moses and Elijah.

85 While the notes to NA28 show that some manuscripts read ὁ ἀγαπητός, this rendering is likely a result of either intentional or accidental harmonisation with that title in Mark and Matthew (Mark 9:7; Matt 17:5). See Marshall, *Luke*, 388.

86 This link, along with its allusion to the servant in Isa 42, is also noted by Green (*Luke*, 821), Marshall (*Luke*, 388), and Nolland (*Luke 9*, 501), though the latter suggests that the term "has a different function" at the crucifixion.

This challenge at Golgotha is not the first time a similar sentiment has been expressed in Luke. The words of the crowd appear to be an alternative resumption of an image from Luke 4, in which Jesus reads Isa 61:1–2 and announces it fulfilled (Luke 4:16–21). He predicts that the people will quote to him a familiar proverb: "'Physician, heal yourself!' Whatever we heard was done in Capernaum, do here in your hometown also" (4:23).

Both in Nazareth and at the crucifixion, Jesus is challenged to prove his identity by acting in a way that the crowd deems suitable for that identity. In both cases, he refuses. In Luke 4, the justification for Jesus' unorthodox choice of ministry context is found in the stories of Elijah and Elisha, both of whom ministered to foreigners at the expense of the larger Israel (4:25–27).[87] As we have seen, the image of Elijah's embodiment of a righteous remnant repeatedly characterises that remnant by means of small, marginalised groups at the expense of the larger institution. A foreign mother and her child are saved, while the established house of Israel is subjected to judgement. The priests of Malachi are harshly rebuked, while those who fear Yhwh will receive healing in the restoration associated with his messenger. In Luke 4, Elijah and Elisha again represent Yhwh's work among unexpected recipients of his salvation, while those who expect to benefit, ironically, reject it.[88]

Jesus' identity as the "chosen one" is therefore worked out in a way that is opposite to what the people expect.[89] At the transfiguration, Luke portrays Jesus as greater than those who have previously held this title: that is, he is the greater Moses, the greater Elijanic/Isaian servant, and the greater Israel.[90] The divine affirmation from heaven confirms Jesus' identity as greater than those who have previously been "chosen," even as he stands with them on the mountain. At the crucifixion, Luke portrays him on a second mountain, again

---

87   "These anecdotes demonstrate that the sort of mission for which [Jesus] has been anointed has as its precedent the prophetic activity of Elijah and Elisha" (Green, *Luke*, 217). The proximity of an Elijah reference to the reading of Isa 61 in Luke 4 may also represent further evidence that later readers identified Elijah with 4Q521. See also Otten, *I Alone*, 99–100; Valve "Lord Elijah," 146.

88   See Jonathan Huddleston: "By comparing Jesus to Elijah and Elisha, perhaps Luke suggests to his audiences (even if unwittingly) that Jesus too is strange, surprising, and confounding" ("What Would Elijah and Elisha Do? Internarrativity in Luke's Story of Jesus," *JTI* 5 [2011], 280).

89   Such a reversal may also be behind Jesus' statements in Luke 12:52–53, where his mission appears to be precisely the opposite of Elijah's in Malachi: "For from now on there will be five divided in one house, three against two and two against three. They will be divided, father against son and son against father, mother against daughter and daughter against mother, mother-in-law against her daughter-in-law and daughter-in-law against mother-in-law."

90   See Teeter and Lyons, "The One and the Many," 29–32.

between two figures, mocked as the "chosen one" for fulfilling his true identity (23:35). To Luke, Jesus' identities as confirmed at the transfiguration are fulfilled at the cross. He suffers as the ideal prophet, both at the hands of and on behalf of the people, and depicts in parallel the two potential responses to a divine encounter: the one that mocks and the one that believes.

2.4.2   The Lord Who Comes

Mark approaches the passion narrative from a somewhat different angle, choosing to present Jesus, in his arrest and sentencing, explicitly in terms of Malachi's coming Lord (Mal 3:1). In Mark 13, Jesus begins to tell of the future conflicts, persecutions, and cosmic phenomena that will accompany his return (13:5–37). In contrast to Luke, Mark does not describe Jesus as the "chosen one"; instead, he uses τοὺς ἐκλεκτούς to refer to those who will be saved (13:20, 22, 27). This usage, as we have seen, is consistent with the title's scriptural application to the community of Israel. The chosen ones, to Mark, are the righteous community. He envisions a still future sending of messengers (ἀποστελεῖ τοὺς ἀγγέλους) to gather the chosen ones (τοὺς ἐκλεκτούς) at Jesus' second coming (13:26–27),[91] possibly in parallel to the sending of Elijah at his first (cf. Mal 3:1; 3:23; Mark 1:2), to establish, finally, this community out of every corner of the earth (Mark 13:27).

The last three verses of Jesus' discourse in this section (13:35–37) form an inclusio via the command to "keep alert" (γρηγορέω). He illustrates his own coming through a parable of the master of a house returning from a journey. The language of this segment appears to allude to the expectation of the Lord's coming in Mal 3, supporting the suggestion of a Malachian background to vv. 26–27 above. Further, this segment introduces temporal touchpoints that will be fulfilled throughout the passion account:

> [35] Therefore keep alert [γρηγορεῖτε], for you do not know when the lord of the house [ὁ κύριος τῆς οἰκίας] is coming [ἔρχεται], whether evening [ὀψέ] or midnight [μεσονύκτιον] or at the rooster's crowing [ἀλεκτοροφωνίας] or early [πρωΐ],
> [36] lest having come suddenly [ἐξαίφνης] he find you sleeping [καθεύδοντας].
> [37] But what I say to you I say to all: Keep alert [γρηγορεῖτε]! (13:35–37)

---

91   Mark L. Strauss notes that the ἄγγελοι in this text could be either human or angelic messengers, but he applies this ambiguity only to the question of whether this "ingathering" refers to missionary expansion in the first century CE (*Mark*, ZECNT, vol. 2, ed. Clinton E. Arnold [Grand Rapids: Zondervan, 2014], 593).

The combination of ἐξαίφνης for "suddenly" with a κύριος τῆς οἰκίας who is "coming" (ἔρχομαι) produces a statement with remarkable similarities to the "Lord" (LXX κύριος) who "suddenly" (ἐξαίφνης) "comes" (ἔρχομαι) to his temple in Mal 3:1.[92] Given the eschatological tenor of Jesus' discourse in this segment, as well as the rarity of ἐξαίφνης in both NT and LXX texts,[93] such an allusion is no exegetical stretch. Simultaneously, however, the segment is given an initial fulfilment within the text of Mark itself. In the Gethsemane pericope that follows, Jesus asks that his disciples "remain here and keep alert [γρηγορεῖτε]" (14:34). He then returns and finds them "sleeping" (καθεύδοντας – 14:37). This sequence repeats itself, using the same vocabulary, in 14:38–41. Further, between the beginning of the last supper account (14:17) and the beginning of Jesus' sentencing before Pilate (15:1), each of the temporal notations mentioned in the parable appears in some form. The last supper occurs at "evening" (ὀψίας – 14:17), Peter's denial is predicted to occur at "night" (νυκτί), before the "rooster crows" (ἀλέκτορα – 14:30, cf. 14:72), and Jesus is handed over to Pilate "early" (πρωῒ – 15:1).[94] The reference to a rooster crowing is found nowhere else in any of the Gospel accounts outside of direct reference to Peter's denial, so its solitary presence here in Mark's parable seems an intentional marker. The coming of the Lord to his temple predicted in Malachi is encased by Mark in a parable that moves toward its fulfilment as Jesus moves toward the cross.

Mark's Gethsemane account also appears to be modelled on the image of a grieving Elijah in 1 Kgs 19. It refers to Jesus' "soul" (ψυχή; cf. LXX 1 Kgs 19:4) being "deeply grieved to the point of death" (Mark 14:34; cf. 1 Kgs 19:4), a position on the ground (Mark 14:35; cf. 1 Kgs 19:4–5), multiple instances of sleep

---

92   John Strachan has proposed Mark's construction of a Malachian inclusio between the book's introduction in 1:2 and this passage in ch. 13, which sections off chs. 1–13 as a warning about the imminent destruction of the temple. While his arguments about Mark's perspective on the temple are beyond the scope of this book, very few scholars have noted an allusion to Malachi in Mark 13:35–37 (Strachan notes only two who suggest it briefly, including Martin, cited below), and this observation, I would argue, is fully defensible and deserving of the consideration I will also allot it here. See John Michael Strachan, "Rewriting the Ending: Malachi's Threat and the Destruction of the Temple in the Gospel of Mark," PhD diss., Marquette University (2022), 48–64.

93   NT Mark 13:36; Luke 2:13; 9:39; Acts 9:3; 22:6; LXX Isa 47:9; Jer 6:26; 15:8; Mic 2:3; Hab 2:7; Mal 3:1; Job 1:19; Prov 24:22.

94   Troy Martin's study is preoccupied with the provenance of these terms as names for four night watches. However, he does observe that they are used to "structure the passion narrative" ("Watch During the Watches [Mark 13:35]," *JBL* 120 [2001], 697 n. 48). See also R.H. Lightfoot, *The Gospel Message of St Mark* (Oxford: Clarendon, 1952), 53; R.W.L. Moberly, "The Coming at Cockcrow: A Reading of Mark 13:32–37," *JTI* 14 (2020), 217. Contra Gundry, who finds the parallels weak (*Mark*, 799–800).

(Mark 14:37, 40, 41; cf. 1 Kgs 19:5–6), a variation of the sentiment "it is enough" (Mark 14:41; cf. 1 Kgs 19:4), and a command to "arise" (Mark 14:42; cf. 1 Kgs 19:7).[95] As Jesus follows his own description of Malachi's Lord coming to his temple, he bears the grief of the Elijah of Kings in the background. His disciples provide the negative contrast: having been asked to keep watch, they are sleeping and must be commanded to "arise" (Mark 14:42; cf. 1 Kgs 19:5). In this sense they assume the negative elements of Elijah's character in 1 Kgs 19, even as Jesus bears the prophet's weight of grief. The resulting image again combines the Elijah of Kings with the expectation of Malachi, but, once again, Jesus' fulfil-ment of the scriptural image is intended to shock. The coming Lord of Malachi approaches a temple that, at least initially, takes the horrifying shape of a cross.

2.4.3   Elijah at the Cross

The final appearance of Elijah by name in the Gospels, recorded in narratives of Mark and Matthew, is found in the context of that cross. In both accounts, the crowd responds to Jesus' cry, "*Eloi, Eloi, lema sabachthani?*' which is trans-lated 'My God, my God, why have you forsaken me?'" (Mark 15:34; cf. the alternative transliteration of the Aramaic in Matt 27:46) with the assumption that he is calling for Elijah (Mark 15:35–36; Matt 27:47, 49). This puzzling reac-tion has been interpreted as a test of Jesus' innocence: Elijah was expected to save the righteous, so the crowd assumes that, if Jesus were righteous, Elijah would come to save him.[96] However, given the arguments formed by both Gospels' uses of Elijah to this point, the rhetorical weight of this refer-ence must be deeper.[97] Both Mark and Matthew have repeatedly shown the ways in which Jesus either assumes or surpasses the Elijah image. The sug-gestion that this same Jesus would still be relying on a future Elijah to save him demonstrates just how thoroughly the onlookers have missed the point.[98]

---

95   See Wolfgang Roth, *Hebrew Gospel: Cracking the Code of Mark* (Oak Park: Meyer-Stone, 1988), 74–75.

96   See Jeremias, "Ἠλ(ε)ίας," 932–33, 937–38. France argues that those standing nearest the cross would have been Roman soldiers, not Jewish onlookers, and therefore unlikely to have held such a tradition (*Matthew*, 1077).

97   Numerous scholars have also argued that Ἐλωί is very difficult to mistake for Ἠλίας (see for discussion Gundry, *Mark*, 967). Mark F. Whitters interprets the quotation as reflect-ing Mark's underlying concern "that Jesus *not* be identified as Elijah" ("Why Did the Bystanders Think Jesus Called upon Elijah before He Died [Mark 15:34–36]? The Markan Position," *HTR* 95 [2002], 120). However, this interpretation does injustice to the other Elijah allusions seen in Mark's presentation of Jesus overall.

98   So also Schreiber: "Gerade durch das eigentlich nicht mißzuverstehende ἐλωί, kommt das radikale Mißverstehen der Menschen unüberhörbar zum Ausdruck!" (*Kreuzigungsbericht*, 174 n. 4).

Jesus is not invoking an eschatological forerunner; that forerunner has long come and gone. Instead, with his cry Jesus invokes the entirety of the righteous sufferer image expressed in Ps 22, which is consistent with the pattern of Elijah as a righteous sufferer affirmed by the same two Gospels (cf. Mark 9:12–13; Matt 17:11–12).[99] He is not calling for Elijah; he is completing Elijah's mission in his suffering, even as he has just demonstrated his identity as Malachi's coming Lord (Mark 13–15). In a final twist of irony, it is the Roman centurion standing at the cross who becomes the unexpected believer, recognising what the more likely onlookers have so utterly missed: "truly this man was the son of God" (Mark 15:39; cf. Matt 27:54; Mark 1:1).[100]

2.5   "Two Men"

This interdependency between suffering and glory that is encapsulated in the Elijah image in all three Synoptics is brought to a final resolution by a clever and provocative thread drawn through Luke's account and into the first chapter of Acts. Luke's transfiguration narrative introduces the figures on the mountain with the announcement "and behold, two men [καὶ ἰδοὺ ἄνδρες δύο] talking with him; they were Moses and Elijah" (9:30). This formulation is unique to Luke; Mark and Matthew simply introduce Moses and Elijah by name (Mark 9:4; Matt 17:3). It is also rare in the New Testament. The combination of δύος and ἄνδρος appears three times in Luke and twice in Acts, but the exact locution καὶ ἰδοὺ ἄνδρες δύο occurs three times in total: once at the transfiguration, once at the resurrection, and once at the ascension.[101]

---

99   See Stephen P. Ahearne-Kroll, *The Psalms of Lament in Mark's Passion* (Cambridge: Cambridge University Press, 2007), 198–214 (Ps 22 is here cited as Ps 21 as per LXX numbering); Michael A. Lyons, "Psalm 22 and the 'Servants' of Isaiah 54; 56–66," *CBQ* 77 (2015): 640–56.

100   "The confusion of the bystanders is an intentional rhetorical device that prepares the reader for the resolution provided by the centurion. When he utters his observation, all other titles and names for Jesus retreat into oblivion" (Whitters, "Bystanders," 124).

101   While I had observed Luke's unique use of "two men," the repetition of the exact phrase καὶ ἰδοὺ ἄνδρες δύο was pointed out and explored in a recent article by Jared Hay, which supported my suspicions about the association of these "men" with Moses and Elijah. See Jared W. Hay, "'And suddenly, two men …': Moses and Elijah in Lukan Perspective," *ExpTim* 134 (2023): 435–44. It is also observed by Mikeal C. Parsons, who does not consider the resurrection and transfiguration accounts to describe Elijah as one of the men, but nonetheless agrees that "it is striking that at three of the most exalted moments of Jesus' ministry – his transfiguration, his resurrection, and his ascension – these two men are present" (*The Departure of Jesus in Luke-Acts*, JSNTSup 21 [Sheffield: Sheffield Academic, 1987], 172–73). See similarly Hoffeditz, "A Prophet," 209; Nolland, *Luke 9*, 498; Zwiep, *Ascension*, 106. Green reflects on the "similar hermeneutical purpose" of these three occurrences, but highlights their differences rather than their similarities (*Luke*, 380–81

The women at the empty tomb are startled by "two men" appearing before them "in dazzling apparel" (24:4). At the ascension, it is "two men" in white clothing who stand before the disciples looking up into heaven (Acts 1:10).[102] Jared Hay argues that the uniqueness of this precise phrase in Luke-Acts and in scriptural texts overall provides "a powerful textual indicator that the men *referred* to in the first instance are to be *inferred* in instances two and three."[103]

The potential presence of Moses and Elijah at the resurrection and the ascension in Luke-Acts bears direct implications for the interpretation of both accounts; indeed, for Luke's presentation of Jesus overall. The "two men" who were said to speak with Jesus at the transfiguration, though no words are quoted (Luke 9:30), also speak in both other contexts. At the resurrection, they ask the women at the tomb, "Why do you seek the living among the dead?" (24:5). While this question is certainly fitting in its narrative context, to imagine it coming from the mouths of Moses and Elijah, two figures thought by many not to have died, is to hear a powerful testimony of the supremacy of Jesus over both. Two prophets who superseded death place themselves in the context of the dead in order to point the women to the ultimate prophet who superseded death; thereby repeating the message of the transfiguration in spectacular form.[104]

---

n. 94). Interestingly, the differences he sees relate to reminders of the past with a view toward the present and the future, which actually perfectly fit an identification of the two men in both cases as Moses and Elijah.

102　The association of angelic men in "shining white appearance" with the Elijah image is also made, as we have seen, by *LivProph* 21:2.

103　Hay, "Two Men," 439; original emphases. While the two men at the resurrection and the ascension are generally assumed to be angels, Luke only specifies them as such in the second-hand report of the disciples on the Emmaus road, quoting the report of the women (24:23). The description of the clothing of the men at the resurrection (ἐν ἐσθῆτι ἀστραπτούσῃ – 24:4) is also linked back to the transfiguration, in which the clothing of Luke's Jesus becomes "dazzling white [λευκὸς ἐξαστράπτων]" (9:29; see also Marshall, *Luke*, 885). The accounts of Mark and Matthew use different terms (λευκὰ ὡς τὸ φῶς in Matt 17:2 and στίλβοντα λευκὰ λίαν in Mark 9:3), highlighting the lexical correspondence present specifically between Luke's transfiguration and resurrection accounts. An identification of the two men with Moses and Elijah does not deny their angelic characteristics, but rather recognises that Moses and Elijah themselves may have been seen as heavenly figures (on Elijah, see Jan-A. Bühner, *Der Gesandte und sein Weg im 4. Evangelium*, WUNT II/2 [Tübingen: Mohr Siebeck, 1977], 344; Jeremias, "Ἠλ(ε)ίας," 932; Joynes, "Returned Elijah," 462–63).

104　The connection between the two accounts is further highlighted by the reminder given to the women by the two men of the passion predictions Jesus had previously made (24:6–7).

At the ascension, the "two men" speak with the disciples (Acts 1:11) after Jesus has ascended to heaven in their sight (1:9). This is a passage that has been recognised to allude directly to the ascension of Elijah in 2 Kgs 2 (Acts 1:6–11).[105] If Luke indeed intends to hint at Elijah's presence as one of the "two men," then this pericope recalls 2 Kgs 2 even more specifically. In Kings, Elijah ascends toward heaven in the sight of his disciple Elisha, upon which the broader community of prophets takes three days to look for him (2 Kgs 2:17). In Acts 1, Elijah becomes one of the "two men" who promise a group of disciples looking for their master that "this Jesus, who ascended from you into heaven, will come in the same way you saw him going into heaven" (1:11).[106] The disciples, in the meantime, will receive the power to carry on Jesus' work when the Holy Spirit falls on them, like the mantle of Elijah fell on Elisha (Acts 1:8; cf. 1 Kgs 19:19).

Luke's evident literary correlation between Moses and Elijah at the transfiguration and the "two men" at the resurrection and the ascension is not necessarily intended to make an empirical claim about the factual identity of the heavenly figures in the latter two passages. Instead, it argues that Moses and Elijah were understood to appear as messengers from the heavenly realm, and again confirms the innate flexibility of these images. Luke creates this literary relationship to make a specific rhetorical and theological claim. To his argument, the role of Elijah as forerunner has finally come full circle. The two men, associated with Elijah, prophesy the return of the greater Elijah to the community which will carry on Elijah's work.[107] The great Mosaic prophet, whose return was promised for the restoration of Israel, now tells those who had waited for him to wait for the greater prophet like Moses (cf. Acts 3:22–23). "This Jesus" is the one who will return "in the same way you saw him going" (Acts 1:11) and effect the restoration of the righteous remnant.

---

105   See e.g. Craig S. Keener, *Acts* (Grand Rapids: Baker, 2012), 1:719; Zwiep, *Ascension*, 194.

106   Valve observes that "Elijah was plausibly generally associated with the notion of 'hiddenness', due to the repeated mention of his behaving like this in 1–2 Kings" ("Elijah, the Servant, and Phinehas," 24).

107   Kee hints at an Elijah pattern present in Jesus' disciples, as well as in Jesus, in the Gospel of Mark as well. He further suggests that the disciples, for Mark, are a model of the community to which the Gospel is written, which is consistent with my theory of the Elijah pattern as an image of God's people. See Kee, *Community*, 87, 120–21. In other words, "the biblical Elijah tradition provided the necessary ingredients for structuring the events that surrounded the end of Jesus' earthly career and the beginning of the early Christian community" (Zwiep, *Christ*, 63–64).

2.6   *Summary*

The Elijah image in each of the Synoptics is initially identified with the forerunner persona of John the Baptist (Mark 1; Luke 1; Matt 11). In various ways, this image is subsequently absorbed by the person and role of Jesus. Jesus' portrayal as the paradigmatic righteous sufferer and as Yhwh's "chosen one" is formed of combined allusions to other Hebrew prophets, patriarchs, messengers, the servant of Isaiah, and the people of Israel themselves. John begins Elijah's work, but Jesus brings it to completion. As the greater Elijah, he embodies both a level of suffering as visceral as the community's and the glorious restoration that has kept their hope alive. His incarnated fulfilment of both these realities transcends any figure that came before him, as he becomes simultaneously the culmination of Israel's prophetic tradition and of their own identity. As Omerzu observes of the Markan writer: "Er schreibt damit jüdische Geschichte ... fort als Geschichte Jesu, die u.a. Teil der Geschichte des Elia, Mose und Jesaja ist, und konstituiert damit zugleich die Geschichte seiner Adressaten."[108]

The synoptic writers, in other words, describe Jesus within the framework of characters already adopted by their communities. Rather than present him as a new paradigm, they portray him as the fulfilment of a multiplicity of paradigmatic images at once. His confirmation as greater than Moses and Elijah at the transfiguration is an unambiguous statement that the personification of Israel's hope now has a new face. He is the prophet like Moses to whom the righteous community must now listen (Matt 17:5; Mark 9:7; Luke 9:35),[109] even as membership within that community once again becomes redefined. The righteous community, to the Gospel writers, represents those who are willing, like Elisha and the disciples, to leave everything behind and follow their Elijah.

3   The Fourth Gospel

3.1   *John, Jesus, and Elijah*

The relationship between the use of the Elijah image in the Synoptics and that in the Gospel of John has evoked much discussion. In the first chapter of the Fourth Gospel, John the Baptist is explicitly asked by a delegation of priests and Levites, following his denial of being the Christ (John 1:20), whether he is then "Elijah" or "the prophet" (1:21; cf. 1:25). Both of these proposals John also

---

108   Omerzu, "Geschichte," 99.
109   So also de la Serna, "Pablo," 165.

flatly denies (1:21). In response, he associates himself with the wilderness voice of Isa 40:3 (1:23), but not with the messenger of Malachi.[110] Outside of this context (1:19–28), Elijah's name is not mentioned in the book again.

This singular reference has raised questions regarding the Fourth Gospel's conception of both the Elijah figure and John the Baptist in relation to the synoptic accounts. Some commentators have argued that the Fourth Gospel is not aware of the John the Baptist/Elijah tradition.[111] This suggestion is less than convincing, given the other synoptic traditions that it does seem to know.[112] Others have suggested significant similarities between the miracles depicted in John's Gospel and those of Elijah and Elisha.[113] Several have concluded that the Baptist's explicit denial of the identities of Christ, Elijah, and "the prophet" effectively projects all three of these identities onto Jesus.[114] Paul Anderson and Maurizio Marcheselli, for example, have argued separately that Jesus is portrayed in the Fourth Gospel not only as the Christ, but also as Elijah and the prophet like Moses.[115] In contrast, Hoffeditz maintains that Elijah imagery

---

110   Further, Hoffeditz notes the Fourth Gospel's substitution of the NT *hapax legomenon* εὐθύνω for LXX Isa 40's ἑτοιμάζω (used in the synoptic quotations [Mark 1:3; Matt 3:3; Luke 3:4]) which, he argues, is made to downplay John's forerunner role ("A Prophet," 234–36).

111   So e.g. Leon Morris: "It is not a contradiction of [the Synoptics], but had John had their statement before him he would scarcely have left his own account in just this form" (*The Gospel According to John*, rev. ed., NICNT [Grand Rapids: Eerdmans, 1995], 118).

112   Edwin D. Freed argues that John was well aware of the synoptic traditions identifying John the Baptist with Elijah, and that he uses elements from several of these to craft his statements regarding the identity of Jesus in 1:19–23 and 6:67–71 ("Jn 1:19–27 in Light of Related Passages in John, the Synoptics, and Acts," in *The Four Gospels 1992: Festschrift Frans Neirynck* [Leuven: Leuven University Press, 1992], 1948). See also a comparison of the introductions of John and Mark in Dietrich-Alex Koch, "Der Täufer als Zeuge des Offenbarers," in *The Four Gospels 1992: Festschrift Frans Neirynck* (Leuven: Leuven University Press, 1992), 1963–84.

113   See e.g. J. Louis Martyn, "We Have Found Elijah," in *Jews, Greeks and Christians*, ed. R. Hammerton-Kelly and R. Scroggs, SJLA 21 (Leiden: Brill, 1976), 191–95; Allan Mayer, "Elijah and Elisha in John's Signs Source," *ExpTim* 99 (1988): 171–73.

114   Henricus Pidyarto Gunawan has argued, in significant detail, for numerous plot-level allusions between Jesus in John's Gospel and Elijah in Kings ("Jesus as the New Elijah: An Attempt to the Question of John 1:21," *SiChrSt* 9 [2010]: 29–53). See also Bernard P. Robinson, "Christ as a Northern Prophet in St John," *Scr* 17 (1965): 104–108. So also Oscar Cullmann: "Im vierten Evangelium kann es keinen Würdetitel geben, der nicht in Jesus Christus seine Erfüllung fände" (*Die Christologie des Neuen Testaments*, WMANT 25 [Tübingen: Mohr Siebeck, 1975], 36).

115   Paul N. Anderson, "Jesus, the Eschatological Prophet in the Fourth Gospel: A Case Study in Dialectical Tensions," *Faculty Publications – George Fox School of Theology* 284 (2018): 7–16; Maurizio Marcheselli, "The Range and Significance of the References to Elijah in John's Gospel," *StBiSl* 12 (2020): 227–51. Similar is Robinson's earlier conclusion ("Elijah, John and Jesus," 266).

is "subdued" in John in general because of its messianic implications, in order to avoid ascribing too high an identity to John the Baptist and too low an identity to Jesus.[116] He argues that subtle analogies between the Baptist and Elijah remain in the Fourth Gospel, but that these "do not spill over in the description of Jesus because to describe Jesus as the eschatological Elijah would also lower John's 'high' christology."[117]

Hoffeditz's conclusion that the Elijah image plays a less obvious role in the Fourth Gospel in comparison to the Synoptics is well taken.[118] On the other hand, he cannot help but observe that Elijah imagery is, nevertheless, still present. In the prologue to the Fourth Gospel, John the Baptist is described as being "sent from God" (ἀπεσταλμένος παρὰ θεοῦ – John 1:6) "as a testimony, to bear witness about the light" (εἰς μαρτυρίαν ἵνα μαρτυρήσῃ περὶ τοῦ φωτός – 1:7). Hoffeditz notes the Malachian tenor in the image of John as a man "sent" (ἀποστέλλω) from God (1:6),[119] and argues that the prologue's repeated emphasis on John as only a witness (1:7, 8) is intended to specify that, while he is an Elijah-like figure, he is not the eschatological "light" envisioned by traditions such as Sir 48:1.[120] He concludes that "the evangelist subdues but does not remove the eschatological Elijanic colors associated with the Baptist. At the same time, he presents Jesus in much of the standard terminology surrounding the expected Elijah, without equating Jesus with Elijah or even attempting to draw connections."[121]

That the image of John the Baptist being "sent" as a witness to Jesus is grounded in Malachi's Elijah is a defensible conclusion, especially given how the motifs of sending, testimony, and light will later be utilised with respect to the Elijah image in Revelation.[122] However, after the point of John's denial

---

116   Hoffeditz, "A Prophet," 227. See also Öhler: "Vor allem aber polemisiert ... der Text gegen eine übermäßige Hochschätzung des Täufers" (*Elia*, 94). Öhler further concludes, wrongly in my view, that the image of Elijah plays no role in the portrayal of Jesus in the Fourth Gospel: "Wäre er Elia gewesen, wäre Jesus nicht der Christus!" (95, cf. 247).

117   Hoffeditz, "A Prophet," 227. Martyn comes to a similar conclusion on the basis of a literary-critical investigation of John 1 ("We Have Found Elijah," 197–219).

118   A more extreme expression of this view is offered by Marinus de Jonge: "Obviously John knew of an identification of the Baptist with Elijah, but he did not regard it worthwhile to give his opinion about a possible identification of Jesus and Elijah" (*Jesus: Stranger from Heaven and Son of God*, SBibSt 11, trans. John E. Steely [Missoula: Scholars, 1977], 54).

119   Hoffeditz, "A Prophet," 231.

120   Hoffeditz notes the association of Elijah with light and life in Ben Sira and suggests that such a conception is behind the insistence of John's Gospel that only the true light – not the Baptist or Elijah – can bring life ("A Prophet," 229–30).

121   Hoffeditz, "A Prophet," 247.

122   See discussion in ch. 7 of this study.

of the Elijah role (1:21), I would argue that there is a strong case to be made that the writer does indeed shift the Elijah image onto Jesus, and that this analogy is even used to draw a distinction between his true and false disciples. The flexibility in character analogies present in nearly every textual source of the Elijah tradition to this point, of course, easily allows for such a shift. Rather than diminishing Jesus' identity, as Hoffeditz has suggested, I would argue that a distinct Elijah-like thread drawn through the Fourth Gospel highlights precisely, in John the Baptist's own words, that "the one coming from heaven is over all" (John 3:31).

3.2   *Heavenly Ascent*

3.2.1   Introduction

I suggest that this Elijanic thread can be most clearly traced via John's motif of heavenly ascent. A pattern of ascent and descent is strikingly central to the Fourth Gospel, both geographically and with respect to a heavenly realm.[123] Some have seen in this motif a refutation of mystic heavenly ascent traditions, in which the author of John denies the legitimacy of any heavenly ascent except that of Jesus.[124] It is difficult to maintain an argument of wholesale denial, however, when several of these ascent traditions, specifically those of Enoch and Elijah, come from precisely the scriptures that Jesus describes as testifying to him (John 5:39–40). A stronger argument can be made that the Fourth Gospel reinterprets these traditions by applying their ultimate outworking directly to Jesus himself.[125]

3.2.2   Ἄγγελοι Ascending and Descending

The opening example in the first chapter of John reawakens a peculiar Pentateuchal image. Jesus is described as promising Nathanael, a sceptical would-be disciple,

---

123   This theme is developed by Theo Witkamp and Jan Krans, "Heavenly Journey and Divine Epistemology in the Fourth Gospel," in *Jewish, Christian, and Muslim Travel Experiences: 3rd Century BCE–8th Century CE*, ed. P.B. Hartog, S. Luther, and C.E. Wilde (Berlin: de Gruyter, 2023), 145–60.

124   See e.g. Jey J. Kanagaraj, *'Mysticism' in the Gospel of John: An Inquiry into its Background*, JSNTSup 158 (Sheffield: Sheffield Academic, 1998), 199–201; Colin G. Kruse, *John: An Introduction and Commentary*, TNTC 4 (Downers Grove: InterVarsity Press, 2003), 112; Hugo Odeberg, *The Fourth Gospel* (Amsterdam: B.R. Grüner, 1929), 72.

125   Witkamp and Krans do argue that "John seems to contradict vehemently certain (apocalyptic) traditions about ascending to heaven … even when they originated from within Scripture itself" ("Heavenly Journey," 151). They then expand this proposal, however, by allowing that John "also is able to incorporate (some of) them by reinterpreting them" (151).

ὄψεσθε τὸν οὐρανὸν ἀνεῳγότα καὶ τοὺς ἀγγέλους τοῦ θεοῦ ἀναβαίνοντας καὶ καταβαίνοντας ἐπὶ τὸν υἱὸν τοῦ ἀνθρώπου.

You will see the heaven opened and the messengers of God ascending and descending on the Son of Man. (1:51)[126]

Commentators have rightly observed this image as a combination of Ezekiel's vision of "heavens opened" (LXX ἠνοίχθησαν οἱ οὐρανοί – Ezek 1:1) and an allusion to Jacob's dream in Gen 28:12.[127] The thrust of this conflated allusion applies the heavenly glory seen in both accounts to Jesus himself. It places Jesus in a position not only superior to the prophet Ezekiel who received the vision and the patriarchs whom the Genesis story originally concerns, but also to any ἄγγελοι who go up to or come down from heaven.[128] This anecdote by itself might not yet constitute an Elijah allusion, though it is interesting to note that Elijah also could be considered an ἄγγελος who ascends to heaven. Jesus also promises that Nathanael will "see" (root ὁράω) the heavenly ascent he describes. In 2 Kgs 2:10, whether or not Elisha "sees" (ראה; LXX ὁράω) Elijah's ascent forms the condition for his double reception of Elijah's spirit.[129] When several additional passages in John are considered, both of these themes will bring the Gospel's larger use of the Elijah image into clearer focus.

---

126   This is the first occurrence of "Son of Man" in the Fourth Gospel, a term which is almost certainly taken from Dan 7, where a "son of man" is presented to the Ancient of Days to receive an eternal kingdom (7:3–14). This title proves inextricably connected to the ascent/descent motif in John, as I demonstrate in the next section. Daniel 7 is linked again to the Elijah motif in Revelation, as we will see in the final chapter of this study.

127   See e.g. Charles K. Barrett, *The Gospel According to St John*, 2nd ed. (London: SPCK, 1978), 186–87; Kanagaraj, *'Mysticism'*, 188–94. Cf. the more sceptical views of Raymond E. Brown (*The Gospel According to John*, AB 29 [New Haven: Yale University Press, 1995], 1:90) and J. Ramsey Michaels (*The Gospel of John*, NICNT [Grand Rapids: Eerdmans, 2010], 136).

128   The role of the angels in both accounts is unclear, and some have protested that an allusion to Gen 28 in John 1 places Jesus in the role of the ladder (see e.g. John Painter, "The Enigmatic Son of Man," in *The Four Gospels 1992: Festschrift Frans Neirynck* [Leuven: Leuven University Press, 1992], 1873)! Kanagaraj smooths over the issue by stating that, in Genesis, "the vision of Yahweh to Jacob and the means of communication with him are emphasized more than the ascent-descent of the angels" (*'Mysticism'*, 191). However, the ἄγγελοι still unquestionably provide examples of other beings who transverse heavenly and earthly realms. Delbert Burkett suggests that this image portrays Jesus as the "link" between heaven and earth (*The Son of the Man in the Gospel of John*, JSNTSup 56 [Sheffield: Sheffield Academic, 1991], 118).

129   Anderson associates Nathanael's subsequent acknowledgement with a recognition of Jesus as the awaited prophet like Moses ("Jesus," 9).

3.2.3   The Son of Man Who Descends

The next usage of ascent/descent language in John appears in ch. 3, in the context of Jesus' dialogue with Nicodemus. Here Jesus takes the superiority established in ch. 1 a step further by declaring that "no one ascends [ἀναβέβηκεν] into heaven except the one who descends [καταβάς], the Son of Man" (3:13).[130] Here again, Jesus' statement can hardly be read as denying that anyone ever ascended according to scriptural tradition, when that tradition explicitly states that the prophet Elijah "went up" (ויעל; LXX ἀνελήμφθη – "he was taken up") to heaven (2 Kgs 2:11).[131] Language of moving up and down is also central to the Kings narrative.[132] However, Elijah only ascends to heaven. He does not come back down. Jesus' statement to Nicodemus declares that the only true "ascender" to heaven is the one who also descends; that is, the Son of Man. His uniqueness, in other words, is grounded in the fact that he first descended *from* heaven, and therefore claims it as his origin and not just his destiny. This is a status that even Moses and Elijah cannot claim.[133]

An argument against Jesus' uniqueness could also be made here from the opposite direction. Jan-A. Bühner has explored the ascent-descent motif in John in relation to traditions of heavenly מלאכים who are sent down from heaven with a message and then return.[134] This motif is indeed explicit in John 1, as we have just observed, in which ἄγγελοι do descend from heaven. In this sense, they also claim heavenly origin. Bühner's contention that Jesus

---

130   This statement has been problematised because of the perfect ἀναβέβηκεν being taken to refer to a past ascension (i.e. "no one has ascended") (see e.g. Painter, "Son of Man," 1878–79). However, Madison N. Pierce and Benjamin E. Reynolds have demonstrated, based on recent conclusions regarding the Greek verbal aspect, that "time value" may be less significant for perfect verbs than previously thought, and that this term can legitimately be translated in a present sense based on the context ("The Perfect Tense-Form and the Son of Man in John 3.13: Developments in Greek Grammar as a Viable Solution to the Timing of the Ascent and Descent," *NTS* 60 [2014], 153–54).

131   Both ἀναλαμβάνω (LXX 2 Kgs 2:11) and ἀναβαίνω (John 3:13) can be used to render the Hebrew עלה, as seen in the use of ἀναβαίνω in e.g. LXX 2 Kgs 2:23; 3:7.

132   See Burnett, "Going Down," 281–97.

133   At least one branch of ascent mysticism explicitly drew its pattern from Moses' ascent at Sinai to meet with Yhwh (see for discussion Peder Borgen, "Some Jewish Exegetical Traditions as Background for Son of Man Sayings in John's Gospel [Jn 3,13–14 and context]," in *L'Évangile de Jean: Sources, rédaction, théologie*, ed. M. de Jonge, BETL 44 [Leuven: Leuven University Press, 1977], 243–52; Wayne A. Meeks, *The Prophet-King*, NovTSup 14 [Leiden: Brill, 1967], 297–301; Klaus Wengst, *Das Johannesevangelium*, TKNT 4 [Stuttgart: Kohlhammer, 2019], 116).

134   Bühner, *Der Gesandte*, 316–41. "Da der מלאך im Himmel seine Heimat hat, muß er, wenn Gott ihn als Boten auf die Erde sendet, dorthin hinabsteigen und entsprechend nach beendetem Auftrag wieder in die himmlische Heimat hinaufsteigen" (335).

in John's Gospel is to be viewed through the lens of "der מלאך als שליח Gottes" raises a serious exception to the claim that Jesus is the only one both to ascend and descend, especially since the current study itself has connected Jesus with just such a "sent messenger" by means of the figure of Elijah.[135]

At this point, Jesus' claim to be the "Son of Man" provides the critical differentiation. Even as his heavenly origin separates him from other humans who ascend, so his human identity as the Son of Man distinguishes him from the status of a mere heavenly messenger. In his dialogue with Nicodemus, Jesus claims to be equally tied to heaven and earth: both one of the people and over the people; both human and simultaneously greater than all other messengers who have come from heaven.[136]

Further, several scholars have argued that John 3:13 displays a compelling allusion to Prov 30:3–4.[137] This passage appears in the context of a dialogue with God (30:1–4), in which Agur laments his lack of understanding:

> [3] And I have not learned wisdom, nor do I know knowledge of the holy ones.
> [4] Who has ascended to the heavens and come down? Who has gathered the wind in his hands? Who has wrapped waters in the mantle? Who has raised up all the ends of the earth? What is his name, and what is his son's name? For you know! (Prov 30:3–4)

In the broader context of John 3, multiple elements of this passage are taken up to portray Jesus' dialogue with a learned Pharisee who suddenly appears to know nothing at all (3:1–21).[138] His self-identification as the Son of Man also provides a point of contact: Jesus claims to be the son who ascended to heaven and came down, who controls the elements and holds knowledge.[139] If the

---

135 Bühner, *Der Gesandte*, 316–22, 340–41.

136 This differentiation also serves to distinguish Jesus from John the Baptist. Regardless of whether the writer of the Fourth Gospel sees John as Elijah, the Baptist is indeed one who is "sent from God" (John 1:6). On the other hand, he is not explicitly associated with heaven, and neither does he experience ascent. Jesus, on the other hand, claims both.

137 See e.g. Burkett, *The Son*, 47–48, 76, 85; Ernest M. Sidebottom, *The Christ of the Fourth Gospel in the Light of First-Century Thought* (London: SPCK, 1961), 206.

138 Witkamp and Krans see this contrast as one of the primary themes of this passage ("Heavenly Journey," 148–55).

139 So Burkett: "What is attributed to God in Prov 30.4, Jesus attributes to himself as 'the Son of the Man' in Jn 3.13" (*The Son*, 85). John 3:13 may also allude to Deut 30:11–14, in which Yhwh's law is depicted as near enough to the people that no one need ascend to heaven and bring it down. This link would support Jesus' presentation in John as Yhwh's "word [that] is very near to you" (Deut 30:14; cf. John 1:14).

Elijah image is indeed part of the background of John's ascension motif, then this allusion fits even more precisely. Though a different word is used, Elijah too controls waters with a garment (2 Kgs 2:8).[140] He too displays power over natural forces, and brings knowledge of Yhwh's word and works (1 Kgs 17:24; 18:37). Yet Jesus is greater, because he has not only ascended to heaven, but also is heavenly by nature. The reader of John's Gospel, placed into the role of Nicodemus, is reminded again, as Nathanael was, that heavenly knowledge – that is, heavenly sight – is required to follow this greater Elijah: "Unless someone is born again/from above [ἄνωθεν], he is not able to see [ὁράω] the kingdom of God" (3:3).

3.2.4   The True Disciples

In John 7, the ascension motif is broadened to include explicitly the perspective of those who remain on earth. Jesus tells the Pharisees, "Yet a short time I am with you; then I go away to the one who sent me. You will seek me and will not find me, and where I am you are not able to go" (7:33–34). The same assertion is reprised in 8:21 (cf. 8:24), with an addition: "I am going away, and you will seek me, *and you will die in your sin* [ἐν τῇ ἁμαρτίᾳ ὑμῶν ἀποθανεῖσθε]; where I am going you are not able to go" (emphasis added). Two allusions appear to be combined in this statement: another plot-level analogy to 2 Kgs 2:15–18, in which the "sons of the prophets" search for Elijah after his ascension and fail to find him,[141] and a lexical allusion via the addition in 8:21 to Ezek 3:20. Here Ezekiel is told that, if he does not warn the righteous person who has turned away, that person "will die in his sin" (MT sg בעונו; LXX pl ἐν ταῖς ἁμαρ-τίαις αὐτοῦ).[142]

Here John engages in a similar type of conflated analogising that we have observed in the synoptic accounts. He places Jesus in the narrative framework of the Elijah story and gives him the prophetic warning voice of Ezekiel. Through this conflation, he draws a distinction between those who follow Jesus and those who do not. Those who die in their sins are the ones who seek Jesus

---

140   Cf. שמלה in Prov 30:4 and אדרת in 2 Kgs 2:8.

141   The same motif is possibly also seen in Obadiah's concern in 1 Kgs 18:10–12 that the spirit of God will carry Elijah away so that Ahab will not be able to find him. Michaels acknowledges the "intriguing possibility" of this reference, but concludes that "the writer could hardly have expected readers to pick up such a subtle allusion here" (*John*, 456). If, however, Valve's conclusion that Elijah was associated with a "hiddenness" motif is correct, then just such an allusion becomes likely ("Elijah, the Servant, and Phinehas," 24).

142   While ἐν τῇ ἁμαρτίᾳ is singular in John 8:21, as per MT Ezek 3:20, the statement is reprised again with the plural ταῖς ἁμαρτίαις in 8:24, as per the LXX. Brown is one of very few commentators who has noticed any allusion to Ezekiel here, though he inexplicably cites LXX Ezek 3:18 which uses ἀδικία rather than the ἁμαρτία of 3:20, 24 (*John*, 1:347, note to viii 21).

and do not find him. They are paralleled to Elijah's disciples *other than* Elisha. Elisha knows that Elijah is in heaven because he witnessed the ascension, and he can tell the other prophets that they will not find him (2 Kgs 2:15–18). The ones still looking, on the other hand, are the ones lacking spiritual sight, and, to John's Gospel, the ones who will die in their sins.[143]

Placed centrally between these paralleled statements (John 7:33–34; 8:21–24) is a prediction that finds its resolution after Jesus' resurrection. After a resumption of his living water discourse in 7:37–38, the writer clarifies that Jesus spoke "concerning the spirit whom those who believed in him were about to receive; for the spirit was not yet there, because Jesus was not yet glorified" (7:39). Gunawan here argues for another parallel with 2 Kgs 2, in the motif of the spirit that is given to followers after the glorious resurrection/ascension of the leader.[144] He further combines this image with Jesus' promise in John 14:12 that "the one who believes in me, the works that I do, he will also; and greater than these he will do, because I am going to the father," noting the tradition of Elisha's performing more miracles than Elijah.[145] What he does not observe is the fulfilment of this very promise in John 20:22, when Jesus appears to his disciples after the resurrection, breathes on them, and pronounces "Receive the holy spirit."[146] At that point, just as Elisha received Elijah's spirit only when his master ascended, Jesus is resurrected, about to ascend, and his disciples can receive his spirit.[147]

John's Gospel, from its beginning, develops a theme of eternal life through Jesus.[148] Simultaneously, the writer emphasises that Jesus' disciples have access to his power, as per 14:12. The book concludes with the cryptic mention of a rumour that one of Jesus' disciples might remain alive until the eschaton (21:23). If my observations about the Elijanic context for Jesus' heavenly origin

---

143   The reprisal of this warning in 8:24 includes the added caveat ἐὰν … μὴ πιστεύσητε ὅτι ἐγώ εἰμι. This ἐγώ εἰμι, of course, famously reappears in 8:58, in which Jesus declares existence prior to Abraham and, as so many have noted, appears to claim the very identity of the God of Israel (see e.g. Brown, *John*, 1:367). The prophetic warning of Ezekiel (John 8:21, 24) is thus linked to an identity that subsumes everything encompassed in Abraham's name, as well as to the perpetual existence of Elijah (7:33–34). The resulting picture of Jesus is not only one of divinity, but also one that simultaneously identifies with the reality of the people and speaks into the larger group as a voice calling for repentance.

144   Gunawan, "New Elijah," 40–42.

145   Gunawan, "New Elijah," 42–43; cf. Sir 48:12 on Elisha.

146   So Brown, *John*, 1:324; Michaels, *John*, 468–69.

147   Marie E. Isaacs argues that the "spirit" within the Gospel of John is presented as a prophetic image, and that the disciples' reception of the spirit renders their role prophetic as well ("The Prophetic Spirit in the Fourth Gospel," *HeyJ* 24 [2007], 391–407).

148   See 1:4; 3:15–16, 36; 4:14, 36; 5:21–26, 39–40; 6:27–68; 8:12; 10:10, 28; 11:25; 12:25, 50; 14:6; 17:2–3; 20:31.

and return are correct, then this statement may be a final indicator that the disciples have now taken over Jesus' Elijah image. They have received the spirit of their resurrected master, as Elisha received the spirit of Elijah, and are starting to entertain the possibility of circumventing death themselves. Though Elisha does not escape death and neither, later, do Jesus' disciples, the possibility is no longer unimaginable. The disciples have seen their glorified master, they have been promised eternal life, and they bear the spirit of Elijah.

3.3   *Summary*

The Fourth Gospel ends, then, with the disciples of Jesus taking on a role that even John the Baptist could not claim. Jesus is the Christ, the ultimate prophet like Moses, and the one both greater than Elijah because of his heavenly origin and greater than other heavenly messengers because of his status as the Son of Man. He is now glorified and ascended, and his successors, like Elisha, bear his spirit and carry on his work. While its approach is different from that of the Synoptics, the Gospel of John is equally resonant in displaying Jesus as the embodiment of a hope for the restoration of the righteous. This restoration comes through the spiritual knowledge and sight that comes only from Jesus, which allows his followers to see him as the greater Elijah, for whom they have waited, and as the incarnate paradigm of a restored people of God.

4   Conclusion: the Story Continues

The use of the Elijah image in the New Testament Gospels is multifaceted and complex, eluding neat correlations in the same way that we have observed in earlier texts. All four Gospels, in various ways, use the Elijah image in relation to both John and Jesus, to express what they are and what they are not via comparison, contrast, and elevation. John is Elijah; so is Jesus. John is the Malachian messenger, the voice in the wilderness, and the patriarchal miracle child; Jesus is the prophet like Moses, the suffering Isaian servant, and the one who is greater than Elijah and the patriarchs. He is portrayed as the sum of Israelite tradition, and represents the presence and work of Yhwh himself. As such, to the Gospel writers, Jesus initiates the awaited, all-encompassing restoration that we have seen envisioned by earlier Second Temple texts.

The rest of the New Testament writings depict the beginnings of an expanding community which purports to carry on Jesus' mission. We have already seen in the ascension narrative of Acts 1 that Jesus' disciples are portrayed in the role of Elisha, as they watch their master be taken to heaven and are empowered to carry on his work. This image is carried through the book of Acts, in which the followers of Jesus are repeatedly placed in Elijah- and Elisha-like roles.[149] Peter takes over John the Baptist's call to a baptism of repentance, and verifies Jesus' identity as the prophet like Moses and the servant of Yhwh (Acts 3:18–26; cf. 2:38). He performs miracles of healing (3:1–10) and even raises the dead (9:36–43). Philip is miraculously translated from one place to another (8:39).[150] Stephen's stoning at the testimony of false witnesses (6:10ff; 7:59–60) evokes the indictment of Naboth (1 Kgs 21:8–14) as well as the crucifixion of Jesus himself (Matt 26:59–64; Luke 23:34, 46). Herod Agrippa's execution of James and imprisonment of Peter (Acts 12:1–19) follows the lines of the similar persecution of John the Baptist at the hands of Herod Antipas (Mark 6:14–29), though Peter, at least initially, escapes John's fate. Paul has a supernatural encounter (Acts 9:1–9), heals the sick and demon-possessed (Acts 14:8–10; 19:11–17), and raises a young man from the dead (20:7–12). He trains his own disciples (15:40; 16:1–5) and focuses his ministry outside of Israel (e.g. 16:6–10).[151] As Otten has noted, "As Luke develops the Elijah motif in connection with Peter, Paul, and the other pillars of the church, he reveals the usefulness of the remnant theme for understanding the complexities of the people of God."[152] I would argue that the presence of the Elijah image in these passages is not specifically concerned with developing a certain theme, but rather that it highlights both the initial intentionality and the continued later reception of the literary presentation of Elijah as an image of Yhwh's righteous community.

Through the Acts narrative, Jesus' fulfilment of the prophetic role of establishing a righteous community is lived out through the disciples, even as they take over the Elijah role that Jesus assumed in the Gospels. A similar Elijah-like characterisation of the early communities of Jesus-followers is further displayed in several New Testament epistles, where it is used less in narrative characterisation and more in the development of an early Christian theology of God's people. Several authors adopt the Elijah image for the purpose of their own unique literary strategies, as we will now see. Fundamentally, their use of this image continues to reflect a narrative in which the people of God carry out the role of Elijah, both in their identity as the righteous remnant and in their eschatological preparation for the second coming of Jesus Christ.

149 Beers even argues for the disciples' continuation of Jesus' Isaian servant role in the narrative of Luke-Acts (*Followers*, e.g. 118–26).
150 For a detailed discussion of Elijah-Elisha analogies in this narrative, see F. Scott Spencer, *The Portrait of Philip in Acts*, JSNTSup 67 (Sheffield: Sheffield Academic, 1992), 135–41.
151 For a recognition of many of these connections to the Elijah narrative, see Josef Zmijewski, *Die Apostelgeschichte* (Regensburg: Friedrich Pustet, 1994), 177, 334, 340, 366, 401, 453, 727. See also Otten, *I Alone*, 143–59.
152 Otten, *I Alone*, 139.

CHAPTER 6

Elijah and the Believers in the Epistles

1   Introduction

> ³² And what more do I say? For the time would fail me a recounting
> of Gideon, Barak, Samson, Jephthah, David and also Samuel and the
> prophets,
> ³³ who through faith conquered kingdoms, worked righteousness,
> obtained promises, stopped the mouths of lions,
> ³⁴ extinguished the power of fire, escaped the mouths of the sword, were
> strengthened out of weakness, became mighty in war, toppled foreign
> armies.
> ³⁵ Women received back their dead by resurrection. But others, being
> tortured, did not accept release, in order that they might obtain a better
> resurrection.
> ³⁶ And others bore suffering by mocking and floggings, and even chains
> and imprisonment.
> ³⁷ They were stoned, sawn apart, killed with the slaughter of the sword.
> They went about in skins of sheep and goats, poor, oppressed, mistreated –
> ³⁸ of whom the world was not worthy – wandering in deserts and moun-
> tains and caves and the holes of the earth.
> ³⁹ And all these, being approved through faith, did not receive the
> promise.
> ⁴⁰ God for our sakes was providing something better, in order that, apart
> from us, none would be made perfect. (Heb 11:32–40)

This vivid conclusion to the so-called "Hall of Faith" of Heb 11 takes up the prophetic pattern of the Hebrew Bible as the background for the early Christian
story. The followers of Jesus are given a critical role in the narrative of God's
people, holding, in the message proclaimed by Jesus and the apostles, the hope
of vindication for all those who witnessed and suffered before them. They
stand in the line of judges, kings, and prophets; of those who supernaturally
controlled fire, were strengthened in weakness, and brought grieving women
back their dead; those who wore animal skins, wandered in deserts, mountains, and caves, and waited for the restoration that Yhwh had promised. Elijah
may not be present in this retelling by name, but it is difficult to imagine that
the outline of his character does not form part of the background to these

descriptions.[1] The greater righteous community of the past, portrayed in the pattern of Elijah and others, now both forms the pattern for, and is dependent on, the faith of the contemporary generation.

Evidence that the Elijah pattern continued to be associated with God's people by the early Christian communities is seen in multiple contexts within the New Testament epistles. He is mentioned by name in Rom 11 and James 5, but significant arguments have been made that the apostle Paul models his own self-portrayal after Elijah in several of his writings.[2] Such a portrayal would be consistent with Paul's miraculous encounters as described in Acts, as well as with a well-demonstrated Hellenistic and Roman literary practice in which writers utilised stories and figures of the past to make rhetorical points.[3] The mention of Elijah in James has been thoroughly under-explored by most commentators, but a close examination reveals that the prophet's inclusion in this book is actually vital to the coherence of its overall argument.

In this chapter I will show that the Elijah image in the New Testament epistles continues to be fundamentally tied to the preservation and restoration of a righteous community. We will see that Paul's connection of Elijah with the remnant in Rom 11 is tied to his own identification with both the prophet and the remnant, and that this identification is underscored by additional Elijanic

---

1 Hebrews 11:35 recalls the widow and her resurrected son of 1 Kgs 17:17–24 (see David M. Moffitt, *Atonement and the Logic of Resurrection in the Epistle to the Hebrews*, NovTSup 141 [Leiden: Brill, 2011], 186), 11:37 uses δέρμα in parallel to the δερμάτινος of Elijah's clothing in LXX 2 Kgs 1:8, and Heb 11:38b utilises the same terms for "desert" (ἔρημος), "mountain" (ὄρος), and "cave" (σπήλαιον) as LXX 1 Kgs 19:4, 8, and 9. See also Eisenbaum, *Jewish Heroes*, 176; Öhler, *Elia*, 260–62; Otten, *I Alone*, 65–66; Valve, "Elijah, Elisha," 65–82.

2 See e.g. Ábel, "Elijah," 266–95; Leithart, *1 & 2 Kings*, 143–44; Martos, "Prophet and Remnant," 258; Chris S. Stevens, "Paul, the Expected Eschatological Phinehas-Elijah Prophet Law-Giver," in *Paul and Gnosis*, Pauline Studies, vol. 9, ed. Stanley E. Porter and David I. Yoon (Leiden: Brill, 2016), 80–104; Vena, "Paul's Understanding," 38. Contra Karl Olav Sandnes (*Paul – One of the Prophets?* WUNT II/43 [Tübingen: Mohr Siebeck, 1991], 156), who argues that "Paul compares himself, not with Elijah ... but with a well-known pattern of prophetic history of OT and Judaism."

3 For a general investigation of exemplarity in the Roman period, see Matthew B. Roller, *Models from the Past in Roman Culture: A World of Exempla* (Cambridge: Cambridge University Press, 2018). For the use of this convention with respect to the figure of Abraham, see Annette Yoshiko Reed, "The Construction and Subversion of Patriarchal Perfection: Abraham and Exemplarity in Philo, Josephus, and the *Testament of Abraham*," *JSJ* 40 (2009): 185–212. For the use of exemplarity as a potential key to both the dating and authorship of James, see Kelsie G. Rodenbiker, "Pseudonymity, Exemplarity, and the Dating of James," in *Die Datierung neutestamentlicher Pseudepigraphen: Herausforderungen und neuere Lösungsansätze*, WUNT 470, ed. Wolfgang Grünstäudl and Karl Matthias Schmidt (Tübingen: Mohr Siebeck, 2021), 219–43. Rodenbiker suggests that Paul's use of scriptural figures generally better fits the category of typology (222), which is certainly true in some cases. I would argue, however, that Paul also utilises Elijah as an exemplary figure in the allusion I discuss below.

imagery in Galatians and 2 Corinthians. We will observe the structural centrality of the Elijah reference in the book of James, concluding that the description "Elijah was a man like-natured to us" endows an Elijah-like eschatological
identity and responsibility on the people of God who receive it.

2   Pauline Literature

2.1   *Romans 11*

The first explicit mention of Elijah in epistolary literature appears in the larger
context of Rom 9–11, in which Paul argues for the salvation of a remnant of
Israel. He refers explicitly to 1 Kgs 19:10, 14 in Rom 11:1–5:

> [1] Therefore I say, has not God rejected his people? Absolutely not! For
> I also am an Israelite, out of the seed of Abraham, of the tribe of Benjamin.
> [2] God has not rejected his people whom he foreknew. Or do you not know
> what the scripture says in Elijah, how he intercedes to God against Israel:
> [3] "Lord, they have killed your prophets, they have torn down your altars,
> and I alone am left, and they seek my life."
> [4] But what does the divine response say to him? "I have kept for myself
> seven thousand men, those who did not bow a knee to Baal."
> [5] Therefore in the same way also in the present time a remnant exists
> according to gracious election.

Two questions generally arise for commentators surrounding this analogy.
First, Paul's quotation of 1 Kgs 19 does not draw directly from any extant textual witness.[4] None of the relatively minor grammatical shifts reflected in the
quotation pose any significant problem, however,[5] and at least one may well be

---

4   Paul abridges Elijah's complaint, reverses the order of the destroyed altars and killed proph-
    ets, and leaves out the forsaken covenant altogether (Rom 11:3; cf. LXX 1 Kgs 19:10, 14). His
    addition of "for myself" (ἐμαυτῷ) is unique, though it is attested by the Vulgate of 1 Kgs 19:18.
    His reference to Baal is preceded by a feminine article, which appears neither in the Hebrew
    nor Greek versions of 1 Kgs 19. See Ernst Käsemann, *An die Römer*, 4th ed., HNT 8a (Tübingen:
    Mohr Siebeck, 1980), 290; Katja Kujanpää, *The Rhetorical Functions of Scriptural Quotations
    in Romans: Paul's Argumentation by Quotations*, NovTSup 172 (Leiden: Brill, 2019), 209–26;
    Christopher D. Stanley, *Paul and the Language of Scripture: Citation Technique in the Pauline
    Epistles and Contemporary Literature*, SNTSMS 69 (Cambridge: Cambridge University Press,
    1992), 147–58.
5   The addition of ἐμαυτῷ clarifies what is already implicit in both Kings and Romans: that the
    remnant is kept by and belongs to Yhwh. The feminine article linked with Baal likely refers
    to the Jewish reading convention of substituting the names of foreign deities with a term
    for "shame," which is feminine in both Hebrew and Greek (בֹשֶׁת; αἰσχύνη). See F.F. Bruce,

intentional. Romans 11:4 shifts the future sense of והשארתי in 1 Kgs 19:18 to the past sense of the aorist κατέλιπον.[6] Where to the viewpoint of the Elijah cycle the preservation of the remnant is still in the future, to Paul's perspective, this remnant has been secured.

A more interesting question is raised by Paul's description of Elijah's intercession as "against Israel" (κατὰ τοῦ Ἰσραήλ – Rom 11:2). This formulation is consistent with the prophet's indictment of Israel on Horeb, and confirms Paul's interpretation of him, along the lines of Blum's argument, as an "Unheilsprophet."[7] Indeed, in Paul's retelling of 1 Kgs 19, Yhwh's promise of a remnant comes *in spite of* Elijah's prayer (Rom 11:2). Numerous scholars have suggested that Paul characterises himself as an Elijah-like prophet in this text,[8] but this analogy is secondary, at least at first, to Paul's identification with the remnant.[9] The fact that God has not rejected his people is demonstrated by Paul's own status as an Israelite who has received salvation:

11:1	11:2–4
Has not God rejected his people? Absolutely not! [μὴ ἀπώσατο ὁ θεὸς τὸν λαὸν αὐτοῦ; μὴ γένοιτο] For I also am an Israelite, out of the seed of Abraham, of the tribe of Benjamin.	God has not rejected his people [οὐκ ἀπώσατο ὁ θεὸς τὸν λαὸν αὐτοῦ], whom he foreknew. Or do you not know what the scripture says in Elijah, how he intercedes to God against Israel: 'Lord, they have killed your prophets, they have torn down your altars, and I alone am left, and they seek my life.' But what does the divine response say to him? 'I have kept for myself seven thousand men, those who did not bow a knee to Baal.'

11:5 – "Therefore in the same way also in the present time a remnant exists according to gracious election."

The Letter of Paul to the Romans, TNTC 6 (Leicester: Inter-Varsity Press, 1985), 210; Joseph A. Fitzmyer, *Romans*, AYB 33 (New Haven: Yale University Press, 2008), 604–605.

6 Cf. the second-person future καταλείψεις of some LXX mss, which McKenzie argues entered the text "under the influence of v. 16" (*Kings*, 143).

7 Blum, "Der Prophet," 288.

8 See e.g. Käsemann, *Römer*, 291; Ulrich B. Müller, *Prophetie und Predigt im Neuen Testament*, SNT 10 (Gütersloh: Mohn, 1975), 110.

9 See Käsemann, *Römer*, 291; Lappenga, *Ζῆλος*, 199; Martos, "Prophet and Remnant," 255; Sandnes, *Paul*, 16 n. 6.

Paul sees himself as the representative of a remnant preserved from judgement. His status as "also an Israelite" (11:1) includes him in the "Israel" against which Elijah intercedes (11:2). He further confirms this analogy by drawing a direct parallel between Elijah's context and his own (11:5). However, Paul's larger argument in the book overall suggests that he does not confine the Elijah analogy to a single direction.[10] Earlier in Romans, Paul takes on something of the role of a judgement prophet himself, in the harsh rebukes he levels against an apostate Israel (e.g. Rom 2:17–29). He applies an image of Elijah-like zeal to his Jewish contemporaries, but laments that it is "zeal for God [ζῆλον θεοῦ] but not according to knowledge" (10:2).[11] At the same time, he speaks of his own fervent intercession that precisely those people would be saved (10:1).

Paul's use of prophetic and Elijah imagery is consistent with the flexibility in patterning we have observed throughout the Elijah texts to this point. The prophet's characteristic zeal is adopted and practised by Paul's contemporaries, who do not realise that Elijah's prophetic voice is the very voice that indicts them (Rom 11:2). Paul's voice, on the other hand, takes up the role of prophetic intercession that Elijah's could not carry (10:2), recognising that Yhwh's remnant is preserved from within a larger group deserving of judgement. Paul identifies himself with both the prophetic voice and the remnant, taking on and extending the Elijah pattern even as he furthers the early Christian shift in this pattern from a representation of a purely Israelite remnant community to a community of the followers of Jesus. Like Elijah, Paul's "existence itself becomes a sign for the fact that God has not forsaken his people."[12]

2.2   *Galatians 1*

Paul's flexible use of the Elijah pattern in Romans is supported by allusions that can be observed in several additional letters. Several scholars have argued for his self-characterisation as an Elijah figure in Gal 1, first evidenced in his own pre-Christian zeal (περισσοτέρως ζηλωτής – 1:14) that is similar to that of

---

10   So Steck: "Paulus steht als Israelit selbst dafür, daß Israel nicht verstoßen ist (11 1–2a), steht aber als Apostel angesichts der Verschlossenheit Israels gegenüber dem Evangelium an der Seite Elias und wird wie dieser auf den Rest hingewiesen" (*Israel*, 278 n. 2). See similarly Lappenga, *Ζῆλος*, 198. Öhler has suggested that the Elijah image here is paralleled, not to Paul, but to Paul's hypothetical interlocutors who ask if God has forsaken his people (*Elia*, 255).

11   For a reference to Elijah in comments on Rom 10:2, see e.g. Käsemann, *Römer*, 270. Fitzmyer states that "In postexilic and late pre-Christian Judaism *zēlos*, 'zeal,' for God, his law, or his Temple was considered the characteristic of the faithful Jew" (*Romans*, 582–83), and cites the references to both Phinehas and Elijah in 1 Macc 2 (583).

12   Martos, "Prophet and Remnant," 260.

his contemporaries in Rom 10:2.[13] Paul describes his encounter with Jesus in terms of a prophetic call (Gal 1:15),[14] before relating a journey away from Jerusalem, in which "I went away into Arabia, and returned again to Damascus" (1:17).[15] N.T. Wright has offered an interpretation of this enigmatic account that draws on the only other mention of Arabia in the New Testament; significantly, also in Galatians.[16] In Gal 4:25, Paul names Arabia as the site of Mount Sinai. Wright, who has since been followed by numerous others, suggests that Paul's journey to Arabia was one of travelling to Sinai in the footsteps of Elijah.[17] In 1 Kgs 19, following a supernatural experience on Carmel, Elijah travels to Horeb, lamenting that his zeal has accomplished nothing. In Gal 1, Paul describes his former zeal (1:14), a supernatural encounter (1:15), and a journey to a location which he himself associates with Horeb/Sinai (4:25). Further, after Arabia, he "again returned [ὑπέστρεψα] to Damascus" (1:17), just as Elijah, after his journey to Horeb, is instructed to "Go, return [LXX ἀνάστρεφε] on your

---

13   See Lappenga, Ζῆλος, 143: "My argument here is that in Gal 1:14, Paul's primary model is Elijah." Even if Paul's self-description here were to function as a reference to his association with the zealot tradition, as suggested by Martin Hengel (*Die Zeloten: Untersuchungen zur jüdischen Freiheitsbewegung in der Zeit von Herodes I. bis 70 n. Chr.*, 3rd ed., ed. Roland Deines and Claus-Jürgen Thornton, WUNT 283 [Tübingen: Mohr Siebeck, 2011], 182), this tradition can hardly be extracted from its roots in the figure and campaign of the conflated Phinehas-Elijah, as Hengel also recognises (see 165–71).

14   So also e.g. James D.G. Dunn, *The Epistle to the Galatians*, BNTC 9 (Peabody: Hendrickson, 1993), 63; Ronald Y.K. Fung, *The Epistle to the Galatians*, NICNT (Grand Rapids: Eerdmans, 1988), 63; Scott J. Hafemann, *Paul, Moses, and the History of Israel*, WUNT 81 (Tübingen: Mohr Siebeck, 1995), 100–106; Müller, *Prophetie und Predigt*, 110; Sandnes, *Paul*, 48–70; de la Serna, "Pablo," 166–70; Krister Stendahl, *Paul Among Jews and Gentiles* (Philadelphia: Fortress, 1976), 7–12. For an opposing perspective, see Martinus C. de Boer, *Galatians*, NTL (Louisville: Westminster John Knox, 2011), 91; Beverly Gaventa, *From Darkness to Light* (Philadelphia: Fortress, 1986), 27–28.

15   This journey is not mentioned in Acts, which has led to significant speculation regarding its timeframe and purpose. Most scholars interpret it as one of evangelism, likely to the kingdom of the Nabateans (see e.g. de Boer, *Galatians*, 96; F.F. Bruce, *The Epistle of Paul to the Galatians*, NIGTC 9 [Exeter: Paternoster, 1982], 95–96; Dunn, *Galatians*, 70; Fung, *Galatians*, 69).

16   Wright, "Arabia," 686.

17   Wright, "Arabia," 686. See further Lappenga, Ζῆλος, 144–45; Leithart, *1 & 2 Kings*, 143–44; de la Serna, "Pablo," 178–79; Stevens, "Paul," 87–88; Vena, "Paul's Understanding," 37–39. Stevens notes that "Even if this position has not adopted the comparison of all three prophets, Moses, Elijah, and Paul, fleeing for their lives into the wilderness is quite significant" ("Paul," 87 n. 38). Bruce mentions this connection in passing, but prefers the interpretation of Pauline evangelism in the Nabatean kingdom (*Galatians*, 96). Jacob M. Myers and Edwin D. Freed note the similarity to the stories of Moses and Elijah, but do not identify Arabia with Sinai ("Is Paul Also Among the Prophets?" *Int* 20 [1966], 47).

way to the wilderness of Damascus" (1 Kgs 19:15).[18] If these points in Paul's initial post-conversion journey are taken as a replication of the Elijah narrative, as I believe they may well be, then the apostle's identification with Elijah moves beyond literary references to lived identification with an Elijah-like role.

2.3   *2 Corinthians 12*

A third Pauline passage which may be named here recalls a motif we have already observed in the Gospel of John. Paul's cryptic description of his ascent to the third heaven in 2 Cor 12 reveals significant lexical correspondences with Gal 1, in which I have just argued that Paul claims an Elijanic identification:

Galatians 1:6–2:10	2 Corinthians 11:1–12:21
Defends his message against ἕτερον εὐαγγέλιον (1:6) and ψευδαδέλφους (2:4)	Defends his message against εὐαγγέλιον ἕτερον (11:4; cf. 11:13); cites danger at the hands of ψευδαδέλφους (11:26)
Claims that even an ἄγγελος ἐξ οὐρανοῦ can preach a false gospel (1:8)	Claims that Satan appears in disguise as ἄγγελον φωτός (11:14)[19]
Former zeal: "being more extremely zealous [περισσοτέρως ζηλωτής] for my ancestral traditions" (1:14)	Current zeal: "For I am jealous for you with a godly jealousy [ζηλῶ γὰρ ὑμᾶς θεοῦ ζήλῳ]" (11:2)[20]
Appeals to Hebrew pedigree (1:14)	Appeals to Hebrew pedigree (11:22)
Returned to Damascus (1:17)	Persecution in Damascus (11:32)[21]
Received the gospel through a "revelation [ἀποκάλυψις] of Jesus Christ" (1:12; cf. 1:16)	Describes "revelations [ἀποκαλύψεις] of the Lord" (12:1)[22]

---

18   De la Serna, "Pablo," 179; Wright, "Arabia," 686–87.

19   Mark Seifrid mentions in passing the connection to Gal 1:8, but only to note the heightened intensity of the charge in 2 Cor 11:14 (*The Second Letter to the Corinthians*, PNTC [Grand Rapids: Eerdmans, 2014], 418–19).

20   Lappenga sees a link to both Elijah and Phinehas in Paul's use of zeal in this verse (*Zῆλος*, 168–73).

21   Gaventa notes this connection via the appearance of Damascus in both accounts (*From Darkness*, 37).

22   De Boer argues for a contrast in the senses of ἀποκάλυψις in these passages, where Galatians refers to the singular revelation of Christ that converted Paul and gave him the gospel message, while 2 Corinthians is intended to downplay the significance of ecstatic experience (*Galatians*, 80–81). However, given the similarities between the two passages, even such a rhetorical contrast would not negate the parallel.

Swears before God to his truthful-ness: ἰδοὺ ἐνώπιον τοῦ θεοῦ ὅτι οὐ ψεύδομαι (1:20)	Swears before God to his truthful-ness: ὁ θεὸς ... οἶδεν ... ὅτι οὐ ψεύδομαι (11:31)
After an interval of fourteen years I went up again to Jerusalem ... It was because of a revelation [ἀποκάλυψις] that I went up (2:1–2)[23]	Experience took place fourteen years prior (12:2)

Both passages revolve around Paul's legitimisation of his ministry, and their lexical and thematic overlap is such that New Testament scholars have repeatedly speculated about whether the two revelations described refer to the same event. Most have determined that they do not, noting the difficulty of any historical correlation of the two within the timeline of Acts.[24] This point is well taken. At the same time, the fact that these are the only two Pauline passages that reference a timespan of fourteen years argues that some sort of correspondence between them should be seriously considered. I suggest that it may be possible to interpret this correspondence as an intentional literary characterisation device, rather than as an invitation to harmonise historical timelines. It is difficult to conceive of Paul producing two such overtly similar *literary* descriptions, supported by a multitude of parallels, without a common event, or at least a common paradigmatic motif, underlying them both. It would further not be unreasonable for Paul to have considered his conversion and his Sinai journey together to encompass a prophetic call, a theophany, and a mountaintop experience such as those of Moses and Elijah. The literary correlation of a heavenly ascent experience with these motifs would certainly fit the larger Mosaic and Elijanic framework through which Paul portrays himself. Whether or not the experience described in 1 Cor 12 is to be historically associated with this larger cluster of occurrences, then, I would argue that he intentionally chooses to speak of them in parallel terms.

---

23 It is notable that Elijah also departs to fulfil a mission as a result of his supernatural revelation in 1 Kgs 19.

24 See e.g. William Baird, "Visions, Revelation, and Ministry: Reflections on 2 Cor 12:1–5 and Gal 1:11–17," *JBL* 104 (1985), 652; Paul Barnett, *The Second Epistle to the Corinthians*, NICNT (Grand Rapids: Eerdmans, 1997), 561; Christian Wolff, *Der zweite Brief des Paulus an die Korinther*, 2nd ed. (Berlin: Evangelische Verlagsanstalt, 2011), 240. Scholars have tried to harmonise Paul's Damascus road experience and his heavenly ascent in various ways, often attempting to locate them within the chronology of Acts (see e.g. Barnett, *Second Corinthians*, 553–55). A few have argued for a correlation of the events in the two accounts, specifically Charles Buck and Greer Taylor (*Saint Paul: A Study of the Development of His Thought* [New York: Charles Scribner's Sons, 1969], 219–26) and John Knox ("'Fourteen Years Later': A Note on the Pauline Chronology," *JR* 16 [1936], 345–49). Knox later retracts his correlation of the two events in idem, *Chapters in a Life of Paul*, rev. ed. (Macon: Mercer University Press, 1987), 34 n. 1.

Both de la Serna and Vena have also observed a thematic link between 2 Cor 12 and the Elijah cycle, specifically to Elijah's final ascent to heaven in 2 Kgs 2.[25] Vena even suggests, similar to my observation regarding the disciples at the end of the Fourth Gospel, that Paul, as a follower of Jesus, might have expected to avoid death and "be transposed alive at the *parousia*."[26] This conclusion does not entirely follow, since Paul recounts a heavenly ascent already in the past.[27] The only other pericope in the Kings cycle which could provide a parallel would be Elijah's ascent onto Horeb in 1 Kgs 19 which, as per Wright, may already be reflected in Paul's journey in Gal 1.[28] Certain literary parallels do suggest that Paul may have 1 Kgs 19 in mind in his description of his heavenly experience and its surrounding context:

1 Kings 19	2 Corinthians 11–12
"I have been very zealous [LXX ζηλῶν ἐζήλωκα] for Yhwh, God of hosts" (19:10, 14)	"For I am jealous for you with a godly jealousy [ζηλῶ γὰρ ὑμᾶς θεοῦ ζήλῳ]" (11:2)
Preceded by royal persecution (19:1–2)	Description of revelation preceded by description of royal persecution (11:32)
"Return ... to Damascus" (19:15)	Persecution in Damascus (11:32)
Witnesses Yhwh passing by (19:11)	Describes "revelations [ἀποκάλυψις] of the Lord" (12:1)
"What are you doing here, Elijah?" (19:9)	"whether in the body I do not know, or out of the body I do not know, God knows" (12:2)
"What are you doing here, Elijah?" (19:13 – verbatim repetition of 19:9)	"whether in the body or apart from the body I do not know, God knows" (12:3 – near verbatim repetition of 12:2)
"after the fire a קול דממה דקה" (19:12)	"heard inexpressible words, which a man is not permitted to speak" (12:4)

---

25   De la Serna, "Pablo," 176–77; Vena, "Paul's Understanding," 38.

26   Vena, "Paul's Understanding," 53, also 38.

27   Wolff has further pointed out that a physical ascension is likely not meant in Paul's case, since Jesus' physical ascent is explicitly said to have been witnessed, whereas Paul's was not (*Zweite Korinther*, 240). Elijah's final ascent is also physically witnessed by Elisha (2 Kgs 2:9–12). If Paul indeed expected to be "taken up" at the *parousia*, as 1 Cor 15:51–53 indicates, such an ascension at the end of earthly life would provide a stronger parallel with 2 Kgs 2 than the experience described in 2 Cor 12.

28   Unlike 2 Kgs 2, Elijah's experience in 1 Kgs 19 was private and unwitnessed, providing a better analogy for Paul's experience in 2 Cor 12.

Admittedly, to argue that Paul might have had a supernatural encounter at Sinai in addition to that on the Damascus road would be pure speculation. However, the presence of a literary allusion, again, would not only clarify some of the unique wording and repetition in the Corinthian passage,[29] but would also support Paul's larger imitation of Elijah, both in his ascent to heaven and his journey to Arabia, as well as in his prophetic persona overall.[30]

Some scholars have protested that the concept of Paul as an Elijah figure in general ignores the identification of John the Baptist as Elijah in the Gospels, or have attempted to harmonise the timelines so that a Pauline Elijah tradition emerges as earlier than the Baptist-Elijah tradition.[31] On the contrary, we have seen in multiple Gospel accounts that the Elijah image is intended to be assumed by Jesus' disciples, and that the application of this image by multiple writers to multiple figures is entirely unproblematic in early Jewish and Christian writings. Even if Paul had known some of the Gospel traditions, his self-portrayal as a prophet like Elijah, and simultaneously as the preserved remnant in Romans, would remain entirely true both to their purpose and intent and to the broader understanding and use of the Elijah figure.

Further, it is possible that Paul also conceived of himself as something of an eschatological forerunner.[32] Far from denying the significance of John the Baptist as the Elijah awaited by Malachi's epilogue, Paul believes that another day of Yhwh is still coming.[33] In 1 Cor 3, he describes a coming day of judgement that is distinctly reminiscent of Mal 3:[34]

---

29   For example, an intentional allusion to 1 Kgs 19 could render the seemingly redundant repetition of Paul's "in or out of the body" statement a stylistic homage to the Kings narrative. An allusion to 1 Kgs 19:12 in 2 Cor 12:4 would confirm further that Paul, at least, interpreted the קול דממה דקה of Elijah's Horeb to be a divine voice, and not the absence of sound, and that he associated the "inexpressible words" he heard with such a divine voice.

30   De la Serna additionally points out the reference in 2 Cor 12:12 to the "signs and wonders" (dat. σημείοις καὶ τέρασιν) evident in Paul's ministry, a locution used in the LXX primarily of the Exodus (see e.g. Deut 34:11!). He draws on this apparent allusion to support a case for Paul as a prophet like Moses and, ultimately, a prophet like Elijah ("Pablo," 169–70). See also Luke Timothy Johnson, who connects this locution specifically to the expectation of a prophet like Moses (*Prophetic Jesus, Prophetic Church: The Challenge of Luke-Acts to Contemporary Christians* [Grand Rapids: Eerdmans, 2011], 33).

31   So Vena, "Paul's Understanding," 49–52. See also Justin Taylor, "The Coming of Elijah, Mt 7,10–13 and Mark 9,11–13: The Development of the Texts," *RB* 98 (1991), 118–19.

32   This is the primary thesis argued by de la Serna, "Pablo."

33   See de la Serna, "Pablo," 170–76.

34   Though Vena's thesis argues that Paul's self-characterisation as Elijah is based in Mal 3, the connection to 1 Cor 3 is not made in his article.

¹² Now if any man builds on the foundation gold, silver, precious stones, wood, hay, straw,

¹³ each man's work will become evident; for the day will show it because it is revealed with fire, and the fire itself will test the quality of each man's work.

¹⁴ If any man's work which he has built on it remains, he will receive a reward.

¹⁵ If any man's work is burned up, he will suffer loss; but he himself will be saved, yet so as through fire. (1 Cor 3:12–15)

² But who can endure the day of his coming, and who can stand in his appearing? For he is like a smelter's fire and like washer's lye,

³ᵃ and he will sit as a smelter and purifier of silver, and he will purify the sons of Levi and refine them like gold and like silver ...

¹⁹ For behold, the day is coming, burning like an oven, and all the insolent and all the doers of evil will be stubble. And the coming day will devour them, says Yhwh of hosts, which will not leave to them root or branch. (Mal 3:2–3a, 19)

If a day of Yhwh like the one predicted by Malachi is still to come, then that future day would logically require its own forerunner.[35] Paul's use of Elijah in Romans confirms his conviction that the gospel he preaches will ultimately determine the preservation of the new remnant. Thus, it is reasonable to conclude that Paul considers himself the Elijah of Israel's eschatological restoration, with the implication that this restoration is imminent because the forerunner is already present.[36] His readers must ensure that they are part of the remnant which will be saved on the new day of Yhwh, because Elijah is here and the day is coming.

---

35   Vena agrees that Paul considered himself to be the forerunner of the end-time appearance of God, and that other early Christians likely viewed him this way as well. He argues, however, that it was only when Paul died without the appearance of the *parousia* that the status of forerunner was transferred by the communities to John the Baptist, in order to explain the expected day of Yhwh as having already come and gone in the person of Jesus ("Paul's Understanding," 51–52).

36   "We suggest then that Paul regarded his ministry as the fulfilment of the prophecies of Joel, Isaiah, and especially Malachi concerning the opportunity for repentance offered by God, in the last days, through the preaching of an eschatological prophet. He believed that he was that prophet playing out the role of the Elijah of Malachi" (Vena, "Paul's Understanding," 53–54). "Paulus hat ... in sich den Elia der Endzeit erblickt" (Käsemann, *Römer*, 291).

3   James

3.1   *Introduction*

The expectation of a still-future eschatological day for which the Christian communities must prepare themselves proves critical to the understanding of Elijah's appearance in the letter of James. At first glance, the logic of this passage in its broader context is anything but clear. The prophet known from the Hebrew Bible as one of fire, miracles, and eschatological restoration is suddenly presented as an everyday model for effective prayer, via the example of a prayer that does not even appear in the Kings cycle it seems to reference:

> ¹⁷ Elijah was a man like-natured to us, and he prayed earnestly that it would not rain, and it did not rain upon the earth for three years and six months.
> ¹⁸ And again he prayed, and the heaven gave rain and the earth sprouted its fruit. (James 5:17–18)

Contrary to James's retelling, Elijah in Kings does not pray for either drought or rain. He simply announces both (1 Kgs 17:1; 18:1, 41). Many scholars appeal to the prophet's bent posture awaiting rain on Carmel as a position of prayer (1 Kgs 18:42), but such a cryptic note is hardly clear enough to justify prayer as the primary lesson to be learned from Elijah's character.[37] The larger landscape of early Jewish and Christian texts does attest to a tradition in which Elijah prays for the return of rain, as seen in the secondary addition to *LivProph* 21. This tradition is further described in 4 Ezra 7:106–11.[38] The relationship of the letter of James to the tradition attested in these texts, of course, depends fundamentally on the dating of James, regarding which no consensus has been

---

37   See e.g. Darlack, "Pray for Reign," 3–4 n. 11; Luke Timothy Johnson, *The Letter of James*, AB 37A (New Haven: Yale University Press, 1974), 337.

38   The tradition related in 4 Ezra 7 bears numerous similarities to the book of James in its descriptions of eschatological reward and judgement, including the question of the effectiveness of righteous intercession in an eschatological context (e.g. 7:102–103). In defence of an affirmative answer are produced examples of righteous intercessors including Elijah, who prayed "for those who received the rain, and for the one who was dead, that he might live" (7:109; translation by Metzger, "Fourth Ezra," 541). James's citing of three years and six months of drought (5:17; in contrast to the return of rain "in the third year" in 1 Kgs 18:1) may correspond to eschatological sets of sevens like the one used in 4 Ezra 7:90–101 (cf. Dan 7:25; 12:7; Rev 11–13). See for discussion Darlack, "Pray for Reign," 2–3; Sophie Laws, *The Epistle of James*, BNTC (Peabody: Hendrickson, 1980), 235–37; Rainer Metzner, *Der Brief des Jakobus*, THKNT 14 (Leipzig: Evangelische Verlagsanstalt, 2017), 310; Pavelčík, "Eliáš," 266, 271–72.

reached.[39] On the one hand, the author of James may have taken his conclusion that Elijah prays for rain from a larger tradition based in an exegetical interpretation of 1 Kgs 18. On the other hand, the existence and accessibility of such a tradition prior to James is not certain. If it did exist, James endows this tradition with significantly more theological weight than it carries in the other texts that witness to it. Further, he chooses a figure that hardly seems to be the strongest intercessory exemplar in the Hebrew Bible, as we have seen. Even within Elijah's own story, other unambiguous examples of prayer are present, including a case of specific intercession in the raising of the widow's son (1 Kgs 17:21; cf. 18:37).[40] This example would arguably have been much more suitable for James's call to interpersonal intercession in the context of sickness and healing (James 5:13–16). Yet it is passed over in favour of Elijah's prayer for rain.

Several recent studies have begun to answer the mystery of this passage by appealing to the book's underlying eschatological thrust, and to Elijah as a recognised eschatological figure.[41] The letter of James awaits the coming of the Lord (e.g. 5:7), and Elijah, according to Malachi and Ben Sira, is meant to appear before the coming of the Lord (Mal 3:23–24; Sir 48:10).[42] If it is indeed this eschatological role that prompts Elijah's appearance in James, then the book's connection of Elijah with community prayer, by implication, endows

39   Fourth Ezra is dated by Metzger to the late first century CE ("Fourth Ezra," 520). As such, potential interdependence between it and the letter of James could go in either direction. As I noted in Chapter 4, the conceptual relationship between *LivProph* 21 and James is also difficult to determine. A first-century form of *LivProph* could be contemporary even with an early date of James. If, however, the Christian origin posited by Satran is to be considered (*Biblical Prophets*, 118), its presentation of Elijah's prayer for rain would more likely presuppose the connection made by James. For opposing conclusions on the dating of James, see Scot McKnight, *The Letter of James*, NICNT (Grand Rapids: Eerdmans, 2011), 13–38 (dating to the 50s CE) and Rodenbiker, "Pseudonymity," 239–40 (dating to the second century CE).

40   See Richard Bauckham, "James, 1 and 2 Peter, Jude," in *It is Written: Scripture Citing Scripture*, ed. D.A. Carson and H.G.M. Williamson (Cambridge: Cambridge University Press, 1988), 306; Kovalishyn, "Prayer of Elijah," 1034; Laws, *James*, 235.

41   See Darlack, "Pray for Reign"; Metzner, *Jakobusbrief*; Pavelčík, "Eliáš," 266–306; also Todd C. Penner, *The Epistle of James and Eschatology*, JSNTSup 121 (Sheffield: Sheffield Academic, 1996). Eng posits that the overarching theme of James is "eschatological vindication," highlighting as key James 1:12 which reads "Blessed is the man who endures trial, for having been tested he will receive the crown of life, which [the Lord] promised to those who love him" (*Eschatological Approval*, 187–90). See the similar conclusion of Taylor and Guthrie, who highlight 1:12 as the central point of two overlapping inclusios within James 1, thus becoming "the central proposition of the first chapter" ("Structure," 684).

42   See Pavelčík, "Eliáš," 293, 295–99.

such prayer with eschatological significance as well. The lexical structure of the book's wider discourses on prayer indeed supports the thesis that prayer, to James, has eschatological impact. This same structure further reveals a fundamental literary and rhetorical interdependency between these prayer discourses, by which the Elijah example comes to be directly tied into the rhetoric of the book overall.

A closer analysis argues that Elijah's place in this larger argument is determined and demonstrated by means of a framework of repeated keywords.[43] These keywords link the book's distinct units of thought together and render them conceptually interdependent. The outcome is a unified rhetorical entity, perhaps best comparable to a musical composition featuring continuous lines of counterpoint. Independent "melodies" of argument converge and diverge in turn, intersecting at harmonious intervals and being sharpened by purposeful dissonance. While the result may appear disorganised at first glance, the interdependent relationship between lexical "notes" in this composition reveals an argument that is internally coherent and works toward a unified conclusion.[44]

The investigation that I will conduct in this section is somewhat longer than those I have presented of the Pauline epistles. Given the historical tendency to read James as a collection of largely unrelated communal instructions,[45] as well as the shortage of satisfactory explanations for Elijah's inclusion, I believe that a more detailed analysis of James 5 and its role in the larger book is called for. My aim is to demonstrate, by means of a lexical-structural analysis, what I consider to be Elijah's critical role in James's presentation of prayer as a means of preparation for the eschaton.

---

43   Eng has demonstrated that James uses strategies of "catchword association" similar to those observed in the Hebrew Bible, LXX texts, and Qumran fragments ("Semitic Catchwords," 245–67). He defines "catchword association" as "the adjacent placing of distinct sections of text, linked by a common lexeme" (246). I would argue that James's use of linked keywords extends to non-adjacent texts as well, and that it is meant to effect the reading of one section in light of another.

44   Taylor and Guthrie have described the overlap of what they argue to be "the body's great central section" (2:12–4:12) and the "final movement of the body" (4:6–5:6) in terms of "a powerful knitting effect" and an "interlocking and weaving pattern" ("Structure," 685). I agree with the markers they have identified to differentiate these sections, and I would further argue that this "interlocking and weaving pattern" extends beyond the overlap of these two macro sections to include the repetition and thematisation of other keywords both within and outside of them.

45   This view was classically held by Martin Dibelius and exerted considerable influence over the scholarship of his time. See Martin Dibelius, *Der Brief des Jakobus* (Göttingen: Vandenhoeck & Ruprecht, 1959), 2. See further the comprehensive discussion of recent scholarship in Mark E. Taylor, "Recent Scholarship on the Structure of James," *CBR* 3 (2004): 86–115.

3.2   *Lexical-Structural Analysis*

3.2.1   Sections under Study

In order to define Elijah's relationship to James's conception of prayer, it is necessary to consider the book's treatment of prayer overall. The root εὔχομαι occurs only in the immediate context of the Elijah illustration (James 5:13–18), but the theme of prayer is raised twice previously, presented in terms of "asking" (αἰτέω) in 1:5–8 and 4:1–3.[46] Both of these passages are located in larger, rhetorically distinct units, which nevertheless share a considerable number of repeated keywords. For the purposes of this study, I define these first two units as 1:2–27 and 3:13–4:12.[47] The third unit on prayer, in which Elijah appears (5:7–20), bears unmistakable lexical links to both earlier units. For ease of reference, I have numbered the sections 1–3, respectively. Table 1 represents a list of the lexemes shared by these three sections, with the shaded rows representing roots that occur nowhere else in the book.[48]

---

46   Pavelčík also comments on the αἰτέω sections and their relationship to the prayer of Elijah, noting that the various aspects of prayer described are interdependent ("Eliáš," 268).

47   Though they account for them somewhat differently than I have chosen to, Taylor and Guthrie note structural breaks at the same points ("Structure," 687). Johnson places the conclusion to the second section at 4:10 rather than 4:12, which is a defensible alternative division (*James*, 268–69; cf. Taylor and Guthrie, "Structure," 692). I have chosen to include 4:11–12 with the preceding section, rather than isolating it as its own transitional unit (cf. Taylor and Guthrie, "Structure," 692), because the larger section of 3:13–4:12 contains lexical combinations which also appear together elsewhere in the book. James 4:11–12 is marked by the use of "judgement" (κρίνω) and "law" (νόμος), which are defining terms in 2:1–13. James 2:1–13, in turn, contain the distinctive terms μοιχεύω and φονεύω, which are reprised only in 4:2–4. James 2:1–13 further concerns partiality (προσωπολημψία), which is found again in the description of earthly wisdom in 3:17. Thus, 3:13–4:12 as a unit reprises keywords from 2:1–13. Simultaneously, 3:13–4:12 is also linked to chs. 1 and 5. The term used for destruction (ἀπόλλυμι) in 4:12 is found elsewhere in James only in 1:11, which is part of the introduction to boasting that is reprised in 3:13–4:10. The image of salvation (σῴζω) introduced in 1:21 is reprised in 2:14, 4:12, and 5:15, 20. Thus, while 4:11–12 in itself does not contain significant commonality with the section immediately preceding it, the larger passage functions as a point of convergence for keywords from nearly every other section of the book.

48   Other scholars have noted the large-scale lexical and thematic inclusio formed by chs. 1 and 5 (see e.g. Pavelčík, "Eliáš," 271; Taylor and Guthrie, "Structure," 700–701). Taylor and Guthrie have argued for the organisation of James 1 on the basis of a tripartite structure (683–84). The division I put forward here sees a similar structure visible at the book level, in which 1:2–27 represents the introduction to the concerns of the book (specifically highlighting the critical role of prayer), 3:13–4:12 provides a mid-point summary, and 5:7–20 presents the concluding arguments.

TABLE 1   Shared lexemes

Keyword root	Section 1 1:2–27	Section 2 3:13–4:12	Section 3 5:7–20
ἀγαθός	1:17	3:17	
αἰτέω	1:5, 6	4:2, 3	
ἁμαρτάνω	1:15	4:8	5:15, 16, 20
βούλομαι	1:18	4:4	
γῆ		3:15	5:7, 12, 17, 18
γινώσκω	1:3		5:20
δίδωμι	1:5, 17	4:6	5:18
δίκη	1:20	3:18	5:16
ἐγγύς		4:8	5:8
ἔργον	1:3, 4, 20, 25	3:13	5:7, 16
θεν/ἄνωθέν	1:17	3:15, 17; 4:1	
θνήσκω	1:15		5:20
θυμός	1:14, 15	4:2	5:7, 8, 10, 13
ἵστημι	1:8	3:13, 16; 4:4, 7	5:9
καθαρός	1:27	4:8	
καρδία	1:26	3:14; 4:8	5:8
καρπός		3:17, 18	5:7, 18
καυχάομαι	1:9	3:14	
κρίνω	1:6	3:17; 4:11, 12	5:9, 12
κόσμος	1:27	4:4	
λάλος	1:19	4:11	5:10
λαμβάνω	1:7, 12, 15	4:3	5:7, 10
λανθάνω	1:18, 24, 25	3:14	5:19
λέγω	1:13, 18, 21, 22, 23	4:5, 6	5:16
μακάριος	1:12, 25		5:11
μένω	1:3, 4, 12, 25		5:11
νόμος	1:25	4:11, 12	
ὁδός	1:8		5:20
πείθω	1:3, 6	3:17	5:15
ποιέω	1:22, 23, 25	3:18; 4:11	5:15
πλάνη	1:16		5:19, 20
πραΰς	1:21	3:13	
σοφός	1:5	3:13, 15, 17	
στρέφω		3:13	5:19, 20
σῴζω	1:21	4:12	5:15, 20

TABLE 1   Shared lexemes (cont.)

Keyword root	Section 1	Section 2	Section 3
	1:2–27	3:13–4:12	5:7–20
ταπεινός	1:9, 10	4:6, 10	
ὕψος	1:9	4:10	
ψύχω/δίψυχος	1:8, 21	3:15; 4:8	5:20

These three sections, somewhat abbreviated for the sake of space, are laid out with their shared keywords below:

Section 1

> 1:5 But if any of you lacks wisdom [σοφίας], let him ask [αἰτείτω] of God, who gives [διδόντος] to all generously and without reproach, and it will be given [δοθήσεται] to him.
>
> 6a But he must ask [αἰτείτω] in faith [πίστει] without wavering [διακρινό-μενος], for the one who wavers [διακρινόμενος] is like a wave of the sea ...
>
> 7 For that man ought not to expect that he will receive [λήμψεταί] anything from the Lord;
>
> 8 a double-souled [δίψυχος] man, unstable [ἀκατάστατος] in all his ways [ὁδοῖς] ...
>
> 14 Each one is tempted when he is carried away and enticed by his own lust [ἐπιθυμίας].
>
> 15 Then when lust [ἐπιθυμία] has conceived, it gives birth to sin [ἁμαρτίαν]; and when sin [ἁμαρτία] is accomplished, it brings forth death [θάνατον].
>
> 16 Do not be deceived [πλανᾶσθε], my beloved brethren.
>
> 17a Every good gift [δόσις ἀγαθή] and every perfect thing given [δώρημα] is from above [ἄνωθέν], coming down from the father of lights ...
>
> 18 Willingly he brought us forth by the word of truth [ἀληθείας], so that we would be a kind of firstfruits among his creatures.
>
> 19 Know this, my beloved brethren, and let everyone be swift to hear, slow to speak [λαλῆσαι], slow to anger,
>
> 20 for human anger does not achieve the righteousness [δικαιοσύνην] of God.
>
> 21 Therefore, putting aside all filthiness and rampant wickedness, in meekness [πραΰτητι] receive the implanted word, which is able to save [σῶσαι] your souls [ψυχάς]. (1:5–8, 14–21)

Section 2

^{3:13} Who among you is wise [σοφός] and understanding? Let him show by his good behaviour [ἀναστροφῆς] his deeds in the meekness of wisdom [πραΰτητι σοφίας].

¹⁴ But if you have bitter jealousy and selfish ambition in your heart [καρδίᾳ], do not be arrogant and lie against the truth [ἀληθείας].

¹⁵ This wisdom [σοφία] is not that which comes down from above [ἄνωθεν], but is earthly [ἐπίγειος], soulish [ψυχική], demonic.

¹⁶ For where jealousy and selfish ambition exist, there is disorder [ἀκαταστασία] and every evil thing.

¹⁷ But the wisdom from above [ἄνωθεν σοφία] is first pure, then peaceable, gentle, reasonable, full of mercy and good fruits [καρπῶν ἀγαθῶν], unwavering [ἀδιάκριτος], without hypocrisy [ἀνυπόκριτος].

¹⁸ And the fruit [καρπός] of righteousness [δικαιοσύνης] is sown in peace by those who make peace.

^{4:1} What is the source of quarrels and conflicts among you? Is it not your pleasures that wage war in your members?

² You lust [ἐπιθυμεῖτε] and do not have … You do not have because you do not ask [αἰτεῖσθαι].

³ You ask [αἰτεῖτε] and do not receive [λαμβάνετε], because you ask [αἰτεῖσθε] wrongly, to spend on pleasures …

^{6a} But he gives [δίδωσιν] a greater grace …

⁸ Draw near [ἐγγίσατε] to God and he will draw near [ἐγγιεῖ] to you. Cleanse [καθαρίσατε] your hands, you sinners [ἁμαρτωλοί], and purify your hearts [καρδίας], you double-souled [δίψυχοι] …

¹² There is one lawgiver [νομοθέτης] and judge [κριτής], who is able to save [σῶσαι] and to destroy; but who are you, the one who judges [κρίνων] your neighbour? (3:13–4:3, 6a, 8, 12)

Section 3

^{5:7} Therefore be patient [μακροθυμήσατε], brethren, until the coming of the Lord. Behold the farmer [γεωργός] waiting for the precious fruit of the earth [καρπὸν τῆς γῆς], being patient for it until it receives [λάβῃ] the early and late [rains].

⁸ You also be patient [μακροθυμήσατε], establish your hearts [καρδίας], because the coming of the Lord has drawn near [ἤγγικεν].

⁹ Do not complain, brethren, against one another, in order that you might not be judged [κριθῆτε]; behold, the judge [κριτής] stands before the door …

¹³ Is anyone among you suffering? Let him pray …

¹⁵ And the prayer of faith [πίστεως] will save [σώσει] the weak, and the Lord will raise him up, and if he has committed [πεποιηκώς] sins [ἁμαρτίας], they will be forgiven him.

¹⁶ Therefore confess your sins [ἁμαρτίας] to one another, and pray for one another so that you may be healed. The prayer of a righteous [δικαίου] man is very powerful in its effects [ἐνεργουμένη].

¹⁷ Elijah was a man like-natured to us, and he prayed earnestly that it would not rain, and it did not rain upon the earth [γῆς] for three years and six months.

¹⁸ And again he prayed, and the heaven gave [ἔδωκεν] rain and the earth [γῆ] sprouted its fruit [καρπόν].

¹⁹ My brethren, if any among you is deceived [πλανηθῇ] away from the truth [ἀληθείας] and someone turns him back [ἐπιστρέψῃ],

²⁰ let him know that the one turning back [ἐπιστρέψας] a sinner [ἁμαρτωλόν] from the deception of his way [πλάνης ὁδοῦ] will save [σώσει] his soul [ψυχήν] from death [θανάτου] and will cover a multitude of sins [ἁμαρτιῶν]. (5:7–9, 13, 15–20)

An initial reading of these sections may object that they are thematically diverse and largely unrelated. However, the sheer volume of common vocabulary suggests something to be gained from reading each section with a view toward the interpretation of the others. Elijah is presented in section 3 as a relatable exemplar of prayer. He must therefore, in the view of the author, somehow embody the qualities necessary to pray effectively. A second reading of the sections delineated above reveals that precisely such necessary qualities are described in sections 1 and 2. Even a sampling of their shared keywords shows that these sections are fundamentally interlocked, and that they reveal a cumulative argument towards James's conception of prayer. The following discussion will outline the rhetorical foundation laid by sections 1 and 2 via a sampling of their shared keywords, which will then allow the resulting description of prayer to be carried forward into the interpretation of Elijah's role in section 3 as a model for the prayers of the community.

3.2.2 Keywords
3.2.2.1 Δίψυχος, Ἄνωθεν, Σοφός
First, the term δίψυχος ("double-souled") appears only twice in James; once each in sections 1 and 2. In section 1, it describes the person whose prayer will not be answered (1:8); in section 2, it represents a reason to repent (4:8). Second, the term ἄνωθεν ("from above") is also found only in sections 1 and 2. In section 1, it describes the "good gift" (δόσις ἀγαθή) that comes down "from

above" (1:17). In section 2, it refers to the kind of wisdom readers are to seek, namely, the wisdom from above (σοφία ἄνωθεν/ἄνωθεν σοφία – 3:15, 17). Third, references to wisdom (σοφός/σοφία) are also unique to these two contexts in James, appearing only as the object of prayer in section 1 ("if any of you lacks wisdom [σοφίας], let him ask of God" – 1:5) and as the contrasting wisdom from above and worldly wisdom in section 2 (3:13–17). This worldly wisdom, in turn, is described as ψυχική (3:15), forming a conceptual link to the double-souled person (δίψυχος) whose prayer will not be answered in 1:8 and who must purify his heart in 4:8. The intentional linking of these three keywords, then, begins to form an image of the characteristics of a holistic spiritual person who both prays for and exhibits the wisdom that is given from above.[49]

3.2.2.2 Καρπός, Ἀγαθός, Δίδωμι, Δικαιοσύνη

James's continued elaboration of this wisdom begins to add in additional descriptors that will later be picked up by the Elijah section. The ἄνωθεν σοφία is described in section 2 as "full of ... good fruits" (μεστὴ ... καρπῶν ἀγαθῶν – 3:17). Surprisingly, both of these latter terms are rare in James. Καρπός is used elsewhere only in the following verse (3:18) and in the immediate context of the Elijah example (5:7, 18). The only other noun James describes with the adjective ἀγαθός is the "good gift" (δόσις ἀγαθή) already noted in section 1 (1:17). Not only are wisdom and the good gift both sent "from above" (ἄνωθεν), but the fruits of wisdom and that same gift are also the only things described as "good" (ἀγαθός). The good gift comes from the father (1:17), and wisdom is explicitly the result of prayer (1:5). Both have a heavenly source. Thus, the "wisdom from above" which is "full of good fruits" may be identified as the same wisdom that results from prayer, and may further be described as a "good gift" that comes from the father.

The description of the "good fruits" is further developed in the next verse (3:18) to become the "fruit of righteousness" (καρπὸς δικαιοσύνης). In contrast to some of the more distinctive keywords, righteousness represents something of a theme in James, describing both a quality to be emulated and an opposing quality (unrighteousness) which is deserving of judgement.[50] In section 1, it renders a characteristic of God that is to be gained by those who follow him:

49 Taylor and Guthrie observe that the purpose of 3:13–18 and its discussion of σοφία ἄνωθεν "appears to extend beyond relationships with the units immediately before and after, encompassing a larger scope than just immediate contextual associations" ("Structure," 697).

50 Pavelčík points out that the adjectival form appears only in 5:16 and 5:6 ("Eliáš," 268). However, the root is much more pervasive, occurring a total of ten times throughout the book (1:20; 2:21, 23, 24, 25; 3:6, 18; 5:6 [×2], 16).

¹⁹ Know this, my beloved brethren, and let everyone be swift to hear, slow to speak, slow to anger,

²⁰ for human anger does not achieve the righteousness of God.

²¹ Therefore, putting aside all filthiness and rampant wickedness, in meekness receive the implanted word, which is able to save your souls. (1:19–21)

In contrast to human anger, which does not attain to the righteousness of God, readers are to receive the "implanted word, which is able to save your souls" (1:21). These verses are organised in a kind of interpretive parallelism of commands and their justification:

> A. Command: be swift to *hear*, slow to speak, slow to anger
> > B. Justification: human anger does not achieve the righteousness of God
> A'. Command: put aside wickedness and receive the implanted *word*
> > B'. Justification: which is able to save your souls

Semantically, the command to be quick to hear in line A is paralleled to receiving the implanted word in line A'. By implication, this "implanted word" does achieve the righteousness of God, as opposed to human anger, which does not. The compound term "implanted" (ἔμφυτος) is a *hapax legomenon* in the New Testament, but it furthers exquisitely and, I would argue, intentionally the image of the righteous qualities borne by this word as "fruit" (i.e., the καρπὸς δικαιοσύνης of 3:18).⁵¹ These distinct lexical and thematic "notes" of righteousness, fruit, and a good and heavenly gift, as well as the backdrop of prayer, finally converge nowhere else than at the introduction of Elijah and his rain.⁵²

3.2.2.3   *Rain and Its Καρπός*

As noted above, the only other uses of καρπός outside of 3:17–18 occur in the immediate context of the Elijah illustration (5:7–20).⁵³ This section (section 3) is delineated by its own inclusio via the theme of rain and its resultant fruit. At the opening, James's readers are told to be patient for the coming of the Lord, like a farmer who waits for the early and late rains and the "precious fruit of the

---

51   Cf. Taylor and Guthrie, "Structure," 691.

52   Metzner also suggests a connection between the prayer of Elijah and the peace that results from the fruit of righteousness in 3:18 (*Jakobusbrief*, 312–13).

53   Other potential thematic references would be the illustration of fig trees and vines producing an inappropriate crop in 3:12, and the reference to firstfruits (ἀπαρχή) in 1:18 discussed below.

earth" (τίμιον καρπὸν τῆς γῆς – 5:7). At the closing, Elijah's prayer has the result that "the earth sprouted its fruit" (ἡ γῆ ἐβλάστησεν τὸν καρπὸν αὐτῆς – 5:18). Other scholars have agreed that the bracketed structure of this section links Elijah's prayer for physical rain with an eschatological result:[54]

> [7] Therefore be patient, brethren, until the coming of the Lord. Behold the farmer waiting for the precious fruit [τὸν τίμιον καρπόν] of the earth [τῆς γῆς], being patient for it until it receives early and late [rains] [πρόϊμον καὶ ὄψιμον].
> [8] You also be patient, establish your hearts, because the coming of the Lord has drawn near.
> [9] Do not complain, brethren, against one another, in order that you might not be judged; behold, the judge stands before the door. (5:7–9)

> [17] Elijah was a man like-natured to us, and he prayed earnestly that it would not rain [βρέξαι], and it did not rain [ἔβρεξεν] upon the earth [τῆς γῆς] for three years and six months.
> [18] And again he prayed, and the heaven gave rain [ὑετὸν ἔδωκεν] and the earth [ἡ γῆ] sprouted [ἐβλάστησεν] its fruit [τὸν καρπὸν αὐτῆς].
> [19] My brethren, if any among you is deceived away from the truth and someone turns him back,
> [20] let him know that the one turning back a sinner from the deception of his way will save his soul from death and will cover a multitude of sins. (5:17–20)

In the opening bracket of this inclusio, the image of eschatological rain is followed by a command toward interpersonal relationships: those who grumble against one another will be judged when the imminent judge appears (5:9). This judge was previously introduced in section 2 as the only one "able to save [σῶσαι] and to destroy" (4:12). In the closing bracket, the description of Elijah's rain is again followed by a command to recognise interpersonal relationships as bearing eschatological significance. Just as negative speech against others brings judgement, positive exhortation in the form of turning another from deception will save (σώσει) that soul from death (5:20).[55]

---

54   See e.g. Darlack, "Pray for Reign," 87–95; Robert Eisenman, "Eschatological 'Rain' Imagery in the War Scroll from Qumran and in the Letter of James," *JNES* 49 (1990), 179; Pavelčík, "Eliáš," 270–71.

55   While numerous scholars have drawn a section break between the Elijah example in 5:17–18 and the exhortation to turn back sinners in 5:19–20 (e.g. Peter H. Davids, *The*

A potential challenge to the legitimacy of this inclusio could be that the two brackets use different descriptors for rain. James 5:7 speaks of the adjectival "early and late" rains (πρόϊμος and ὄψιμος), while 5:17–18 uses the verb βρέχω and the noun ὑετός.[56] This objection somewhat counteracts itself from the outset, since the Elijah verses alone use two different terms. A far stronger argument for the link between the brackets, however, is the allusion they form to Joel 2 when taken together. Several scholars have heard echoes of the Greek of Joel 2:23 in James's use of πρόϊμος and ὄψιμος:[57]

> And children of Zion, rejoice and be glad in the Lord your God, because he has given [ἔδωκεν] to you the food that leads to righteousness, and he will rain [βρέξει] for you the rain [ὑετόν] – the early and late [πρόϊμον καὶ ὄψιμον] – just as before.

While πρόϊμος and ὄψιμος are found together, alongside ὑετός, in a few other LXX verses, Joel 2:23 alone utilises all four terms together.[58] Further, the broader images of restoration seen in Joel 2:22–23 are thoroughly integrated by James 5, including righteousness (Joel 2:23), food/rain being "given" (LXX δίδωμι) by God (2:22–23), the desert "sprouting" (βλαστάνω – 2:22), and a tree bearing fruit (καρπός) (2:22).[59] Not only does this allusion support the inclusio around the thematic use of rain in James 5, but it also establishes the underlying eschatological context for the entire passage. Joel's promise of fruit-producing early and late rains is given in the context of the day of Yhwh (2:1ff), which will bring both judgement and restoration. A recognition of this context as the backdrop for James 5 strengthens the parallel between Elijah's rain, which causes "sprouting" (βλαστάνω) and "fruit" (καρπός) (5:17–18), and the rain and precious fruit which is awaited like the coming of the Lord (5:7).

Epistle of James, NIGTC 16 [Grand Rapids: Eerdmans, 1983], 198; Laws, *James*, 237), a few have noted that they may be connected (e.g. Pavelčík, "Eliáš," 301; Taylor and Guthrie, "Structure," 700–701, 703–704).

56   For a discussion of πρόϊμον καὶ ὄψιμον in 5:7 as referring to early and late rains, rather than early and late fruit, see Metzner, *Jakobusbrief*, 280–81.

57   See e.g. Darlack, "Pray for Reign," 90; Laws, *James*, 211–12.

58   Cf. LXX Deut 11:14; Jer 5:24; Hos 6:3; Zech 10:1.

59   See Darlack, "Pray for Reign," 90 for an alternative discussion of thematic links between these texts. Laws, while suggesting only briefly the possibility of a literary allusion, comments that "because *the early and the late rain* is always in the OT explicitly the gift of God, and in Hos. vi. 3, indeed, an image of the coming of God, the farmer's waiting is seen to be even more closely analogous to their own. He waits upon God the giver of rain, and they may wait upon the coming of the Lord" (*James*, 212–13; original emphasis).

3.2.3 The Firstfruits

The image that emerges from this interdependent concert of keywords begins to reveal the logic behind James's use of Elijah. He is associated with rain through the Kings cycle and with the day of Yhwh through Malachi.[60] His character provides a perfect point of intersection for the agricultural imagery and eschatology evoked by the allusion to Joel, which promises the restoration of the people, like early and late rains, in the context of the day of Yhwh. In Joel 2, rain is the blessing that accompanies repentance (2:12–17). It results in "vindication," or "righteousness" (צדקה – 2:23). In James, as we have seen, the righteousness of God is produced through the implanted word, which ultimately results in salvation (James 1:21). The same passage reveals James's readers themselves to be a kind of fruit; more specifically, the "firstfruits" (ἀπαρχή):[61]

> [16] Do not be deceived, my beloved brethren.
> [17] Every good gift and every perfect thing given is from above, coming down from the father of lights ...
> [18] Willingly he brought us forth by the word of truth, so that we would be a kind of firstfruits among his creatures.
> [19] Know this, my beloved brethren, and let everyone be swift to hear, slow to speak, slow to anger,
> [20] for human anger does not achieve the righteousness of God. (1:16–20)

The fruit named here is the choicest of the crop, and it is identified as the people. Here again, the lexical structure of the unit elaborates this identity: the firstfruits are paralleled with "every good gift," in that both are produced by the father of lights. We have already seen that this good gift is linked with wisdom, which is the result of prayer. This wisdom is also linked with fruit (3:17), which, according to Elijah's example, also results from prayer and is also given by heaven (5:18).[62] The fruit is called "precious" (5:7), and it will come into fullness at the coming of the Lord.[63] This consistent motif of fruit in all

---

60   Malachi's epilogue also alludes to Joel 2 even as it predicts the coming of Elijah, referring to the day of Yhwh as "great and fearful" (יום יהוה הגדול והנורא – Mal 3:23) in a near-direct parallel to Joel 2:11 (כי־גדול יום־יהוה ונורא מאד).

61   This term is used in the New Testament primarily in reference to salvation (see e.g. Rom 8:23; 1 Cor 16:15; 2 Thess 2:13; Rev 14:4). LXX usage of ἀπαρχή, while not consistently rendering any single Hebrew word, appears in contexts referring to the first gifts offered to Yhwh in worship, often including agricultural fruits (see e.g. Exod 22:28; 23:19; Lev 23:10; Num 18:29–30; Deut 18:4; 26:2; 2 Sam 1:21; 2 Chron 31:5; Neh 10:39).

62   For a similar conclusion, see Metzner, *Jakobusbrief*, 311–12.

63   Johnson notes that, "although the main point is the desired attitude of patience, the characterization of the fruit as 'precious' (*timion*) is noteworthy. This is certainly the only time

three sections concerning prayer reveals an underlying exhortation to James's readers to pray that they might both bear and be good fruit. This is precisely the call to community prayer that is exemplified by the character of Elijah (5:13–18). The lexical and thematic interdependency formed by this motif may be graphed as in Figure 1:

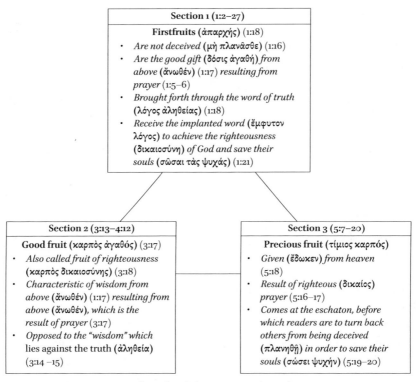

FIGURE 1   Prayer in James: lexical and thematic interdependency

Not only is each of these sections based in a call to prayer, but they also all describe a specific type of fruit that results from prayer (firstfruits, good fruit, precious fruit). The firstfruits, introduced in section 1, are revealed to be the

in the biblical literature that something so lowly as produce has been given a designation usually associated with jewels and crowns" (*James*, 314). Here he misses the opportunity set up by his own description to associate this fruit with the "crown of life promised to those who love him" that comes to those who endure in 1:12, and the paralleled "kingdom which he promised to those who love him" in 2:5.

people themselves (1:18). Section 2 elaborates the motif of fruit to include righteousness and wisdom, while the Elijah illustration in section 3 reveals that
this righteous, precious fruit is an eschatological image. The people themselves, identified by their righteous deeds, are the fruit which will come to full
maturity at the coming of the Lord. Elijah's rain, in parallel form, is also demonstrated to be an eschatological motif.[64] Just like the good fruit, this eschatological rain can only be the result of prayer. It is prayer which gives the wisdom
that rains down from heaven. It is prayer which prepares the people for the
coming of the Lord, and it is prayer which will hasten that coming like Elijah's
rain. If the people are not prepared for the Lord's coming – that is, if they suffer
or lack wisdom (1:5; 5:13) – it is because they simply do not ask (4:2). They are
called to pray for wisdom from above, which has the power to effect the fruit
of righteousness in their own lives. By their prayers – that is, by their imitation of Elijah – they ensure the ongoing life of the community (5:13–16). When
they do pray, then, both for themselves and for the community, they follow the
example of the ὁμοιοπαθὴς ἡμῖν (5:17); the one who causes the Lord's rain of
restoration to fall upon the land.

3.3   Why Elijah?

The question of why Elijah in particular is summoned to conclude a specific
biblical book has, of course, been asked before. In the epilogue to Malachi,
he represents an eschatological forerunner to the day of Yhwh who will turn
back the hearts of the people (3:23–24). When the endings of the two books
are compared, the conclusion to Malachi emerges looking distinctly like a thematic pattern for the conclusion of James.[65] In both books, Elijah is mentioned
only once, abruptly, in the final verses of the extant text, and is followed by a
description of turning people to avert judgement:

> [23] Behold, I am sending to you Elijah the prophet before the coming of
> the great and fearful day of Yhwh.
> [24] And he will turn back the heart of fathers together with sons, and the
> heart of sons together with their fathers, lest I come and strike the land
> with a curse. (Mal 3:23–24)

---

64   See n. 38 above.
65   Kovalishyn only briefly raises the possibility of James's use of the Malachi tradition
      ("Prayer of Elijah," 1036), but likewise suggests that "the example of Elijah works as a sum-
      mative illustration to highlight a key theme of the letter and to draw together the conclu-
      sion" (1028).

¹⁷ Elijah was a man like-natured to us, and he prayed earnestly that it would not rain, and it did not rain upon the earth for three years and six months.
¹⁸ And again he prayed, and the heaven gave rain and the earth sprouted its fruit.
¹⁹ My brethren, if any among you is deceived away from the truth and someone turns him back,
²⁰ let him know that the one turning back a sinner from the deception of his way will save his soul from death and will cover a multitude of sins. (James 5:17–20)

While some have argued that the final two verses of James are disconnected from the Elijah example prior to it, lexical interdependency between these final verses and the other two prayer sections, again, does not allow for this conclusion.[66] The deception (πλάνη) from which readers turn each other back (5:19–20) is the same deception against which James warns them in 1:16, immediately before introducing them as the firstfruits (1:17–18). The truth (ἀλήθεια) from which the deceived have wandered (5:19) recalls the "word of truth" again from section 1; the same word by which the firstfruits are brought forth (1:18). It is also found in section 2 (3:14). The connection in James's conclusion between sin (ἁμαρτία) and death (θάνατος) is seen in section 1 immediately prior to the warning against deception: lust breeds sin (ἁμαρτία) and sin brings forth death (θάνατος). Such "sinners" are the double-souled who need to cleanse their hearts in section 2 (4:8). Finally, the only other reference to "saving the soul" is in 1:21 (σῶσαι τὰς ψυχὰς ὑμῶν), where it is credited to the "implanted word" which brings about the righteousness of God. Its context, like that of ch. 5, describes a distinction between the righteous and the wicked, in line with the "saving" that is credited to the one lawgiver and judge in section 2 (4:12).

This lexical interdependency, combined with the Malachian pattern, argues that James's entire conclusion may still have the figure of Elijah in mind. The author has artfully conflated the prophetic images produced by Kings and Malachi, in order to point readers to a single exemplar who summarises their identity and call. This figure must simultaneously be considered righteous and wise, associated with rain and its produce, associated with heaven, and linked to the coming of the Lord. In short, the exemplar must be Elijah.

---

66   See e.g. Davids, *James*, 198; Laws, *James*, 237.

3.4   *Summary*

Thus, James's use of Elijah is far from a superficial, misquoted example. A lexical analysis of the book's sections on prayer demonstrates that he is not only connected but fundamental to the argument structure of the entire book. The goal of James's conclusion is to present readers with Elijah's mission. They, like the prophet, are eschatological agents of repentance who are to turn back those who stray. As they pray mutually for one another, they ensure the preservation of life in the community (5:13–15). James strategically links Elijah's eschatological work with prayer in order to give his readers a weapon for this mission: the prophet's power over rain in Kings is the power believers exercise when they pray. They can imitate Elijah because he is like them: equally glorious and vulnerable; heavenly and down-to-earth. The simultaneous patterns of Malachi and Joel that underlie James's exhortation to prayer underscore its eschatological objective, in which readers become essentially their own end-time forerunners: praying for rain and turning back sinners as they wait for the coming of the Lord. In other words, the righteous community of God's people is, once again, to identify itself with Elijah.

4   Conclusion: God's People as Prophet and Remnant

To the early Christian communities represented by the New Testament epistles, Elijah remains a point of identification and expectation. He forms a part of the pattern of their experiences of hardship and suffering in Heb 11, which are presented as the road by which their salvation will be attained. He lies behind the prophetic identity of Paul, as the apostle both calls readers to faith and embodies the remnant saved by grace. To the readers of James, Elijah becomes the pattern by which they pray for both physical and spiritual restoration as they await the eschatological day of the Lord.

The epistles reiterate the flexibility of the Elijah image that we have observed throughout early Jewish and Christian texts. From various angles, they utilise both the prophetic and remnant facets of the preexisting Elijah pattern. In a continuation of the motif begun in the Gospels, the followers of Jesus take the role of Elijah upon themselves. At the same time, they look ahead to the return of the greater Elijah who represents their very reason for existence: the one they await as returning from heaven so that the entire righteous community together may finally "receive the promise" (Heb 11:39).

CHAPTER 7

Elijah and the Witnesses in Revelation

1   Introduction

The final book of the New Testament offers what may well be the most compelling example in all of our texts of an Elijah image conflated with other images to portray the people of God. It does not mention Elijah by name, but the description in Rev 11 of two prophetic figures who call down plagues like Moses and also control rain and fire (11:5–6) can hardly fail to evoke Israel's two most paradigmatic prophets.[1] These Moses- and Elijah-like "witnesses" (μάρτυρες) are given prophetic power and authority for a limited time (11:3), after which they die a martyr's death (11:7). Though the world celebrates their vanquishing (11:9–10), the witnesses do not remain dead. After three and a half days, they receive "breath of life from God" (11:11), are resurrected, and are taken to heaven in a cloud (11:12).

To the reader who knows the Elijah traditions, these motifs are immediately familiar. They present something of a summary image of Elijah as he is portrayed throughout early Jewish and Christian texts. At the same time, they are conflated in and around the same passage with numerous other scriptural

---

1   Cf. Exod 7:17–21ff; 1 Kgs 17; 2 Kgs 2. See Traugott Holtz's conclusion that Rev 11 "setzt die beiden Zeugen durch ihre Fähigkeiten, mit denen sie den Menschen begegnen, zu Elija ... und Mose ... in Parallele, ohne sie namentlich zu nennen" (*Die Offenbarung des Johannes*, NTD 11 [Göttingen: Vandenhoeck & Ruprecht, 2008], 85). Historically, conclusions regarding the identity and significance of these characters have ranged from a physical Moses and Elijah (Paolo Byong-Seob Min investigates Rev 11 in light of the expectations of Deut 18 and Mal 3, though he concludes that various identifications may be possible [*I Due Testimoni di Apocalisse 11,1–13: Storia, Interpretazione, Teologia*, PhD diss., Pontifical Gregorian University {1991}, 123–29]), a different prophetic pairing such as Enoch and Elijah (see David E. Aune, *Revelation 6–16*, WBC 52B [Nashville: Thomas Nelson, 1993], 599–600 for a discussion of this view held already in the patristic period; also Holtz re: the Apocalypse of Elijah [*Offenbarung*, 85]), new prophetic figures (see Daniel K.K. Wong, "The Two Witnesses in Revelation 11," *BSac* 154 [1997]: 344–54), or some form of representation of the people of God. This latter view has recently been widely adopted and is held by scholars such as G.K. Beale (see e.g. *Revelation*, 585–87), Robert H. Mounce (*The Book of Revelation*, NICNT [Grand Rapids: Eerdmans, 1997], 217), and Richard Bauckham (*The Climax of Prophecy* [Edinburgh: T&T Clark, 1993], 273–74). For an overview of positions, see Aune, *Revelation 6–16*, 599–603. The imagery itself unmistakably portrays Moses and Elijah; other conclusions must be derived exegetically. I would argue that the significance of the use of precisely these images indeed lies in their identification with the people of God.

images, including the temple measurement motif of Ezekiel (Rev 11:1–2; Ezek 40–42), temporal notations out of Daniel (Rev 11:2–3; Dan 7:25), and the olive trees and lampstands of Zechariah (Rev 11:4; Zech 4:1–14). This literary interweaving brings the reader once again to a sensation that should, by this point in our study, be very familiar: that of facing a literary work so tightly composed and interpretively dense that it cannot be unravelled in a meaningful way without continual reference to multiple source texts at the same time.

A comprehensive treatment of all the allusions potentially traceable within Rev 11 is, again, beyond the scope of this book.[2] The focus of this chapter will be held on those intertexts most relevant to the portrayal and effect of the Elijah image within its context. As such, I will highlight three parallel images within Rev 11 that inform the interpretation of the witnesses: a measured temple, a holy city, and the olive trees/lampstands. I will then locate these images in the larger framework of the pericope, arguing that both the close details and the larger frame of Rev 11:1–13 present them as analogous and cumulative lenses through which to view the same reality: that of the survival and vindication of the endangered people of God.

2   Lenses of Analogy

2.1   *The Measured Temple*

> [1] And there was given to me a measuring rod like a staff, saying, "Get up and measure the temple of God and the altar and the ones worshipping in it."
>
> [2a] But the court outside the temple cast outside and do not measure it, because it has been given to the nations. (Rev 11:1–2a)

---

2   Allusions to Jeremiah, Isaiah, Esther, and other books within the Book of the Twelve have also been recognised, both in the portrayal of the witnesses themselves and in the surrounding context. The classic pairing of Moses and Elijah has been characteristic of many of our texts. However, the conflation of additional characters with this image is completely consistent with the nature both of Revelation and of analogical literary characterisation as we have observed it. See Aune's comments on Jer 5:14, Dan 7, and Esther (*Revelation 6–16*, 613, 617, 623–24). For references to Jonah and Micah, see Beale, *Revelation*, 604, 606. For example lists of intertexts, see Bauckham, *Climax*, 169–70; Andrew Harker, "Prophetically Called Sodom and Egypt: The Affective Power of Revelation 11:1–13," in *The Book of Revelation: Currents in British Research on the Apocalypse*, ed. Garrick V. Allen, Ian Paul, and Simon P. Woodman, WUNT II/411 (Tübingen: Mohr Siebeck, 2015), 37. For a significant text-critical analysis with Revelation's use of Zechariah as a test case, see Garrick V. Allen, *The Book of Revelation and Early Jewish Textual Culture* (Cambridge: Cambridge University Press, 2017).

Revelation 11 opens with a motif of "measuring" (μετρέω) the temple with a rod (κάλαμος), an image which alludes to Ezek 40–42.[3] The latter text also begins with a visionary who is introduced to a man holding a "measuring rod" (κάλαμος μέτρον – LXX Ezek 40:3, cf. 40:5) to measure the various aspects of the temple.[4] These measurements make up the majority of chs. 40–42. In the final dialogue of ch. 42, the guide describes the chambers in which the priests are to leave those artifacts too holy to be taken into the "outer court" (τὴν αὐλὴν τὴν ἐξωτέραν – LXX Ezek 42:14). The concluding measurement of the chapter then describes the purpose of the wall that had been measured: "to distinguish between the holy and the profane" (MT Ezek 42:20).[5]

Revelation's adoption of this motif illustrates the same pattern of separation: the area measured (the temple, altar, and worshippers) is separated from the "court outside" (τὴν αὐλὴν τὴν ἔξωθεν) which "has been given to the nations" (11:2). There is general agreement that the measured temple in this chapter is presented in some way as an analogy of the people of God.[6] Broader use of temple, altar, and worship imagery in Revelation argues further that these motifs cannot be definitively distinguished, as they are all made to represent the visceral experience of a persecuted community.[7] Revelation 3:12 for example, in the context of the church letters, promises to make the one who overcomes "a pillar in the temple of my God." The altar provides shelter for the souls of

---

3 See e.g. Beale, *Revelation*, 559–65; Elisabeth Schüssler Fiorenza, *Revelation: Vision of a Just World* (Minneapolis: Augsburg Fortress, 1991), 76; Beate Kowalski, *Die Rezeption des Propheten Ezechiel in der Offenbarung des Johannes* (Stuttgart: Verlag Katholisches Bibelwerk, 2004), 345–57; Mounce, *Revelation*, 213. Ezekiel 40–42 is located within a larger unit spanning chs. 40–48. Of particular significance beyond chs. 40–42 is the measuring of the altar in 43:13–17, which corresponds to the command to measure the altar, as well as the temple and its worshippers, in Rev 11:1. Steven J. Friesen has noted the numerous Ezekielian allusions worked into Rev 10–11, and argues that "John was positioning his text among those of the prophets, comparing his message of judgement and preservation to theirs" (*Imperial Cults and the Apocalypse of John* [Oxford: Oxford University Press, 2001], 142–43).

4 Ezekiel 40–42 is the only text in the Hebrew Bible or the New Testament outside of Revelation whose Greek rendering uses the terms κάλαμος (reed, chaff) and μέτρον (measure) in the same immediate context.

5 Cf. the alternative τοῦ διαστέλλειν ἀνὰ μέσον τῶν ἁγίων καὶ ἀνὰ μέσον τοῦ προτειχίσματος τοῦ ἐν διατάξει τοῦ οἴκου of LXX Ezek 42:20.

6 See e.g. Beale, *Revelation*, 561–62; Holtz, *Offenbarung*, 84.

7 Contrary to Marko Jauhiainen's protest that these diverse depictions of a single referent are too tightly packed to be plausible ("The Measuring of the Sanctuary Reconsidered," *Bib* 83 [2002], 512–13) and Aune's similar reservation ("How, one asks, can the temple, the altar, and the worshipers *all* stand for the people of God?" [*Revelation 6–16*, 598]), this is precisely the type of conflated analogy we have observed as prolifically present in early Jewish and Christian literature, and which easily fits the apocalyptic style of Revelation.

martyrs in 6:9–11, before it takes on a sentient voice of its own in 16:7 that appears to be the voice of the martyrs themselves (cf. 16:6).[8] The προσκυνοῦντας ἐν αὐτῷ, in Revelation's usage, can fall into only one of two camps: those who worship God or those who worship God's antagonists.[9]

As the temple, the righteous themselves become the locus of God's presence, and they are the ones to be "measured." Scholarly consensus has largely interpreted this motif of measurement as one of protection, either physical or spiritual.[10] Such protection, however, can only be an interpretive implication of the primary purpose of the measured portions stated in Ezekiel: to establish an impenetrable boundary between the holy and the profane; to prepare a pure sanctuary for the presence of Yhwh (Ezek 43).[11] While the preservation of God's people is the ultimate result of this distinction, this outcome is only realised at the end of the entire book. In Rev 21:15–17, a μέτρον κάλαμος

---

8   "Though the participle 'saying' is singular, it is possible that the voice represents the corporate declaration of the souls of the martyrs whom John heard crying out for justice in 6:9–10" (Beale, *Revelation*, 820).

9   See worship of God in 4:10; 5:14; 7:11; 11:16; 14:7; 15:4; 19:4, 10; 22:8–9. See worship of antagonists in 9:20; 13:4–15; 14:9–11; 16:2; 19:20; 20:4. The only other uses of προσκυνέω in Revelation are in 3:9, in reference to "those who say they are Jews and are not" bowing at the feet of God's true people, and here in 11:1.

10 See e.g. Aune, *Revelation 6–16*, 604; Beale, *Revelation*, 558–59; Brian K. Blount, *Revelation: A Commentary*, NTL (Louisville: Westminster John Knox, 2009), 202–203; R.H. Charles, *The Revelation of St. John*, vol. 1, ICC (Edinburgh: T&T Clark, 1920), 274–75; Holtz, *Offenbarung*, 84; Kowalski, *Rezeption*, 345–46; Mounce, *Revelation*, 213–14, 219. The discussion surrounding the relationship of Revelation's temple measurement motif with the destruction of Jerusalem in 70 CE misses the point of the allusion. Readers are not asked to imagine the most recent Jerusalem temple being physically measured, nor are they to conjure an image of a purely metaphorical temple. Instead, they are immediately to be transported to the text of Ezekiel, and to place themselves within that oracle's explicit separation between the holy and the profane. See the similar conclusions of Beale, *Revelation*, 556, 561; Friesen, *Imperial Cults*, 141–43. For extensive treatment of this discussion, see Aune, *Revelation 6–16*, 593–98; Adela Yarbro Collins, *Crisis and Catharsis: The Power of the Apocalypse* (Philadelphia: Westminster, 1984), 64–69.

11 While Jauhiainen's critique of the consensus interpretation is somewhat distracted by its need for a physically measurable configuration of the temple, altar, and worshippers, it does offer a helpful refocus on the purpose of Ezekiel's measurement motif as "not to signify security or protection but to reveal to Ezekiel Yahweh's plan regarding the return of the Glory, the restoration of pure worship, and the reordering of the tribes" ("Measuring," 516–17; cf. 509–10). Holtz, ironically, downplays an allusion to Ezekiel precisely because the Ezekiel text does not fit a motif of protection (*Offenbarung*, 84)! See also Michael A. Lyons on the Ezekiel text: "The focus is on boundaries" ("Envisioning Restoration: Innovations in Ezekiel 40–48," in *'I Lifted My Eyes and Saw': Reading Dream and Vision Reports in the Hebrew Bible*, ed. Elizabeth R. Hayes and Lena-Sofia Tiemeyer [London: Bloomsbury, 2014], 80).

reappears; the only context in which it occurs in Revelation outside of ch. 11.[12] This time, it is a golden rod in the hand of a heavenly messenger, measuring not the temple but the new city of Jerusalem. The temple and its holy separation from the profanity outside is no longer needed, because the entire city is the perfectly recreated centre of the glory and presence of God (21:22–23). Only at this point can the impenetrable barrier be dissolved. The city's gates can remain perpetually open because nothing unclean will ever threaten it again (21:24–27).

In the context of Rev 11, however, the distinction is still needed. This passage must therefore be read in light of its Ezekielian intertext as an image of separation between the measured portion, representing God's people, and the excluded portion, representing those outside.[13] This identification will be further developed by the unfolding arrangement of the chapter and the addition of further analogical lenses in the following verses.

2.2   *The Holy City*

The same nations to whom the outer court is given are further said to "trample the holy city for forty-two months" (Rev 11:2b). The time notation, which works out to three and a half years, undoubtedly alludes to the "time, times, and half a time" of Dan 7:25.[14] The image of a "holy city" has not been seen to this point in Revelation, and could derive from a number of scriptural contexts.[15] However,

---

12   So also Blount, *Revelation*, 202.

13   This polemic is explicitly described in Ezek 44:5–9, in which profane outsiders are not allowed to enter the sanctuary. Scholars arguing for a motif of protection in Revelation have pointed out that the outer courts of the Jerusalem temples were also legitimate places of worship, and therefore should not represent the analogical foil to God's people (see e.g. Beale, *Revelation*, 560–61). However, as I will demonstrate, the effect of the images in Rev 11:1–4 is to present multiple interpretive lenses in quick succession in order to deepen and colour a single image, without requiring that the extended implications of each of those images be taken to their full conclusions. Further, since the backdrop to the Ezekiel image is one of distinction between the holy and the profane, the distinction drawn in Revelation should be interpreted through this lens unless further evidence demonstrates otherwise. For a summary of the various identifications of those "cast out" (Rev 11:2), see Aune, *Revelation 6–16*, 597–98; Beale, *Revelation*, 557–59.

14   Cf. Rev 12:14; Dan 8:9–14; 12:7. See e.g. Aune, *Revelation 6–16*, 609; Beale, *Revelation*, 565; Charles, *Revelation*, 279.

15   עיר קדוש appears in Dan 9:24 in the context of a seventy-week time period of preparation. Other potential intertexts include Israel's mistaken self-identification with the "holy city" in Isa 48:2 and the subsequent promise of this city's (Jerusalem's) restoration in 52:1, as well as associations between a city and Yhwh's holy mountain/dwelling place/people in Ps 46:4; 48:1; Isa 62:12; Zech 8:3. See also references to Jerusalem as "the holy city" in Neh 11:1, 18.

where Daniel's time notation denotes oppression of the "holy ones of the most high" (קַדִּישֵׁי עֶלְיוֹנִין; LXX τοὺς ἁγίους τοῦ ὑψίστου), Revelation characterises these saints of God in terms of a city, a second lens that follows immediately on the heels of the temple metaphor described above.

Nations (ἔθνη) and a city (πόλις) are mentioned together again in 11:8–9, after the two witnesses are killed for their prophesying. The cities of 11:2 and 11:8 appear to be intentionally paralleled, as descriptions related to Jerusalem are used of both.[16] However, the city where the witnesses lie is no longer the holy city. It is the "great city" (τῆς πόλεως τῆς μεγάλης – 11:8), which also has not appeared in Revelation prior to this point. In every subsequent mention of it, this great city becomes the paradigm of wickedness that is "Babylon."[17] The holy city, on the other hand, vanishes from the narrative of Revelation after 11:2, and the reader is left to wonder whether it, like the witnesses, has ultimately succumbed to its opposition.

A powerful image of hope appears when the dead witnesses are resurrected and taken to heaven (Rev 11:11–12). However, the reader still hears nothing of the holy city. Further vignettes portray the great city's downfall and eventual destruction (Rev 16–17), which culminates in Rev 18 where its complete overthrow is predicted, with the note that "in her the blood of prophets and of saints was found, and of all who have been slain on the earth" (18:24). It is only after this point that the holy city reappears. In the final restoration that begins in Rev 21, the holy city is mentioned for the first time since ch. 11 as "the holy city, new Jerusalem, coming down out of heaven from God, prepared like a bride adorned for her husband. And I heard a loud voice from the throne saying, 'Behold, the tabernacle of God is with mankind, and he will dwell with them, and they will be his people'" (21:2–3).

If the great city is an image of wickedness and antagonism against the work and people of God, then the holy city is an image of precisely those people themselves.[18] They are downtrodden, persecuted, and martyred, but

---

16   The city of 11:2 appears to contain the temple, while that of 11:8 is described as the place "where also their Lord was crucified."

17   See Adela Yarbro Collins, *The Combat Myth in the Book of Revelation* (Missoula: Scholars, 1976), 195 n. 60. Beale sees a similar contrast in John's use of the two city images, arguing that those who are trampled represent the true believers while "the great city" is a reference to the persecutors (*Revelation*, 569; cf. 591).

18   Similarly, see Fiorenza: "Since the author uses the name 'Jerusalem' just for the New Jerusalem, his characterization of the city as the 'holy city' seems to refer to neither the eschatological nor the historical Jerusalem, which in 11:8 is called 'the great city.' If the expression 'holy city' means the same circle of persons as the figures 'temple, altar, and worshiper,' then 11:2 speaks of the Christian community" (*Revelation*, 77). I would argue

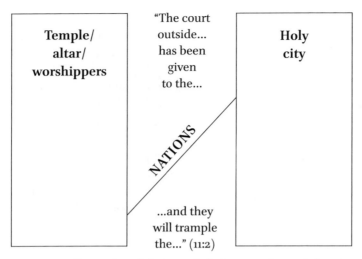

FIGURE 2   The temple and the city with the nations as literary link

the promise of the book is that they will ultimately be gloriously vindicated. Thus, the "holy city" in Rev 11:2 represents another lens, like that of the temple, through which to view the people of God.

One of the interpretive obstacles to identifying the referents of Rev 11:1–2 is that the "cast out" outer court could be taken as a parallel to the trampled holy city (11:2): the court is given to the nations just as the city is trampled by the nations. From this perspective, if the holy city is to represent the people of God, then so must the outer court, but the outer court is rejected by the measurement motif. This difficulty is resolved, however, if the two images are seen as two separate allusions; two distinct interpretive lenses that contribute unique nuances to a portrait of the same reality, as in Figure 2.

In this schema, the reference to the nations provides the literary link between the two lenses. While the temple, altar, and worshippers are designated as holy, the outer court outside the temple is rejected and given to the nations. These nations, in turn, will execute the trampling against the holy city. As such, it is not the outer court and the holy city that are paralleled, but the measured temple and the city. Both of these images can therefore be understood to represent distinct perspectives – literary lenses – through which to view the holy and endangered identity of God's people within the book.

that Rev 11 depicts the holy city as the community endangered, while Rev 21–22 describes it as the community restored.

2.3   *The Two Witnesses*
2.3.1   The Witnesses as the Temple and the City

> [3] And I will grant to my two witnesses, and they will prophesy 1260 days, clothed in sackcloth.
> [4] These are the two olive trees and the two lampstands who are standing before the Lord of the earth.
> [5] And if anyone wishes to harm them, fire comes forth out of their mouth and consumes their enemies. And if anyone might wish to harm them, he must be killed in this way.
> [6] These have the power to shut the heavens in order that rain might not fall during the days of their prophecy; and they have power over the waters to turn them into blood and to strike the earth with every plague as often as they might wish. (Rev 11:3–6)

The introduction of the two witnesses in Rev 11:3 has often been treated separately from the temple measurement motif and the holy city of vv. 1–2, with some scholars arguing that 11:3 represents the start of a new unit based on a distinct literary source.[19] In the composite image that begins Rev 11, however, the witnesses are presented as literary parallels both to the temple and to the holy city, and provide a third overlaid lens in the portrayal of the people of God.[20] We have already seen that the literary reference to the "nations" provides the link between the measured temple, with its altar and worshippers, and the paralleled holy city. In similar form, the holy city and the two witnesses are linked by equal time notations: the forty-two months of the city's trampling correspond to the 1260 days of the witnesses' prophesying, both of which equal three and a half years.[21] Further, all three lenses are preceded in turn by a form of the root δίδωμι: the visionary is "given" a rod to measure the temple, the outer court is "given" to the nations who will trample the city, and it is "granted" to the two witnesses to prophesy. The resulting literary structure

---

19   See e.g. Aune, *Revelation 6–16*, 611; George R. Beasley-Murray, *The Book of Revelation*, NCB (London: Oliphants, 1974), 37–38; Charles, *Revelation*, 270–273; Collins, *Combat Myth*, 195 n. 60.

20   For an affirmation of the literary unity of this section, see Holtz, *Offenbarung*, 83.

21   Aune notes this parallel time notation as "one of the few formal links between 11:1–2 and 11:3–13" (*Revelation 6–16*, 610). So also Collins, *Combat Myth*, 915 n. 60; Holtz, *Offenbarung*, 83. For an extensive discussion of the 42 months/1260 days, see Beale, *Revelation*, 565–68. He notes that the identification of both the witnesses and the holy city with the persecuted community is confirmed by the parallel persecution of the woman and the saints of chs. 12–13 for the same period of time (568).

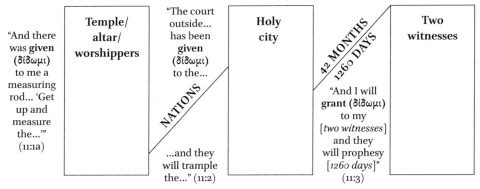

The temple, the city, and the witnesses with the nations and time notations as literary links

effectively connects both adjacent units to each other and links all three units together, as in Figure 3.

Based on this structural arrangement, the identity of the temple and the city as analogies for God's people effectively identifies the witnesses with the people as well. This third image will be much further developed in this context than either of the others, and it finds its basis in Zech 4, as described below. Zechariah 2, located in the same series of visions as Zech 4, has been suggested as a further source text for the temple measurement image.[22] It describes a man intending to measure the city of Jerusalem (2:1–2; LXX 2:5–6).[23] Jauhiainen has argued against the direct dependence of Rev 11:1 on Zech 2 based on differences in form and theme, and he may well be correct.[24] Nevertheless, the measuring motif in Rev 11, in the context of the olive trees and lampstands, acts as a thematic trigger. Zechariah's measuring motif concerns not the temple but the city (Zech 2), in the same context as the olive trees and lampstand (Zech 4). All three of these images converge in Rev 11:1–3, supporting the conclusion that they are indeed meant to inform each other and underscoring the passage's threefold description of the people of God. The close of the measurement pericope in Zech 2 poignantly highlights both the imminent arrival of Yhwh's presence and his choice of a holy people, which correspond to the larger message of Revelation: "Many nations will be joined to Yhwh on that

---

22   Lyons notes the presence of the temple measurement motif in Ezekiel, Zechariah, and Revelation ("Envisioning," 75 n. 15).

23   See e.g. Aune, *Revelation 6–16*, 604; Bauckham, *Climax*, 269 n. 46.

24   Marko Jauhiainen, *The Use of Zechariah in Revelation*, WUNT II/199 (Tübingen: Mohr Siebeck, 2005), 68. However, he also notes that "the most likely connection between Zech 2 and Rev 11 is in the way that measuring is used as a literary device to communicate something to the audience" (68).

day, and they will be to me a people, and I will dwell in your midst … Yhwh will possess Judah as his portion upon the holy land, and he will again choose Jerusalem" (Zech 2:11–12).

2.3.2 The Witnesses as the Olive Trees and Lampstands

The two witnesses of Rev 11, then, identified with imagery of Moses and Elijah, are portrayed as analogous to the temple of God's people, chosen apart from the larger group, and to an endangered holy city. By this point, we have repeatedly observed Elijah's consistent identification in early Jewish and Christian literature with a chosen and endangered righteous remnant. The portrait of the two witnesses builds on the images of election and endangerment innate in the temple and the holy city to depict, once again, two individuals who embody the suffering and survival of a righteous community. The fact that Moses and Elijah appear together recalls, similarly to the transfiguration, the foundational law and prophetic word upon which that people's identity is based.

The description of these figures as olive trees and lampstands, however, is rather unexpected. This image derives unmistakably from Zech 4, in which a visionary is awakened by a heavenly messenger and shown a golden lampstand with an olive tree on either side.[25] This vision, like the one in Rev 11, is given in the context of a temple (Zech 3–4) and a measurement pericope (Zech 2). Twice, the visionary asks his guide to explain the identity of the implements (Zech 4:4, 11–12). The second time, he receives the cryptic answer, "These are the two sons of fresh oil [שְׁנֵי בְנֵי־הַיִּצְהָר] who are standing by the Lord of the whole earth" (Zech 4:14). This description is assumed and condensed in Revelation's introduction of the witnesses as "the two olive trees and the two lampstands who are standing before the Lord of the earth" (Rev 11:4).

Many scholars have suggested that the figures behind Zechariah's lampstand and two olive trees are the priest Joshua and the temple-builder Zerubbabel portrayed in Zech 2–4, which may well be the case in the immediate context.[26]

---

25 For a "nearly unanimous" list of scholars recognising this allusion, see Garrick V. Allen, "Reusing Scripture in the Book of Revelation: Reworking Zechariah 4 in the Apocalypse," in *The Book of Revelation: Currents in British Research on the Apocalypse*, ed. Garrick V. Allen, Ian Paul, and Simon P. Woodman, WUNT II/411 (Tübingen: Mohr Siebeck, 2015), 2–3 n. 3. Blount argues that Revelation's use of the definite article to introduce these terms implies the expected familiarity of his readers with the image of Zech 4 (*Revelation*, 209). For an extensive discussion regarding specifically the text of Zech 4 as reused by Revelation, see Garrick V. Allen, "Textual Pluriformity and Allusion in the Book of Revelation: The Text of Zechariah 4 in the Apocalypse," ZNW (2015): 136–45.

26 See e.g. Aune, *Revelation 6–16*, 599, 631; Blount, *Revelation*, 209; Fiorenza, *Revelation*, 78; Michael R. Stead, *The Intertextuality of Zechariah 1–8*, LHBOTS 506 (London: T&T Clark,

Strangely, however, בני־היצהר is not used in the sense of anointed ministers, as it is often translated in Zech 4, in any other context in the Hebrew Bible.[27] In the vast majority of uses, יצהר refers to the oil that represents both Yhwh's blessing upon the land and people and the sacrifice they are to offer to him in return.[28] An example of this usage which should inform the interpretation of Zech 4 is Hag 1, a text fundamentally linked to the first six chapters of Zechariah through the corresponding work of Zech 7–8.[29] Here Yhwh declares that the "heavens withheld dew and the earth withheld its produce [כלאו שמים מטל והארץ כלאה יבולה]" (Hag 1:10), including יצהר (1:11), because the people have neglected the rebuilding of the temple (1:9). I have already suggested that Haggai's designation as מלאך יהוה in this passage (Hag 1:13), along with the declaration of drought, may be a factor behind the identification of Malachi's messenger as Elijah. In the completed arrangement of the Book of the Twelve, it is on the other side of Zechariah's lampstand vision that the drought is reversed. In Zech 8:12, Yhwh states that "the land will give its produce and the heavens will give their dew [והארץ תתן את־יבולה והשמים יתנו טלם], and I will cause the remnant of this people [שארית העם הזה] to inherit all these things." The return of this blessing is linked to the obedience of the שארית העם in Hag 1:12, 14.[30] Simultaneously, the designation of the lampstand/olive trees in Zech 4 as "sons of fresh oil" may indicate that whoever filled these roles was expected to break the curse of drought declared by the מלאך יהוה in Haggai. In other words, an Elijah-like figure appears in Revelation as a בן יצהר to complete the work of a drought-pronouncing מלאך יהוה and restore the proper worship of Yhwh.[31]

2009), 184. In contrast, see Mark Boda, "Oil, Crowns and Thrones: Prophet, Priest and King in Zechariah 1:7–6:15," in *Perspectives on Hebrew Scriptures I*, ed. Ehud Ben Zvi (Piscataway: Gorgias, 2007), 393–94; Jauhiainen, *Zechariah*, 48–49.

27   So also Jauhiainen, *Zechariah*, 48; David L. Petersen, *Haggai & Zechariah 1–8*, OTL (London: SCM, 1984), 230–31; Stead, *Intertextuality*, 182. It is, remarkably, used in the name of the Levite Korah בן־יצהר in Num 16 (and related references), who becomes a paradigm of one who establishes himself against the ministers Yhwh has chosen. It is possible that the locution in Zech 4 represents an ironic inversion of Korah's name and thus underscores the status and identity of the implements as Yhwh's chosen servants.

28   See Num 18:12; Deut 7:13; 11:14; 12:17; 14:23; 18:4; 28:51; Jer 31:12; Hos 2:10 (Eng 8), 24 (22); Joel 1:10; 2:19, 24; Hag 1:11; Neh 5:11; 10:38 (Eng 37), 40 (39); 13:5, 12; 2 Chron 31:5; 32:28. So also Jauhiainen, *Zechariah*, 48–49; Petersen, *Haggai*, 230–31.

29   For the link between Haggai and Zech 1–6 via Zech 7–8, see e.g. John R. Barker, "Haggai," in *The Oxford Handbook of the Minor Prophets*, ed. Julia M. O'Brien (Oxford: Oxford University Press, 2021), 521–22; Wöhrle, *Abschluss*, 16–17.

30   See Wöhrle, *Abschluss*, 17: "Durch die in Sach 7–8 eingebrachten Nachträge ... wird sodann festgehalten, dass nicht nur der Tempelbau, sondern auch alle weitere Zuwendung Jhwhs von der anhaltenden Umkehr des Volkes abhängig ist."

31   Jauhiainen has astutely suggested that the identity of the olive trees and lampstand might be left intentionally undisclosed in Zech 4, expressed in terms of "ideal *future* servants

Rather than breaking the curse of drought as their title suggests, however, the sackcloth-clad figures of Rev 11 call it down, like Elijah in 1 Kgs 17 (Rev 11:6), indicating that their time is still one of judgement rather than restoration.[32]

Commentators have routinely raised the question of Revelation's discrepancy in numbers relative to Zech 4: where Rev 11 describes the witnesses as two olive trees and two lampstands, Zechariah has only one lampstand.[33] The answer could simply be that Rev 11 has two individuals to fit into a single image. However, a better solution may be found in Revelation's subtly conflated interpretation of Zechariah's lampstand imagery in both the two witnesses of Rev 11 and the lampstands that represent the churches in Rev 1–3.[34] John's first vision in Rev 1 describes "seven golden lampstands, and in the midst of the lampstands one like a son of man" (1:12–13). There are few details implicit in this passage to tie its lampstand image specifically to Zechariah, rather than simply to the tabernacle descriptions of Exodus and Numbers.[35] Revelation 11, however, provides the missing link. The specific term translated "lampstand" (λυχνία) appears in Revelation only in chs. 1–2 and ch. 11, the latter of which unmistakably uses Zechariah. The numerical designation of seven lamps or lampstands, on the other hand, is unique to Rev 1–3, the Pentateuch, and Zech 4.[36]

---

of Yahweh" so that this restoration might be applied to multiple contexts (*Zechariah*, 48–49). This strategy indeed seems to be applied by the author of Rev 11, in which two unnamed witnesses take up the roles of בני־היצהר.

32   This role of judgement is likely highlighted by the witnesses' sackcloth apparel (see e.g. Aune, *Revelation 6–16*, 611; Beale, *Revelation*, 576; Blount, *Revelation*, 209). Contra Bauckham, who sees in this mournful attire a message of repentance couched in judgement (*Climax*, 278).

33   See e.g. Aune, *Revelation 6–16*, 612; Jauhiainen, *Zechariah*, 91. Allen notes that neither the phrase καὶ αἱ δύο λυχνίαι nor its Hebrew retroversion are "present in any version or manuscript that preserves Zech 4:14," and that "the material seems to be, at least superficially, John's innovation" ("Reusing Scripture," 5; also 7). He offers a thoughtful textual reconstruction of an alternative reading tradition of Zech 4:2 that could explain John's identification of two lampstands in Revelation ("Reusing Scripture," 7–12). While ultimately unprovable, his reading is compelling. However, I find an interpretation based in the literary links between Rev 1–3 and 11 to be equally compelling, as I describe below.

34   A connection here is also noted by e.g. Beale (*Revelation*, 574) and Martin Kiddle (*The Revelation of St. John*, MNTC [New York: Harper, 1940], 181).

35   So Jauhiainen, *Zechariah*, 85. See Exod 25, 37; Num 8.

36   Another potential intertext in this discussion is Rev 4:5, which describes the "seven spirits of God" as "seven lamps of fire" (see e.g. Bauckham, *Climax*, 165–66; Beale, *Revelation*, 206–207). The images are clearly connected, but must be differentiated because of the distinction in terms. Only the lampstand churches of Rev 1–3 and the witnesses of Rev 11 are called λυχνίαι. The masculine cognate term λύχνος is further used to designate the "lamp" whose light will no longer shine in the destroyed Babylon (Rev 18:23), as well as the "lamp" no longer needed in the restored Jerusalem (22:5) because its "lamp" is the lamb (21:23). The term for the seven lamps which equate to the seven spirits in Rev 4:5,

As such, both Rev 1–3 and Rev 11 must be understood in light of their mutual background in Zech 4 and their resultant link with each other.[37]

The interpretive payoff of this connection is significant. In Zech 4, seven lamps are connected to a single golden lampstand in their centre, with an olive tree on each side to supply the lampstand with oil (4:2–3). Revelation 1–3 turns the seven lamps into the seven lampstand churches, connected to the "one like a son of man" who is placed at their centre and walks among them (1:13; 2:1).[38] Revelation 11 further adapts that image of the churches and personifies it as two individuals, adding in Zechariah's olive trees to give the witnesses the power of sustaining the life of the lamp/lampstand churches.

The two witnesses, then, personify both the churches and the power that keeps them alive. As both the lampstands and the source of oil, they are self-sustaining. As long as they survive, the light of God's righteous communities survives. The reader knows from the narrative of Rev 11, however, that there is a period during which the witnesses are overcome and killed. At this

---

on the other hand, is λαμπάς, which is used elsewhere in Revelation almost exclusively to denote brightness or splendour (15:6; 18:14; 19:8; 22:1, 16). The only exception is in 8:10 in the third trumpet judgement, where a star fell "burning like a torch [λαμπάς]." Bauckham has argued that the lamps/spirits of Rev 4 should be interpreted as the power borne by the church/witness lampstands to enable their prophetic message (*Climax*, 165; similarly Jauhiainen, *Zechariah*, 90). It is noteworthy that LXX Zech 4:2–3 uses the rare term λαμπαδεῖον (found only in two other passages in the LXX [Exod 38:16 {MT 37:22} and 1 Kgs 7:35 {MT 7:49}] and nowhere in the NT) to render the Hebrew גלה ("bowl") that sits atop the lampstand (LXX λυχνία) of Zechariah's vision. Any argument for a literary connection between the seven spirits who are lamps (Rev 4) and the seven lampstands (Rev 1–3), then, should be based in a potential mutual allusion to Zechariah and in the common use of the number seven, rather than in any English association between lamps and lampstands.

37   Jauhiainen comes to a very similar conclusion: "In 11:4 John finally draws together various threads from Zech 4 that he has been developing. First … John identifies his two witnesses as the two mysterious Zecharian olive trees. Just as the olive trees in Zech 4 are necessary for the realization and proper functioning of the coming temple, so the witnesses are crucial in the building of the eschatological temple. Second, just as the two 'sons of oil' in Zech 4 suggests two individuals, so the two witnesses are, on the narrative level, two individuals. However, the witnesses also symbolize the church(es), hence their identification with two lampstands. Third, the temple in Revelation is not to be built by [human] might, nor by [military] power, but by God's Spirit (Zech 4:6) … Finally, just as with the lampstand in Zech 4, so also two lampstands in Rev 11 have lamps (though not explicitly mentioned), and lamps were earlier identified with God's seven spirits. The lampstands give their light and are able to fulfil their prophetic vocation only insofar as they have lamps that are burning" (*Zechariah*, 92–93).

38   Beale notes that the "one like a son of man" is presented with imagery of both a king and a priest, "which would have precedent in the two figures of Zech 4:3, 11–14 (see on Rev. 11:4)" (*Revelation*, 209).

point, the only thing that can resurrect the life of the endangered churches is the "breath [πνεῦμα] of life from God" (11:11); the same πνεῦμα that lights the lampstands of Revelation (4:5) and is associated with the lamb (5:6), who is also the "son of man" in the midst of the churches (1:16, 20; cf. 3:1; 4:5; 5:6). This combination of images ultimately provides to Revelation's readers the hope of restoration promised in Zech 4:6: "'Not by might nor by power, but by my spirit,' says Yhwh of hosts."[39]

2.4   *Summary*

Thus, the highly composite pattern of literary allusions just within Rev 11:1–13 provides three distinct, yet complementary and interwoven, lenses through which to view God's people. They are simultaneously the measured temple of Ezek 40–42, the endangered holy city, and the witnesses who are killed for their testimony to Jesus but ultimately resurrected by his spirit. All three images combine to demonstrate, in microcosm, the fate of the people of God: their endangerment as well as their ultimate preservation and restoration.

The temple and the city are specifically linked to the two witnesses, depicted as Moses and Elijah. These are given a prophetic voice to the surrounding world, knowing that it will not listen. Simultaneously, as Zechariah's olive trees and lampstands, the witnesses also represent both the life of the people of God and their continuous survival. In other words, Elijah here is once again portrayed both as a prophet and as the embodiment of the remnant. When the two witnesses are taken to heaven, just like Elijah in Kings, the reader is implicitly prepared to see the holy city descend back down (21:2), in a day when all opposition is vanquished and God is perfectly present with his people.

3   The Prophet and the People: Ezekiel 37 and Ezekiel 2–3

This conflated depiction of the people of God places Elijah squarely back in the composite role which his character has filled throughout the texts we have examined: that of an embodiment of both the paradigmatic prophet and the endangered righteous community. One further set of intertexts, which play both a structural and an analogical role in the narrative of Rev 11, offers additional evidence that the author indeed intends to merge these realities in the persons of the two witnesses.

---

39   Bauckham sees this verse as central to the reason behind Revelation's repeated use of Zech 4 (*Climax*, 162–63).

The resurrection of the witnesses in Rev 11:11, at which point "spirit of life from God entered into them [πνεῦμα ζωῆς ἐκ τοῦ θεοῦ εἰσῆλθεν ἐν αὐτοῖς] and they stood upon their feet [καὶ ἔστησαν ἐπὶ τοὺς πόδας αὐτῶν]," is widely recognised as an allusion to Ezek 37 and the revivification of the dry bones.[40] The agent there is once again a visionary, who is told to prophesy over a valley of dry bones. What is often translated as a "noise" and a "rattling" that follows as the bones arise is actually קול and רעש, rendered elsewhere as "voice" and "earthquake."[41] While LXX Ezek 37:7 is missing the reference to a voice, it translates רעש as σεισμός, the same phenomenon that occurs in Rev 11:13 after the witnesses receive πνεῦμα (11:11) and hear a "voice" (φωνή – 11:12). The result, in Ezekiel's dry bones pericope, is that "the breath came into them and they lived [εἰσῆλθεν εἰς αὐτοὺς τὸ πνεῦμα, καὶ ἔζησαν], and they stood on their feet [καὶ ἔστησαν ἐπὶ τῶν ποδῶν αὐτῶν]" (LXX Ezek 37:10).

These dry bones that receive "breath" or "spirit" (רוח/πνεῦμα) are explicitly identified in Ezekiel as the people of Israel, and described in resurrection imagery like that seen in the witnesses of Rev 11:

> [11] And he said to me, "Son of man, these bones are all the house of Israel. Behold, they are saying, 'Our bones have dried up and our hope has perished; we are cut off.'
> [12] Therefore prophesy and say to them, 'Thus says the Lord Yhwh, "Behold, I am opening your graves and I will cause you to come up from your graves, my people, and I will bring you into the land of Israel.
> [13] And you will know that I am Yhwh when I open your graves and when I cause you to come up from your graves, my people.
> [14] I will put my spirit in you and you will live, and I will cause you to rest upon your land, and you will know that I am Yhwh; I have spoken and I will act." The oracle of Yhwh.'" (Ezek 37:11–14)

On the basis of this allusion, Revelation's resurrected witnesses who stand on their feet fill the analogical slot of Ezekiel's endangered people of God and their restoration. This image is consistent both with the portrayal of the witnesses as Elijah and with the conflated image of the people of God that is presented at the beginning of Rev 11.

At the same time, some of the primary locutions in Rev 11 that trigger the connection to Ezek 37 can also be found in the context of Ezekiel's call narrative

---

40   See e.g. Aune, *Revelation 6–16*, 623; Bauckham, *Climax*, 170 n. 35; Beale, *Revelation*, 596–97; Blount, *Revelation*, 215–16; Charles, *Revelation*, 290; Mounce, *Revelation*, 222.

41   As, for example, in 1 Kgs 19:11–12!

in Ezek 2–3. This text is also unmistakably present in the context of Rev 11, as it forms the source for the image of the "little book" which John is given to eat and then to prophesy in Rev 10:8–11. The content of Rev 11 may be considered to be a portion of this prophetic call and the book that accompanies it, which turns John's stomach bitter but is "sweet as honey" in his mouth (10:9–10).[42] When Ezekiel is called, he is commanded to eat a scroll containing words of woe which "was in my mouth like honey for sweetness" (Ezek 3:3). This call narrative is introduced in Ezek 2:1 with the command to "stand upon your feet [LXX στῆθι ἐπὶ τοὺς πόδας σου] and I will speak with you." Immediately, "spirit entered into me and caused me to stand upon my feet [ἦλθεν ἐπ' ἐμὲ πνεῦμα ... καὶ ἔστησέ με ἐπὶ τοὺς πόδας μου]" (2:2).[43] In the course of the subsequent call and its accompanying vision, the prophet encounters the glory of Yhwh along-side a קול רעש (φωνὴ τοῦ σεισμοῦ – LXX Ezek 3:13). He falls on his face, from which position again "spirit entered into me and caused me to stand upon my feet [ἦλθεν ἐπ' ἐμὲ πνεῦμα καὶ ἔστησέ με ἐπὶ πόδας μου]" (3:24).[44]

Thus, while the shape of Ezek 37 is immediately visible in the resurrection of the witnesses, the presence of Ezek 2–3 must be acknowledged by its role at the end of Rev 10. As such, this latter intertext forms a structural frame around the witness pericope (Rev 10:8–11; 11:11), which is merged with an allusion to the dry bones. The interpretive implications of this composite image are, again, significant. In Ezek 37, the dry bones who receive life are explicitly said to be the people of God. In Ezek 2–3, however, the same terms are used to character-ise the prophet. Both texts are undeniably present in the imagery within and surrounding Rev 11, and both appear to be linked to the same phrase. Their interpretive outworkings must be held together. On the basis of Ezek 2–3, at an individual level, the witnesses are an analogy for the prophet. On the basis of Ezek 37, at a corporate level, they portray the community of the people of God.

---

42   That Rev 11:1–13 functions as the content of John's prophetic call in ch. 10 has been noted
       by e.g. Beale, *Revelation*, 556; Blount, *Revelation*, 198–201. Aune notes the link between
       10:8–11 and 11:3–13 through the use of προφητεύω (10:11; 11:3) (*Revelation 6–16*, 594). For
       the structural integration of 10:1–11:13, see Felise Tavo, *Woman, Mother, and Bride: An
       Exegetical Investigation in the "Ecclesial" Notions of the Apocalypse* (Leuven: Peeters, 2007),
       173–77.

43   The Hebrew and Greek texts of Ezek 2:2 each contain clauses missing by the other. Where
       MT reads ותעמדני על־רגלי כאשר דבר אלי רוח בי ותבא; LXX states καὶ ἦλθεν ἐπ' ἐμὲ
       πνεῦμα καὶ ἀνέλαβέ με καὶ ἐξῆρέ με καὶ ἔστησέ με ἐπὶ τοὺς πόδας μου.

44   The use of ἐβασάνισαν for "tormented" in Rev 11:10 may be intended as another trigger of
       Ezek 3, which uses מכשול (LXX βάσανος) as an "obstacle" intended for the destruction of
       the formerly righteous person who turns to wickedness (3:20 – cf. discussion of John 7–8).

That such dual characterisation is given to a composite figure undeniably identified with Elijah argues that the writer of Rev 11 recognised the capacity of the Elijah figure to hold conflated identifications, as established throughout Second Temple literature. In the literary background to the two witnesses, the character roles of prophet and people cannot be separated. The figures able to hold back rain, control fire, and ascend to heaven represent both the prophetic voice and the righteous people.

Just as the measuring motif of Ezek 40–42 reappears in Rev 21–22, so, apparently, does the conclusion to the prophetic mission of Ezek 2–3. Revelation 22:10 announces that the time of prophetic fulfilment is approaching, and therefore "let the unrighteous one still be unrighteous, and let the unclean one still be unclean, and let the righteous one still practise righteousness, and let the holy one still be holy" (22:11). This expression of the immutability of the people's fate appears to draw on Ezek 3:27: "the one who hears will hear and the one who refuses will refuse, because they are a rebellious house."[45] The distinction between the holy and the profane set up by the measurement motif of Ezek 40–42 would then be underscored by the allusion to Ezek 2–3. Both are reprised in Revelation's conclusion, which represents the conclusion of the witnesses' prophetic mission: the spirit of God will give life to his people and the righteous community will be permanently and irrevocably established.

4   The Prophet and the People at the Beginning and the End

In light of the key role Rev 11 plays in the interpretation of both the beginning of the book of Revelation and its end, it may be argued that this chapter provides a key juxtaposing and comparative link.[46] The identification of the prophetic figures as "witnesses" (μάρτυρες) integrates them into a description of the people of God that runs through Revelation.[47] Both μάρτυς (witness, martyr) and μαρτυρία (testimony) are terms consistently used to refer to the righteous and

---

45   The statement in Rev 22 may represent a conflated allusion to Ezek 3 and Dan 12:10, as noted by Beale (*Revelation*, 1131).

46   For a discussion of the role of Rev 11 in the centre portion of Revelation (10:1–15:4), see Elisabeth Schüssler Fiorenza, *The Book of Revelation: Justice and Judgment* (Philadelphia: Fortress, 1985), 53–55.

47   Aune notes that the designation μάρτυρες is "a critical term within the theology of the book as a whole" (*Revelation 6–16*, 610). See also Beale, *Revelation*, 572; Blount, *Revelation*, 211–12.

their message and faith.[48] Remarkably, the paradigmatic witness presented in the book is not the Mosaic/Elijanic figure(s) of Rev 11, but rather Jesus himself, the "faithful witness [ὁ μάρτυς, ὁ πιστός], the firstborn of the dead, and the ruler of the kings of the earth" (1:5; cf. 3:14; 22:20).[49] The Moses/Elijah figures therefore not only embody the broader body of witnesses, but also stand along with them in the pattern of Jesus as they prove their faithfulness in death and are raised back to life.

As the book progresses, the righteous communities and their message continue to be described in μάρτυς-terms, particularly after the introduction of the witnesses in Rev 11. That these are meant to embody the larger identity of God's people is evident from their links with the churches in Rev 1–3, as well as from the threefold image of temple, holy city, and witness that forms the background to their introduction. The image of the temple, as well as of the Zecharian olive trees/lampstands, provides a priestly nuance, while the images of Moses and Elijah dressed in sackcloth endow them with the responsibility of prophetic judgement.

On the other side of Rev 11, all of these images are linked to the final restoration of chs. 21–22.[50] The measurement motif that opens Rev 11 is concluded in Rev 21, where it reappears as a golden rod in the hand of a heavenly messenger, measuring the perfectly holy city (21:15). The literary presence of this "holy city," vanished from the narrative entirely since Rev 11, is now reintroduced as the new and restored Jerusalem is released from heaven (21:2).[51] The image of the lampstands that connect Moses and Elijah with the churches disappears after Rev 11, until the light such lampstands produce is used as a contrast

---

48   As also of the witnesses' testimony in 11:7. See Rev 1:2, 9; 2:13; 6:9; 12:11, 17; 17:6; 19:10; 20:4; 22:16, 18. Beale notes the relationship between the death of the witnesses in 11:7 and the martyrs killed for their witness in 6:9–11 (*Revelation*, 587–88).

49   Beale points out the use of μάρτυς in reference to Israel in LXX Isa 43:10–13 and 44:6–8, and argues that these texts may "contribute to John's understanding of 'witness' in 1:5 and elsewhere in Revelation" (*Revelation*, 213–14).

50   Scholars have noted the connections that exist between Rev 1–3 and 21–22 (see e.g. Ian Paul, "Source, Structure, and Composition in the Book of Revelation," in *The Book of Revelation: Currents in British Research on the Apocalypse*, ed. Garrick V. Allen, Ian Paul, and Simon P. Woodman, WUNT II/411 [Tübingen: Mohr Siebeck, 2015], 42). Less common is an acknowledgement of the role of ch. 11 within this structural framework.

51   As Beale (*Revelation*, 1089) has observed, the πλατείας τῆς πόλεως on which the bodies of the witnesses lie in Rev 11:8 are now transformed into ἡ πλατεῖα τῆς πόλεως χρυσίον καθαρὸν – the city street of pure gold (21:21). See also Robert W. Wall, *Revelation*, NIBC 18 (Peabody: Hendrickson, 1991), 255: "the street of their former shame has now been replaced by the street of their eternal glory."

between the great city's destruction (ch. 18) and the holy city's perfection (chs. 21–22). The feminine term λυχνία (lampstand) only appears in Rev 1–2 and 11, but its masculine cognate λύχνος is used in the downfall of "Babylon" in 18:23, where no lamp will ever shine again.[52] The new Jerusalem, on the other hand, will need no sun because the lamb/the Lord God is its light (λύχνος – 21:23; 22:5). In this context, "the role of God's people as 'lampstands' bearing the light of the divine lamp finally will be perfected."[53] In the restored holy city, the light-giving work of the community will be done when it experiences the unmediated presence of God.

The use of Elijah in Revelation, then, is based firmly in the overarching purpose of the book; namely, to describe the final and complete establishment of God's righteous community in his presence. It develops the theme of faithful witnesses who follow the ultimate witness, Jesus, and who are willing to give their lives for the message. They are the temple that is separated and chosen; the holy city that will die but ultimately be restored. If Jesus is the paradigm witness, the secondary witnesses are also portrayed as both human and heavenly, victorious over death, associated both with the prophetic message and the people whom they represent. No traditional portrait, I would argue, better encompasses all of these realities than the figure of Elijah.

Revelation's transformation of the scriptural Elijah figure for early Christian communities is summarised and repeated at the end of the book:

> [6] And the Lord, the God of the spirits of the prophets [τῶν πνευμάτων τῶν προφητῶν] has sent his messenger [ἀπέστειλεν τὸν ἄγγελον αὐτοῦ] to show to his servants the things which must take place in a short time.
>
> [7] And behold, I am coming swiftly [ταχύ]. Blessed is the one who keeps the words of the prophecy of this book ...
>
> [12] Behold, I am coming swiftly [ταχύ], and my recompense with me, to repay each person according to his work ...
>
> [16] I, Jesus, have sent my messenger [ἔπεμψα τὸν ἄγγελόν μου] to testify [μαρτυρῆσαι] to you these things for the churches ...
>
> [20] The one testifying [μαρτυρῶν] these things says "Yes, I am coming swiftly [ταχύ]." Amen. Come Lord Jesus. (Rev 22:6–7, 12, 16, 20)

---

52   Rev 18:23 is likely an allusion to Jer 25:10, which uses נר to describe the lamp that will
       no longer exist in Babylon; the same term used for the seven lamps on the lampstand of
       Zech 4:2.

53   Beale, *Revelation*, 1115.

This benediction both completes a frame around the book of Revelation itself (cf. ἀποστείλας διὰ τοῦ ἀγγέλου αὐτοῦ in Rev 1:1) and lexically produces a conclusion to the promise linked in Malachi with the coming of Elijah: "Behold, I am sending my messenger [LXX ἐξαποστέλλω τὸν ἄγγελόν μου], and he will prepare a way before me, and suddenly the Lord whom you are seeking will come to his temple ... And I will come near to you for judgement, and I will be a swift witness [LXX μάρτυς ταχύς]" (Mal 3:1, 5).[54]

The reference to the "spirits of the prophets" further supports a background in the Elijah image. Where Malachi's epilogue identified Elijah as a future coming messenger, Revelation's conclusion states that the messenger has come and has testified for the churches.[55] The Gospel of John, as we have seen, presents John the Baptist as one "sent" (ἀπεσταλμένος – John 1:6) from God as a "witness to bear witness about the light [μαρτυρίαν ἵνα μαρτυρήσῃ περὶ τοῦ φωτός]" (1:7, cf. v. 8). As an interim Elijah figure, the Baptist fulfilled the role of Malachi's sent messenger who testified in preparation for Jesus' initial appearance, and who paid for his testimony with his life. To Revelation, however, the swift witness of judgement in Malachi, the Lord who comes suddenly to his temple, is ultimately none other than Jesus himself, and the churches are those who testify to him.

The book of Revelation, then, reawakens the Elijah image because it purports to conclude his story. In the establishment of the righteous community, embodied in the new and restored Jerusalem, the messenger-prophet's role will finally be complete. He has been sent, he has come, and he has testified. He has represented the people both as one of them and as over them, both in their victory and in their suffering. He has embodied simultaneously the undying prophetic word and the endangered people, to an extent surpassed only by Jesus himself. Whether under the threat of Jezebel, the endangerment of exile, the persecution of a Roman emperor, or the dread of supernatural forces, Elijah has lived on to demonstrate that Yhwh yet preserves a remnant.

---

54   "Insofar as John can be seen in the same prophetic tradition and Jesus was perceived by the early church as the ultimate fulfilment of many ancient prophecies, it would not be surprising if John's vision contained a number of such attempts at prophetic closure of unfulfilled prophecies" (Jauhiainen, *Zechariah*, 153–54; see also 161).

55   Ἄγγελοι play significant roles throughout Revelation, most of which contain no connection to Elijah. The combination of a "sent messenger" and the witness image (Rev 22:16), however, allows the identification to be made in this case.

5   Conclusion: a Remnant Preserved and Restored

Thus, the witnesses in Rev 11 represent the survival of both the prophetic voice
and the endangered righteous community. We have seen how the Elijah image
was demonstrably and repeatedly used to portray the preservation of a righteous remnant in the context of Second Temple interpretive communities. As
such, the portrayal of Revelation's prophetic witnesses with Elijanic imagery
allow the other μάρτυρες throughout the book, and within its readership, to
claim the confident hope of ultimate vindication. When Elijah has finished
his mission, all that is left is for Revelation's ultimate paradigmatic witness
to say "Yes, I am coming quickly," and for hearers to respond "Amen. Come,
Lord Jesus" (22:20).

CHAPTER 8

Conclusion

In this study, I have sought to demonstrate that Elijah's significance as a literary figure in the Second Temple period is a result of his characterisation and reception as a prophet who embodies the righteous community. The assessment of Ben Zvi, quoted in my introduction, argues that a figure's literary centrality in this period was a byproduct of its receiving communities' identification with it, and vice versa.[1] "The power," Ben Zvi further notes, "of [such a] site of memory is that it can be seen from multiple perspectives and shifting arrays of light and shadow and thus can embody, balance and communicate all of them."[2] This kind of multivalence is precisely what we have seen in the many facets and presentations of the single figure of Elijah. That this figure continues to grip hearts and imaginations to this day argues that he reflects, in some way and form, the depth of the human experience. All of the diverse facets of his character come together to give voice and form to the lament, triumph, despair, and, ultimately, restoration of the people of God.

Beginning from his presentation in Kings, I argued that Elijah's characterisation as both a prophet and the embodiment of the righteous community hinges on a recognition of the Second Temple literary strategy of conflated allusion, the presence of which has been demonstrated in other texts.[3] Based on the diachronic frameworks of McKenzie and Blum, I presented the narrative Elijah cycle, in its current form, as a post-exilic insertion into the storyline of DtrH. Building on the foundation of Carr and Ben Zvi, I further proposed that Elijah's endangerment and survival in the Kings cycle is literarily constructed to function as a point of identification for post-exilic communities, and that this literary presentation forms the basis for his ongoing relevance in early Jewish and Christian texts.

My analysis of Elijah's narrative characterisation in Kings demonstrated that a recognition of the conflated allusions at play is critical to his interpretation. These allusions show Elijah characterised with imagery of Moses, Hagar, and Ishmael, forming a composite figure simultaneously patterned after a prophetic parent and an endangered child, which can further be identified with Israel. I showed that the jarring narrative contrast between 1 Kgs 17–18 and

---

1 Ben Zvi, "Memory of Moses," 335.
2 Ben Zvi, "Memory of Moses," 353.
3 See Grossman, "Dynamic Analogies."

1 Kgs 19 is the result of an intentional inversion of the results of Carmel on Horeb, in which Elijah must fail as a prophet like Moses in order to account for the exile. At the same time, this contrast is also intended to remind a post-exilic audience that Yhwh preserves a remnant, even when the nation as a whole does not repent and must face judgement.

This study then examined Elijah's identification as the priestly-prophetic messenger of Malachi, demonstrating that all four uses of the term מלאך within the book are interpreted by the later writer of the epilogue as a single figure. This figure is exegetically identified as the Elijah of Kings, who is also linked with the zealous figure of Phinehas in Num 25. I described the confla-tion in Mal 3:1 of the preparation of Yhwh's way from Isa 40 with the guarding of the people's way from Exod 23 via a similar strategy to that demonstrated by Stromberg in Isa 57: that is, the messenger prepares Yhwh's way by guarding the people on the way of obedience. This mission is represented in Malachi's epilogue as Elijah's "turning of hearts," by which the entire community is to be turned back to Yhwh. In its function as a link between the corpora of the Hebrew Bible, Malachi's epilogue presents Elijah's return as a second chance for the success of the Mosaic mission, in which Yhwh's righteous community will finally be established when Elijah comes again.

Among the later Second Temple texts, I observed that Sir 48:1–11 is the first to offer a presentation of Elijah based unequivocally in both Kings and Malachi. Ben Sira further alludes to Isa 49 in his interpretation of Elijah's mis-sion, thereby linking Elijah with Isaiah's servant figure – an image applied both to a prophet and to Yhwh's people as a whole. First Maccabees 2 adopts Elijah's association with Phinehas from Malachi and possibly even from Kings, dem-onstrating that later readers recognised the allusions present in earlier texts. *Lives of the Prophets* 21 recognises Elijah's dual priestly and prophetic role. The Apocalypse of Zephaniah appears to have some conception of Elijah as a righteous figure who continues to exist in a state beyond death. 4Q558 likely connects Elijah with the day of Yhwh, demonstrating further consistency with earlier traditions. 4Q521 has frequently been argued to identify Elijah with a messianic image, but this claim promises more than can be substantiated by the fragmentary text. What it does show is a collage of allusions to multiple scriptural passages that portray Yhwh's coming restoration as comprehensive and sure. An allusion to Mal 3:24 in one of its fragments encompasses Elijah in a future restoration that spans Israelite tradition. He is one prophetic figure whose identity is part of a much greater reality in which Yhwh preserves and restores his people.

An analysis of the New Testament Gospels revealed their writers' thor-oughgoing familiarity with and use of techniques of conflated allusion. These writers adeptly apply various facets of an already-conflated Elijah image in turn to John the Baptist, Jesus, and Jesus' disciples, thereby perpetuating this image further as one of both the quintessential prophet and the embodiment of God's people. In the Synoptics, the combination of Elijah with images of Moses and Isaiah's servant results in a presentation of Jesus as surpassing any traditional prophetic expectation, both in suffering and in glorification. I argued for a similar conclusion in the Gospel of John, particularly by means of the ascent/descent motif. As the one who descended from a heavenly origin, Jesus is greater than any human who claims ascent, Elijah and Moses included. Simultaneously, as the Son of Man, Jesus is greater than any celestial messenger who descends, only to deliver a message, and then returns. He is at once more heavenly than Elijah and more human than the angels, thus presenting a superior paradigm of both the prophet and the people.

This identification of the Elijah image with the righteous community is carried on via allusions in Acts and the New Testament epistles. I argued that Paul applies the Elijah image to himself both before and after his conversion, via descriptions of zeal reminiscent of 1 Kgs 18 and a potential reference to a trip to Sinai in Gal 1:17, and even, possibly, through his description of a heavenly ascent in 2 Cor 12. In Rom 11, on the other hand, Paul highlights Elijah's function as a judgement prophet, and identifies himself with the remnant that is saved by grace. As such, Paul sees in himself both of Elijah's core roles: that of the prophet like Moses who sees Israel's endangerment and pronounces judgement on those who do not repent, and that of the righteous remnant that is preserved. In the letter of James, Elijah functions as a fundamental rhetorical link in urging readers to prepare for the eschaton. Here I argued that the Elijah analogy is lexically and structurally central to the book's argument, and that it endows readers with the same power wielded by the prophet as they pray. In other words, the Elijah example in James reawakens the prophet's forerunner role in the letter's early Christian readers, and calls them to identify themselves with the prophet who is like them. Once again, then, Elijah functions as a living description of God's people.

In an analysis of Rev 11, finally, I proposed that the Elijah image in the form of the two witnesses functions as a hinge point for the presentation of God's people in the entire book. The witnesses are given prophetic power, presented as paradigmatic sufferers, and supernaturally caught up to heaven. They are paralleled with the temple as the locus of the presence of God. Simultaneously, they are described as lampstands corresponding to the churches in Rev 1–3, and literarily paralleled with the holy city that is critically endangered in Rev 11:2 but then restored in chs. 21–22. This holy city descends from heaven, where the Elijah-like witnesses have been waiting, as the gloriously restored new Jerusalem, in which God's preserved people will never be endangered again.

The answer to the question of "why Elijah" in Second Temple Jewish and early Christian literature, then, is found in Elijah's dual characterisation as the paradigmatic prophet and the preserved people of God. He is the prophet who is also the people, and his immortality in the narrative of Kings, as well as his ongoing literary life, ensures readers of the continued survival of a righteous community. This image is one of identification and of hope; one that acknowledges endangerment and simultaneously promises glorious restoration. I have sought to show the consistent evidence for this motif throughout the Elijah texts of the broader Second Temple period, which provides a visceral expression of the suffering and hope of the communities who produced and received these texts. Elijah embodies their reality. His predicted return as expressed in Malachi raises the hope that a prophet like Moses will yet succeed in establishing them as a restored people. The ascension of Jesus into heaven in the footsteps of Elijah projects this hope into the future a second time for the early Christian communities, promising that their suffering and martyrdom will also not be in vain. The Elijah image promises that the souls which cry out "how long?" from under the altar (Rev 6:10) will become the holy city that descends from heaven restored (21:2). At this point, Elijah's prophetic mission will be accomplished, and the righteous community embodied by his perpetual existence will declare with one voice, הנה אליהו – "Behold, Yhwh is my God" (1 Kgs 18:11, 14).

Bibliography

Ábel, František. "Elijah in the Message of Paul the Apostle: Typology of the Elijah Figure in Paul's Missionary Zeal for the Gospel." *StBiSl* 13 (2021): 266–95.

Achenbach, Reinhard. "'A Prophet Like Moses' (Deuteronomy 18:15) – 'No Prophet Like Moses' (Deuteronomy 34:10): Some Observations on the Relation between the Pentateuch and the Latter Prophets." Pages 435–58 in *The Pentateuch: International Perspectives on Current Research*. Edited by Thomas B. Dozeman, Konrad Schmid, and Baruch J. Schwarz. FAT 78. Tübingen: Mohr Siebeck, 2011.

Aernie, Jeffrey W. *Is Paul Also Among the Prophets? An Examination of the Relationship between Paul and the Old Testament Prophetic Tradition in 2 Corinthians.* LNTS 467. London: T&T Clark, 2012.

Ahearne-Kroll, Stephen P. *The Psalms of Lament in Mark's Passion.* Cambridge: Cambridge University Press, 2007.

Albertz, Rainer. *Elia: Ein feuriger Kämpfer für Gott.* 4th edition. Leipzig: Evangelische Verlagsanstalt, 2015.

Allen, Garrick V. *The Book of Revelation and Early Jewish Textual Culture.* Cambridge: Cambridge University Press, 2017.

Allen, Garrick V. "Reusing Scripture in the Book of Revelation: Reworking Zechariah 4 in the Apocalypse." Pages 1–17 in *The Book of Revelation: Currents in British Research on the Apocalypse*. Edited by Garrick V. Allen, Ian Paul, and Simon P. Woodman. WUNT II/411. Tübingen: Mohr Siebeck, 2015.

Allen, Garrick V. "Textual Pluriformity and Allusion in the Book of Revelation: The Text of Zechariah 4 in the Apocalypse." *ZNW* 106 (2015): 136–45.

Allen, Ronald Barclay. "Elijah the Broken Prophet." *JETS* 22 (1979): 193–202.

Allison, Dale C. Jr. "Elijah Must Come First." *JBL* 103 (1984): 256–58.

Allison, Dale C. Jr. *The New Moses: A Matthean Typology.* Eugene: Wipf & Stock, 1993.

Anderson, Paul N. "Jesus, the Eschatological Prophet in the Fourth Gospel: A Case Study in Dialectical Tensions." *Faculty Publications – George Fox School of Theology* 284 (2018): 7–16.

Assis, Elie. "Moses, Elijah and the Messianic Hope: A New Reading of Malachi 3,22–24." *ZAW* 123 (2011): 207–20.

Assmann, Jan. *Das kulturelle Gedächtnis.* 8th edition. Munich: C.H. Beck, 2018.

Aune, David E. *Revelation 6–16.* WBC 52B. Nashville: Thomas Nelson, 1998.

Aus, Roger. *Water into Wine and the Beheading of John the Baptist.* Atlanta: Scholars, 1988.

Baird, William. "Visions, Revelation, and Ministry: Reflections on 2 Cor 12:1–5 and Gal 1:11–17." *JBL* 104 (1985): 651–62.

Baldwin, Joyce G. *Haggai, Zechariah and Malachi*. TOTC 28. Nottingham: Inter-Varsity Press, 1972.

Balentine, Samuel E. "The Prophet as Intercessor: A Reassessment." *JBL* 103 (1984): 161–73.

Barker, John R. "Haggai." Pages 511–23 in *The Oxford Handbook of the Minor Prophets*. Edited by Julia M. O'Brien. Oxford: Oxford University Press, 2021.

Barnett, Paul. *The Second Epistle to the Corinthians*. NICNT. Grand Rapids: Eerdmans, 1997.

Barrett, Charles K. *The Gospel According to St John*. 2nd edition. London: SPCK, 1978.

Bauckham, Richard. *The Climax of Prophecy*. Edinburgh: T&T Clark, 1993.

Bauckham, Richard. "James, 1 and 2 Peter, Jude." Pages 303–17 in *It is Written: Scripture Citing Scripture*. Edited by D.A. Carson and H.G.M. Williamson. Cambridge: Cambridge University Press, 1988.

Bauckham, Richard. "The Restoration of Israel in Luke-Acts." Pages 435–87 in *Restoration: Old Testament, Jewish, and Christian Perspectives*. Edited by James M. Scott. Leiden: Brill, 2001.

Beal, Lissa M. Wray. *1 & 2 Kings*. ApOTC. Downers Grove: InterVarsity Press, 2014.

Beal, Lissa M. Wray. "Setting the Table for Christ in the Elisha Narratives in 1 and 2 Kings." Pages 165–75 in *Interpreting the Old Testament Theologically: Essays in Honor of Willem A. VanGemeren*. Edited by Andrew T. Abernethy. Grand Rapids: Zondervan, 2018.

Beale, G.K. *The Book of Revelation*. NIGTC. Grand Rapids: Eerdmans, 1999.

Beare, Francis Wright. *The Gospel According to Matthew*. Oxford: Blackwell, 1981.

Beasley-Murray, George R. *The Book of Revelation*. NCB. London: Oliphants, 1974.

Becker, Eve-Marie. *Das Markus-Evangelium im Rahmen antiker Historiographie*. WUNT 194. Tübingen: Mohr Siebeck, 2006.

Becker, Michael. "'4Q521' und die Gesalbten." *RevQ* 18 (1997): 73–96.

Beentjes, Pancratius C. "Ben Sira's Portrayal of Aaron and Phinehas (Sir 45:6–25): An Interaction between Tradition and Innovation." Pages 51–63 in *Ben Sira in Conversation with Traditions*. Berlin: de Gruyter, 2022.

Beentjes, Pancratius C. *The Book of Ben Sira in Hebrew*. VTSup 68. Leiden: Brill, 1997.

Beentjes, Pancratius C. "Canon and Scripture in the Book of Ben Sira." Pages 591–605 in *"Happy the One who Meditates on Wisdom."* Leuven: Peeters, 2006.

Beentjes, Pancratius C. "In Search of Parallels: Ben Sira and the Book of Kings." Pages 118–31 in *Intertextual Studies in Ben Sira and Tobit: Essays in Honor of Alexander A. Di Lella*. Edited by Vincent Skemp and Jeremy Corley. Washington: Catholic Biblical Association of America, 2005.

Beentjes, Pancratius C. "Inverted Quotations in the Bible: A Neglected Stylistic Pattern." *Bib* 63 (1982): 506–23.

Beentjes, Pancratius C. *Jesus Sirach en Tenach*. PhD diss., Catholic Theological University Amsterdam, 1946.

Beentjes, Pancratius C. "Prophets and Prophecy in the Book of Ben Sira." Pages 135–50 in *Prophets, Prophecy, and Prophetic Texts in Second Temple Judaism*. Edited by Robert D. Haak and Michael H. Floyd. New York: T&T Clark, 2006.

Beentjes, Pancratius C. "Relations between Ben Sira and the Book of Isaiah." Pages 201–206 in *"Happy the One who Meditates on Wisdom."* Leuven: Peeters, 2006.

Beentjes, Pancratius C. "Some Major Topics in Ben Sira Research." Pages 3–16 in *"Happy the One who Meditates on Wisdom."* Leuven: Peeters, 2006.

Beers, Holly. *The Followers of Jesus as the 'Servant': Luke's Model from Isaiah for the Disciples in Luke-Acts*. LNTS 535. London: Bloomsbury T&T Clark, 2015.

Ben Zvi, Ehud. "Exploring the Memory of Moses 'The Prophet' in Late Persian/Early Hellenistic Yehud/Judah." Pages 335–64 in *Remembering Biblical Figures in the Late Persian and Early Hellenistic Periods: Social Memory and Imagination*. Edited by Diana V. Edelman and Ehud Ben Zvi. Oxford: Oxford University Press, 2013.

Ben Zvi, Ehud. "Jonah 4:11 and the Metaprophetic Character of the Book of Jonah." *JHebS* 9 (2009). Accessed November 14, 2024. https://jhsonline.org/index.php/jhs/article/view/6234.

Ben Zvi, Ehud. "The Memory of Abraham in Late Persian/Early Hellenistic Yehud/Judah." Pages 3–37 in *Remembering Biblical Figures in the Late Persian and Early Hellenistic Periods: Social Memory and Imagination*. Edited by Diana V. Edelman and Ehud Ben Zvi. Oxford: Oxford University Press, 2013.

Ben Zvi, Ehud. *Social Memory among the Literati of Yehud*. Berlin: de Gruyter, 2019.

Ben Zvi, Ehud. "The Study of Forgetting and the Forgotten in Ancient Israelite Discourse/s: Observations and Test Cases." Pages 139–57 in *Cultural Memory in Biblical Exegesis*. Edited by Pernille Carstens, Trine Bjørung Hasselbach, and Niels Peter Lemche. PHSC 17. Piscataway: Gorgias, 2012.

Ben-Porat, Ziva. "The Poetics of Literary Allusion." *PTL: A Journal for Descriptive Poetics and Theory of Literature* 1 (1976): 105–28.

Berger, Yitzhak. *Jonah in the Shadows of Eden*. Bloomington: Indiana University Press, 2016.

Blaylock, Richard M. "My Messenger, the LORD, and the Messenger of the Covenant: Malachi 3:1 Revisited." *SBJT* 20 (2016): 69–95.

Blenkinsopp, Joseph. *Isaiah 56–66*. AB 19B. New York: Doubleday, 2003.

Blenkinsopp, Joseph. *Prophecy and Canon: A Contribution to the Study of Jewish Origins*. Notre Dame: University of Notre Dame Press, 1977.

Blount, Brian K. *Revelation: A Commentary*. NTL. Louisville: Westminster John Knox, 2009.

Blum, Erhard. "Der Prophet und das Verderben Israels: Eine ganzheitliche, historisch-kritische Lektüre von 1 Reg XVII–XIX." *VT* 47 (1997): 277–92.

Boda, Mark. "Oil, Crowns and Thrones: Prophet, Priest and King in Zechariah 1:7–6:15." Pages 379–404 in *Perspectives on Hebrew Scriptures I*. Edited by Ehud Ben Zvi. Piscataway: Gorgias, 2007.

de Boer, Martinus C. *Galatians*. NTL. Louisville: Westminster John Knox, 2011.

Borgen, Peder. "Some Jewish Exegetical Traditions as Background for Son of Man Sayings in John's Gospel (Jn 3,13–14 and context)." Pages 243–58 in *L'Évangile de Jean: Sources, rédaction, théologie*. Edited by M. de Jonge. BETL 44. Leuven: Leuven University Press, 1977.

Botner, Max. "The Role of Transcriptional Probability in the Text-Critical Debate on Mark 1:1." *CBQ* 77 (2015): 467–80.

Bottini, Giovanni Claudio. "Continuity and Innovation in Biblical Tradition: Elijah from 1 Kgs 17–18 to Jas 5:17–18." *StBiSl* 11 (2019): 120–29.

Brady, Christian M.M. "What Shall We Remember, the Deeds or the Faith of Our Ancestors? A Comparison of 1 Maccabees 2 and Hebrews 11." Pages 107–19 in *Earliest Christianity within the Boundaries of Judaism: Essays in Honor of Bruce Chilton*. Edited by Alan Avery-Peck, Craig A. Evans, and Jacob Neusner. Boston: Brill, 2016.

Brodie, Thomas L. *The Crucial Bridge*. Collegeville: Liturgical, 2000.

Brown-Driver-Briggs Hebrew and English Lexicon, The Enhanced. Oxford: Clarendon, 1959.

Brown, Raymond E. *The Gospel According to John*. 3 volumes. AB 29. New Haven: Yale University Press, 1995.

Bruce, F.F. *The Epistle of Paul to the Galatians*. NIGTC. Exeter: Paternoster, 1982.

Bruce, F.F. *The Letter of Paul to the Romans: An Introduction and Commentary*. TNTC 6. Leicester: Inter-Varsity Press, 1985.

Buck, Charles and Greer Taylor. *Saint Paul: A Study of the Development of His Thought*. New York: Charles Scribner's Sons, 1969.

Bühner, Jan-A. *Der Gesandte und sein Weg im 4. Evangelium*. WUNT II/2. Tübingen: Mohr Siebeck, 1977.

Burkett, Delbert. *The Son of the Man in the Gospel of John*. JSNTSup 56. Sheffield: Sheffield Academic, 1991.

Burnett, Joel S. "'Going Down' to Bethel: Elijah and Elisha in the Theological Geography of the Deuteronomistic History." *JBL* 129 (2010): 281–97.

Cameron, Peter Scott. *Violence and the Kingdom: The Interpretation of Matthew 11:12*. ANTJ 5. Frankfurt: Peter Lang, 1984.

Carlson, R.A. "Élie à l'Horeb." *VT* 19 (1969): 416–39.

Carr, David M. *Holy Resilience: The Bible's Traumatic Origins*. New Haven: Yale University Press, 2014.

Carr, David M. "Method of Determination of Direction of Dependence: An Empirical Test of Criteria Applied to Exodus 34,11–26 and Its Parallels." Pages 107–40 in *Gottes*

Volk am Sinai: Untersuchungen zu Ex 32–34 und Dtn 9–10. Edited by Matthias Köckert and Erhard Blum. Gütersloh: Kaiser/Gütersloher, 2001.

Chapman, Stephen B. "A Canonical Approach to Old Testament Theology? Deuteronomy 34:10–12 and Malachi 3:22–24 as Programmatic Conclusions." *HBT* 25 (2003): 121–45.

Charles, R.H. *The Revelation of St. John*. Volume 1. ICC. Edinburgh: T&T Clark, 1920.

Childs, Brevard S. *Introduction to the Old Testament as Scripture*. London: SCM, 1979.

Clark, David George. "Elijah as Eschatological High Priest: An Examination of the Elijah Tradition in Mal. 3:23–24." PhD diss., University of Notre Dame, 1975.

Cogan, Mordechai. *1 Kings*. AB 10. New York: Doubleday, 2001.

Cohn, Robert L. "The Literary Logic of 1 Kings 17–19." *JBL* 101 (1982): 333–50.

Collins, Adela Yarbro. *The Combat Myth in the Book of Revelation*. Missoula: Scholars, 1976.

Collins, Adela Yarbro. *Crisis and Catharsis: The Power of the Apocalypse*. Philadelphia: Westminster, 1984.

Collins, John J. "The Afterlife in Apocalyptic Literature." Pages 119–39 in *Judaism in Late Antiquity 4: Death, Life-After-Death, Resurrection and The World-to-Come in the Judaisms of Antiquity*. Edited by Alan Avery-Peck and Jacob Neusner. HdO. Leiden: Brill, 2000.

Collins, John J. *The Scepter and the Star: Messianism in Light of the Dead Sea Scrolls*. New York: Doubleday, 1995.

Collins, John J. *Sibylline Oracles*. Pages 317–472 in *The Old Testament Pseudepigrapha*. Volume 1. Edited by James H. Charlesworth. Garden City: Doubleday, 1983.

Corley, Jeremy. "Elijah Among the Former Prophets in Hebrew Ben Sira 48:1–12." *StBiSl* 12 (2020): 198–226.

Cronauer, Patrick T. *The Stories about Naboth the Jezreelite*. LHBOTS 424. New York: T&T Clark, 2005.

Crüsemann, Frank. *Elia – die Entdeckung der Einheit Gottes*. Gütersloh: Kaiser/Gütersloh, 1997.

Cullmann, Oscar. *Die Christologie des Neuen Testaments*. WMANT 25. Tübingen: Mohr Siebeck, 1975.

Cummins, S. Anthony. "Integrated Scripture, Embedded Empire: The Ironic Interplay of 'King' Herod, John and Jesus in Mark 6.1–44." Pages 31–48 in *Biblical Interpretation in Early Christian Gospels*. Volume 1: The Gospel of Mark. Edited by Thomas R. Hatina. London: T&T Clark, 2006.

Curtis, Edward L. and Albert A. Madsen. *The Books of Chronicles*. ICC. Edinburgh: T&T Clark, 1952.

Danker, Frederick William, ed. *A Greek-English Lexicon of the New Testament and other Early Christian Literature* (BDAG). 3rd edition. Chicago: University of Chicago Press, 2000.

Darlack, James M. "Pray for Reign: The Eschatological Elijah in James 5:17–18." MA Thesis. Gordon-Conwell Theological Seminary, 2007.

Dautzenberg, Gerhard. "Elija im Markusevangelium." Pages 1077–94 in *The Four Gospels 1992: Festschrift Frans Neirynck*. Leuven: Leuven University Press, 1992.

Davids, Peter H. *The Epistle of James*. NIGTC. Grand Rapids: Eerdmans, 1983.

Davies, W.D. and Dale C. Allison, Jr. *The Gospel According to St Matthew*. 3 volumes. ICC. Edinburgh: T&T Clark, 1991.

DeJong, David N. *A Prophet Like Moses (Deut 18:15, 18): The Origin, History, and Influence of the Mosaic Prophetic Succession*. JSJSup 205. Leiden: Brill, 2022.

Dentan, Robert C. and William L. Sperry. "Malachi." Pages 1115–44 in *IB*. Volume 6. New York: Abingdon, 1956.

DeVries, Simon J. *1 Kings*. 2nd edition. WBC 12. Dallas: Word, 2003.

Dharamraj, Havilah. *A Prophet Like Moses? A Narrative-Theological Reading of the Elijah Stories*. Milton Keynes: Paternoster, 2011.

Dibelius, Martin. *Der Brief des Jakobus*. Göttingen: Vandenhoeck & Ruprecht, 1959.

Diebner, Bernd Jørg. "Überlegungen zum 'Brief des Elia' (2Chr 21,12–15)." DBAT 23 (1986): 66–97.

Dietrich, Walter. *Prophetie und Geschichte: Eine redaktionsgeschichtliche Untersuchung zum deuteronomistischen Geschichtswerk*. FRLANT 108. Göttingen: Vandenhoeck & Ruprecht, 1972.

Docherty, Susan. "Israel's Scriptures in the Dead Sea Scrolls." Pages 138–61 in *Israel's Scriptures in Early Christian Writings: The Use of the Old Testament in the New*. Edited by Matthias Henze and David Lincicum. Grand Rapids: Eerdmans, 2023.

Dozeman, Thomas B. "The Wilderness and Salvation History in the Hagar Story." *JBL* 117 (1998): 23–43.

Dumbrell, William J. "Malachi and the Ezra-Nehemiah Reforms." *RTR* 35 (1976): 42–52.

Dunn, James D.G. *The Epistle to the Galatians*. BNTC 9. Peabody: Hendrickson, 1993.

Eckey, Wilfried. *Das Lukasevangelium*. 2 volumes. Neukirchen-Vluyn: Neukirchener, 2004.

Edwards, James R. "The Servant of the Lord and the Gospel of Mark." Pages 49–63 in *Biblical Interpretation in Early Christian Gospels*. Volume 1: The Gospel of Mark. Edited by Thomas R. Hatina. London: T&T Clark, 2006.

Eisenbaum, Pamela Michelle. *The Jewish Heroes of Christian History: Hebrews 11 in Literary Context*. SBLDS 156. Atlanta: Scholars, 1996.

Eisenman, Robert. "Eschatological 'Rain' Imagery in the War Scroll from Qumran and in the Letter of James." *JNES* 49 (1990): 173–84.

Eissfeldt, Otto. "'Bist du Elia, so bin ich Isebel' (1 Kön. xix 2)." Pages 65–70 in *Hebräische Wortforschung: Festschrift zum 80. Geburtstag von Walter Baumgartner*. VTSup 16. Leiden: Brill, 1967.

Eng, Daniel K. *Eschatological Approval: The Structure and Unifying Motif of James.* Sheffield: Sheffield Phoenix, 2022.

Eng, Daniel K. "The Role of Semitic Catchwords in Interpreting the Epistle of James." *TynBul* 70 (2019): 245–67.

Facsimiles of the Fragments Hitherto Recovered of the Book of Ecclesiasticus in Hebrew. London: Oxford University Press and Cambridge University Press, 1901.

Faierstein, Morris. "Why Do the Scribes Say That Elijah Must Come First." *JBL* 100 (1981): 75–86.

Ferguson, Anthony. "The Elijah Forerunner Concept as an Authentic Jewish Expectation." *JBL* 137 (2018): 127–45.

Fiorenza, Elisabeth Schüssler. *The Book of Revelation: Justice and Judgment.* Philadelphia: Fortress, 1985.

Fiorenza, Elisabeth Schüssler. *Revelation: Vision of a Just World.* Minneapolis: Augsburg Fortress, 1991.

Fischer, Georg. "Jeremiah – 'The Prophet like Moses'?" Pages 45–66 in *The Book of Jeremiah: Composition, Reception, and Interpretation.* Leiden: Brill, 2018.

Fitzmyer, Joseph A. "More about Elijah Coming First." *JBL* 104 (1985): 295–96.

Fitzmyer, Joseph A. *Romans.* AYB 33. New Haven: Yale University Press, 2008.

Flannery, Frances. "'Go Back by the Way You Came:' An Internal Textual Critique of Elijah's Violence in 1 Kings 18–19." Pages 161–73 in *Writing and Reading War: Rhetoric, Gender, and Ethics in Biblical and Modern Concepts.* Edited by Brad E. Kelle and Frank Ritchel Ames. Atlanta: Society of Biblical Literature, 2008.

Fohrer, Georg. *Elia.* ATANT 31. Zürich: Zwingli-Verlag, 1957.

France, R.T. *The Gospel of Mark.* NIGTC. Grand Rapids: Eerdmans, 2002.

France, R.T. *The Gospel of Matthew.* NICNT. Grand Rapids: Eerdmans, 2007.

Frankfurter, David. *Elijah in Upper Egypt: The Apocalypse of Elijah and Early Egyptian Christianity.* Minneapolis: Fortress, 1993.

Freed, Edwin D. "Jn 1:19–27 in Light of Related Passages in John, the Synoptics, and Acts." Pages 1943–61 in *The Four Gospels 1992: Festschrift Frans Neirynck.* Leuven: Leuven University Press, 1992.

Friesen, Steven J. *Imperial Cults and the Apocalypse of John.* Oxford: Oxford University Press, 2001.

Fung, Ronald Y.K. *The Epistle to the Galatians.* NICNT. Grand Rapids: Eerdmans, 1988.

García Martínez, Florentino and Eibert J.C. Tigchelaar. *The Dead Sea Scrolls Study Edition.* 2 volumes. Leiden: Brill, and Grand Rapids: Eerdmans, 1997–98.

Garsiel, Moshe. *From Earth to Heaven: A Literary Study of Elijah Stories in the Book of Kings.* Bethesda: CDL Press, 2014.

Gaventa, Beverly. *From Darkness to Light.* Philadelphia: Fortress, 1986.

Genette, Gérard. *Palimpsests: Literature in the Second Degree.* Translated by Channa Newman and Claude Doubinsky. Lincoln: University of Nebraska Press, 1997.

Gesenius, Wilhelm. *Hebräisches und Aramäisches Handwörterbuch.* 18th edition. Heidelberg: Springer, 2013.

Gibson, Jonathan. *Covenant Continuity and Fidelity: A Study of Inner-Biblical Allusion and Exegesis in Malachi.* London: Bloomsbury T&T Clark, 2016.

Glazier-McDonald, Beth. *Malachi: The Divine Messenger.* Atlanta: Scholars, 1987.

Glover, Neil. "Elijah versus the Narrative of Elijah: The Contest between the Prophet and the Word." *JSOT* 30 (2006): 449–62.

Green, Joel B. *The Gospel of Luke.* NICNT. Grand Rapids: Eerdmans, 1997.

Gregory, Russell. "Irony and the Unmasking of Elijah." Pages 93–169 in *From Carmel to Horeb: Elijah in Crisis.* JSOTSup 85. Sheffield: Almond, 1990.

Grelot, Pierre. "Michée 7,6 dans les évangiles et dans la littérature rabbinique." *Bib* 67 (1986): 363–77.

Groenewald, Alphonso. "Isaiah 1:2–3 and Isaiah 6: Isaiah 'a prophet like Moses' (Dt 18:18)." *HTS Theological Studies* 68 (2012): 1–7.

Grossman, Jonathan. "'Dynamic Analogies' in the Book of Esther." *VT* 59 (2009): 394–414.

Grossman, Jonathan. "The Expulsion of Ishmael Narrative: Boundaries, Structure, and Meaning." Pages 27–37 in *Doubling and Duplicating in the Book of Genesis.* Edited by Elizabeth R. Hayes and Karolien Vermeulen. University Park: Penn State University Press, 2021.

Grossman, Jonathan. "Hagar's Characterization in Genesis and the Explanation of Ishmael's Blessing." *Beit Mikra* (2018): 269–74.

Grundmann, Walter. *Das Evangelium nach Lukas.* 9th edition. THKNT 3. Berlin: Evangelische Verlagsanstalt, 1981.

Guelich, Robert A. *Mark 1–8:26.* WBC 34A. Dallas: Word, 1989.

Gunawan, Henricus Pidyarto. "Jesus as the New Elijah: An Attempt to the Question of John 1:21." *SiChrSt* 9 (2010): 29–53.

Gundry, Robert H. *Mark: A Commentary on His Apology for the Cross.* Grand Rapids: Eerdmans, 1993.

Gundry, Robert H. *Matthew: A Commentary on His Literary and Theological Art.* Grand Rapids: Eerdmans, 1982.

Gunkel, Hermann. *Elias, Jahve und Baal.* Tübingen: J.C.B. Mohr, 1906.

Hadjiev, Tchavdar S. "Elijah's Alleged Megalomania: Reading Strategies for Composite Texts with 1 Kings 19 as an Example." *JSOT* 39 (2015): 433–49.

Hafemann, Scott J. *Paul, Moses, and the History of Israel.* WUNT 81. Tübingen: Mohr Siebeck, 1995.

Hagner, Donald A. *Matthew 1–13.* WBC 33A. Dallas: Word, 1993.

Halbwachs, Maurice. *La mémoire collective.* Paris: Presses Universitaires de France, 1950.

Hare, D.R.A. "The Lives of the Prophets." Pages 379–99 in *The Old Testament Pseudepigrapha*. Volume 2. Edited by James H. Charlesworth. Garden City: Doubleday, 1985.

Harker, Andrew. "Prophetically Called Sodom and Egypt: The Affective Power of Revelation 11:1–13." Pages 19–39 in *The Book of Revelation: Currents in British Research on the Apocalypse*. Edited by Garrick V. Allen, Ian Paul, and Simon P. Woodman. WUNT II/411. Tübingen: Mohr Siebeck, 2015.

Hasel, Gerhard F. *The Remnant: The History and Theology of the Remnant Idea from Genesis to Isaiah*. 2nd edition. AUMSR 5. Berrien Springs: Andrews University Press, 1974.

Hatina, Thomas R. "Embedded Scripture Texts and the Plurality of Meaning: The Announcement of the 'Voice from Heaven' in Mark 1.11 as a Case Study." Pages 81–99 in *Biblical Interpretation in Early Christian Gospels*. Volume 1: The Gospel of Mark. Edited by Thomas R. Hatina. London: T&T Clark, 2006.

Hauser, Alan J. "Yahweh versus Death." Pages 11–89 in *From Carmel to Horeb: Elijah in Crisis*. JSOTSup 85. Sheffield: Almond, 1990.

Hay, Jared W. "'And suddenly, two men …': Moses and Elijah in Lukan Perspective." *ExpTim* 134 (2023): 435–44.

Hays, Richard B. "'Who Has Believed Our Message?' Paul's Reading of Isaiah." Pages 25–49 in *The Conversion of the Imagination: Paul as Interpreter of Israel's Scripture*. Grand Rapids: Eerdmans, 2005.

Hebel, Udo J. "Towards a Descriptive Poetics of Allusion." Pages 135–64 in *Intertextuality*. Research in Text Theory 15. Edited by Heinrich F. Plett. Berlin: de Gruyter, 1991.

Hein, Alicia R. "Rhetoric through Allusion: A Literary Solution to the Letter from Elijah in 2 Chronicles 21." In *Citations and Allusions in the Former Prophets*. BN. Edited by Walter Bührer, Friedrich-Emanuel Focken, and Joachim J. Krause. Freiburg: Herder, forthcoming 2026.

Hendel, Ronald S. "The Two Editions of the Royal Chronology in Kings." Pages 99–114 in *Textual Criticism and Dead Sea Scrolls Studies in Honour of Julio Trebolle Barrera*. Edited by Andrés Piquer Otero and Pablo A. Torijano Morales. JSJSup 158. Leiden: Brill, 2012.

Hengel, Martin. *Die Zeloten: Untersuchungen zur jüdischen Freiheitsbewegung in der Zeit von Herodes I. bis 70 n. Chr.* 3rd edition. Edited by Roland Deines and Claus-Jürgen Thornton. WUNT 283. Tübingen: Mohr Siebeck, 2011.

Hentschel, Georg. *Die Elijaerzählungen: zum Verhältnis von historischem Geschehen und geschichtlicher Erfahrung*. ETS 33. Leipzig: St Benno, 1977.

Hill, Andrew E. *Malachi*. AB 25D. New York: Doubleday, 1998.

Hoffeditz, David M. "A Prophet, a Kingdom, and a Messiah: The Portrayal of Elijah in the Gospels in Light of First-Century Judaism." PhD diss., University of Aberdeen, 2000.

Holtz, Traugott. *Die Offenbarung des Johannes.* NTD 11. Göttingen: Vandenhoeck & Ruprecht, 2008.

Huddleston, Jonathan. "What Would Elijah and Elisha Do? Internarrativity in Luke's Story of Jesus." *JTI* 5 (2011): 265–82.

Isaacs, Marie E. "The Prophetic Spirit in the Fourth Gospel." *HeyJ* 24 (2007): 391–407.

Isbell, Charles D. *Malachi: A Study Guide Commentary.* Grand Rapids: Zondervan, 1980.

Jacobs, Mignon R. *The Books of Haggai and Malachi.* NICOT. Grand Rapids: Eerdmans, 2017.

Jacobson, Howard. *A Commentary on Pseudo-Philo's Liber Antiquitatum Biblicarum.* 2 volumes. Leiden: Brill, 1996.

Japhet, Sara. *1 & 11 Chronicles.* OTL. London: SCM, 1993.

Jassen, Alex P. *Mediating the Divine: Prophecy and Revelation in the Dead Sea Scrolls and Second Temple Judaism.* Leiden: Brill, 2007.

Jauhiainen, Marko. "The Measuring of the Sanctuary Reconsidered." *Bib* 83 (2002): 507–26.

Jauhiainen, Marko. *The Use of Zechariah in Revelation.* WUNT 11/199. Tübingen: Mohr Siebeck, 2005.

Jeremias, Joachim. "Ἠλ(ε)ίας." Pages 930–43 in *TWNT.* Volume 2. Edited by Gerhard Kittel. Stuttgart: Kohlhammer, 1935.

Johnson, Luke Timothy. *The Letter of James.* AB 37A. New Haven: Yale University Press, 1974.

Johnson, Luke Timothy. *Prophetic Jesus, Prophetic Church: The Challenge of Luke-Acts to Contemporary Christians.* Grand Rapids: Eerdmans, 2011.

de Jonge, Marinus. *Jesus: Stranger from Heaven and Son of God.* SBibSt 11. Translated by John E. Steely. Missoula: Scholars, 1977.

Joyce, Paul M. "The Prophets and Psychological Interpretation." Pages 133–48 in *Prophecy and the Prophets in Ancient Israel: Proceedings of the Oxford Old Testament Seminar.* Edited by John Day. LHBOTS 531. New York: T&T Clark, 2010.

Joynes, Christine E. "The returned Elijah? John the Baptist's angelic identity in the Gospel of Mark." *SJT* 58 (2005): 455–67.

Kanagaraj, Jey J. *'Mysticism' in the Gospel of John: An Inquiry into its Background.* JSNTSup 158. Sheffield: Sheffield Academic, 1998.

Karnawalski, Michal. "Proper Names in the Prophetic Narratives of the Hebrew Bible: Examples of Exodus and 1–2 Kings." Paper presented at the Annual Meeting of the European Association of Biblical Studies. Syracuse, 11 July 2023.

Käsemann, Ernst. *An die Römer.* 4th edition. HNT 8a. Tübingen: Mohr Siebeck, 1973.

Katzin, David. "A Paradigm for Identifying the Use of Scriptural Allusion in Lemma-Based Exegesis Within the Qumran Library Using 4QpPsa (4Q171) as an Example." *HUCA* 87 (2016): 61–92.

Kearns, Conleth. *The Expanded Text of Ecclesiasticus.* Edited by Pancratius C. Beentjes. Berlin: de Gruyter, 2011.

Kee, Howard Clark. *Community of the New Age.* NTL. London: SCM, 1977.

Keener, Craig S. *Acts.* 4 volumes. Grand Rapids: Baker, 2012.

Keil, Carl Friedrich. *Biblischer Commentar über die nachexilischen Geschichtsbücher: Chronik, Esra, Nehemia und Esther.* BCAT 5. Leipzig: Dörfling und Franke, 1870.

Keil, Carl Friedrich and Franz Delitzsch. *Commentary on the Old Testament.* Volume 10. Peabody: Hendrickson, 1996.

Kessler, Rainer. *Maleachi.* HThKAT. Freiburg: Herder, 2011.

Kiddle, Martin. *The Revelation of St. John.* MNTC. New York: Harper, 1940.

Kissling, Paul J. *Reliable Characters in the Primary History.* JSOTSup 224. Sheffield: Sheffield Academic, 1996.

Knauf, Ernst Axel. *1 Könige 15–22.* HThKAT. Freiburg: Herder, 2019.

Knowles, Michael. *Jeremiah in Matthew's Gospel: The Rejected-Prophet Motif in Matthaean Redaction.* JSNTSup 68. Sheffield: Sheffield Academic, 1993.

Knox, John. *Chapters in a Life of Paul.* Revised edition. Macon: Mercer University Press, 1987.

Knox, John. "'Fourteen Years Later': A Note on the Pauline Chronology." *JR* 16 (1936): 341–49.

Knuteson, Roy E. "Elijah's Little-Known Letter in 2 Chronicles 21:12–15." *BSac* 162 (2005): 23–32.

Koch, Dietrich-Alex. "Der Täufer als Zeuge des Offenbarers." Pages 1963–84 in *The Four Gospels 1992: Festschrift Frans Neirynck.* Leuven: Leuven University Press, 1992.

Koet, Bart J. "Elijah as Reconciler of Father and Son: From 1 Kings 16:34 and Malachi 3:22–24 to Ben Sira 48:1–11 and Luke 1:13–17." Pages 173–90 in *Essays on Chronicles and Ben Sira in Honor of Pancratius C. Beentjes.* Edited by Jeremy Corley and Harm van Grol. Berlin: de Gruyter, 2011.

Kohn, Risa Levitt. "A Prophet Like Moses? Rethinking Ezekiel's Relationship to the Torah." *ZAW* 114 (2002): 236–54.

Körting, Corinna. "Days of Old and the Day to Come – Malachi between Protology and Eschatology." Pages 85–107 in *Herald of Good Tidings: Essays on the Bible, Prophecy, and the Hope of Israel in Honour of Antti Laato.* Edited by Pekka Lindqvist and Lotta Valve. Sheffield: Sheffield Phoenix, 2021.

Kovalishyn, Mariam Kamell. "The Prayer of Elijah in James 5: An Example of Intertextuality." *JBL* 137 (2018): 1027–45.

Kowalski, Beate. *Die Rezeption des Propheten Ezechiel in der Offenbarung des Johannes.* Stuttgart: Verlag Katholisches Bibelwerk, 2004.

Krause, Joachim J. "Citations, Allusions, and Marking Them in the Hebrew Bible: A Theoretical Introduction with Some Examples." *BibInt* 31 (2023): 440–56.

Kruse, Colin G. *John: An Introduction and Commentary*. TNTC 4. Downers Grove: InterVarsity Press, 2003.

Kugel, James L. *In Potiphar's House: The Interpretive Life of Biblical Texts*. San Francisco: HarperCollins, 1990.

Kujanpää, Katja. *The Rhetorical Functions of Scriptural Quotations in Romans: Paul's Argumentation by Quotations*. NovTSup 172. Leiden: Brill, 2019.

Kynes, William J. *My Psalm Has Turned into Weeping: Job's Dialogue with the Psalms*. BZAW 437. Berlin: de Gruyter, 2012.

Lappenga, Benjamin J. *Paul's Language of Ζῆλος: Monosemy and the Rhetoric of Identity and Practice*. Leiden: Brill, 2015.

Lasine, Stuart. "Matters of Life and Death: The Story of Elijah and the Widow's Son in Comparative Perspective." *BibInt* 12 (2004): 117–44.

Lau, Wolfgang. *Schriftgelehrte Prophetie in Jes 56–66*. BZAW 225. Berlin: de Gruyter, 1994.

Laws, Sophie. *The Epistle of James*. BNTC. Peabody: Hendrickson, 1980.

Lear, Sheree. *Scribal Composition: Malachi as a Test Case*. FRLANT 270. Göttingen: Vandenhoeck & Ruprecht, 2018.

Leithart, Peter J. *1 & 2 Kings*. BTC. Grand Rapids: Brazos, 2006.

Leonard, Jeffery M. "Identifying Inner-Biblical Allusions: Psalm 78 as a Test Case." *JBL* 12 (2008): 241–65.

Leonard, Jeffery M. "Identifying Subtle Allusions." Pages 91–113 in *Subtle Citation, Allusion, and Translation in the Hebrew Bible*. Edited by Ziony Zevit. Sheffield: Equinox, 2017.

Leuchter, Mark. "Samuel: A Prophet Like Moses or a Priest Like Moses?" Pages 147–68 in *Israelite Prophecy and the Deuteronomistic History*. Edited by Mignon R. Jacobs and Raymond F. Person, Jr. Atlanta: Society of Biblical Literature, 2013.

Levenson, Jon D. *The Death and Resurrection of the Beloved Son: The Transformation of Child Sacrifice in Judaism and Christianity*. New Haven: Yale University Press, 1993.

Levin, Christoph. *Der Jahwist*. FRLANT 157. Göttingen: Vandenhoeck & Ruprecht, 1993.

Levinson, Bernard M. *"The Right Chorale": Studies in Biblical Law and Interpretation*. FAT 54. Tübingen: Mohr Siebeck, 2008.

Levinson, Hanne Løland. *The Death Wish in the Hebrew Bible: Rhetorical Strategies for Survival*. SOTSMS. Cambridge: Cambridge University Press, 2021.

Lightfoot, R.H. *The Gospel Message of St Mark*. Oxford: Clarendon, 1952.

Lindbeck, Kristen H. *Elijah and the Rabbis: Story and Theology*. New York: Columbia University Press, 2010.

Loewenstamm, Samuel E. "The Death of Moses." Pages 185–217 in *Studies on the Testament of Abraham*. Edited by George W.E. Nickelsburg. SBLSCS 6. Missoula: Scholars, 1976.

Lyons, Michael A. "The Aqedah as 'Template'? Genesis 22 and 1 Kings 17–18." *JSOT* 46 (2021): 161–76.

Lyons, Michael A. "Envisioning Restoration: Innovations in Ezekiel 40–48." Pages 71–83 in *'I Lifted My Eyes and Saw': Reading Dream and Vision Reports in the Hebrew Bible*. Edited by Elizabeth R. Hayes and Lena-Sofia Tiemeyer. London: Bloomsbury, 2014.

Lyons, Michael A. *From Law to Prophecy: Ezekiel's Use of the Holiness Code*. LHBOTS 507. New York: T&T Clark, 2009.

Lyons, Michael A. "'He Will Call His Servants by Another Name': Concluding Reflections on Community Identity and the Exegesis of Isaiah." Pages 337–72 in *Isaiah's Servants in Early Judaism and Christianity*. Edited by Michael A. Lyons and Jacob Stromberg. WUNT II/554. Tübingen: Mohr Siebeck, 2021.

Lyons, Michael A. "'I also could talk as you do' (Job 16:4): The Function of Intratextual Quotation and Allusion in Job." Pages 169–77 in *Reading Job Intertextually*. Edited by Katharine J. Dell and William J. Kynes. LHBOTS 574. New York: Bloomsbury T&T Clark, 2013.

Lyons, Michael A. "Psalm 22 and the 'Servants' of Isaiah 54; 56–66." *CBQ* 77 (2015): 640–56.

Macho, Alexandro Diez, ed. *Targum Palaestinense in Pentateuchum*. Volume 2: Exodus. Biblia Polyglotta Matritensia IV. Madrid, 1980.

Macho, Alexandro Diez, ed. *Targum Palaestinense in Pentateuchum*. Volume 4: Numeri. Biblia Polyglotta Matritensia IV. Madrid, 1977.

Malchow, Bruce V. "The Messenger of the Covenant in Mal 3:1." *JBL* 103 (1984): 252–55.

Malone, Andrew S. "Is the Messiah Announced in Malachi 3:1?" *TynBul* 7 (2006): 215–28.

Marcheselli, Maurizio. "The Range and Significance of the References to Elijah in John's Gospel." *StBiSl* 12 (2020): 227–51.

Marshall, I. Howard. *The Gospel of Luke*. NIGTC. Exeter: Paternoster, 1978.

Martin, Troy. "Watch During the Watches (Mark 13:35)." *JBL* 120 (2001): 685–701.

Martos, Levente Balázs. "Prophet and Remnant, Crisis and Renewal: Paul's Use of the Elijah Story in Romans 11." *StBiSl* 12 (2020): 252–65.

Martyn, J. Louis. "We have Found Elijah." Pages 181–219 in *Jews, Greeks and Christians*. Edited by R. Hammerton-Kelly and R. Scroggs. SJLA 21. Leiden: Brill, 1976.

Mason, Rex. *The Books of Haggai, Zechariah and Malachi*. CBC. Cambridge: Cambridge University Press, 1977.

Matt, Daniel C. *Becoming Elijah: Prophet of Transformation*. New Haven: Yale University Press, 2022.

Mayer, Allan. "Elijah and Elisha in John's Signs Source." *ExpTim* 99 (1988): 171–73.

McKeating, Henry. "Ezekiel the 'Prophet Like Moses'?" *JSOT* 61 (1994): 97–109.

McKenzie, Steven L. *1 Kings 16–2 Kings 16*. IECOT. Stuttgart: Kohlhammer, 2019.

McKenzie, Steven L. "My God Is YHWH." Pages 92–110 in *Congress Volume 21: Munich 2013*. Edited by Christl M. Maier. Leiden: Brill, 2014.

McKenzie, Steven L. "The Priority of the MT Chronology in Kings." Pages 185–89 in *Biblical and Ancient Near Eastern Studies in Honor of P. Kyle McCarter, Jr.* Edited by Chris A. Rollston, Neal H. Walls, and Susanna Garfein. ANEM 27. Atlanta: SBL, 2022.

McKenzie, Steven L., Rhiannon Graybill, and John Kaltner. "Underwater Archaeology: The Compositional Layers of the Book of Jonah." *VT* 70 (2020): 83–103.

McKenzie, Steven L. and Howard N. Wallace. "Covenant Themes in Malachi." *CBQ* 45 (1983): 549–63.

McKnight, Scot. *The Letter of James*. NICNT. Grand Rapids: Eerdmans, 2011.

Meeks, Wayne A. *The Prophet-King*. NovTSup 14. Leiden: Brill, 1967.

Meinhold, Arndt. *Maleachi*. BKAT 14/8. Neukirchen-Vluyn: Neukirchener, 2006.

Metzger, B.M. "The Fourth Book of Ezra." Pages 518–59 in *The Old Testament Pseudepigrapha*. Volume 1. Edited by James H. Charlesworth. Garden City: Doubleday, 1983.

Metzner, Rainer. *Der Brief des Jakobus*. THKNT 14. Leipzig: Evangelische Verlagsanstalt, 2017.

Michaels, J. Ramsey. *The Gospel of John*. NICNT. Grand Rapids: Eerdmans, 2010.

Min, Paolo Byong-Seob. *I Due Testimoni di Apocalisse 11,1–13: Storia, Interpretazione, Teologia*. PhD diss., Pontifical Gregorian University, 1991.

Miner, Earl. "Allusion." Pages 13–15 in *The New Princeton Handbook of Poetic Terms*. Edited by T.V.F. Brogan. Princeton: Princeton University Press, 1994.

Moberly, R.W.L. "The Coming at Cockcrow: A Reading of Mark 13:32–37." *JTI* 14 (2020): 213–25.

Moffitt, David M. *Atonement and the Logic of Resurrection in the Epistle to the Hebrews*. NovTSup 141. Leiden: Brill, 2011.

Morris, Leon. *The Gospel According to John*. Revised edition. NICNT. Grand Rapids: Eerdmans, 1995.

Mounce, Robert H. *The Book of Revelation*. NICNT. Grand Rapids: Eerdmans, 1997.

Mowinckel, Sigmund. *He That Cometh*. Translated by G.W. Anderson. New York: Abingdon, 1954.

Müller, Ulrich B. *Prophetie und Predigt im Neuen Testament*. SNT 10. Gütersloh: Gerd Mohn, 1975.

Müller, Wolfgang G. "Interfigurality: A Study on the Interdependence of Literary Figures." Pages 101–21 in *Intertextuality*. Research in Text Theory 15. Edited by Heinrich F. Plett. Berlin: de Gruyter, 1991.

Myers, Jacob M. *II Chronicles*. AB 13. Garden City: Doubleday, 1965.

Myers, Jacob M. and Edwin D. Freed. "Is Paul Also Among the Prophets?" *Int* 20 (1966): 40–53.

Naudé, Jackie A. "חרם." Pages 276–77 in *NIDOTTE*. Volume 2. Edited by Willem A. VanGemeren. Grand Rapids: Zondervan (1997).

Nelson, Richard D. *First and Second Kings*. IBC. Louisville: Westminster John Knox, 1987.

Nickelsburg, George W.E. *1 Enoch 1*. Hermeneia. Minneapolis: Fortress, 2001.

Nihan, Christophe. "'Moses and the Prophets': Deuteronomy 18 and the Emergence of the Pentateuch as Torah." *SEÅ* 75 (2010): 21–55.

Nikaido, Scott. "Hagar and Ishmael as Literary Figures: An Intertextual Study." *VT* 51 (2001): 219–42.

Noble, John T. *A Place for Hagar's Son: Ishmael as a Case Study in the Priestly Tradition.* Philadelphia: Fortress, 2016.

Noetzel, Jutta. *Maleachi, ein Hermeneut.* Berlin: de Gruyter, 2015.

Nogalski, James D. *The Book of the Twelve: Micah–Malachi.* SHBC. Macon: Smyth & Helwys, 2011.

Nolland, John. *Luke 9:21–18:34.* WBC 35B. Dallas: Word, 1993.

Nora, Pierre. "From *Lieux de mémoire* to Realms of Memory." Pages i–xxiv in *Realms of Memory: The Construction of the French Past.* Volume 1. Edited by Pierre Nora. New York: Columbia University Press, 1996.

von Nordheim, Eckhard. "Ein Prophet kündigt sein Amt auf (Elia am Horeb)." *Bib* 59 (1978): 153–73.

Noth, Martin. *Überlieferungsgeschichtliche Studien.* 3rd edition. Darmstadt: Wissenschaftliche Buchgesellschaft, 1967.

Novakovic, Lidija. *Messiah, the Healer of the Sick.* WUNT II/170. Tübingen: Mohr Siebeck, 2003.

Odeberg, Hugo. *The Fourth Gospel.* Amsterdam: B.R. Grüner, 1929.

Oeming, Manfred. "Das Alte Testament als Buch der Kirche?: Exegetische und hermeneutische Erwägungen am Beispiel der Erzählung von Elija am Horeb (1 Kön 19), alttestamentlicher Predigttext am Sonntag Okuli." *TZ* 52 (1996): 299–325.

Oettli, Samuel. "Die Bücher der Chronik, Esra und Nehemia." Pages 1–208 in *Die geschichtlichen Hagiographen und das Buch Daniel.* KKAT 8. Nördlingen: C.H. Beck, 1889.

Öhler, Markus. *Elia im Neuen Testament.* BZNW 88. Berlin: de Gruyter, 1997.

Olley, John W. "YHWH and His Zealous Prophet: The Presentation of Elijah in 1 and 2 Kings." *JSOT* 80 (1998): 25–51.

Olson, Daniel C. *A New Reading of the Animal Apocalypse of 1 Enoch.* Leiden: Brill, 2013.

Omerzu, Heike. "Geschichte durch Geschichten: Zur Bedeutung jüdischer Traditionen für die Jesusdarstellung des Markusevangeliums." *EC* 2 (2011): 77–99.

Otten, Jeremy D. *I Alone Am Left: Elijah and the Remnant in Luke–Acts.* Eugene: Pickwick, 2021.

Otto, Susanne. *Jehu, Elia und Elisa.* BWANT 152. Stuttgart: Kohlhammer, 2001.

Owens, Robert J. "Christian Features in the Peshitta Text of Ben Sira: The Question of Dependency on the Syriac New Testament." Pages 177–96 in *The Texts and Versions of the Book of Ben Sira.* JSJSup 150. Edited by Jean-Sébastien Rey and Jan Joosten. Leiden: Brill, 2011.

Painter, John. "The Enigmatic Son of Man." Pages 1869–87 in *The Four Gospels 1992: Festschrift Frans Neirynck.* Leuven: Leuven University Press, 1992.

Pamment, Margaret. "Moses and Elijah in the Story of the Transfiguration." *ExpTim* 92 (1981): 338–39.

Parsons, Mikeal C. *The Departure of Jesus in Luke–Acts.* JSNTSup 21. Sheffield: Sheffield Academic, 1987.

Paul, Ian. "Source, Structure, and Composition in the Book of Revelation." Pages 41–54 in *The Book of Revelation: Currents in British Research on the Apocalypse.* Edited by Garrick V. Allen, Ian Paul, and Simon P. Woodman. WUNT II/411. Tübingen: Mohr Siebeck, 2015.

Pavelčík, Július. "Eliáš v Jakubovom liste." *StBiSl* 12 (2020): 266–306.

Pellegrini, Silvia. *Elija – Wegbereiter des Gottessohnes.* Freiburg: Herder, 2000.

Penner, Todd C. *The Epistle of James and Eschatology.* JSNTSup 121. Sheffield: Sheffield Academic, 1996.

Perkins, Larry. "Kingdom, Messianic Authority and the Re-constituting of God's People – Tracing the Function of Exodus Material in Mark's Narrative." Pages 100–15 in *Biblical Interpretation in Early Christian Gospels.* Volume 1: The Gospel of Mark. Edited by Thomas R. Hatina. London: T&T Clark, 2006.

Petersen, David L. *Haggai & Zechariah 1–8.* OTL. London: SCM, 1984.

Petersen, David L. *Late Israelite Prophecy.* Missoula: Scholars, 1977.

Petersen, David L. *Zechariah 9–14 & Malachi.* OTL. London: SCM, 1995.

Petterson, Anthony R. "The Identity of 'The Messenger of the Covenant' in Malachi 3:1 – Lexical and Rhetorical Analyses." *BBR* 29 (2019): 277–93.

Pierce, Madison N. and Benjamin E. Reynolds. "The Perfect Tense-Form and the Son of Man in John 3.13: Developments in Greek Grammar as a Viable Solution to the Timing of the Ascent and Descent." *NTS* 60 (2014): 149–55.

Poirier, John C. "The Endtime Return of Elijah and Moses at Qumran." *DSD* 10 (2003): 221–42.

Puech, Émile. "Une apocalypse messianique (4Q521)." *RevQ* 15 (1992): 475–522.

Puech, Émile. "Ben Sira 48:11 et la résurrection" Pages 81–89 in *Of Scribes and Scrolls: Studies on the Hebrew Bible, Intertestamental Judaism, and Christian Origins.* Edited by Harold W. Attridge, John J. Collins, and Thomas H. Tobin, S.J. Lanham: University Press of America, 1990.

Puech, Émile. "Ben Sira and Qumran." Pages 79–118 in *The Wisdom of Ben Sira.* Edited by Angelo Passaro and Giuseppe Bellia. Berlin: de Gruyter, 2008.

Puech, Émile. *La croyance des Esséniens en la vie future: immortalité, résurrection, vie éternelle?* 2 volumes. Paris: Gabalda, 1993.

Puech, Émile. "L'attente du retour d'Élie dans l'Ancien Testament et les écrits péritesta-mentaires: 4Q558 et 4Q521." *RevQ* 30 (2018): 3–26.

Rashi. *Mikra'ot Gedolot.* "Haketer." Volume 4. Edited by Menachem Cohen. Ramat Gan: Bar Ilan University Press, 1992.

Reed, Annette Yoshiko. "The Construction and Subversion of Patriarchal Perfection: Abraham and Exemplarity in Philo, Josephus, and the *Testament of Abraham*." *JSJ* 40 (2009): 185–212.

Reeder, Caryn A. "Malachi 3:24 and the Eschatological Restoration of the 'Family.'" *CBQ* 69 (2007): 695–709.

Reid, Barbara E. "Violent Endings in Matthew's Parables and Christian Nonviolence." *CBQ* 66 (2004): 237–55.

Reiss, Moshe. "Elijah the Zealot: A Foil to Moses." *JBQ* 32 (2004): 174–80.

Reventlow, Henning Graf. *Die Propheten Haggai, Sacharja und Maleachi.* 9th edition. ATD 25/2. Göttingen: Vandenhoeck & Ruprecht, 1993.

Rey, Jean-Sébastien. "L'espérance post-mortem dans les différentes versions du Siracide." Pages 257–79 in *The Texts and Versions of the Book of Ben Sira*. Edited by Jean Sébastien Rey and Jan Joosten. Leiden: Brill, 2011.

Rey, Jean-Sébastien and Jan Joosten, eds. *The Texts and Versions of the Book of Ben Sira*. Leiden: Brill, 2011.

Rice, Gene. "Elijah's Requirement for Prophetic Leadership (2 Kings 2:1–18)." *JRT* 59/60 (2006/2007): 1–12.

Richelle, Matthieu. "Élie et Élisée, Auriges en Israël: Une Métaphore Militaire Oubliée en 2 R 2,12 et 13,14." *RB* 117 (2010): 321–36.

Robinson, Bernard P. "Christ as a Northern Prophet in St John." *Scr* 17 (1965): 104–108.

Robinson, Bernard P. "Elijah at Horeb, 1 Kings 19:1–18: A Coherent Narrative?" *RB* 94 (1991): 513–36.

Robinson, John A.T. "Elijah, John and Jesus: An Essay in Detection." *NTS* 4 (1958): 263–81.

Rodenbiker, Kelsie G. "Pseudonymity, Exemplarity, and the Dating of James." Pages 219–43 in *Die Datierung neutestamentlicher Pseudepigraphen: Herausforderungen und neuere Lösungsansätze*. WUNT 470. Edited by Wolfgang Grünstäudl and Karl Matthias Schmidt. Tübingen: Mohr Siebeck, 2021.

Rofé, Alexander. *The Prophetical Stories*. Jerusalem: Magnes, 1988.

Rogland, Max. "Elijah and the 'Voice' at Horeb (1 Kings 19): Narrative Sequence in the Masoretic Text and Josephus." *VT* 62 (2012): 88–94.

Roi, Micha. "Phinehas Is Not Elijah: The Zeal at Shittim (Num 25:6–15) in Light of the Zeal at Horeb (1 Kgs 19), and the Altar at Gilgal (Josh 22:9–34) in Light of the Altar at Mount Carmel (1 Kgs 18)." *RB* 127 (2020): 487–93.

Roller, Matthew B. *Models from the Past in Roman Culture: A World of Exempla*. Cambridge: Cambridge University Press, 2018.

Rossi, Benedetta. "Reshaping Jeremiah: Scribal Strategies and the *Prophet Like Moses*." *JSOT* 44 (2020): 575–93.

Roth, Wolfgang. *Hebrew Gospel: Cracking the Code of Mark*. Oak Park: Meyer-Stone, 1988.

Rudolph, Wilhelm. *Chronikbücher*. HAT 1/21. Tübingen: Mohr Siebeck, 1955.

Rudolph, Wilhelm. *Haggai; Sacharja 1–8; Sacharja 9–14; Maleachi*. KAT. Gütersloh: Mohn, 1976.

Ruzer, Serge. *Mapping the New Testament: Early Christian Writings as a Witness for Jewish Exegesis*. Leiden: Brill, 2007.

Sandnes, Karl Olav. *Paul – One of the Prophets?* WUNT II/43. Tübingen: Mohr Siebeck, 1991.

Satran, David. *Biblical Prophets in Byzantine Palestine: Reassessing the* Lives of the Prophets. Leiden: Brill, 1995.

Savran, George W. *Encountering the Divine: Theophany in Biblical Narrative*. London: T&T Clark, 2005.

Schechter, Solomon and Charles Taylor. *The Wisdom of Ben Sira*. Cambridge: Cambridge University Press, 1899.

Scholtz, Jacob J. "One Messiah, Two Advents, Three Forerunners: The Chiastic Structure of Matthew 11:2–17:13." *IDS* 50 (2016): 1–10.

Schreiber, Johannes. *Der Kreuzigungsbericht des Markusevangeliums*. Berlin: de Gruyter, 1986.

Schwartz, Daniel R. *1 Maccabees*. AYB 41B. New Haven: Yale University Press, 2022.

Schweizer, Eduard. *Das Evangelium nach Markus*. 17th edition. NTD 1. Göttingen: Vandenhoeck & Ruprecht, 1989.

Schwemer, Anna Maria. "Die Elijagestalt im Wandel der Zeiten." *BK* 66 (2011): 229–33.

Seifrid, Mark. *The Second Letter to the Corinthians*. PNTC. Grand Rapids: Eerdmans, 2014.

Sellin, Ernst. *Das Zwölfprophetenbuch*. KAT 12. 2 volumes. Leipzig: Deichert, 1929–30.

de la Serna, Eduardo. "¿Pablo, el Precursor? Pablo y las tradiciones sobre Elías." *RevistB* 3/4 (2013): 161–80.

Shacham-Rosby, Chana. "Elijah the Prophet: The Guard Dog of Israel." *JH* 30 (2016): 165–82.

Shaver, Brenda J. "The Prophet Elijah in the Literature of the Second Temple Period: The Growth of a Tradition." PhD. diss., University of Chicago, 2001.

Sidebottom, Ernest. *The Christ of the Fourth Gospel in the Light of First-Century Thought*. London: SPCK, 1961.

Skehan, Patrick W. and Alexander A. Di Lella. *The Wisdom of Ben Sira*. AB 39. New York: Doubleday, 1987.

Smend, Rudolf. "Das Wort Jahwes an Elia: Erwägungen zur Komposition von 1 Reg. XVII–XIX." *VT* 25 (1975): 525–43.

Smith, John M.P. *A Critical and Exegetical Commentary on the Book of Malachi*. ICC. Edinburgh: T&T Clark, 1912.

Smith, Ralph L. *Micah–Malachi*. WBC 32. Dallas: Word, 1984.

Snaith, John G. "Biblical Quotations in the Hebrew of Ecclesiasticus." *JTS* 18 (1967): 1–12.

Snyman, S.D. "Malachi 4:4–6 (Heb 3:22–24) as a Point of Convergence in the Old Testament or Hebrew Bible: A Consideration of the Intra and Intertextual Relationships." *HTS Theological Studies* 68 (2012): 1–6.

Snyman, S.D. "Malachi's Controversial Conclusion: Problems and Prospects." *AcT* 40 (2020): 124–36.

Snyman, S.D. "Once Again: Investigating the Identity of the Three Figures Mentioned in Malachi 3:1." *VEccl* 27 (2006): 1031–44.

Söding, Thomas. *Das Evangelium nach Markus*. THKNT 2. Leipzig: Evangelische Verlagsanstalt, 2022.

Sommer, Benjamin D. *A Prophet Reads Scripture: Allusion in Isaiah 40–66*. Stanford: Stanford University Press, 1998.

Spencer, F. Scott. *The Portrait of Philip in Acts*. JSNTSup 67. Sheffield: Sheffield Academic, 1992.

Stanley, Christopher D. *Paul and the Language of Scripture: Citation Technique in the Pauline Epistles and Contemporary Literature*. SNTSMS 69. Cambridge: Cambridge University Press, 1992.

Starcky, Jean. "Les quatre étapes du messianisme à Qumran." *RB* 70 (1963): 481–505.

Stead, Michael R. *The Intertextuality of Zechariah 1–8*. LHBOTS 506. London: T&T Clark, 2009.

Steck, Odil Hannes. *Der Abschluß der Prophetie im Alten Testament*. BiThSt 17. Neukirchen-Vluyn: Neukirchener, 1991.

Steck, Odil Hannes. *Israel und das gewaltsame Geschick der Propheten*. WMANT 23. Neukirchen-Vluyn: Neukirchener, 1967.

Steck, Odil Hannes. *Überlieferung und Zeitgeschichte in den Elia-Erzählungen*. WMANT 26. Neukirchen-Vluyn: Neukirchener, 1968.

Steins, Georg. *Die "Bindung Isaaks" im Kanon (Gen 22)*. HBS 20. Freiburg: Herder, 1999.

Stendahl, Krister. *Paul Among Jews and Gentiles*. Philadelphia: Fortress, 1976.

Stevens, Chris S. "Paul, the Expected Eschatological Phinehas-Elijah Prophet Law-Giver." Pages 80–104 in *Paul and Gnosis*. Pauline Studies. Volume 9. Edited by Stanley E. Porter and David I. Yoon. Leiden: Brill, 2016.

Stipp, Hermann-Josef. *Elischa – Propheten – Gottesmänner*. ATSAT 24. St Ottilien: EOS, 1987.

Strachan, John Michael. "Rewriting the Ending: Malachi's Threat and the Destruction of the Temple in the Gospel of Mark." PhD diss., Marquette University, 2022.

Strauss, Mark L. *Mark*. ZECNT. Volume 2. Edited by Clinton E. Arnold. Grand Rapids: Zondervan, 2014.

Stromberg, Jacob. "Isaiah's Interpretive Revolution: How Isaiah's Formation Influenced Early Jewish and Christian Interpretation." Pages 214–32 in *The Book of Isaiah:*

Enduring Questions Answered Anew. Edited by Richard J. Bautch and J. Todd Hibbard. Grand Rapids: Eerdmans, 2014.

Sweeney, Marvin A. *1 & 11 Kings.* OTL. Louisville: Westminster John Knox, 2007.

Sweeney, Marvin A. *The Twelve Prophets.* 2 volumes. Collegeville: Liturgical, 2000.

Sweeney, Marvin A. "Prophets and Priests in the Deuteronomistic History: Elijah and Elisha." Pages 35–49 in *Israelite Prophecy and the Deuteronomistic History.* Edited by Mignon R. Jacobs and Raymond F. Person, Jr. Atlanta: Society of Biblical Literature, 2013.

Tavo, Felise. *Woman, Mother, and Bride: An Exegetical Investigation in the "Ecclesial" Notions of the Apocalypse.* Leuven: Peeters, 2007.

Taylor, Justin. "The Coming of Elijah, Mt 7,10–13 and Mk 9,11–13: The Development of the Texts." *RB* 98 (1991): 107–19.

Taylor, Mark E. "Recent Scholarship on the Structure of James." *CBR* 3 (2004): 86–115.

Taylor, Mark E. and George H. Guthrie. "The Structure of James." *CBQ* 68 (2006): 681–705.

Teeter, D. Andrew and Michael A. Lyons. "The One and the Many, the Past and the Future, and the Dynamics of Prospective Analogy: The Servant(s) as the Vindication of Moses and the Prophets." Pages 15–43 in *Isaiah's Servants in Early Judaism and Christianity.* Edited by Michael A. Lyons and Jacob Stromberg. WUNT II/554. Tübingen: Mohr Siebeck, 2021.

Thiel, Winfried. "Deuteronomistische Redaktionsarbeit in den Elia-Erzählungen." Pages 148–71 in *Congress Volume: Leuven 1989.* Edited by J.A. Emerton. Leiden: Brill, 1991.

Thiel, Winfried. "Essen und Trinken in der Elia- und Elisa-Tradition." Pages 375–88 in *Diasynchron: Beiträge zur Exegese, Theologie und Rezeption der hebräischen Bibel.* Edited by Thomas Naumann and Regine Hunziker-Rodewald. Stuttgart: Kohlhammer, 2009.

Thiel, Winfried. *Könige.* BKAT 9/2. Göttingen: Vandenhoeck & Ruprecht, 2019.

Tiemeyer, Lena-Sofia. "God's Hidden Compassion." *TynBul* 57 (2006): 191–213.

Tilly, Michael. *Johannes der Täufer und die Biographie der Propheten.* Stuttgart: Kohlhammer, 1994.

Tooman, William A. *Gog of Magog. Reuse of Scripture and Compositional Technique in Ezekiel 38–39.* FAT II/52. Tübingen: Mohr Siebeck, 2011.

Torrey, Charles Cutler. *The Lives of the Prophets: Greek Text and Translation.* JBLMS 1. Philadelphia: SBL, 1946.

Vallançon, Henri. *Le développement des traditions sur Élie et l'histoire de la formation de la Bible.* Leuven: Peeters, 2019.

Valve, Lotta. "The Case of Messenger-Elijah: The Origins of the Final Appendix to Malachi (3:23–24)." Pages 93–103 in *'My Spirit at Rest in the North Country' (Zechariah 6.8): Collected Communications to the xxth Congress of the International*

Organization for the Study of the Old Testament, Helsinki 2010. Edited by Hermann Michael Niemann and Matthias Augustin. Frankfurt: Peter Lang, 2011.

Valve, Lotta. *Early Modes of Exegesis: Ideal Figures in Malachi as a Test Case.* Åbo: Åbo Akademi University Press, 2014.

Valve, Lotta. "Elijah, Elisha, and Other 'Prophets' in Hebrews 11:33–38." Pages 65–82 in *From Text to Persuasion: Festschrift in Honour of Professor Lauri Thurén on the Occasion of His 60th Birthday.* Edited by Anssi Voitila, Niilo Lahti, Mikael Sundkvist, and Lotta Valve. Helsinki: Finnish Exegetical Society, 2021.

Valve, Lotta. "Elijah, the Servant, and Phinehas." Pages 1–30 in *Take Another Scroll and Write: Studies in the Interpretive Afterlife of Prophets and Prophecy in Judaism, Christianity and Islam.* Edited by Pekka Lindqvist and Sven Grebenstein. Åbo: Åbo Akademi University Press, 2016.

Valve, Lotta. "Isaiah 61 in Reception: Elijah and Elisha in Luke 4." Pages 232–49 in *Herald of Good Tidings: Essays on the Bible, Prophecy and the Hope of Israel in Honour of Antti Laato.* Edited by Pekka Lindqvist and Lotta Valve. Sheffield: Sheffield Phoenix, 2021.

Valve, Lotta. "The Lord Elijah in the Temple as in Malachi 3.1: 'Overkilling' Elijah Traditions in Luke 2." Pages 144–59 in *Luke's Literary Creativity.* Edited by Jesper Tang Nielsen and Mogens Müller. London: T&T Clark, 2016.

Vena, Osvaldo D. "Paul's Understanding of the Eschatological Prophet of Malachi 4:5–6." *BR* 44 (1999): 35–54.

Verhoef, Pieter A. *The Books of Haggai and Malachi.* NICOT. Grand Rapids: Eerdmans, 1987.

Wall, Robert W. *Revelation.* NIBC 18. Peabody: Hendrickson, 1991.

Walsh, Jerome T. *1 Kings.* Berit Olam. Collegeville: Liturgical Press, 1996.

Watts, Rikki E. *Isaiah's New Exodus and Mark.* WUNT II/88. Tübingen: Mohr Siebeck, 1997.

Weingart, Kristin. "My Father, My Father! Chariot of Israel and Its Horses!" (2 Kings 2:12// 13:14): Elisha's or Elijah's Title?" *JBL* 137 (2018): 257–70.

Wengst, Klaus. *Das Johannesevangelium.* TKNT 4. Stuttgart: Kohlhammer, 2019.

Weyde, Karl William. "The Priests and the Descendants of Levi in the Book of Malachi." *AcT* 35 (2015): 238–53.

Weyde, Karl William. *Prophecy and Teaching: Prophetic Authority, Form Problems, and the Use of Traditions in the Book of Malachi.* BZAW 288. Berlin: de Gruyter, 2000.

White, Hugh C. "The Initiation Legend of Ishmael." *ZAW* 87 (1975): 267–306.

Whitters, Mark F. "Why Did the Bystanders Think Jesus Called upon Elijah before He Died (Mark 15:34–36)? The Markan Position." *HTR* 95 (2002): 119–24.

Wieder, Naphtali. "The 'Law-Interpreter' of the Sect of the Dead Sea Scrolls: The Second Moses." *JJS* 4 (1953): 158–75.

Wiefel, Wolfgang. *Das Evangelium nach Matthäus*. THKNT 1. Leipzig: Evangelische Verlagsanstalt, 1998.

Wiener, Aharon. *The Prophet Elijah in the Development of Judaism*. London: Routledge & Kegan Paul, 1978.

Wilcox, Peter and David Paton-Williams. "The Servant Songs in Deutero-Isaiah." *JSOT* 42 (1988): 79–102.

Willi, Thomas. *Die Chronik als Auslegung*. FRLANT 106. Göttingen: Vandenhoek & Ruprecht, 1972.

Willitts, Joel. "The Remnant of Israel in 4QpIsaiah^a (4Q161) and the Dead Sea Scrolls." *JSJ* 57 (2006): 11–25.

Wink, Walter. *John the Baptist in the Gospel Tradition*. Cambridge: Cambridge University Press, 1968.

Winn, Adam. *Mark and the Elijah-Elisha Narrative*. Eugene: Pickwick, 2010.

Wintermute, O.S. "Apocalypse of Elijah." Pages 721–53 in *The Old Testament Pseudepigrapha*. Volume 1. Edited by James H. Charlesworth. Garden City: Doubleday, 1983.

Wintermute, O.S. "The Apocalypse of Zephaniah." Pages 497–515 in *The Old Testament Pseudepigrapha*. Volume 1. Edited by James H. Charlesworth. Garden City: Doubleday, 1983.

Witkamp, Theo and Jan Krans. "Heavenly Journey and Divine Epistemology in the Fourth Gospel." Pages 145–60 in *Jewish, Christian, and Muslim Travel Experiences: 3rd Century BCE–8th Century CE*. Edited by P.B. Hartog, S. Luther, and C.E. Wilde. Berlin: de Gruyter, 2023.

Wöhrle, Jakob. *Der Abschluss des Zwölfprophetenbuches*. BZAW 389. Berlin: de Gruyter, 2008.

Wöhrle, Jakob. "Jacob, Moses, Levi: Pentateuchal Figures in the Book of the Twelve." Pages 997–1014 in *The Formation of the Pentateuch*. Edited by Jan C. Gertz, Bernard M. Levinson, Dalit Rom Shiloni, and Konrad Schmid. FAT 111. Tübingen: Mohr Siebeck, 2016.

Wolff, Christian. *Der zweite Brief des Paulus an die Korinther*. 2nd edition. Berlin: Evangelische Verlagsanstalt, 2011.

Wong, Daniel K.K. "The Two Witnesses in Revelation 11." *BSac* 154 (1997): 344–54.

van der Woude, Adam Simon. "Der Engel des Bundes: Bemerkungen zu Maleachi 3,1c und seinem Kontext." Pages 289–300 in *Die Botschaft und die Boten: Festschrift für Hans Walter Wolff zum 70. Geburtstag*. Neukirchen-Vluyn: Neukirchener, 1981.

Wright, Benjamin G. "Eschatology without a Messiah in the Wisdom of Ben Sira." Pages 313–23 in *The Septuagint and Messianism*. Edited by Michael A. Knibb. Leuven: Leuven University Press, 2006.

Wright, Benjamin G. *No Small Difference*. SCS 26. Atlanta: Scholars, 1989.

Wright, David P. "The Covenant Code Appendix (Exodus 23:20–33), Neo-Assyrian Sources, and Implications for Pentateuchal Study." Pages 47–85 in *The Formation of the Pentateuch.* Edited by Jan C. Gertz, Bernard M. Levinson, Dalit Rom Shiloni, and Konrad Schmid. FAT 111. Tübingen: Mohr Siebeck, 2016.

Wright, J. Edward. "Whither Elijah? the Ascension of Elijah in Biblical and Extrabiblical Traditions." Pages 123–38 in *Things Revealed: Studies in Early Jewish and Christian Literature in Honor of Michael E. Stone.* Edited by Esther G. Chazon, David Satran, and Ruth Clements. JSJSup 89. Leiden: Brill, 2004.

Wright, N.T. "Paul, Arabia, and Elijah (Galatians 1:17)." *JBL* 115 (1996): 683–92.

Würthwein, Ernst. *Die Bücher der Könige: 1. Kön 17–2 Kön 25.* ATD 11/2. Göttingen: Vandenhoeck & Ruprecht, 1984.

Würthwein, Ernst. *Studien zum Deuteronomistischen Geschichtswerk.* BZAW 227. Berlin: de Gruyter, 1994.

Xeravits, Géza G. *From Qumran to the Synagogues.* Berlin: de Gruyter, 2019.

Yamasaki, Gary. *John the Baptist in Life and Death.* JSNTSup 167. Sheffield: Sheffield Academic, 1998.

Yonge, C.D., trans. *The Works of Philo.* Peabody: Hendrickson, 1993.

Zakovitch, Yair. "Do the Last Verses of Malachi (Mal 3:22–24) Have a Canonical Function?" Pages 60–81 in *The Book of the Twelve – One Book or Many?: Metz Conference Proceedings, 5–7 November 2015.* Edited by Elena Di Pede and Donatella Scaiola. FAT II/91. Tübingen: Mohr Siebeck, 2016.

Zakovitch, Yair. "Juxtaposition in the Abraham Cycle." Pages 509–24 in *Pomegranates and Golden Bells: Studies in Biblical, Jewish, and Near Eastern Ritual, Law, and Literature in Honor of Jacob Milgrom.* Edited by D.P. Wright, D.N. Freedman, and A. Hurvitz. Winona Lake: Eisenbrauns, 1995.

Zenger, Erich and Christian Frevel. *Einleitung in das Alte Testament.* 9th edition. Edited by Christian Frevel. Stuttgart: Kohlhammer, 2016.

Zeron, Alexander. "Einige Bemerkungen zu M.F. Collins 'The Hidden Vessels in Samaritan Traditions.'" *JSJ* 4 (1973): 165–68.

Zeron, Alexander. "The Martyrdom of Phineas-Elijah." *JBL* 98 (1979): 99–100.

Ziesler, J.A. "The Transfiguration Story and the Markan Soteriology." *ExpTim* 81 (1970): 263–68.

Zimmerli, Walther. "Zur Sprache Tritojesajas." Pages 62–74 in *Gottes Offenbarung: Gesammelte Aufsätze.* Munich: Kaiser, 1969.

Zmijewski, Josef. *Die Apostelgeschichte.* Regensburg: Friedrich Pustet, 1994.

Zwiep, Arie W. *The Ascension of the Messiah in Lukan Christology.* NovTSup 87. Leiden: Brill, 1997.

Zwiep, Arie W. *Christ, the Spirit and the Community of God.* WUNT II/293. Tübingen: Mohr Siebeck, 2010.

Index of Authors

Index of Ancient Sources

Later Jewish Literature

Printed in the United States
by Baker & Taylor Publisher Services